MODELING HUMAN BEHAVIOR WITH INTEGRATED COGNITIVE ARCHITECTURES

Comparison, Evaluation, and Validation

MODELING HUMAN BEHAVIOR WITH INTEGRATED COGNITIVE ARCHITECTURES

Comparison, Evaluation, and Validation

Edited by

Kevin A. Gluck
Air Force Research Laboratory

Richard W. Pew
BBN Technologies

Routledge
Taylor & Francis Group
New York London

First published 2005 Lawrence Erlbaum Associates, Inc.

Published 2019 by Routledge
52 Vanderbilt Avenue, New York, NY 10017
2 Park Square Milton Park, Abingdon Oxon OX14 4RN

Routledge is an imprint of the Taylor & Francis Group, an informa business

Library of Congress Cataloging-in-Publication Data

Modeling human behavior with integrated cognitive architectures : comparison, evaluation, and validation / edited by Kevin A. Gluck, Richard W. Pew.
    p. cm.
  Includes bibliographical references and index.
  ISBN 0-8058-5047-3 (cloth : alk. paper)
  ISBN 0-8058-5048-1 (pbk. : alk. paper))
  1. Psychology, Military. 2. Human behavior—Simulation methods.
3. Organizational behavior—Simulation methods. 4. Expert systems (Computer science)—Validation. I. Gluck, Kevin A. II. Pew, Richard W.
U22.3.M576 2005
355.4'8—dc22   2005040143
                                                         CIP

To our families.
—KAG and RWP

Contents

PART II   MODELS OF MULTITASKING AND CATEGORY LEARNING

SECTION III   CONCLUSIONS, LESSONS LEARNED, AND IMPLICATIONS

Contributors

Brett Benyo
BBN Technologies
10 Moulton Street
Cambridge, MA 02138
Email: bbenyo@bbn.com

Amy E. Bolton
NAVAIR Orlando, AIR-4651
12350 Research Pkwy.
Orlando, FL 32826-3275
Email: amy.bolton@navy.mil

Gwendolyn E. Campbell
NAVAIR Orlando, AIR-4651
12350 Research Pkwy.
Orlando, FL 32826-3275
Email: gwendolyn.campbell@navy.mil

Ronald S. Chong
George Mason University
Dept. of Psychology, MS3f5
Fairfax, VA 22030-4444
Email: rchong@gmu.edu

Stephen Deutsch
BBN Technologies
10 Moulton Street
Cambridge, MA 02138
Email: sdeutsch@bbn.com

David E. Diller
BBN Technologies
10 Moulton Street
Cambridge, MA 02138
Email: ddiller@bbn.com

Robert G. Eggleston
Air Force Research Laboratory
2255 H Street
Wright-Patterson AFB, OH 45433-7022
Email: robert.eggleston@wpafb.af.mil

Laura Feinerman
The MITRE Corporation
7515 Colshire Drive, MS H200
McLean, VA 22102
Email: feiner@mitre.org

Floyd Glenn
CHI Systems, Inc.
1035 Virginia Drive
Fort Washington, PA 19034
Email: fglenn@chisystems.com

Kevin A. Gluck
Air Force Research Laboratory
6030 S. Kent St.
Mesa, AZ 85212-6061
Email: kevin.gluck@mesa.afmc.af.mil

Katherine Godfrey
BBN Technologies
10 Moulton Street
Cambridge, MA 02138
Email: kgodfrey@bbn.com

Christian Lebiere
Micro Analysis and Design
6800 Thomas Blvd.
Pittsburgh, PA 15208
Email: clebiere@maad.com

Jean-Christophe Le Mentec
CHI Systems, Inc.
1035 Virginia Drive
Fort Washington, PA 19034
Email: jclementec@chisystems.com

Bradley C. Love
The University of Texas at Austin
University Station A8000
Austin, TX 78712-0187
Email: love@psy.utexas.edu

Katherine L. McCreight
N-Space Analysis
305 Winding Trail
Xenia, OH 45385-1437
Email: nspaceanalysis@earthlink.net

Richard W. Pew
BBN Technologies
10 Moulton Street
Cambridge MA 02138
Email: pew@bbn.com

Joan Ryder
CHI Systems, Inc.
1035 Virginia Drive
Fort Washington, PA 19034
Email: jryder@chisystems.com

Thomas Santarelli
CHI Systems, Inc.
1035 Virginia Drive
Fort Washington, PA 19034
Email: tsantarelli@chisystems.com

James Stokes
CHI Systems, Inc.
1035 Virginia Drive
Fort Washington, PA 19034
Email: jstokes@chisystems.com

Yvette J. Tenney
BBN Technologies
10 Moulton Street
Cambridge, MA 02138
Email: ytenney@bbn.com

Robert E. Wray
Soar Technology, Inc.
3600 Green Road Suite 600
Ann Arbor, MI 48105
Email: wray@soartech.com

Michael J. Young
Air Force Research Laboratory
Building 190, Area B
2698 G Street
Wright-Patterson AFB, OH 45433-7022
Email: michael.young@wpafb.af.mil

Wayne Zachary
CHI Systems, Inc.
1035 Virginia Drive
Fort Washington, PA 19034
Email: wzachary@chisystems.com

Preface

In recent years, the Human Effectiveness directorate of the Air Force Research Laboratory (AFRL/HE) has increased its investment in science and technology for human behavior representation. This increase has occurred as a result of a convergence of evidence in the mid to late 1990s that there was an existing and future need for increased realism in models of human and organizational behavior for use in military simulations.

At the request of the Defense Modeling and Simulation Office (DMSO), the National Research Council (NRC) established a panel to review the state of the art in human behavior representation as applied to military simulations. The panel consisted of leading experts in individual behavior, organizational behavior, decision making, human factors, computational modeling, and military simulations. Results of the panel's efforts were published in a book (Pew & Mavor, 1998) in which they concluded that, "The modeling of cognition and action by individuals and groups is quite possibly the most difficult task humans have yet undertaken. Developments in this area are still in their infancy" (pp. 341–342).

Having established the need for more research in this area, the panel suggested short-, intermediate-, and long-term goals for stimulating progress. These were intended to serve as suggested research directions for DMSO and other DoD agencies with an interest in modeling and simulation. A short-term suggestion was for increased human performance data collection. Real-world, wargame, and laboratory data all can and should be used to constrain the development of new and improved human behavior models. A second short-term suggestion was for the development of human model accreditation procedures because none existed (and they still do not today). In the intermediate term, the panel recommended that substantial resources be allocated for sustained model development in focused areas of interest to the DoD. In the long term, the panel suggested support for theory development and basic research in areas such as decision making, situation awareness, learning, and organizational modeling.

Armed with these recommendations, AFRL/HE created a cognitive process modeling initiative for improving the realism of human behaviors as represented in military simulation environments. This initiative is called the Agent-Based Modeling and Behavior Representation (AMBR) project. A portion of the AMBR project is committed to comparing models of complex human behavior. We refer to this as the AMBR model comparison, and the first 4 years' results from the AMBR model comparison and their implications for the science of formal human behavior representation are the focus of this book.

Publication of this book accomplishes three goals. The first is that the book provides a single, coherent reference source documenting the human data and models from the AMBR model comparison. This was a rather large research effort involving four modeling teams, a moderator, and several related model development and comparison efforts over approximately 4 years. Interim results have been reported in a variety of conference papers and conference symposia, but these are snapshots of isolated portions of the project. It would be more typical of a government lab-sponsored project of this sort to let the contractors go about publishing their own individual papers on what they had accomplished and to be satisfied with the resulting set of separate publications. However, we felt it would be of greater utility to the various communities of interest to combine those papers into an integrated product. This book is that product.

Although it is desirable to document what was accomplished in the AMBR model comparison, it is also important to explain what is vital about those accomplishments and what we have learned that can be of benefit to others. Thus, a second goal of the book is to share our lessons learned and insights with the members of the scientific and technical communities who are most likely to benefit from them.

A third goal of the book is to stimulate and motivate additional research and future model comparisons. We have found the model comparison approach adopted in this project to be a fruitful means to improve the state of the science in cognitive modeling, and we encourage others to adopt some variant of this cooperative comparison approach in future research efforts. Large-scale model comparisons are not easy to accomplish and involve an assortment of constraints, trade-offs, and interim decisions. We did not do everything right the first time. Future projects of this sort will benefit from avoiding the mistakes we made along the way and adopting the successful characteristics of the AMBR model comparison. We hope you find this book to be a useful and informative resource.

Acknowledgments

Both the AMBR model comparison and this book summarizing its results and implications have been sizable efforts. There are many people and organizations deserving mention for their contributions.

The Air Force Research Laboratory (AFRL) provided the majority of the funding for this research under contract F33615-99-C-6002 with BBN Technologies, contracts F33615-99-C-6005 and F33615-01-C-6077 with Soar Technology and George Mason University, and contracts F33615-99-C-6007 and F33615-01-C-6078 with CHI Systems. Jim Brinkley was Director of AFRL's Human Effectiveness Directorate (AFRL/HE) during the initial approval of funds and most of the technical effort; although not personally involved in the conduct of the research, he was an advocate for this project. Mike Young is a Senior Research Psychologist and Chief of the Cognitive Systems Branch in AFRL's Human Effectiveness Directorate. Mike was the driving force behind the AMBR model comparison from its inception to its completion. It is Mike's passion for cognitive science and his commitment to human behavior representation models that got this project started and kept it going in the face of myriad challenges and changes. Our deep gratitude to AFRL and especially to Mike Young.

In addition to the substantial investment by AFRL, both the Defense Modeling and Simulation Office (DMSO) and the Office of Naval Research (ONR) provided funds for portions of the project. Ruth Willis provided DMSO support for an extension of the Experiment 1 models and air traffic control (ATC) simulation to communicate over the high-level architecture (see chap. 3, this volume, for more details about the HLA effort). She also participated in many of the planning and comparison meetings for the

AMBR model comparison. Harold Hawkins provided ONR support to enable the participation of the Carnegie Mellon (ACT-R) modeling team and for data collection to support the concept learning experiment. Harold also served on the expert advisory panel throughout the project. Our sincere thanks to Ruth and Harold for their intellectual involvement and financial support.

The design of Experiment 2, which focused on concept learning, required the collection of significantly more human subject data than originally planned at the beginning of the project. As noted earlier, ONR stepped up with funds to support this new requirement. Amy Bolton and Gwen Campbell were instrumental in making this possible, but it was actually Randolph Astwood, Jr., of Jardon Howard Technologies, and David Holness, of the NAVAIR Orlando Training Systems Division, who collected the data. We appreciate their involvement.

It was apparent going into this unique research project that we were entering unexplored territory, and we figured we could use all the help we could get. Therefore, one of the programmatic decisions made early in the planning of the project was to request the participation of a panel of experts who would advise us on various design decisions and assist in the actual conduct of the comparisons. The expert panel for the first comparison, which focused on models of multitasking, consisted of Sheldon Baron, Wayne Gray, Harold Hawkins, and Peter Polson. The expert panel for the second comparison, which focused on models of concept learning, consisted of Gwen Campbell, Harold Hawkins, Bonnie John, and Brad Love. These people gave generously of their time and effort, and it is unquestionably the case that the AMBR model comparison benefited from their participation. Any flaws or weaknesses in the design, execution, or reporting of the project are the responsibility of the project team and were outside our expert panelists' realm of control. We thank them for their guidance. Brad Love deserves special recognition for his willingness not only to serve on the panel, but also to volunteer to contribute his knowledge and experience by preparing chapter 9, which includes much more insight into category learning than the project team could have provided.

As the technical portion of the project came to a close, discussion turned to the possibility of reporting the entire body of research as a book. This possibility has become a reality thanks to Lawrence Erlbaum Associates, where Bill Webber, Kristin Duch, Lori Stone, Art Lizza, and Heather Jefferson have supported the publication of the book with enthusiasm and vigor. For that we are grateful.

Naturally, once the writing got underway, we turned to colleagues in the cognitive science community for assistance in improving the final product. Stephanie Doane, Ken Funk, Amy Henninger, Bonnie John, Peter Polson, Frank Ritter, Chris Schunn, Jim Staszewski, and Paul Ward all read one or more chapters and provided substantial constructive criticism. Our sincere thanks to all of these reviewers for insightful and thorough feedback that had a significant positive impact on the organization, content, and readability of the book.

Finally, we must acknowledge the hard work of the contributors to the AMBR model comparison and to this book. Throughout the research and final reporting, they endured delays, changes, deadlines, questions, criticisms, and revisions with patience and good humor. We hope they feel as enriched as we do by the experience of it all, and we thank them for their continuing hard work and dedication to improving the state of the science of human behavior representation.

—*Kevin A. Gluck*
—*Richard W. Pew*

OVERVIEW, EXPERIMENTS, AND SOFTWARE

Chapter 1

Background, Structure, and Preview of the Model Comparison

Kevin A. Gluck
Air Force Research Laboratory

Richard W. Pew
BBN Technologies

Michael J. Young
Air Force Research Laboratory

The U.S. military services have developed a variety of systems that allow for synthetic human behavior representation (HBR) in virtual and constructive simulation. Examples include the Army's Modular Semi-Automated Forces (ModSAF), the Navy and Marine Corps' Small Unit Tactical Trainer (SUTT), the Air Force's Advanced Air-to-Air System Performance Evaluation Model (AASPEM), and the Joint Services' Command Forces (CFOR) project. Pew and Mavor (1998) described these systems and others and then noted that, although it is possible to represent human behavior in these systems, the state of the human representation is almost always rudimentary. In the words of Pew and Mavor:

> This lack of human performance representation in models becomes more significant as the size, scope, and duration of wargaming simulations continues to grow. In the future, these limitations will become more noticeable as greater reliance is placed on the outcomes of models/simulations to support training and unit readiness, assessments of system performance, and key development and acquisition decisions. (p. 44)

To begin addressing the problems associated with limited HBR capability, developers of these and future military modeling and simulation systems should begin to draw more from cognitive, social, and organizational theory. In particular, Pew and Mavor (1998) suggested that these modeling systems would benefit from a closer association with the developers of integrative HBR architectures.

3

In the psychology literature, the term *architecture* is often used instead of *system* (e.g., Anderson, 1983, 1993; Newell, 1990; Pylyshyn, 1991). A psychological architecture differs from other modeling and simulation systems in that it makes a priori assumptions that constrain the representations and processes available for use in a model on the basis of the theories underlying the architecture. By virtue of these constraints, architectures are a distinct subset of the total set of possible human representation systems. Chapter 3 of the Pew and Mavor (1998) text provides a description of the major characteristics of 11 integrative architectures. Ritter et al. (2003) described seven more. Morrison (2004) reviewed the characteristics of many of the same architectures and added still another six to the list. This totals at least 24 human representation architectures included in recent reviews.

We recently went through that list of two dozen architectures to confirm the availability of each as implemented in software that can be used to develop models and that perhaps also could be integrated into a larger simulation system. The subset of psychologically inspired human representation architectures that meet this availability criterion[1] is listed in Table 1.1. We do not review the characteristics of these architectures here because that would be redundant with the three recent reviews, but we encourage the interested reader to seek out these references or read about the architectures on their respective Web sites.

The existence of such an assortment of HBR architectures is an indication of the health and vitality of this research area. Yet there is considerable room for improvement. All of the architectures have shortcomings in their modeling capabilities, and none of them is as easy to use as we would like them to be. There is enormous interest in greater breadth, increased predictive accuracy, and improved usability in models of human performance and learning. These interests motivated the creation of a research project that would move the field in those directions.

THE AMBR MODEL COMPARISON

This unique project, called the Agent-Based Modeling and Behavior Representation (AMBR) model comparison, was sponsored primarily by the U.S. Air Force Research Laboratory (AFRL), with additional funding from the

---

[1]Absent from this list are Sparse Distributed Memory (SDM; Kanerva, 1993), Contextual Control Model (CoCoM; Hollnagel, 1993), and 4CAPS (Just, Carpenter, & Varma, 1999). SDM does not exist in simulation form (P. Kanerva, personal communication, October 10, 2003). CoCoM does not exist as executable code in the public domain (E. Hollnagel, personal communication, October 13, 2003). 4CAPS exists in simulation form, but is not being released publicly until adequate documentation and pedagogical materials are in place (S. Varma, personal communication, February 26, 2004).

TABLE 1.1
Human Behavior Representation Architectures Available for Use

Architecture	For Additional Information . . .
ACT-R	http://act-r.psy.cmu.edu/
APEX	http://www.andrew.cmu.edu/~bj07/apex/
ART	http://web.umr.edu/~tauritzd/art/
Brahms	http://www.agentisolutions.com/home.htm
CHREST	http://www.psyc.nott.ac.uk/research/credit/projects/CHREST
C/I	http://www.inst.msstate.edu/SAL/adapt.html
Clarion	http://www.cogsci.rpi.edu/~rsun/clarion.html
CogAff	http://www.cs.bham.ac.uk/~axs/cogaff.html
Cogent	http://cogent.psyc.bbk.ac.uk
COGNET/iGEN	http://www.chiinc.com/
D-OMAR	http://omar.bbn.com/
EPAM	http://www.pahomeschoolers.com/epam/
EPIC	http://www.umich.edu/~bcalab/epic.html
MicroPsi	http://www.informatik.hu-berlin.de/~bach/artificial-emotion/
Micro Saint, HOS, IPME	http://www.maad.com/MaadWeb/products/prodma.htm
MIDAS	http://caffeine.arc.nasa.gov/midas/
PDP++	http://psych.colorado.edu/~oreilly/PDP++/PDP++.html
SAMPLE[2]	http://www.cra.com
Soar	http://www.soartechnology.com

Defense Modeling and Simulation Office (DMSO) and the Office of Naval Research (ONR). The AMBR model comparison involved a series of human performance model evaluations in which the behaviors of computer models were compared to each other and to the behaviors of actual human operators performing the identical tasks.

The Approach

Considered in isolation, there is nothing unique about developing models and comparing them to human data. Cognitive science and other related disciplines are replete with such activities. The unique nature of the project is revealed only through consideration of the details of our approach and how it relates to similar efforts.

A previous research project with which the AMBR comparison shares a close affinity is the Hybrid Architectures for Learning Project sponsored by ONR in the mid- to late 1990s. Hybrid Architectures was committed to improving our understanding of human learning by funding the development of various cognitive architecture-based and machine learning-based models in three different learning contexts. The modeling goal was ". . . to run the basic hybrid model on a selected task to verify the model's performance rela-

---

[2]Contact Karen Harper (kharper@cra.com) directly to obtain the SAMPLE software.

tive to the actual human data and to evolve the model, increasing the match between the learned performances, to obtain a better predictive/explanatory model of the human process" (Gigley & Chipman, 1999, p. 2). The emphases on (a) iterative improvements to computational models and model architectures, and (b) evaluating these improvements through comparison to human data both find parallel emphases in AMBR. There was even an intention in Hybrid Architectures to eventually conduct a thorough comparison of the models that had been developed for the various tasks, but unfortunately the funding for the project disappeared before a final comparison took place. The major methodological differences between the two projects are that (a) all of the AMBR modelers developed models of the same tasks to facilitate comparison, and (b) detailed comparison of the models was an integral part of AMBR and took place on a recurring basis.

Another effort that can help illuminate some of the distinctive characteristics of the AMBR model comparison is the comparison of models of working memory that took place in the late 1990s. The working memory model comparison initially took the form of a symposium and eventually evolved into a book on the topic (Miyake & Shah, 1999). Their goal was to compare and contrast existing models of working memory by having each modeler address the same set of theoretical questions about their respective model's implementation. There are probably more differences than similarities between their effort and AMBR, although both approaches were effective in achieving their objectives. One distinction is that the AMBR models were all implemented in computational process models that can interact with simulated task environments, whereas the working memory models came from an assortment of modeling approaches, including verbal/conceptual theories. Another distinction is that the AMBR model comparison was partially motivated by an interest in encouraging computational modelers to improve the implementations and/or applications of their architectures by pushing on their limits in new ways, whereas the working memory model comparison did not fund the development of new models or architectural changes. A third distinction is that, as mentioned previously, all of the AMBR modelers were required to address the same task scenarios, whereas the working memory modelers each focused on a task of their own choosing. In chapter 12 of the Miyake and Shah (1999) book, Kintsch, Healy, Hegarty, Pennington, and Salthouse (1999) applaud the success of the editors' "common questions" approach to comparing the models. It is noteworthy that they then go on to recommend the following for model comparisons:

> ... we would like to emphasize that, to the extent that direct experimental face-offs among models are possible, they should certainly be encouraged. Obviously, such comparisons would be very informative, and much more could be and should be done in this respect than has heretofore been attempted. (p. 436)

Although not originally inspired by this quote, the strategy adopted in AMBR of having each model address the same experiment scenarios is consistent with the Kintsch et al. recommendation. It is also consistent with the proposal a decade earlier by Young, Barnard, Simon, and Whittington (1989) that HCI researchers adopt the use of scenarios as a methodological route to models of broader scope.

Hopefully the previous paragraphs gave the reader an appreciation for the general research approach selected for the AMBR model comparison, but this tells us little of the precise process that was followed. There were two experiments in the AMBR model comparison pursued sequentially. The first focused on multitasking, and the second focused on category learning. Each of the two experiments involved the following steps:

1. Identify the modeling goals—what cognitive/behavioral capabilities should be stressed?
2. Select a task domain that requires the capabilities identified in (1) and that is of relevance to AF modeling and simulation needs.
3. Borrow/modify/create a simulation of the task domain that either a human-in-the-loop or a human performance model can operate.
4. Hold a workshop at which the model developers learn about the task and modeling environment and exchange ideas with the moderator concerning potential parameters that can be measured and constraints of the individual models that need to be accommodated.
5. Moderator team collects and disseminates human performance data.
6. Modeling teams develop models that attempt to replicate human performance when performing the task.
7. Expert panel convenes with the entire team to compare and contrast the models that were developed and the underlying architectures that support them.
8. Share the results and lessons learned with the scientific community to include making available the simulation of the task domain and the human performance data.

We should note that some of the data were withheld from the modelers in the second comparison, which focused on category learning. We say more about that later.

Manager, Moderator, and Modelers

The project involved people from a variety of organizations representing government, industry, and academia. The Air Force Research Laboratory's Warfighter Training Research Division managed the effort. BBN Technologies served in the role of model comparison moderator. They designed the experiments, provided the simplified air traffic control (ATC) simulation environment implemented in D-OMAR (Deutsch & Benyo, 2001; Deutsch, MacMillan, & Cramer, 1993), and collected data on human operators performing the task. Additional data for the second comparison (category learning) were collected at the University of Central Florida, with supervision from colleagues at NAVAIR Orlando (Gwen Campbell and Amy Bolton). There were four modeling teams. Two of the teams (CHI Systems and a team from George Mason University and Soar Technology) were selected as part of the competitive bidding process at the beginning of the first comparison. A team from Carnegie Mellon University joined the first comparison in mid-course, with funding from the Office of Naval Research. Finally, a fourth modeling team, this one from the Air Force Research Laboratory's Logistics and Sustainment Division, participated on their own internal funding.

Goals

There were three goals motivating the AMBR model comparison, all of which bear a striking resemblance to the recommendations made by the National Research Council (NRC) Panel on Modeling Human Behavior and Command Decision Making (Pew & Mavor, 1998).

Goal 1: Advance the State of the Art. The first goal was to advance the state of the art in cognitive modeling. This goal is consistent with the spirit of the entire set of recommendations from the NRC panel because their recommendations were explicitly intended as a roadmap for improving human and organizational behavior modeling. The model comparison process devised for this project provides a motivation and opportunity for human modelers to extend and test their architectures in new ways. As should be apparent in the subsequent chapters in this book, there is ample evidence that these modeling architectures were challenged and improved as a direct result of their participation in this project.

Goal 2: Develop Mission-Relevant HBR Models. The second goal was to develop HBR models that are relevant to the Department of Defense (DoD) mission, and therefore provide possible transition opportunities. This is consistent with the NRC panel recommendation to support model development in focused areas of interest to the DoD. The two modeling focus areas selected for AMBR were multitasking and category learning. We say more about each of those areas shortly.

Goal 3: Make Tasks, Models, and Data Available. The third goal was to make all of the research tasks, human behavior models, and human process and outcome data available to the public. This is consistent with the NRC panel recommendation for increased collection and dissemination of human performance data. We have described various subsets of the results from the AMBR model comparison at several different conferences over the last 3 years, resulting in almost three dozen conference papers and technical reports. This book, however, is the most comprehensive source of information regarding the scientific output of the AMBR model comparison.

Experiment 1: Multitasking

The AMBR model comparison was divided into two experiments, with a different modeling focus in each. The modeling focus for Experiment 1 was multiple task management because this area represents a capability that is not widely available in existing models or modeling architectures, and because more knowledge regarding how to represent this capability provides an opportunity to improve the fidelity of future computer-generated forces (CGFs). It was the responsibility of the moderator (BBN) to select a task for simulation that emphasized multiple-task management.

Two approaches, representing ends of a continuum of intermediate possibilities, were considered. One approach is to select a high-fidelity task that is of direct operational relevance, realistic complexity, and requires highly trained operators to be the participants. Alternatively, the task could be highly abstracted, almost like a video game that anyone could be expected to learn, but that captures the task management requirements of interest.

Clearly the high-fidelity approach would have greater practical significance and be more challenging from a modeling perspective. However, it would require extensive knowledge acquisition on the part of each modeling team—an investment that would detract from the time and effort that could be put into the model development. The moderator could supply that knowledge, but it is well known that first-hand knowledge is really required to address all the context-sensitive requirements of computational process models. An overlay on this debate was whether the developers would be required to model experienced or novice operators. There were strong arguments against modeling novices in complex simulation environments, mostly centering on concerns that the likely variability they would produce in the data would mask the behaviors we were trying to measure. Using a task of realistic complexity also had implications for the moderator team, which had limited resources for collecting data. Either they would have had to identify and recruit experienced operators from the domain under study or invest in an extensive period of training. Finally, high-fidelity, DoD-relevant simulation environments are often classified at a level that prohibits release in the public domain, and that would conflict with our goal of making all materials from the project available for use by others.

Having weighed these concerns, the moderator opted to use a highly abstracted version of an ATC task and use participants who had played a lot of video games, but had no previous experience with this task. Data were obtained from novice human participants in 4-hour sessions, and the modelers were able to develop the requisite knowledge based on their own experience or by testing a small set of previously untrained participants.

Experiment 2: Category Learning

As the first comparison was wrapping up, the decision was made to focus the second comparison on learning. Considerable effort was devoted to meeting the same constraints considered for Experiment 1. We wanted the task to be fairly abstract so that extensive content knowledge would not be required. It was important that participants have no previous exposure to the material to be learned and that they would not need extensive training to understand the task required of them. The resulting decision was to use the same basic ATC scenario already available from Experiment 1, but to modify it to embed a category learning task. The learning task was based on the Shepard, Hovland, and Jenkins (1961) classic category learning paradigm and its more recent replication and extension by Nosofsky, Gluck, Palmeri, McKinley, and Glauthier (1994). The availability of data from these classic experiments was considered a valuable feature of the task because it allowed the modeling teams to get started on preliminary model developments using existing published results, while the moderator made task modifications and collected the new human data. The second comparison challenged the modelers to build computational process models that simulated the learning of new concepts in the context of executing the ATC task, which is an interesting and novel dual-task requirement. The second comparison also challenged them to make *a priori* predictions of human behavior in a transfer condition. The transfer data were actually withheld from the model developers until after they shared their predictions with the group.

Preview of the Remainder of the Book

The book is divided into three parts. Part I (chaps. 1–3) is background material leading up to the model descriptions. Chapter 1, obviously, is an overview of the effort. Chapter 2 describes, for each of the experiments, more about the rationale for the choice of tasks, a detailed description of the task, its dynamics, and the human operator requirements. It then presents the method and results from the human experiments. Chapter 3 describes the hardware and software that were used and how the software was set up to allow seamless introduction of either a human operator or a model of the behavior of a human operator and the way in which the models were connected into the simulation.

Part II (chaps. 4–7) presents each of the models that were developed in response to the modeling challenges. The authors of these chapters were given a detailed structure to follow to ensure that the chapters would cover similar topics and the reader would find it easier to follow the model descriptions and modeling results. At the end of each of these chapters, the authors were asked to answer a set of summary questions about their models.

Part III is comprised of variations on conclusions, lessons learned, and implications for future research. Chapter 8 offers a discussion of how the models compared in terms of how the architectures and models were similar and different and how they performed the target tasks as compared with human data. Included are comments on how the results of the models' performances were related to and derived from the architectures and assumptions that went into the models. Chapter 9 relates the AMBR models of category learning to other models of category learning in the contemporary psychological literature. Chapter 10 covers a variety of important issues associated with the validation of computational process models. Chapter 11 is composed of reflections on the results of the project and proposes a research agenda to carry the field of human behavior representation forward.

A CD is included with this book. The primary content is loadable/ runnable versions of the D-OMAR ATC simulations and the human data that have been collected. Modelers were asked to include, at a minimum, a readable text file for each model they developed so interested persons can inspect the knowledge content and representation for each model. Additional functionality, such as a model that will actually load and run, is optional, at the discretion of the respective modeling teams. We hope this book and its supporting material are informative resources for all those interested in improving our human behavior representation capabilities.

REFERENCES

Anderson, J. R. (1983). *The architecture of cognition*. Cambridge, MA: Harvard University Press.

Anderson, J. R. (1993). *Rules of the mind*. Mahwah, NJ: Lawrence Erlbaum Associates.

Deutsch, S. E., & Benyo, B. (2001). The D-OMAR simulation environment for the AMBR experiments. In the *Proceedings of the 10th Annual Conference on Computer-Generated Forces and Behavior Representation* (pp. 7–14). Orlando, FL: Division of Continuing Education, University of Central Florida.

Deutsch, S. E., MacMillan, J., & Cramer, N. L. (1993). *Operator Model Architecture (OMAR) demonstration final report (AL/HR-TR–1996-0161)*. Wright-Patterson AFB, OH: Armstrong Laboratory, Logistics Research Division.

Gigley, H. M., & Chipman, S. F. (1999). Productive interdisciplinarity: The challenge that human learning poses to machine learning. In *Proceedings of the 21st Conference of the Cognitive Science Society* (p. 2). Mahwah, NJ: Lawrence Erlbaum Associates.

Hollnagel, E. (1993). *Human reliability analysis: Context and control*. London: Academic Press.

Just, M. A., Carpenter, P. A., & Varma, S. (1999). Computational modeling of high-level cognition and brain function. *Human Brain Mapping, 8*, 128–136.

Kanerva, P. (1993). Sparse distributed memory and related models. In M. H. Hassoun (Ed.), *Associative neural memories: Theory and implementation* (pp. 50–76). New York: Oxford University Press.

Kintsch, W., Healy, A. F., Hegarty, M., Pennington, B. F., & Salthouse, T. (1999). Models of working memory: Eight questions and some general issues. In A. Miyake & P. Shah (Eds.), *Models of working memory: Mechanisms of active maintenance and executive control* (pp. 412–441). New York: Cambridge University Press.

Miyake, A., & Shah, P. (Eds.). (1999). *Models of working memory: Mechanisms of active maintenance and executive control*. New York: Cambridge University Press.

Morrison, J. E. (2004). *A review of computer-based human behavior representations and their relation to military simulations (IDA Paper P-3845)*. Alexandria, VA: Institute for Defense Analyses.

Newell, A. (1990). *Unified theories of cognition*. Cambridge, MA: Harvard University Press.

Nosofsky, R. M., Gluck, M., Palmeri, T. J., McKinley, S. C., & Glauthier, P. (1994). Comparing models of rule-based classification learning: A replication and extension of Shepard, Hovland, and Jenkins (1961). *Memory & Cognition, 22*, 352–369.

Pew, R. W., & Mavor, A. S. (Eds.). (1998). *Modeling human and organizational behavior: Applications to military simulations*. Washington, DC: National Academy Press.

Pylyshyn, Z. W. (1991). The role of cognitive architecture in theories of cognition. In K. VanLehn (Ed.), *Architectures for intelligence* (pp. 189–223). Hillsdale, NJ: Lawrence Erlbaum Associates.

Ritter, F. E., Shadbolt, N. R., Elliman, D., Young, R. M., Gobet, F., & Baxter, G. D. (2003). *Techniques for modeling human performance in synthetic environments: A supplementary review (HSIAC-SOAR-2003-01)*. Wright-Patterson Air Force Base, OH: Human Systems Information Analysis Center.

Shepard, R. N., Hovland, C. L., & Jenkins, H. M. (1961). Learning and memorization of classifications, *Psychological Monographs, 75*(13,Whole No. 517).

Young, R. M., Barnard, P., Simon, T., & Whittington, J. (1989). How would your favourite user model cope with these scenarios? *SIG CHI Bulletin, 20*(4), 51–55.

Chapter 2

The AMBR Experiments: Methodology and Human Benchmark Results

Yvette J. Tenney
David E. Diller
Stephen Deutsch
Katherine Godfrey
BBN Technologies

This chapter describes two experiments in which performance data were collected from humans as a benchmark for comparing the ability of four different modeling teams to replicate and predict the observed data. Our goal was to stress and extend existing modeling architectures by collecting a rich set of data that would require models to successfully integrate and coordinate memory, learning, multitasking, cognitive, perceptual, and motor components. The first experiment focused on multiple task management and attention sharing. The second experiment expanded on the first, embedding a category learning paradigm in a multitasking paradigm.

An unusual feature of the AMBR program was our development of an experimental testbed in which both humans and model participants could function. The testbed was instrumented so that a model could "perceive" the same events as a human participant and had the ability to perform the same actions as its human counterparts. All actions were time stamped and recorded for later analysis. The details of this environment are described in chapter 3.

In this chapter, we describe the experimental task and the human benchmark results, which served as the "ground truth" for assessing the performance of the models. Discussion of how well each of the models fared in predicting the observed human data is deferred until later chapters, where each of the modeling teams has a chance to talk about its model and present its results in depth. Finally, in chapter 8, we take a broad look across models, illustrating where they produce results similar to one another, as well as where they make their own unique predictions. It is these similarities and differences, as highlighted in model performance, that raise questions that can help us better understand the processes by which we as humans operate effectively in complex tasks.

EXPERIMENT 1: INTEGRATIVE MULTITASKING

The initial experiment of the AMBR project was designed to examine human multiple-task management, dynamic priority setting, and attention management as the modeling foci. These areas represent capabilities that were not widely available in existing models or modeling architectures, and they will be important to future computer-generated forces (CGF) representation.

A simplified air traffic control situation was used because of the potential for human operator overload and the need for effective information management strategies. The goal was to foster understanding of multitasking strategies—a capability not widely available in existing models—while providing a relatively straightforward task for initiating the model comparisons.

OVERVIEW

Decision making in complex, fast-paced environments has been studied through simulations in a number of domains, including air traffic control (e.g., Ackerman & Kanfer, 1994; John & Lallement, 1997; MacMillan, Deutsch, & Young, 1997), military command and control (Anderson et al., in press; Cannon-Bowers & Salas, 1998), and team sports (Kirlik, Walker, Fisk, & Nagel, 1996). An air traffic control (ATC) task developed by Mac-Millan, Deutsch, and Young (1997) was adapted for purposes of the present study. The focus was on individual rather than team performance. The task was loosely based on that of a real air traffic controller, but was designed to require minimal participant training. It was chosen because it exhibited the characteristics typical of mentally and perceptually demanding, multitask situations: information arrives at inconvenient or unexpected times, information interrupts an ongoing chain of thought, information relevant to one task may be obscured by information from another, and information irrelevant to the current task may be salient and distracting. In addition, this task readily accommodated variations in display and workload conditions that were expected to have a predictable impact on performance.

The task, although simpler than its real-life equivalent, presented a host of challenges to the modelers. For example, they had to decide how the model would manage the scenario as a whole, choose when to shift between tasks, remember and update tasks awaiting service, and prioritize among them. An additional challenge for the modelers was to ensure that the behavior of the model changed appropriately under different conditions (e.g., with different display types and workload time pressures).

The task involved transferring aircraft in and out of a central sector by reading and sending messages to the aircraft and adjoining controllers. Penalty points were accrued for not carrying out actions within a critical time period, causing aircraft to go "on hold," and not attending to holding aircraft in a timely manner. Smaller penalties were accrued for skipping optional actions and for sending inappropriate, unnecessary, or inefficiently executed messages. The player's goal was to complete the scenario with a minimum of penalties. Optimal performance required staying ahead of the situation (e.g., anticipating the needs of aircraft approaching a sector boundary), attending to high-priority aircraft, remembering to complete actions following an interruption, and developing optimal scanning and reading strategies.

In the ATC task just described, the messages carry no ambiguity (i.e., requests could not be refused). As a result, the tasks across different aircraft and flight stages all had a similar flavor. To help capture the greater variety that characterizes realistic multitasking situations, we introduced a decision task that took the form of a speed change request. Each time there was a speed request, the controller had to answer yes or no depending on the aircraft's alignment. Penalty points were accrued for delayed or incorrect responses. The correct rule was explained at the outset in Experiment 1. In Experiment 2, using a similar task, participants had to discover the correct response (i.e., learn the concept) on the basis of feedback.

Each participant in Experiment 1 experienced six scenarios derived from a combination of three workload levels (two, three, or four aircraft per minute) and two display conditions—a text condition in which all messages had to be read and a color condition in which color codes signaled the action required and obviated the need for reading. The purpose of the experiment was to see to what extent human performance differed as a function of workload and display conditions and to see how well the models would replicate the human results.

METHOD

Participants

Sixteen BBN Technologies employees—4 females and 12 males—participated in the experiment. All were experienced video game players under the age of 36.

Display

Participants were presented with a visual display consisting of a simulated radar screen, six action buttons, and three message boards, with each board associated with two of the action buttons (see Fig. 2.1). The simulated radar screen consisted of a central sector, bounded by yellow lines, representing a 200 × 200 nautical mile (NM) region. A "+" marked the center of the sector. The sector had both an outer and inner border (yellow and green lines), with 25 NM between the borders. The radar display includes four graphic icons representing neighboring controllers and may contain icons for the aircraft moving through the sector. Adjoining controllers (simulated) are located above, below, right, and left of the central sector and are represented graphically by the words *north, south, east,* and *west.*

The icons for the aircraft identify their direction of flight and are labeled with their flight designators (e.g., NW301). Aircraft traveled at a speed of 1,000 NM/hr or .28 NM/second, taking 3.6 seconds to travel 1 mile. Aircraft could enter and exit from all sides of the sector, flying across the sector on straight vertical or horizontal paths. Both incoming and outgoing messages appear over time on one of three message boards located beneath the appro-

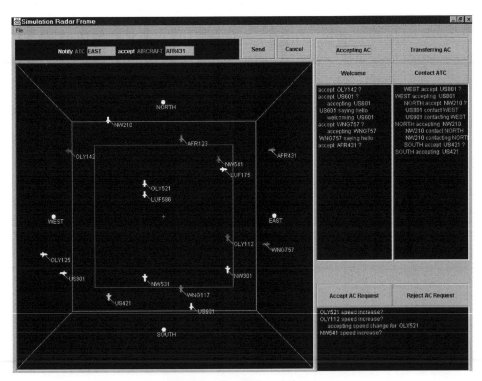

FIG. 2.1.   The ATC workplace.

priate actions buttons (see Fig. 2.1). The aircraft labels within the text message boards are printed in a different color to make them stand out. Within each board, a message can be either left-adjusted or indented. The left-adjusted messages serve as triggers for actions. Indented messages reflect actions already taken and can be ignored unless the player wants to check whether an action is still pending. New messages appear below previous text.

Participants received one of two possible display conditions. In the text display, the information required to determine what actions to take appeared in text form on the message boards on the right side of the display. In the color display (see Fig. 2.1), the aircraft icons were color coded to indicate required actions.

Design

The design was a within-participants comparison of two display conditions (text, color) and three workload levels (low, medium, high). Workload was manipulated by keeping the number of aircraft and their speed constant, but reducing the length of the scenario, by judiciously spacing aircraft closer together in the high-workload scenarios. In this way, the number of possible penalty points remained constant across workload conditions. There were 20 aircraft requesting a hand-off and and three requesting a speed change in every scenario. These requests arrived over a period of 10 minutes for the low-workload condition, 7½ minutes for the medium-workload condition, and 5 minutes for the high-workload condition. The actual scenario length was 11.5, 9, and 6.5 minutes, for the three conditions, respectively, to allow time for all requests to be processed.

Four equivalent sets of scenarios were developed for the experiment. Two sets of scenarios (A and B) were constructed, each with a random assignment of aircraft starting location, aircraft identification labels, and start times to make the sets as equivalent as possible. Two additional scenario sets (A* and B*) were generated by rotating each aircraft in the original scenarios by 180 degrees and randomly reassigning aircraft labels. For example, an aircraft that would enter from the northern portion of the west sector in the original scenario A would enter from the southern portion of the east sector in the new scenario A*. Half the participants were trained on the A and A* scenarios and tested on the B and B* scenarios. The other half were trained on the B and B* scenarios and tested on A and A*. Within each group, half the participants received the unstarred scenarios in the text display condition and the starred scenarios in the color condition. The other half received the starred scenarios in the text condition and unstarred in the color condition. The starred and unstarred versions, mirror images of each other, were structurally equivalent and, therefore, directly comparable in difficulty.

Task Activities

In the experimental task, the "player" (human participant or cognitive model) assumes the role of the air traffic controller in the central sector bounded by the outer yellow line (see Fig. 2.1). The player is responsible for managing all the aircraft as they enter and leave the central sector. An aspect of this ATC task that sets it apart from the real one is that collisions are not of concern. Players are told that aircraft which appear to be colliding are actually at different altitudes. The objective of the task is to complete the required actions in a timely fashion and avoid accumulating penalties for missed, delayed, or incorrect actions.

There are six actions that players can take by using the six action buttons (see Fig. 2.1). An action is initiated by pressing one of the action buttons. For aircraft coming into the central sector, the player should ACCEPT and WELCOME each aircraft. For aircraft within the sector, the player should reply to a request for a speed increase by using the ACCEPT/REJECT AC REQUEST buttons. For aircraft leaving the sector, the player can TRANSFER the aircraft to the next controller and tell the aircraft to CONTACT ATC. Each of these actions and the penalties accrued by incorrectly performing or not performing these actions are described in further detail later and in Table 2.1.

Pressing an action button brings up a message template in the upper left-hand corner above the radar screen, with slots indicating the required information (e.g., aircraft label and ATC). Template slots are filled in by selecting the appropriate icons on the radar display. The template can help the player avoid the penalty for extraneous clicks by serving as a reminder (e.g., only half the commands require clicking on ATC).

Accept.   When the aircraft is 25 miles outside the outer boundary (yellow square), a message appears on the left-most board (e.g., "ACCEPT TWA555?"). In the color display condition, the aircraft icon also turns green. The player must ACCEPT the plane as soon as possible after the message appears.

If the player does not ACCEPT an aircraft before it reaches the outer border, the aircraft will turn red and enter a holding pattern. The player can release the aircraft by clicking on the aircraft and doing an ACCEPT. There are penalties associated with an AC turning red and staying red (see Table 2.1). Aircraft turn red in both the text and color display conditions.

Welcome.   Some time after an aircraft has been accepted, a message appears on the left-most board (e.g., "TWA555 saying hello"). In the color display condition, the aircraft also turns blue. The WELCOME action is an op-

TABLE 2.1
Penalty Points in the Experiment 1 ATC Task

Penalty Category	Player's Goal	Penalty
Hold	Prevent aircraft from holding either while incoming or outgoing	50 points each time an aircraft turns red
Holding Delay	Get aircraft out of holding	10 points each time unit[a] aircraft stays red
Speed Error	Respond to speed change requests correctly	50 points for an incorrect response to a speed change request
Speed Delay	Respond to speed change request in timely manner	2 points each time unit[a] request not answered
Welcome Delay	Welcome aircraft in a timely manner	1 point each time unit[a] aircraft not welcomed
Duplication	Avoid sending the same message twice	10 points for duplication of a message
Extraneous Click	Avoid clicking on an ATC center when not required	10 points for an extraneous click
Incorrect Message	Avoid sending a message when proper trigger not present	10 points for an incorrect message

[a]The time unit was 60 seconds for low-workload, 45 seconds for medium-workload, and 30 seconds for high-workload scenarios, respectively, to keep the maximum number of penalty points that could be earned in each condition constant.

tional action. Omitting it will not cause the aircraft to turn red. There are small penalties, however, associated with a delay in welcoming an aircraft.

Accept/Reject Request. Aircraft within the bounds of the central sector may, from time to time, request a speed increase. A message appears in the bottom-most message area (e.g., "TWA555 speed increase?"), and in the color display condition the aircraft turns magenta. Players can respond with an ACCEPT AC REQUEST or a REJECT AC REQUEST action. Participants are instructed that the judgment of whether to accept or reject the request for a speed increase is entirely straightforward and does not require any calculation of speed or distance. If the aircraft requesting a speed increase has no aircraft traveling in a direct line in front of it, the players must ACCEPT AC REQUEST; otherwise they must REJECT AC REQUEST. An incorrect response to a speed request carries a heavy penalty, whereas a delay in responding to the request carries a lighter penalty.

Transfer. This action is the only one that is not triggered by a message, but rather by the position of the aircraft. When an aircraft in the central sector reaches the inner border (green line), the player should initiate a TRANSFER to hand the aircraft off to the controller in the next sector. In the color display condition, the aircraft icon turns brown.

Contact ATC. As soon as the next controller accepts the aircraft, a message appears on the right board (e.g., "EAST accepting TWA555"). In the color display condition, the aircraft icon turns yellow. If both actions— TRANSFER and telling the aircraft to CONTACT ATC—are not completed by the time the aircraft reaches the outer boundary, the aircraft will turn red and enter a holding pattern, with an ensuing penalty. The aircraft can be released by carrying out the missing TRANSFER and/or CONTACT actions. The player may have to read the messages to determine whether a TRANSFER, CONTACT, or both are required (assuming this information is not remembered). If the player responds to a red outgoing aircraft by doing a TRANSFER and it turns out the TRANSFER had already been carried out, the player accrues a small penalty for a duplicate action. There is a penalty for delaying the release.

In the color display condition, the icon color turns back to white when the SEND is completed. If the SEND is pressed at the last minute, just before the aircraft reaches the border, the aircraft may turn red for a few seconds before turning white. The red indicates that a penalty has been accrued. (Note: In both the color and text displays, the assignment of a penalty in this situation depends on when the simulated adjoining controller actually receives the message and has time to act on it, which can vary depending on how busy the controller is.)

Procedure

Each participant took part in two sessions scheduled no more than a few days apart. The first session, 2½ hours in length, involved an initial phase of training and a practice block of six blocks (covering two display conditions × three workload levels). The initial training began with the text display for all participants. The initial training phase included a demonstration, coached and uncoached practice with simple and complex scenarios, written figures and diagrams, a short quiz to ensure that material was understood, and, finally, the practice block, which served as a dress rehearsal for the actual test blocks.

The second session, 2 hours in length, involved the actual test block of six scenarios. The block consisted of three scenarios with one display followed by three with the other. Half the participants started with text and half with color. Within each display condition, the workload level increased over the three scenarios. A single practice scenario, with the text display, preceded this block. Performance measures on the practice and test blocks were collected and compiled automatically during and after each run.

At the end of each scenario, for both the practice and test blocks, participants completed the unweighted Task Loading Index (TLX) workload rating sheet (Vidulich & Tsang, 1986). Ratings are made by circling a tick mark on a drawing of a 10-unit scale (yielding rankings from 0 to 10) on six different workload scales (mental demand, physical demand, temporal demand, performance, effort, frustration). TLX was selected because of the two most widely used subjective assessment tools, TLX (Hart & Staveland, 1988) and SWAT (Reid & Nygren, 1988). TLX is easier to administer and was potentially easier to manage conceptually in a model.

A debrief questionnaire concerned with the participant's strategies was administered at the conclusion of the experiment (Pew, Tenney, Deutsch, Spector, & Benyo, 2000). Participants were asked about the difficulty of using the two displays, to what extent they read the text messages under different conditions (color/text display when busy/not busy), their strategies for scanning the radar screen, and how much they relied on their memory versus other means for determining what actions to take when an outgoing aircraft turned red (i.e., TRANSFER, CONTACT ATC, or both).

Procedure for Human Performance Models

Data from the first eight human participants were given to the modelers during model development (development data) while data from the second half of the participants were being collected (intended comparison data). The original plan of using data from the unseen half of the subjects for the comparison had to be abandoned, however, because of the variability related to the small sample size. Instead the models were compared against the full, more reliable data set, although it was not entirely new to them. The procedure for the models was the same as for the humans, with one exception: Models did not answer debrief questions, although as an extra challenge they were encouraged to provide workload ratings.

RESULTS

The human results—concerning performance, reaction time, and strategies—are now discussed. The model descriptions and results are deferred until chapters 4 to 7, while chapter 8 provides a comparison of the model results and their architectures.

Accuracy Measures

Figure 2.2 illustrates the human data with respect to mean accumulated penalty points by condition. Error bars represent dual-sided 95% standard error of the mean confidence intervals. The graph clearly shows that more penalty points were accrued with the text display than with the color display, especially at higher workloads. These trends were supported by a two-

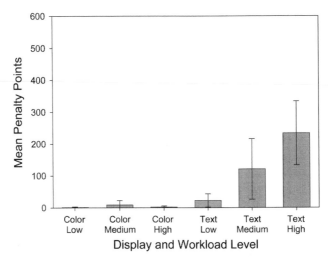

FIG. 2.2.   Penalty scores as a function of display and workload.

factor repeated measures analysis of variance (ANOVA), with significant main effects of display [$F(1, 14) = 23.27$, $p < .001$] and workload [$F(2, 28) = 10.80$, $p < .001$] and a significant interaction of display × workload [$F(2, 28) = 9.76$, $p < .001$].

Penalty scores were explored in greater detail in the most demanding condition: text display with high workload. The upper panel in Fig. 2.3 shows the penalty points in each of the penalty subcategories for the text high-workload condition. It is clear from the graph that the overriding source of points for humans was hold penalties (at 50 points each).

The lower panel in Fig. 2.3 shows the actual number of occurrences of each type of error. The results suggest that participants prioritized their actions so as to minimize overall penalties. Thus, welcome delay, which carries the lowest penalty (1 point per minute), was the most frequent penalty obtained by humans. The next largest category of observed errors was speed delay (2 points per unit of time). The strategy of postponing actions carrying low penalties to focus on preventing aircraft from turning red, which carries a higher penalty (50 points), is a reasonable strategy for coping with high workloads.

Response Time Measures

Figure 2.4 illustrates the mean response times for each display and workload condition. Response times were calculated as the time interval between the appearance of the trigger for an action and the activation of the SEND button to complete that action. All types of actions were included in the average.

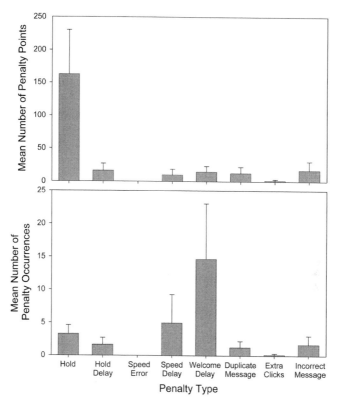

FIG. 2.3. Detailed analysis of penalty categories for text high-workload condition.

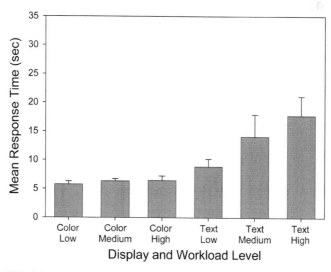

FIG. 2.4. Mean response times as a function of display and workload.

As can be seen in the graph, participants responded to the triggers more quickly with the color display than with the text display, and workload effects were more pronounced in the text than in the color condition. These results show a similar pattern to the results seen in accuracy measures, suggesting there was no speed accuracy tradeoff occurring for the conditions. An ANOVA showed significant main effects of display [$F(1, 14) = 60.78$, $p < .0001$] and workload [$F(2, 28) = 19.69$, $p < .0001$], as well as an interaction of workload × display [$F(2, 28) = 12.73$, $p < .0001$].

Workload Measures

An overall subjective workload rating was obtained for each participant by averaging across the six individual workload scales that are part of the TLX (mental demand, physical demand, temporal demand, performance, effort, frustration). The workload rating scale ranged from 0 to 10 representing *low* to *high workload*, respectively.

The human results, shown in Fig. 2.5, demonstrate that participants rated their workload as higher for the text than for the color display. There was also an increase in subjective workload as actual workload increased, especially for the text display. An ANOVA showed significant main effects of display [$F(1, 14) = 43.97$, $p < .0001$] and workload [$F(2, 28) = 24.43$, $p < .0001$] and a significant interaction of display × workload [$F(2, 28) = 13.21$, $p < .0001$].

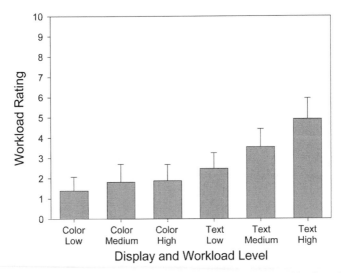

FIG. 2.5.   Subjective workload as a function of display and workload condition.

Debrief Questionnaire for Human Participants

The debrief questionnaire provided insight into human strategies and experiences. Many of the strategies reported by the human participants are reflected in the rationale presented by the modelers for their modeling decisions (see the chapters describing each individual model).

All participants rated the unaided text display as more difficult than the color-coded display (Question 1). The average rating on a scale of 1 to 10—where 1 was *very easy* and 10 was *very difficult*—was 7.5 (range 4–10) for text and 1.94 (range 1–4) for color.

Participants reported adjusting their strategy for accomplishing the task when they switched from one display to another (Question 2). The following answer was typical: "Yes, where color was involved [I] only had to watch for color changes and take appropriate action. No color—had to keep mental 'list' of items in queue." Another response alluded to a possible loss of situation awareness with the color display: "When it got busier, I relied more on colors than knowing which planes were at what point in their trip."

Participants were asked to rate how much they looked at the messages on a scale of 1 to 5 (*never, rarely, sometimes, often, always*) under various conditions (Question 3). Their responses indicate that they rarely looked at the messages in the color display, whether busy (1.8) or not busy (2.4), whereas they often looked at them in the text condition, both when busy (4.06) and when not busy (4.13).

Almost three quarters of the participants answered "yes" when asked whether they had scanned the radar screen in a consistent manner (Question 4). Of those participants, almost half mentioned scanning in a "clockwise" or "north, east, south, west" pattern. Almost all participants mentioned focusing attention on the critical boundaries: the green and yellow borders, the area between the two borders, and the area just inside the green border, and the area just outside the yellow border.

A final question concerned strategies for when an aircraft turned red (Question 5). Participants were asked to indicate on a scale of 1 to 5 (*never, rarely, sometimes, often, always*) how often they engaged in a particular strategy. Their responses indicate that participants sometimes (3.1) remembered what they had already done for that plane and knew immediately what action(s) needed to be taken.

When they did not remember what they had already done for that plane, they sometimes (3.2) scanned the list of messages to see which action(s) they had omitted, rarely (2.4) ignored the message screen and instead did a CONTACT ATC to see whether the red would disappear, and rarely or sometimes (2.5) ignored the message screen and immediately did a TRANSFER AC, followed in due time by a CONTACT ATC.

DISCUSSION

This experiment was, in many ways, successful in producing a domain and data set suitable for evaluating and comparing human performance models. The experimental paradigm provided a relatively rich data set, although a larger sample of participants might have reduced some of the observed variability and inconsistencies seen in the data. Unfortunately, the experimental conditions were such that the color display condition produced little challenge to the human participants and resulted in a less challenging condition than had been desired. With respect to reaction time measures, reaction times increased with workload level. In addition, response times in the color display conditions were faster than the easiest text display condition. With respect to the main focus of this experiment, multiple task management, the results show evidence of load shedding, with more occurrences of welcome delays and speed delays than of holds. Finally, subjective workload ratings clearly reflected workload condition. Subsequent chapters reveal how successfully each of the different human performance models predicted all these results.

EXPERIMENT 2: CATEGORY LEARNING

Another challenging avenue for model development, exploration, and comparison was sought for Experiment 2. We decided to focus on category learning in the context of a dynamic multitasking environment, given that two of the architectures (COGNET/iGEN and DCOG) did not yet have a learning component, whereas the other two (ACT-R and EASE through its predecessor SOAR) had already been applied to category learning phenomena. We were curious to what extent each of the models would borrow from or reuse existing approaches to categorization and adapt them for multitasking purposes. The large literature and rich set of findings associated with concept learning made this capability appealing. The classic category learning study by Shepard, Hovland, and Jenkins (1961) and its more recent replication and extension by Nosofsky, Gluck, Palmeri, McKinley, and Glauthier (1994a) serve as benchmarks against which most models with category learning capabilities are compared (Anderson, 1991; Gureckis & Love, 2003; Kruschke, 1992; Nosofsky, Palmeri, & McKinley, 1994b). Although there are many category learning models, the majority address category learning in isolation, rather than integrated with other behavioral phenomena. By including a variant of the classic study by Shepard et al. (1961) in the ATC task from Experiment 1, we hoped to develop a complex task with a rich set of findings against which to compare the models.

OVERVIEW

In the study by Shepard et al. (1961), participants were asked to classify eight stimulus items varying on three binary valued dimensions (size, color, shape). Stimulus items were organized into two categories, with four items in each category. Given these constraints, there are six possible category structures, illustrated in Fig. 2.6, with the eight stimulus items represented by the eight numbered circles at the corners of the cube. Category assignment is represented by the filled and unfilled circles. Every possible assignment of stimulus items to categories falls into one of the shown category structures or problem types. The main finding of Shepard et al. (1961) was that the six problem types varied in their difficulty to learn, with Problem Type I the easiest to learn, and Problem Type VI the most difficult to master.

Problem Type I requires information about only one dimension. Problem Type II requires knowledge of two dimensions and is the exclusive-or (X-OR) problem with an irrelevant dimension. Problem Types III, IV, and V require information from all three dimensions, with varying degrees of relevance. Problem Type VI requires information from all three dimensions and places equal importance on all dimensions. The results from the Shepard et al. (1961) original study and the Nosofsky et al. (1994a) replication and extension found that Problem Type I was learned most easily, followed by Problem Type II, then by Problem Type III, IV, and V, which were approximately equal in difficulty, and, last, Problem Type VI. Nosofsky et al. (1994a) tested a larger number of participants than in the original Shepard et al. study, collecting enough data to produce learning curves and provide insights into the time course of category learning.

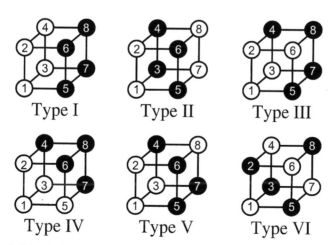

FIG. 2.6. Logical structure of the six types of problems tested by Shepard et al. (1961).

We embedded this classic category learning task in the basic air traffic control situation, couching it as an altitude change request from an aircraft pilot. Participants had to learn to make correct decisions to accept or reject altitude change requests based on three bivariate properties of the aircraft (percent fuel remaining, aircraft size, and turbulence level). In addition to the altitude change requests (the concept learning task), the participant had to hand off a number of aircraft to adjoining controllers (secondary task), similar to what they had done in Experiment 1.

Concept learning also lent itself well to the addition of a transfer test—something our expert panel recommended as critical for model validation. Another advantage was that psychologists studying categorization had developed debriefing techniques for inducing subjects to verbalize their strategies. We felt this kind of information would be valuable to the modelers (Love & Markman, 2003).

The learning requirement provided an opportunity to compare the different ways models could be made to expand their capabilities. By adding a category learning component to the ATC task, modelers were required to either activate and adapt learning algorithms already existing in their models or, in several cases, develop an entirely new learning mechanism. The degree to which learning mechanisms were integrated into existing model architectures could vary from a separate submodule implemented as a black box, and able to be manipulated independently from the rest of the system, to a fundamental component and constraint on the model architecture. We were interested in the different approaches the models would take and how successful they would be in matching human learning.

METHOD

Participants

Participants were 90 college undergraduates (mean age 21.75, range 18–33) with at least sophomore status and an intended or declared psychology major. Seventy-three percent were female. Fifty-four students were recruited from colleges in the Boston area, predominantly from Boston University, and were tested at BBN Technologies in Cambridge, MA. Thirty-six additional participants were recruited from and tested at the University of Central Florida in Orlando. Participants were randomly assigned to conditions. One of the BBN experimenters observed several testing sessions in Florida to ensure that identical procedures were followed. One participant was replaced due to an inability to understand the secondary airspace management task, indicated by a lack of responsiveness to a large number of task action cues. As a non-native English speaker, it is possible she had not understood the instructions because of insufficient mastery of English.

Display

The visual display and stimulus items were adapted from the color display condition in Experiment 1 (the text display was not used in this experiment). Two changes were made to the color display. First, three properties of the aircraft were on occasion displayed on the simulated radar screen just below the aircraft label. These three properties represented percent fuel remaining, aircraft size, and turbulence level, each with one of five possible values. Possible values for percent fuel remaining were "10," "20," "30," "40," or "50." Values for aircraft size were "XS," "S," "M," "L," or "XL," while values for turbulence level were "0," "1," "2," "3," or "4." Of the five values for each property, only two—the second and the fourth—appeared in the learning portion of the experiment. The remaining three values were reserved for the transfer task described next. Second, the action buttons previously labeled ACCEPT AC REQUEST and REJECT AC REQUEST were relabeled ACCEPT ALTITUDE REQUEST and REJECT ALTITUDE REQUEST, respectively.

Design

The design consisted of two between-participants factors each containing three levels and one within-participants factor. The two between factors were category problem type and workload level; the within factor was blocks. Three different problem types (i.e., category structures) were used and were identical to problem types I, III, and VI used in Shepard et al. (1961) and Nosofsky et al. (1994a). The logical structures of the three problem types are shown in Fig. 2.6. Three workload levels—low, medium, and high—were explored, each with a different number of required secondary task actions. Participants were randomly assigned to one of these nine groups.

Procedure

Participants completed eight presentation blocks or scenarios. This procedure was similar to that used in Nosofsky et al. (1994a). Each of the eight scenarios contained 16 category judgment requests, with each stimulus item appearing twice per block. The stimulus ordering within each block was randomized. The workload level and problem type remained constant over the eight blocks.

The task and procedures were based on the task and procedures used in Experiment 1 with several extensions. A category learning component was added to the task, as was a transfer condition completed at the end of the eight blocks. The category learning task was emphasized as the primary task and is described later. The multitasking airspace management portion of Experiment 1 was treated as a secondary task and is also discussed later.

Primary Task. The category learning task was couched as a request from a pilot to change altitude. Altitude change requests were used in place of speed change requests from Experiment 1. Just like speed requests, altitude requests were signaled by an aircraft turning magenta and by a message appearing in the bottom-most message area (e.g., "UAL250 altitude change?"). Participants were instructed that their main task was to determine the correct responses to altitude change requests based on three properties of the aircraft. These properties were displayed at the same time the aircraft turned magenta and remained until either feedback was provided for a response to an altitude change request or until a 30-second deadline for responding had been exceeded. If a participant did not respond to the altitude change request within 15 seconds, a warning was provided of the impending time limit. The aircraft icon started flashing, and all secondary task action buttons were disabled until the participant responded. Participants not responding prior to the deadline incurred a penalty of 200 points, while making an incorrect response only accrued 100 points. Thus, it was advantageous to make a guess rather than not respond. Participants were warned that they might also incur additional penalties by not being able to perform needed actions during the time the secondary task buttons were grayed out.

Feedback was given after each response in both visual and auditory form. Feedback to an incorrect response consisted of a low "buzz" tone presented for 350 msec as well as an "X" icon presented next to the aircraft label. Positive feedback consisted of a high chime sound presented for 1 second and a smiley face icon. The visual feedback icons were presented for 5 seconds.

Secondary Task. The secondary task involved handling aircraft that are either entering or leaving the central sector in the same manner as in Experiment 1. This time, however, the length of the scenario was held constant, and the number of hand-off requests was varied to create different workload conditions. Each of the eight blocks/scenarios contained 16 aircraft, with the number of these aircraft requiring airspace management actions by the participant varying by workload condition. In the high-workload condition, all 16 aircraft made a hand-off request, with 8 entering and 8 exiting the airspace. In the medium-workload condition, 12 hand-offs were required, with half entering and half exiting the airspace. In the low-workload condition, no aircraft required hand-offs, but all made altitude change requests. In summary, high-workload scenarios consisted of 32 requests (16 altitude changes and 16 hand-offs), medium workload consisted of 28 requests (16 altitude changes and 12 hand-offs), and low-workload scenarios consisted of 16 requests (16 altitude changes and no hand-offs). Each of the scenarios lasted 10 minutes.

Penalty Point Structure. The penalty point structure was identical to that used in Experiment 1, with the exception that speed errors and speed delays were replaced with penalties for incorrectly responding or not responding to the altitude change request. An incorrect response to the primary task (altitude change request) garnered 100 penalty points, while failure to respond to the altitude change request within the allotted time earned 200 penalty points. Failure to respond to the secondary task (hand-off request) carried lower penalties. This penalty point structure ensured that participants gave priority to the primary category learning task and did not skip any category judgments. This procedure did, in fact, result in a complete set of learning data from each participant even in the most difficult condition.

Transfer Task. Following the training phase, a transfer task was conducted to provide insight into what participants had learned and retained from the training phase (see Table 2.2). The transfer test consisted of 25 items—8 old and 17 new. The 8 old items (trained) were identical to those in the training phase. Eight of the new items (extrapolated) had values for all three properties that were more extreme than the values presented during the training phase and therefore could be responded to by analogy with the trained stimuli. The remaining nine new items (internal) had a value for one or more of the properties that was halfway in between the values during the training phase. They were included to force participants to make new classification decisions, but are not included in these analyses because there were no clear predictions for these items.

Table 2.3 shows the complete set of eight different training items followed by the 25 transfer test items. The left column (Items) shows the value

TABLE 2.2
Aircraft Properties During Training and Transfer Phases

| | Stimulus Properties | | | Example Items |
Phase of Experiment	% Fuel Remaining	Size	Turbulence Level	(Three Properties)
Training	20, 40	S, L	1, 3	20 L 1
Transfer	10, 20, 30, 40, 50	XS, S, M, L, XL	0, 1, 2, 3, 4	50 L 2

for the three properties of the aircraft (percent fuel remaining, aircraft size, and turbulence level). The numbers 1 to 5 in this column refer to the five possible values for each property as shown in Table 2.2. The letters A and R in the top half of Table 2.3 refer to the binary responses accept and reject that are required by the structure of the different problem types. The particular items that were to be accepted versus rejected, in the training phase, were counterbalanced across subjects.

The aircraft were all simultaneously present in the display and did not move. A static display was used to allow ample time for participants to consider each new stimulus item. Participants were told that they would be seeing some new property values in addition to those they had seen before, and they were instructed to make their decisions to accept or reject an altitude change based on what they had learned previously. In a randomly chosen sequence, each aircraft, one at a time, turned magenta, and the three aircraft property values were presented on the screen. Participants judged whether to accept or reject each aircraft based on the property values. The presentation was self-paced, with the aircraft reverting to white and its properties disappearing after the aircraft was judged. No feedback was given during the transfer task.

Procedure for Human Participants. Participants were tested individually by one of two experimenters in Cambridge or one of three experimenters

TABLE 2.3
Structure of the Training and Transfer Task Items

		Training Phase	
		Problem Type	
Items	*I*	*III*	*VI*
2 2 2	A	A	A
2 2 4	A	A	R
2 4 2	A	A	R
2 4 4	A	R	A
4 2 2	R	R	R
4 2 4	R	A	A
4 4 2	R	R	A
4 4 4	R	R	R

	Transfer Phase
Item Set	*Item*
Trained	222, 224, 242, 244, 422, 424, 442, 444
Extrapolated	111, 115, 151, 155, 511, 515, 551, 555
Internal	133, 233, 433, 533, 313, 323, 343, 353, 333

in Florida. The experiment took about 4 hours: 1½ hours for instruction and practice and 2½ hours to complete the tasks and debriefing. At the onset of the experiment, participants were given a color vision test to ensure they could differentiate the colors used in the experiment. Participants were trained in the general task through the viewing of several short instructional videos illustrating the main parts of the display and the possible actions and penalties. After viewing the videos, participants responded to several short training scenarios designed to help them understand the mechanical characteristics of the task, after which participants filled out an online, multiple-choice quiz to ensure they had understood the instructions. Correct answers were displayed to any incorrect responses, and participants were retested until they achieved a perfect score on the test.

After completing the quiz, participants took part in the eight learning scenarios. Each scenario lasted 10 minutes. A workload questionnaire was completed online at the beginning, middle, and end of the training after Blocks 1, 4, and 8. The questionnaire was similar to the one used in Experiment 1, but used a 7-point rating scale and the following format: Question 1: Mental Demand: How mentally demanding was the task? Question 2: Physical Demand: How physically demanding was the task? Question 3: Temporal Demand: How hurried or rushed was the pace of the task? Question 4: Performance Errors: How likely were you to make mistakes on this task? Question 5: Effort: How hard did you have to work to accomplish your level of performance? Question 6: Frustration: How insecure, discouraged, irritated, and annoyed were you?

Following the eight blocks, participants were given the transfer task, which was self-paced. Finally, human participants completed an online questionnaire designed to elicit details about their learning strategies on the primary task (see Table 2.4).

Procedure for Human Performance Models

Early in the model development cycle, we shared the data from the human learning phase, including primary and secondary task performance, reaction times, workload ratings, and debrief responses, with the modeling teams. These data were provided to facilitate the modeling efforts. However, to test the model's ability to predict, and not simply replicate, human behavior, the results of the transfer task were not revealed to the modeling teams until after an initial round of model predictions was produced by the modeling teams. Modeling teams were then provided with the results of the transfer task and allowed to revise their models in light of these results. Results for the human performance models are presented individually in chapters 4 to 7 and compared as a whole in chapter 8.

TABLE 2.4
Debriefing Questionnaire

Question	*Response Type*
Screen 1	
On the last of the eight blocks (the ones with the moving planes and smiley faces):	
1. How did you decide whether to accept or reject an altitude change request?	Open Ended
2. Did your strategy change over the 8 blocks? [Please explain]	Open Ended
Screen 2	
On the last of the eight blocks (the ones with the moving planes and smiley faces):	
1. Did you use a rule? (check) Yes No	Yes/No
2. If yes, I accepted an altitude request when:	Open Ended
3. If no, what did you do?	Open Ended

RESULTS AND DISCUSSION

We originally planned to analyze the results in terms of three variables: problem type, secondary task workload (between participants), and blocks (within participants). However, preliminary analysis revealed, surprisingly, almost no effect of the workload manipulation. Although there were significantly more hand-off errors in the high- than in the medium-workload condition, confirming that the manipulation had in fact made the hand-off task more difficult, there were no significant effects of the secondary task on the category learning task for either accuracy or response time. For this reason, the workload variable was omitted from the analyses reported here. We speculate on possible reasons for the lack of a workload effect later.

Primary Task

Accuracy Measures. The category learning data are shown in Fig. 2.7. The graph shows the mean probability of error for each block of 16 categorization judgments in each of the Type I, III, and VI problems. It is clear that, despite the difference in the domains, the human results closely replicate those of previous studies (Nosofsky et al., 1994a; Shepard et al., 1961). The fewest number of errors occurred for the Type I problem, followed by the Type III problem. The Type VI problem showed the greatest occurrence of errors.

A two-factor mixed ANOVA, with problem type as the between-participant variable and blocks as the within-participant variable, yielded a significant main effect of problem type [$F(2, 87) = 23.47$, $p < .0001$] and of blocks

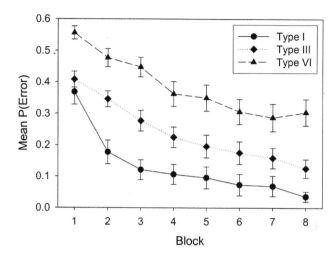

FIG. 2.7. Category learning data for Type I, III, and VI problems.

$[F(7, 609) = 56.70, p < .0001]$ and no significant interaction of problem type × blocks $[F(14, 609) = 1.31, p > .10]$. A Tukey pairwise contrasts test ($p < .05$) confirmed that the three problem types were each acquired at significantly different rates from each other.

A more fine-grained analysis of the data for Problem Type III is shown in Fig. 2.8. In Problem Type III, there are two sets of stimulus items, where each item in the set has the same structural relationship to other items and is logically equivalent. Four stimulus items—1, 2, 7, and 8 (see Fig. 2.6, Problem Type III)—are members of what can be described as the "central" set because they share at least two feature values with other members of the category, whereas Items 3, 4, 5, and 6 are members of the "peripheral" set. Members of these sets are logically equivalent, meaning they can be interchanged with one another by rearranging the stimulus dimension labels. Because of their logical equivalence, it is possible to aggregate the responses to these stimulus items. Another way to think about the distinction between central versus peripheral sets is in terms of rules. Problem Type III can be thought of as a rule with two exceptions. If the rule is "Accept if dimension 1 is maximal," Items 4 and 6 are exceptions. If the rule is "Accept if dimension 2 is maximal," Items 3 and 5 are exceptions. Items 1, 2, 7, and 8 are members of the "central" set because they are never the exceptions, whereas Items 3, 4, 5, and 6 are members of the "peripheral" set because they can be exceptions.

Replicating the results of Nosofsky et al. (1994a) for Problem Type III, the data show that items from the central set were learned more quickly than peripheral items. A two-factor repeated measures ANOVA with item (central vs. peripheral) and block as within-subject variables resulted in sig-

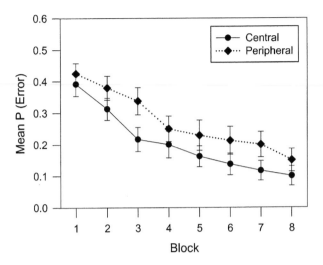

FIG. 2.8.   Category learning data for the Type III problem.

nificant main effects of item [$F(1, 29)$ = 6.00, $p < .05$)] and block [$F(7, 203)$ = 20.50, $p < .0001$], with no interaction of item × block [$F(7, 203) < 1.0$, $p >$ .10].

Response Time Measures.   Figure 2.9 shows the mean response times to the primary category learning task. The pattern of results was similar to the accuracy results. Again there were significant effects of problem type [$F(2, 87)$ = 4.52, $p < .05$] and block [$F(7, 609)$ = 24.14, $p < .0001$)], with no significant interaction of problem type × block [$F(14, 609)$ = 1.28, $p > .10$]. A Tukey test revealed that responses were faster in Problem Type I than Problem Type III or VI ($p < .05$), which did not differ from each other.

Secondary Task

Penalty Score Measures.   An ANOVA of the penalties on the secondary task showed no significant effect of problem type [$F(2, 57) < 1$, $p > .10$], block [$F(7, 399) < 1$, $p > .10$], or block × problem type [$F(14, 399)$ = 1.21, $p > .10$]. The mean penalty score was low (10.84), suggesting that performance on the hand-off task was quite accurate. Surprisingly, accuracy was not affected by the difficulty of the problem type on the category task, as would be expected if participants were multitasking and shedding the hand-off task when the primary category learning task became more difficult. Evidently neither task was sacrificed for the sake of the other. Difficulties caused by harder problem types in the altitude request task or more planes

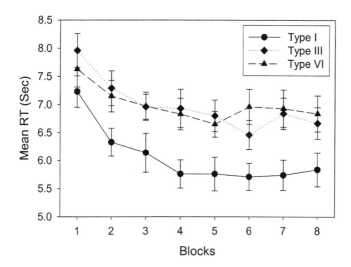

FIG. 2.9. Response times to the category learning task as a function of category learning problem type.

to transfer in the hand-off task did not spill over into the other task as expected.

Response Time Measures. Response times for the secondary task again showed no main effect of the primary task [$F(2, 57) < 1, p > .10$]. There was a significant main effect of blocks [$F(7, 399) = 2.83, p < .01$], with participants responding more quickly on later blocks (see Fig. 2.10). However, this decrease in response time was not affected by the difficulty of the category task, as would be expected if participants were sacrificing time on one task to work on the other. The nonsignificant interaction of problem type × block [$F(14, 399) = 1.68, p > .10$] suggests that participants were simply becoming more familiar with the hand-off task, rather than benefiting from the improved performance across blocks on the category task. The average response time for a hand-off was fairly fast (8.5 seconds) considering that three to four clicks of the mouse were required.

There are several possible reasons for the lack of multitasking within our paradigm. One is that the secondary workload levels may not have been sufficiently high to cause interference on the category task. We may have simply failed to find the "sweet spot" that would lead to task interference on the category task. Alternatively, our procedure may have discouraged multitasking and not facilitated the use of spare time while performing the secondary task to work on the categorization task. In pilot testing, using a slightly different procedure in which aircraft properties were visible at all times, rather than being extinguished after each response, participants did

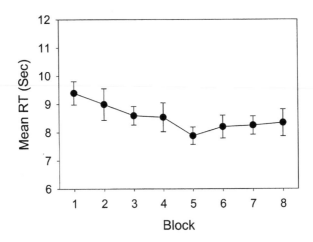

FIG. 2.10.   Response times to the secondary task as a function of blocks.

seem to be dividing their time between the two tasks (e.g., by looking at the aircraft properties and reviewing what had happened during a break in the secondary task). In the final version of the procedure, in which aircraft properties vanished as soon as a response was made, perhaps there was less incentive to time-share. This change in procedure (removing the properties shortly after the participant made a response) was incorporated to replicate more closely traditional concept learning paradigms.

Subjective Workload Ratings

Participants were asked to rate the required workload of the task in its entirety (i.e., both primary and secondary task components together) after Blocks 1, 4, and 8. The results, illustrated in Fig. 2.11, were similar to those found for the error measures. An ANOVA showed a significant main effect of problem type [$F(2, 87) = 3.25$, $p < .05$], with higher workload ratings for Problem Types III and VI than for Problem Type I ($p < .05$). There was a main effect of block [$F(2, 174) = 39.32$, $p < .0001$], with workload ratings declining across blocks and no interaction of problem type × block [$F(4, 174) = 1.08$, $p > .10$].

Debrief Questionnaire

Responses to the debrief questionnaire were analyzed to determine strategies participants used for each of the three problem types on the primary task. We first analyzed whether participants reported using a rule during the last of the eight blocks when asked a yes/no question pertaining to rule use (see Table 2.4, Screen 2). Eighty-one percent of the participants reported using a rule. Results mirror the ease with which participants learned the different problem types. Participants in the Problem Type I condition reported using a rule most often (29 of 30) followed by Problem Type III (26 of 30) and last for Problem Type VI (18 of 30).

Second, we examined responses to the open-ended questions to determine which strategies were reported by participants during the last of the eight blocks (see Table 2.4, Screen 1). Most responses were indicative of rule use (77%), followed by a memorization strategy (18%) where participants reported remembering or memorizing the instances, and with a small number of participants reporting having guessed (3%). Two percent of the participants could not be identified as having any discernable strategy. Reports of memorization or guessing increased with problem type complexity. No participants indicated memorization or guessing strategies for Problem Type I. Of the participants in the Problem Type III condition, 6 indicated memorizing the instances, 1 participant reported guessing, and the remainder, 23, reporting rule-based strategies. The number of individuals reporting memorizing the instances increased to 10 for Problem Type VI, with 2 participants indicating they were guessing, and the rest (18) reporting rule-based strategies.

To better analyze the open-ended questions, we organized participants into *perfect* and *imperfect* learners. Perfect learners had achieved a perfect score on the category learning task on the last block. Perfect learner status was achieved by 80% of the participants in the Problem Type I, 50% in Problem Type III, and 30% in Problem Type VI. Of the perfect learners,

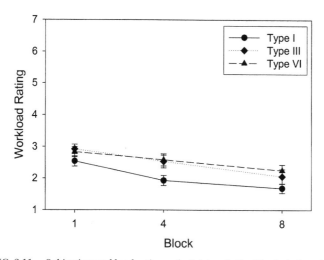

FIG. 2.11. Subjective workload ratings administered after Blocks 1, 4, and 8.

100% reported using a rule in Problem Types I and III, while 89% reported using a rule in Problem Type VI.

The striking finding about perfect learners was that they tended to report a limited set of common strategies as described later. Nonlearners rarely mentioned these strategies, and almost no one who mentioned one of them failed to achieve a perfect score. In other words, subjects' verbal reports of strategy use strongly correlated with performance at the end of the learning phase of the experiment.

For Problem Type I, all of the perfect learners reported using a one-feature rule (e.g., "Accept if turbulence is 3"). Two of the imperfect learners also reported using a one-feature rule and may have simply discovered the rule at the last minute. The other imperfect learners tended to report rules that were more complicated than necessary, containing extraneous or incorrect features.

In Problem Type III, 11 of the 15 perfect learners could be classified as using one of four strategies. Three of these strategies involved feature-based rules, and one consisted of enumerating the four, presumably memorized, instances. The first strategy is a single feature rule with two exceptions or instances. For example, accept small aircraft, except small planes with 20% fuel in turbulence level 3; also accept large planes with 40% fuel remaining in turbulence level 3. The second strategy involves 2 two-feature rules. For example, accept if aircraft is small in turbulence level 1 or the plane has 40% fuel remaining in turbulence level 3. This strategy is a clever alternate way to describe the structure inherent in Category 3. The third strategy is a two-feature rule with two memorized instances. For example, accept small planes with 40% fuel remaining. In addition, accept "20 S 1" and "40 L 3." The last strategy reported was to memorize all four instances. Participants were judged as using a memorization strategy if they recited all four exemplars in response to the question of how they decided which aircraft to accept. Interestingly, none of the imperfect learners in Problem Type III reported using any of these "winning" strategies. They tended to report partial, but insufficient, rules, incorrect rules, or they said something vague, like "memorization," without going into detail.

In Problem Type VI, five of the perfect learners reported memorizing the instances. Four of these five reported four of the exemplars. The other four perfect learners reported using a correlated values rule. We define a correlated values rule as a rule in which participants recall two values as positively correlated (either two low or two high values) or negatively correlated (one high value and one low value). For example, accept large planes with high fuel and high turbulence or low fuel and low turbulence; also accept small planes with low fuel and high turbulence or high fuel and low turbulence.

Transfer Task

We begin our analysis of the transfer data by first comparing performance on the transfer items that had previously been encountered (transfer trained items) with performance on those same items from the last block of training (training Block 8 items; see Fig. 2.12). We contrast these results with performance on extrapolated transfer items more extreme than the trained items (transfer extrapolated items). Extrapolated items were scored in the same manner as the nearest previously trained item. The transfer trained versus transfer extrapolated comparison was designed to assess how well strategies generalized from one type of item to another. The training Block 8 versus transfer trained comparison allowed for an evaluation of how well performance transferred from the learning portion of the experiment to the transfer condition.

A two-factor mixed ANOVA, with problem type as the between-participants factor and items (training Block 8, transfer trained, transfer extrapolated) as the within-participants factor, showed there were significant main effects of problem type [$F(2, 87) = 26.96$, $p < .0001$] and items [$F(2, 174) = 18.91$, $p < .0001$] and no interaction of problem type × items [$F(4, 174) = 1.16$, $p > .10$]. The results show a significantly greater number of errors on the trained items on the transfer test than on the identical items in training Block 8. Less surprising was the finding that extrapolated items were missed more frequently than trained items on the transfer test. A Tukey analysis showed that all three types of items differed significantly from each other ($p < .05$).

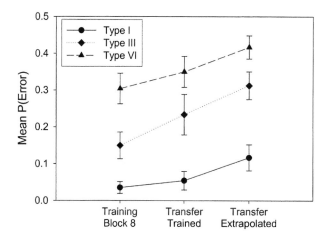

FIG. 2.12.   Transfer task results for Block 8 learning data and trained and extrapolated transfer test items.

CONCLUSION

We included a classic study of category learning as part of a multitasking ATC task. The category learning component of Experiment 2 provided a replication of results found in earlier studies by Shepard et al. (1961) and Nosofsky et al. (1994a)—in particular the finding that certain problem types could be learned more easily than others. The transfer task extended these results by examining the generalization of category learning to a new context. The results show that both context and item changes produced a deterioration in performance. Accuracy was forfeited when learners had to switch contexts, from training to transfer test, even for those items that were identical in the two contexts. Performance declined even more when the items were analogous, but not identical to those previously learned. The loss of information across contexts may have been accelerated by the need to generate additional rules (e.g., such as rounding up) for the internal items. These new rules may have interfered with the retention of the original rules.

A striking finding was pervasiveness of rules reported in the debrief session and the extent to which particular strategies correlated with success on the task. The rules reported by the successful learners were uniformly simple for Problem Type I and became more complex and varied for Type III. For Type VI, some participants discovered a surprisingly complex rule involving positively and negatively correlated values. Another successful strategy involved realizing there were only four items to accept and committing them to memory. This strategy was not as obvious as it seemed because there were 16 items in each block (the 8 items were each repeated). Many of the strategies reported by those who were unable to master the task in the time allotted resembled "buggy" versions of the winning strategies (e.g., incorrect rules and inaccurate memorization of instances).

Although we desired to produce an interaction between category learning performance and a secondary task workload manipulation, no evidence was found for time-sharing between the primary and secondary tasks. Perhaps a more difficult workload manipulation or a more integrated task structure would have led to time-sharing. Even without this finding, a rich set of learning and performance data were collected on which to extend, evaluate, and compare the four models. These models' ability to replicate and predict the human results described in this chapter and the implications for an emerging and exciting discipline provide the theme for the remainder of this book.

ACKNOWLEDGMENTS

We gratefully acknowledge the sponsorship of this research by the Human Effectiveness Directorate of the Air Force Research Laboratory. We thank

AFRL Program Manager Mike Young and COTR Kevin Gluck for their guidance and support. We are extremely grateful to the modeling teams for their contributions to the AMBR project, including Bob Eggleston and Katherine McCreight (AFRL); Wayne Zachary, Jim Stokes, and Joan Ryder (Chi Systems, Inc.); Christian Lebiere (CMU); Ron Chong (George Mason University); and Robert Wray (Soar Technology, Inc.). We are indebted to Randy Astwood, David Holness (Naval Air Warfare Center, Training Systems Division), and Sandra Spector (BBN Technologies) for their help in collecting human participant data.

REFERENCES

Ackerman, P. L., & Kanfer, R. (1994). *Air Traffic Controller Task CD-ROM database, data collection program and playback program.* Office of Naval Research, Cognitive Science Program.

Anderson, J. R. (1991). The adaptive nature of human categorization. *Psychological Review, 98,* 409–429.

Anderson, J. R., Bothell, D., Byrne, M. D., Douglass, S., Lebiere, C., & Qin, Y. (in press). An integrated theory of mind. *Psychological Review.*

Cannon-Bowers, J. A., & Salas, E. (Eds.). (1998). *Making decisions under stress: Implications for individual and team training.* Washington, DC: American Psychological Association.

Gureckis, T. M., & Love, B. C. (2003). Towards a unified account of supervised and unsupervised learning. *Journal of Experimental and Theoretical Artificial Intelligence, 15,* 1–24.

Hart, S., & Staveland, L. (1988). Development of the NASA-TLX: Results of empirical and theoretical research. In P. Hancock & N. Meshkati (Eds.), *Human mental workload* (pp. 139–184). Amsterdam: North-Holland.

John, B. E., & Lallement, Y. (1997, August 7–10). *Strategy use while learning to perform the Kanfer–Ackerman Air Traffic Controller task.* Proceedings of the Ninteenth Annual Conference of the Cognitive Science Society, Palo Alto, CA.

Kirlik, A., Walker, N., Fisk, A. D., & Nagel, K. (1996). Supporting perception in the service of dynamic decision making. *Human Factors, 38,* 288–299.

Kruschke, J. K. (1992). ALCOVE: An exemplar-based connectionist model of category learning. *Psychological Review, 99,* 22–44.

Love, B. C., & Markman, A. B. (2003). The non-independence of stimulus properties in human category learning. *Memory & Cognition, 31,* 790–799.

MacMillan, J., Deutsch, S. E., & Young, M. J. (1997, September 22–26). *A comparison of alternatives for automated decision support in a multi-task environment.* Proceedings of the 41st annual meeting of the Human Factors and Ergonomics Society, Albuquerque, NM.

Nosofsky, R. M., Gluck, M., Palmeri, T. J., McKinley, S. C., & Glauthier, P. (1994a). Comparing models of rule-based classification learning: A replication and extension of Shepard, Hovland, and Jenkins (1961). *Memory & Cognition, 22,* 352–369.

Nosofsky, R. M., Palmeri, T. J., & McKinley, S. C. (1994b). Rule-plus-exception model of classification learning. *Psychological Review, 101,* 53–79.

Pew, R. W., Tenney, Y. J., Deutsch, S., Spector, S., & Benyo, B. (2000). *Agent-based modeling and behavior representation (AMBR) evaluation of human performance models: Round 1—Overview, task simulation, human data, and results.* Cambridge: Distributed Systems & Logistics, BBN Technologies, A Verizon Company.

Reid, G. B., & Nygren, T. E. (1988). The subjective workload assessment technique: A scaling procedure for measuring mental workload. In P. A. Hancock & N. Meshkati (Eds.), *Human mental workload* (pp. 185–218). New York: North-Holland.

Shepard, R. N., Hovland, C. L., & Jenkins, H. M. (1961). Learning and memorization of classifications. *Psychological Monographs, 75* (13, Whole No. 517).

Vidulich, M. A., & Tsang, P. S. (1986). *Collecting NASA workload ratings: A paper-and-pencil package (Version 2.1), working paper.* Moffet Field, CA: NASA Ames Research Center.

Chapter 3

The Simulation Environment for the AMBR Experiments

Stephen Deutsch
David E. Diller
Brett Benyo
BBN Technologies

Laura Feinerman
The MITRE Corporation

One of the goals of the AMBR Model Comparison was to make the simulation environment for the comparison available to other researchers so that they might have the opportunity to use it to extend our initial accomplishments in novel ways. This book and its accompanying CD accomplish that goal. Nevertheless, the development and use of computational process models and the simulation environments with which they will interact are challenging endeavors. Each simulation engine (such as that used in AMBR) has particular requirements and limitations, and these should be understood as well as possible before starting a new modeling and simulation effort. This chapter provides detailed information regarding the simulation environment used in the AMBR Model Comparison and serves as a useful resource for anyone considering the use of this software in future research or for those considering the development of new software for similar human behavior representation (HBR) research purposes.

D-OMAR SIMULATION FOR THE AMBR EXPERIMENT

The Distributed Operator Model Architecture[1] (D-OMAR) served as the distributed simulation environment for the AMBR experiments. It provided the simulation environment for both the real-time human participant

---

[1] Detailed information on D-OMAR is available at http://omar.bbn.com.

trials and the fast-time human performance model runs (Deutsch & Benyo, 2001). In the Experiment 1 Phase 1 trials and the Experiment 2 trials, socket-based native-mode connectivity linked the D-OMAR simulator to the simulators for the human performance models. In the Experiment 1 Phase 2 trials, native-mode connectivity was replaced by the HLA RTI for half of the trials.

The Scenarios for the AMBR Experiment Trials

The experiment trials were based on a simplified air traffic control environment where the human participant or human performance model played the role of an air traffic controller who was responsible for managing the aircraft in a sector and the transfer of aircraft to and from adjacent sectors. In Experiment 1, the modeling teams were challenged to build human performance models that reflected the management of multiple tasks and attention sharing as evidenced by the human participants. In Experiment 2, the scenarios were revised to challenge the modeling teams with a concept learning task.

The starting points for the development of the AMBR experiment software were the scenarios (Deutsch & Cramer, 1998) that supported the MacMillan experiments (MacMillan, Deutsch, & Young, 1997). The MacMillan experiments had been implemented in an older all-Lisp version of the OMAR simulation system, hence software changes were required to update the scenarios to operate in the current D-OMAR simulation environment. The scenarios were then revised to meet the requirements of the new experiment designs.

Scenario scripts were developed for each of the AMBR experiment trials. Additional scripts were developed to support the training scenarios for the experiment participants. A detailed description of the content of these scenarios is contained in chapter 2. The scripts defined the behaviors of the aircraft necessary to create the situations dictated by the experiment designs. They defined the timing and flight path for each aircraft and requests of the air traffic controller made by each aircraft.

In Experiment 1, scenario scripts were manually generated for the different experimental conditions. Aircraft position, routing, and velocity were chosen to produce the desired activities within the scenario, while other aircraft characteristics such as starting locations, aircraft identification labels, and aircraft start times were randomly assigned. For Experiment 2, a script generation program was developed. The script generator randomly constructed a set of scenario scripts for each participant in the experiment. Constraints were built into the script generator to ensure the scripts met the requirements for the each of the various experimental conditions.

The ATC Workplace

The ATC workplace for the AMBR experiment trials is shown in Fig. 3.1. It includes a synthetic radar display and a message system to support communication among the players in the airspace—the air traffic controllers and the flight crews of the aircraft in the sectors.

The radar portion of the display includes icons for the aircraft and neighboring controllers. The aircraft icons are labeled with flight designators (e.g., NW301) and identify the aircraft's direction of flight. The icons for the neighboring controllers are labeled with their names (e.g., EAST), reflecting their location with respect to the central sector. The aircraft and ATC icons are mouse sensitive and are used to provide slot values when generating messages. The sector boundaries for the air traffic control regions are painted in yellow (the outer square and radial lines in Fig. 3.1). The notification boundary, painted in green (the inner square in Fig. 3.1), just inside the boundary for the center sector, marks the beginning of the region in which to initiate the transfer of aircraft to an adjacent sector.

The message system supports communication among air traffic controllers and between air traffic controllers and the aircraft in their sectors. A prompt line above the radar screen displays the current state of the message being prepared (see Fig. 3.1). Screen buttons are available for message selection by type (e.g., the button labeled "CONTACT ATC" in the upper

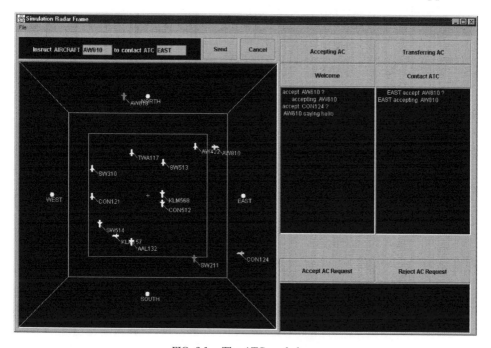

FIG. 3.1. The ATC workplace.

right-hand panel of Fig. 3.1 initiated the message shown in the prompt line). Message slots are filled by using the mouse to select an aircraft or ATC icon from the radar screen. In the prompt line, the icons for the EAST controller and the aircraft AW810 have been selected. Using the mouse to select the "Send" button initiates the transmission of the message to the designated recipient. The message then appears in the appropriate message panel. A message can be canceled explicitly using the "Cancel" button or implicitly by selecting another message type.

For the AMBR experiments, messages were sorted to three separate screen panels by category (see Fig. 3.1): Those related to inbound aircraft appeared in the left-hand message panel, those related to outbound aircraft appeared in the right-hand message panel, and those related to aircraft requesting speed changes (Experiment 1) or altitude changes (Experiment 2) appeared in the lower message panel. Messages requiring a response from the local controller (e.g., an incoming request to accept an aircraft) were left justified within the panel, whereas those that did not require a response (e.g., an outgoing message for an adjacent ATC to accept an aircraft) were indented.

In Experiment 1, there were two treatment conditions: the "text" condition and the "color" condition. Experiment 2 used only the color condition. In the text trials, participants had to watch for aircraft approaching the notification and sector boundaries and monitor the message screens to determine when actions were required. In the color condition, when an action was required, that aircraft's icon was painted in a color selected to indicate the specific action required. When the correct action was taken, the aircraft icon became white again. As expected, the text case proved significantly more challenging than the color case.

The Experiment 2 concept learning task was based on learning the correct response to an aircraft's altitude change request. As the request was made, the aircraft's color was changed from white to magenta. The experiment defined three situational properties—fuel remaining, aircraft size, and turbulence—as the basis for the controller's decision to accept or reject the request. Single-character alphanumeric symbols were presented beneath the aircraft's flight designator to denote the aircraft's current state for each property. A correct response was followed by a smiley face and a bell-like tone; an incorrect response was followed by an X and a growl-like tone. In the absence of a response within 15 seconds, the aircraft icon began to flash, and nonaltitude-related responses were inhibited. At 30 seconds, the opportunity to respond to the request was terminated.

Model's View of the Workplace

An application-programming interface (API) was developed that defined the interface between the ATC workplace and the human performance models. The models' simulators were provided with information on each item as it appeared or moved on the ATC workplace screen. The form of "viewing" of the screen was determined by the model. The human performance models performed actions analogous to those performed by the human participants—viewing the radar and message panels of the ATC workplace screen, and constructing and sending of messages.

Basic static information such as map scaling and the location of sector and notification boundaries was made available to the model developers off-line. Online updates took several forms. The appearance of new aircraft was noted, and aircraft positions were subsequently updated once per second. During the color trials, the models were notified of aircraft color changes as they occurred. The models were also notified of incoming messages and their content, and of the panel on which the message appeared. As outgoing messages were constructed, information on the updating of the prompt line above the radar display was conveyed. For Experiment 2, aircraft parameter values were made available as altitude change requests were made, and the models were notified of correct or incorrect responses and the erasure of the aircraft's parameter values shortly after their response.

Inputs at the workplace were generated by experiment participants: human participants or human performance models. They consisted of the mouse selects used to construct messages to adjacent controllers and sector aircraft. Message type was determined by a button select (e.g., "ACCEPTING AC"). Slot values to complete the message were filled in by icon selects to identify an ATC (e.g., "EAST" in Fig. 3.1) and an aircraft (e.g., "AW810"). Selection of the "Send" button initiated the transfer of the message to its designated recipient. As the message was sent, it appeared in the appropriate message panel.

The AMBR Scenario Agents

The principal agent in the AMBR scenarios—the experiment subject— played the role of the air traffic controller for the center sector. The controller was either a human participant or one of the four human performance models. When a human participant was acting as the center sector controller, a "lightweight" agent was used to track and record the actions of the human player. When a human performance model played the role of the controller for the center sector, the model typically, but not always, operated in its own simulator, in some cases operating on the same machine as the D-OMAR simulator and in other cases operating on a separate machine.

The remaining air traffic controllers—those for the four adjacent sectors—were played by D-OMAR human performance models. Aircraft transiting the sector were also active scenario agents, as were the radar systems provided for each of the sector controllers. The radar systems provided the information to drive the ATC workplace display for the experiment participant and the "displays" used by the D-OMAR models acting as controllers for the adjacent sectors. Air traffic controller models for the adjacent sectors used their radar systems to track aircraft and made use of the messaging system to handle communication with adjacent controllers and the aircraft in their sectors. Aircraft used the messaging system in communicating with the air traffic controllers.

In real-world air traffic control situations, exchanges between controllers and the aircraft in their sector take place at a rapid pace. Responses from the aircraft and adjacent sector models in the AMBR scenarios were consistent, but leisurely. This was done to extend transaction times to create situations in which there were concurrent pending transactions—multitasking situations.

Automating the Experiment 2 Trials

Because of the fairly large number of participants involved in Experiment 2, human data were collected at two different facilities. To standardize the experimental process and minimize any procedural differences that might occur between the two different facilities, we automated much of the experimental process for Experiment 2. Most materials were presented and all information was collected using the automated system, with the exception of the background form and some illustrations. Training materials, including movies with instructional voice-over, example scenarios, and a quiz, were all part of the automated experimental process. Additionally, several questionnaires and the experiment debrief were performed online. These materials are on the CD that accompanies this book.

The experimenter began by launching the application and inputting the participant number for the session. The system then displayed the appropriate experimental session for the chosen participant. Although some parts of the session were paced by the instructor or participant, others such as the videos and scenarios could not be interrupted or paused once initiated. All data collected during the experiment were automatically logged for off-line evaluation. Although the system required both Lisp and Java processes to be initiated to run a scenario, the system was structured so that only a single application required launching by the experimenter.

D-OMAR Basics

D-OMAR was developed initially as a discrete event simulator with the flexibility to explore a range of architectures for human performance modeling. It has been used as a general-purpose simulation environment.

More recently, it has been used extensively as the foundation for agent-based system development. Today there are two implementations of D-OMAR: the hybrid Lisp and Java implementation, now known as OmarL, and the newer all Java implementation, OmarJ. The AMBR experiments were supported using OmarL; OmarJ was not available at the beginning of the AMBR project.

The basic elements of the D-OMAR simulation environment for the AMBR experiment trials are the:

- Simulation engine
- Scenario scripting capability
- Simulation control panel
- Application user interface
- Interface to the human performance models
- Data recording subsystem

Architecturally, the simulation engine, Core-OMAR, is configured as a peer in a distributed computing environment. A D-OMAR simulation environment can be configured with a single Core-OMAR node for the entire environment, with multiple Core-OMAR peers in a distributed simulation environment or for operation with one or more heterogeneous simulators.

The two principal elements of Core-OMAR, implemented in Lisp, are the simulator and representation languages used in developing the scenarios that the simulator executes. The Core-OMAR simulator is an event-based simulator that can be run in either real- or fast-time modes. The representation languages include a frame language, a rule language, and a procedural language. The Simple Frame Language (SFL) is a classical frame language derived from KL-ONE (Brachman & Schmolze, 1985). In addition to its representational role as a frame language, it is used to provide object-oriented definitions for scenario agents and entities. The rule language, one of the several versions of Flavors Expert (FLEX; Shapiro, 1984), is a forward chaining rule language with collections of rules segregated into individual rule sets. The procedure language, the Simulation Core (SCORE) language, is used to define the behaviors of all scenario agents. It includes forms for defining proactive behaviors as goals and procedures and reactive behaviors initiated by impinging events. Multiple-task behavior is mediated via priority-based procedure conflict resolution.

A publish-subscribe protocol forms an important component of the SCORE language. *Signal-event* and *signal-event-external* are the basic forms for "publish"; the former broadcasts a message within a node, whereas the latter broadcasts a message locally and to remote nodes. The message is in the form of a list where the first element of the list is the message type. One or more agents may subscribe to a signal by type in one or more procedures. The individual elements of the message may be vetted before deciding to accept the message for further processing. The subscription to a message type expires when a message is accepted for processing and must be renewed if further messages of that type are to be processed.

In a distributed simulation environment, simulator-to-simulator communication is required in addition to agent-to-agent communication. The form *signal-event-simulator-external* is provided to support this functionality. Simulator-to-simulator communication is used primarily for time management in distributed simulation.

Data recording forms an important subsystem within the Core-OMAR simulator. The SCORE language includes forms to support data recording. The objects recorded are event objects defined using the *defevent* form. Two built-in event types, stimulus and response events, were used to capture the timing of the events that reflected human or model performance. Data collected reflected the timing of a response to a given stimulus or the failure to respond to the stimulus. Additional event types were defined to record scoring data associated with participant errors and timing penalties. At the end of a simulation run, data relevant to the run, including stimulus–response event and scoring data, were recorded to disk.

In addition to its role as a peer in a network of homogeneous or heterogeneous simulators, each Core-OMAR node can act as a server supporting several clients used to complete the simulation environment. The clients, all implemented in Java, provide user interfaces to support scenario development and execution. The developer's interface includes a graphical editor to support the definition of SFL concept and roles, and a browser to examine the detailed and large-scale structure of the goal and procedures that make up a scenario. The simulation control panel is used to select and control scenario execution.

The ATC workplace (Fig. 3.1) as operated by a human participant was implemented as an application interface. For the experiment trials, the simulation control panel enabled the experimenter to select and initiate the scenario to be executed.

D-OMAR Native-Mode Distributed Simulation

The AMBR Experiment 1 Phase 1 and Experiment 2 trials were run using D-OMAR native-mode connectivity between simulation nodes. For human participant trials, the D-OMAR simulator was run in real-time mode. For Experiment 1, the experimenter selected and initiated a scenario using the control panel, and the human participant interacted with the ATC workplace as required by the unfolding events. For Experiment 2, a scripting mechanism was developed to automatically sequence through the training scenarios and the subsequent trial scenarios. This significantly reduced the workload for the experimenters.

For model trials, the D-OMAR simulator was run in fast-time mode. System configurations for the four human performance models were each slightly different. The Experiment 1 DCOG model was developed as a D-OMAR model. As such it operated as a D-OMAR agent in the same Lisp image as the experiment scenario. The Experiment 2 DCOG model was written in Java, operated in its own Java virtual machine, and communicated with D-OMAR through a socket.

The ACT-R and EASE models are Lisp models that each operated in its own simulator. Hence, each was configured as a two-node network. The ACT-R model was run in the same Lisp image as the D-OMAR simulator. The EASE model ran under Linux. It ran on a single machine with the Linux version of D-OMAR. In this instance, D-OMAR and EASE each operated in its own Lisp image connected via a socket.

Last, the COGNET/iGEN model, a C++ model, ran in its own simulator and used a CORBA interface to support connectivity with D-OMAR. The varied distributed computing environments employed for the AMBR experiments made it essential that time management and data exchange be carefully addressed.

Native-Mode Time Management

For the Experiment 1 DCOG model, time management was not an issue; it simply ran within the D-OMAR simulator alongside the standard AMBR scenario entities. Each of the other three models ran in its own simulator interacting with the D-OMAR simulator. From the perspective of the D-OMAR simulator, the basic time management cycle was to complete an event-based time step in which an update of the ATC workplace took place and then grant the model's simulator the opportunity to respond to the new screen events and act on any of its pending initiatives. The grant included notification of the time at which the D-OMAR simulator required control again. The model simulator was free to run up to the grant time or to an earlier time at which it generated an input to the workplace. At this point, the model's simulator would issue a symmetrical grant specifying the current time and the time at which it next needed control. With the grant now passed back to D-OMAR, the basic time cycle then repeated once again. The pattern continued until reaching the stop time dictated by the scenario for the trial.

In addition to the basic time grant, the API included start-of-run and end-of-run notifications. On the D-OMAR side, the API was implemented using the standard publish-subscribe protocol with the *signal-event-simulator-external* form used to generate outbound messages and the *with-signal* form used to capture and process inbound messages. The ACT-R and EASE teams using Lisp and the DCOG team using Java were provided code to support these exchanges. D-OMAR and COGNET/iGEN handled these exchanges using CORBA.

Native-Mode Data Exchange

Data exchange between D-OMAR and each of the HBR models included: (a) information that was presented at the workplace to be viewed by the model, and (b) actions that the model could take to construct messages to adjacent controllers and aircraft in the sector. D-OMAR provided information on what was presented on the screen; it was the responsibility of the model simulator to determine how the model "saw" the data. D-OMAR provided the models with updates of aircraft positions and, in the color case, updates of the color changes that specified when actions were pending on an aircraft.

Actions taken by the models emulated the mouse object selects used to construct messages to adjacent controllers and sector aircraft. The messages included a message type and the slot values necessary to complete the message. Some message types required a single argument, an aircraft select, whereas others required an aircraft select and an ATC select. A mouse select of the "Send" button initiated the transmission of the message. As messages were constructed, the model was notified of updates to the prompt panel above the radar screen, first with the template for the message type and then with the slot values as they were entered. When a message was transmitted, the model was notified of the clearing of the prompt panel and of the message's appearance as an outgoing message in the appropriate message panel. The models were also notified of the appearance of inbound messages from adjacent controllers and sector aircraft and the message panel in which they were to appear.

The API for data exchange was implemented much like that for time management. The *signal-event-external* form was used to generate the messages notifying the model of new or updated information appearing at the ATC workplace. Messages arriving from the models that detailed mouse selects were captured and processed using the *with-signal* form.

HLA-Mode Distributed Simulation

For Experiment 1 Phase 1, the central focus was the conduct of the multitasking experiment. For Experiment 1 Phase 2, the focus was on replicating the Phase 1 results in the High Level Architecture (HLA; Kuhl, Weatherly, & Dahmann, 1999) simulation environment. Earlier work in D-OMAR included an HLA interface for real-time execution using HLA interactions for data exchange. For the AMBR experiments, the D-OMAR interface to HLA was upgraded to also address fast-time time management and the attribute-value model for data exchange. MITRE (Feinerman, Prochnow, & King, 2001) provided expert advice in the development of the HLA federates. DMSO release 1.3 NG V3.2 of the RTI was used for the AMBR HLA-based experiment.

Implicit in the design for the HLA experiment was the separation of the workplace from the entities reflected in that workplace—the aircraft and the air traffic controllers for the four adjacent sectors. In moving to the HLA implementation, two federates were developed. The first federate, the workplace federate, provided the ATC workplace to be operated either by a human participant or a human performance model. The second federate, the world federate, included models for the aircraft transiting the airspace and the human performance models for the controllers for the adjacent sectors.

When running with a human participant, the simulation environment included just two federates (not including the HLA federation tools)—the world federate and the workplace federate operated by the human participant. When running with a human performance model, the model operated as an agent in a third federate interacting solely with the workplace federate.

HLA-Mode Time Management

Time management in an HLA federation is handled by the HLA Run Time Infrastructure (RTI). Federates send requests to the RTI when the federates are ready to advance their local clocks, either to a specified time or the time of the next incoming event. The RTI is responsible for keeping all federates synchronized by appropriately granting time advances.

When running in fast time with a human performance model, the world and workplace federates used the RTI's next-event-request (NER) command with a time-out value to advance their clock. The D-OMAR native-mode time-grant message mapped directly onto the RTI next-event-request command. The RTI allows the federate to advance its logical clock either to the time of the specified request or the time at which a new event for the federate was generated, whichever is earlier. When a federate advances its logical clock, the next possible time at which it can generate an event is equal to the time of the federate's time-advance-request plus the federate's lookahead value. When a human performance model hits the "Send" button, the workplace federate is notified immediately and must then notify the model's federate of the updated screen state. We used a lookahead value of zero so that a federate could immediately generate events at the time to which it had advanced. Larger lookahead values facilitate increased parallel processing by the federates in an HLA federation. The requirements of the experiment prevented taking advantage of this HLA capability.

For the human participant trials, no formal RTI time management protocol was necessary because the human interaction must occur in real time. In this case, the RTI acted as a message passing system, forwarding events to other federates as quickly as possible. Because there is no mechanism to guarantee hard real-time performance, the hardware was selected to be fast enough to ensure that all messages were processed in a timely manner.

HLA-Mode Data Exchange

To handle data exchanges in the HLA federation, we created a one-to-one mapping from the D-OMAR native mode API to HLA exchanges using a mix of interaction and attribute-value updates. We created HLA objects to represent the aircraft and ATC regions. Updates of aircraft positions were transmitted from the world simulation federate to the workstation federate and from there to the human performance model federate through the HLA attribute-value update function. Data exchanges such as communication messages from an ATC to an airplane, or button presses at the ATC workplace either by a human participant or human performance model, were transmitted as HLA interactions.

Additional interactions were needed for the HLA federation because the world simulation and workplace were implemented as two separate federates. In addition to the standard aircraft position-change messages, the world-simulation federate had to inform the workstation whenever an aircraft crossed the notification boundary. This allowed the workstation to accurately record the time of the boundary crossing as a stimulus event and thus pair it with the appropriate subsequent button-press response event.

HLA Impact on Model Performance

An important goal for Experiment 1 Phase 2 was to demonstrate that the HLA provided a simulation environment in which it was reasonable to conduct human performance experiments and that human performance models could reasonably interact with a simulated workplace. The HLA implementation met these goals, but was found to have a significant negative impact on the run times for most of the human performance model trials. The HLA configuration was also found to require significantly more computer power for the human participant trials.

For the HLA human participant trials, additional computer power was required to ensure adequate real-time system response. For Phase 1, the experiment control panel and the simulation were run on a 200 MHz Pentium desktop machine. The workplace display operated on a 500 MHz Pentium laptop machine. For Phase 2, the HLA implementation required the replacement of the 200 MHz machine with a 266 MHz machine and the addition of a second 500 MHz machine. All three machines had 128 Mbytes of memory and operated under Windows NT. The world federate ran on the 266 MHz Pentium laptop, the workplace federate and the HLA RTI ran on a 500 MHz Pentium laptop, and the workplace display ran on the second 500 MHz Pentium laptop. The experiment was controlled from the laptop running the workplace federate. For Experiment 2, the machine configuration was the same as Experiment 1 Phase 1, with the 200 MHz desktop machine replaced by a 500 MHz laptop machine.

For the model runs, there was a price to pay for the distributed computation. Table 3.1 provides data on run times relative to real time (e.g., the DCOG model ran more than 14 times faster than real time in native mode and two-thirds real time in HLA mode). The data in Table 3.1 reflect DCOG, ACT-R, and COGNET/iGEN trials that were run on 950 MHz Pentium with 512 Mbytes of memory operating under Windows NT. The Phase 1 DCOG, ACT-R, and EASE trials used native-mode D-OMAR connectivity. The Phase 1 COGNET/iGEN trials used a CORBA interface between the model and the D-OMAR simulator. As indicated in Table 3.1, the HLA RTI interface was actually more efficient than the CORBA interface. It was the one case in which HLA provided improved performance over Phase 1.

The EASE trials were run on a 400 MHz Pentium with 256 Mbytes of memory operating under Linux, hence the EASE timing data are not directly comparable with the data for the other models. The relative speeds of native mode and HLA modes for the EASE runs are relevant—HLA was slower by a factor of two.

The human performance models that ran very fast (see Table 3.1) in native mode lost this advantage in HLA mode. The dominant performance factor was not in the models, but rather the mode of connectivity between the model's simulator and the D-OMAR simulator. Socket connections, the HLA RTI, and particularly the CORBA implementation each had a high cost associated with its use.

TABLE 3.1
Run Time as a Multiple of Real Time in Native-Mode
and HLA-Mode AMBR Trials

Mode	950 MHz 512 Mbytes			400 MHz 256 Mbytes
	AFRL DCOG	CMU ACT-R	CHI Sys COGNET	Soar Tech EASE
Native	0.07	0.11	1.30	2.27
HLA	1.48	0.86	0.94	5.55

A second factor impacting performance was the necessary implementation of the scenarios as two federates—a world federate and a workplace federate—for the HLA implementation. It was important to demonstrate a generic workplace readily adaptable to operate with a broad range of vehicle federates, but this did have an unfavorable impact on performance. Message traffic that was local to a single simulator in Phase 1 became message traffic moving between two federates in the HLA implementation.

Operating in D-OMAR native mode, the DCOG and ACT-R model trials were dramatically faster than real time. This is clearly the regime in which one would prefer to operate. Short run times facilitated model development and model trials by compressing AMBR experiment trials with wall clock times of 6½, 9, and 11½ minutes to 1 minute or less. The Phase 1 DCOG model ran internal to D-OMAR and did not require a socket connection. The ACT-R model ran in the same Lisp image as D-OMAR. Native-mode D-OMAR code recognized the shared image and bypassed the socket connection required between Lisp images or between nodes. This optimization led to significant time savings.

EASE ran in a separate Lisp image and required a socket connection to D-OMAR for non-HLA trials. The COGNET/iGEN model used CORBA to connect to D-OMAR for non-HLA trials. The necessary socket connection significantly slowed execution times for these model runs.

The results of the Phase 1 trials were reproduced in the HLA environment, but were found to require significantly more computer power to maintain adequate system response for the human participant trials. For three of the four human performance models, trial run times were significantly longer in HLA mode than in D-OMAR native mode. HLA provides another time management mechanism—the time advance request (TAR). It is possible that TAR would have proved more efficient, but time and resources were not available to explore this option.

When computer resource utilization is a concern in an HLA simulation environment, consideration should be given to implementing the workplace and the human performance model as a single federate. The efficiency of within-simulator communication can be used to efficiently accommodate the demand for high-frequency data exchange between the workplace and the human performance model.

HLA Federate Compliance Testing

The world-simulation federate and the workstation federate both completed the DMSO-sponsored HLA compliance testing on March 22, 2001. This certifies that the two federates are fully compliant with HLA version 1.3 and makes them available to other researchers. The world-simulation federate is quite domain specific, useful only for simulating aircraft and

ATCs in this simplified air traffic control environment. The workstation, however, is more generic. The workplace displays and functionality have been used in scenarios unrelated to the AMBR project and could readily be extended to operate in related domains. The federates are included on the CD that accompanies this book.

CONCLUSION

The computing environment to support the AMBR experiments was necessarily complex. It had to support the implementation of the design for the two experiments, and it also had to provide a real-time simulation environment in which to conduct the human participant trials and a fast-time simulation environment to support the model trials. Data collection and scoring had to operate identically for human participants and models as subjects. Connectivity with the simulators for each of the human performance models was slightly different in each instance. For Experiment 1 Phase 2, it was necessary to provide an HLA simulation environment for human participant and model trials. For the most part, we were able to rely on existing D-OMAR simulation capabilities to meet the demands of the AMBR experiment. It was sufficient to use existing capabilities to implement the scenarios required by the experiment designs, make modest improvements to the existing HLA simulation capability, and provide scripting to support the Experiment 2 human participant trials and ease the burden of doing large numbers of human performance model runs.

ACKNOWLEDGMENTS

The authors wish to acknowledge the assistance of David Prochnow and Ron King from the MITRE Corporation in developing HLA simulation environment for Experiment 1.

REFERENCES

Brachman, R. J., & Schmolze, J. G. (1985). An overview of the KL-ONE knowledge representation system. *Cognitive Science, 9,* 171–216.

Deutsch, S., & Benyo, B. (2001, May). *The D-OMAR simulation environment for the AMBR experiments.* Proceedings of the 10th Conference on Computer Generated Forces and Behavior Representation, Orlando, FL.

Deutsch, S. E., & Cramer, N. L. (1998, October). *OMAR human performance modeling in a decision support experiment.* Proceedings of the 42nd annual meeting of the Human Factors and Ergonomics Society, Chicago, IL.

Feinerman, L. E., Prochnow, D. L., & King, R. A. (2001, May). *Icarus: An HLA federation for HBR models.* Proceedings of the 10th Conference on Computer Generated Forces and Behavior Representation, Orlando, FL.

Kuhl, F., Weatherly, R., & Dahmann, J., (1999). *Creating computer simulation systems: An introduction to the High Level Architecture.* Upper Saddle River, NJ: Prentice-Hall.

MacMillan, J., Deutsch, S. E., & Young, M. J. (1997, September). *A comparison of alternatives for automated decision support in a multi-tasking environment.* Proceedings of the Human Factors and Ergonomic Society 41st annual meeting, Albuquerque, NM.

Shapiro, R. (1984). *FLEX: A tool for rule-based programming* (BBN Report No. 5843). Cambridge, MA: BBN Technologies.

MODELS OF MULTITASKING
AND CATEGORY LEARNING

Constrained Functionality: Application of the ACT-R Cognitive Architecture to the AMBR Modeling Comparison

Christian Lebiere
Carnegie Mellon University

THE ACT-R COGNITIVE ARCHITECTURE

Symbolic Level

ACT-R is a production system theory that models the steps of cognition by a sequence of production rules that fire to coordinate retrieval of information from the environment and from memory. It is a cognitive architecture that can be used to model a wide range of human cognition. It has been used to model tasks from memory retrieval (Anderson, Bothell, Lebiere, & Matessa, 1998) to visual search (Anderson, Matessa, & Lebiere, 1997). The range of models developed—from those purely concerned with internal cognition to those focused on perception and action—makes ACT-R a plausible candidate to model a task like the air traffic control (ATC) simulation in this project because the task includes all of these various components. In all domains, ACT-R is distinguished by the detail and fidelity with which it models human cognition. It makes claims about what happens cognitively every few hundred milliseconds in the performance of a task. ACT-R is situated at a level of aggregation considerably above basic brain processes, but considerably below significant tasks like ATC. The new version of the theory has been designed to be more relevant to tasks that require deploying significant bodies of knowledge under conditions of time pressure and high information-processing demand. This is because of the increased concern with the temporal structure of cognition and the coordination of perception, cognition, and action.

Figure 4.1 displays the information flow in the ACT-R 4.0 architecture (Anderson & Lebiere, 1998). There are essentially three memories—a goal stack that encodes the hierarchy of intentions guiding behavior, a procedural memory containing production rules, and a declarative memory containing chunks of information. These are all organized through the current goal that represents the focus of attention. The current goal can be temporarily suspended when a new goal is pushed on the stack. The current goal can be popped, in which case the previous goal is retrieved from the stack. Productions are selected to fire through a conflict resolution process that chooses one production from among the productions that match the current goal. The selected production can cause actions to be taken in the outside world, can transform the current goal (possibly resulting in pushes and pops to the stack), and can make retrieval requests of declarative memory (such as what is the sum of 3 and 4?). The retrieval result (such as 7) can be returned to the goal. The arrows in Fig. 4.1 also describe how new declarative chunks and productions are acquired. Chunks can be added to declarative memory either as popped goals reflecting the solutions to past problems or perceptions from the environment. Productions are created from a process called *production compilation*, which takes an encoding of an execution trace resulting from multiple production firings and produces a new production that implements a generalization of that transformation in a single production cycle.

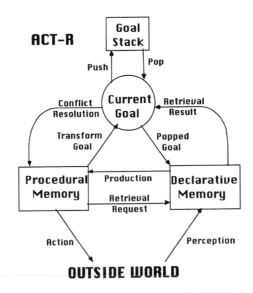

FIG. 4.1. The overall flow of control in ACT-R 4.0.

Anderson et al. (in press) described the new version of the theory, ACT-R 5.0. It differs from this version primarily in providing a further integration of perception and action on an equal footing with cognition and in removing the goal stack. Because the models presented here made limited use of these features, they should run in ACT-R 5.0 with few modifications and produce substantially similar results.

Subsymbolic Level

ACT-R can be described as a purely symbolic system in which discrete chunks and productions interact in discrete cycles. However, ACT-R also has a subsymbolic level in which continuously varying quantities are processed, often in parallel, to produce much of the qualitative structure of human cognition. These subsymbolic quantities participate in neural-like activation processes that determine the speed and success of access to chunks in declarative memory as well as the conflict resolution among production rules. ACT-R also has a set of learning processes that can modify these subsymbolic quantities. The activation of a chunk reflects the log posterior odds that that chunk is relevant in a particular situation. The activation A_i of a chunk i is computed as the sum of its base-level activation B_i plus its context activation:

$$A_i = B_i + \sum_j W_j S_{ji} \qquad \text{Activation Equation}$$

In determining the context activation, W_j designates the attentional weight given the focus element j. An element j is in the focus, or context, if it is part of the current goal chunk (i.e., the value of one of the goal chunk's slots). S_{ji} stands for the strength of association from element j to a chunk i. ACT-R assumes that there is a limited capacity of source activation and that each goal element emits an equal amount of activation. Source activation capacity is typically assumed to be 1 (i.e., if there are n source elements in the current focus, each receives a source activation of $1/n$). The associative strength S_{ji} between an activation source j and a chunk i is a measure of how often i was needed (i.e., retrieved in a production) when chunk j was in the context. Associative strengths provide an estimate of the log likelihood ratio measure of how much the presence of a cue j in a goal slot increases the probability that a particular chunk i is needed for retrieval to instantiate a production. The base-level activation of a chunk is learned by an architectural mechanism to reflect the past history of use of a chunk i:

$$B_i = \ln \sum_{j=1}^{n} t_j^{-d} \approx \ln \frac{nL^{-d}}{1-d} \qquad \text{Base-Level Learning Equation}$$

In the prior formula, t_j stands for the time elapsed since the *jth* reference to chunk i, d is the memory decay rate, and L denotes the lifetime of a chunk (i.e., the time since its creation). As Anderson and Schooler (1991) showed, this equation produces the Power Law of Forgetting (Rubin & Wenzel, 1990) as well as the Power Law of Learning (Newell & Rosenbloom, 1981). When retrieving a chunk to instantiate a production, ACT-R selects the chunk with the highest activation A_i. However, some stochasticity is introduced in the system by adding gaussian noise of mean 0 and standard deviation σ to the activation A_i of each chunk. To be retrieved, the activation of a chunk needs to reach a fixed retrieval threshold τ that limits the accessibility of declarative elements. If the gaussian noise is approximated with a sigmoid distribution, the probability P of chunk i to be retrieved by a production is:

$$P = \frac{1}{1 + e^{-\frac{A_i - \tau}{s}}} \qquad \text{Retrieval Probability Equation}$$

where $s = \sqrt{3}\sigma / \pi$. The activation of a chunk i is directly related to the latency of its retrieval by a production p. Formally, retrieval time T_{ip} is an exponentially decreasing function of the chunk's activation A_i:

$$T_{ip} = Fe^{-fA_i} \qquad \text{Retrieval Time Equation}$$

where F is a time scaling factor. In addition to the latencies for chunk retrieval as given by the Retrieval Time Equation, the total time of selecting and applying a production is determined by executing the actions of a production's action part, whereby a value of 50 ms is typically assumed for elementary internal actions. External actions, such as pressing a key, usually have a longer latency determined by the ACT-R/PM perceptual-motor modules (Byrne & Anderson, 1998). In summary, subsymbolic activation processes in ACT-R make a chunk active to the degree that past experience and the present context (as given by the current goal) indicate that it is useful at this particular moment.

Just as subsymbolic activation processes control which chunk is retrieved from declarative memory, the process of selecting which production to fire at each cycle, known as *conflict resolution*, is also determined by subsymbolic quantities called *utility* that are associated with each production. The utility, or expected gain, E_i of production i is defined as:

$$E_i = P_i \bullet G - C_i \qquad \text{Expected Gain Equation}$$

where G is the value of the goal to which the production applies, and P_i and C_i are estimates of the goal's probability of being successfully completed and the expected cost in time until that completion, respectively, after production i fires. Just as for retrieval, conflict resolution is a stochastic process through the injection of noise in each production's utility, leading to a probability of selecting a production i given by:

$$p(i) = \frac{e^{\frac{E_i}{t}}}{\sum_j e^{\frac{Ej}{t}}}$$ Conflict Resolution Equation

where $t = \sqrt{6}\sigma/\pi$. Just as for the base-level activation, a production's probability of success and cost are learned to reflect the past history of use of that production—specifically, the past number of times that that production lead to success or failure of the goal to which it applied, and the subsequent cost that resulted, as specified by:

$$P_i = \frac{Successes}{Successes + Failures}$$ Probability Learning Equation

$$C_i = \frac{\sum Costs}{Successes + Failures}$$ Cost Learning Equation

Costs are defined in terms of the time to lead to a resolution of the current goal. Thus, the more/less successful a production is in leading to a solution to the goal and the more/less efficient that solution is, the more/less likely that production is to be selected in the future.

These equations at the subsymbolic level strongly constrain and determine the quantitative behavior of a model specified through symbolic chunks and productions and provide the bulk of the predictive power of the theory.

EXPERIMENT 1 MODEL

Modeling Methodology

If it is to justify its structural costs, a cognitive architecture should facilitate the development of a model in several ways. It should limit the space of possible models to those that can be expressed concisely in its language and work well with its built-in mechanisms. It should provide for significant transfer from models of similar tasks, either directly in the form of code or more generally in the form of design patterns and techniques. Finally, it should provide learning mechanisms that allow the modeler to only specify in the model the structure of the task and let the architecture learn the details of the task in the same way that human cognition constantly adapts to the structure of its environment. These architectural advantages not only reduce the amount of knowledge engineering required and the number of trial-and-error development cycles, providing significant savings in time and labor, but also improve the predictiveness of the final model. If the natural model derived a priori from the structure of the task, the constraints of the architecture and the guidelines from previous models of related tasks provides a good fit of the empirical data, one can be more confident that it will generalize to unforeseen scenarios and circumstances than if it is the result of post hoc knowledge engineering and data analysis. That is the approach that we have adopted in developing a model of this task and indeed more generally in our use of the ACT-R architecture.

When faced with developing a model of this task, we did not try to reverse engineer from their data and protocols which techniques and strategies subjects used when confronted with the task, but instead we asked ourselves which ACT-R model would best solve the task given the architectural constraints. An additional emphasis in developing the model was on simplicity because of the time constraints provided by the flyoff and, because the subjects had only had a limited amount of practice with the task, it was fairly unlikely that they had developed highly elaborate strategies. Generally, for each phase, the total development time, including the time-consuming process of finding the best way to interface with the simulation, was less than 6 weeks, and the time to develop the model was less than 1 week. A more time-consuming part of the process is the repeated tweaking of the model (both in terms of real-valued parameters as well as symbolic knowledge structures) to attempt to improve the fit to the data. This practice, however widespread, can take arbitrarily large amounts of time and often results in little meaningful improvements to the model. Our experience here confirmed that it would be best left to a minimum if tolerated at all. Indeed from our perspective, this project illustrated quite nicely the dual advantage of cognitive architectures. Because they provide considerable constraints on the mechanisms and parameters to be used for building human performance models, they limit the degrees of freedom where other, non-first-principled methods have to resort to parameter fitting and further validation. Moreover, because of those constraints and the leverage of built-in mechanisms, the development of the model is much more efficient, making human performance models more affordable for their many potential applications.

One common design pattern in ACT-R models of similar tasks (e.g., Lee & Anderson 2001) is the concept of unit task (Card, Moran, & Newell, 1983). Unit tasks correspond to subtasks of more complex tasks that are associated with a specific goal in a given context. That decomposition has been shown to have significant psychological validity in the prediction of subject performance (Corbett, Anderson, & O'Brien, 1995). Unit tasks further the goal of simplicity because they provide a way to decompose a model of a complex task into independent sets of productions applying in specific situations. Moreover, unit tasks correspond directly to the concept of goal type in ACT-R, with each goal of that type corresponding to a specific instance of that unit task and productions that match that goal type corresponding to the knowledge required to solve that unit task. The decomposition of ACT-R models is similar to the software engineering concept of object-oriented programming, with classes corresponding to goal types, instances of those classes corresponding to chunks (goals) of that type, and methods applying to objects of that class corresponding to productions that apply to goals of that type.

Of course unit task decomposition is not merely a software engineering principle for developing cognitive models, but rather it corresponds to an underlying psychological reality as well. The unit tasks for this simulation are fairly clearly identified. In both the aided and unaided conditions, processing an aircraft that requires action by the central controller is a clearly defined unit task. In the color (aided) condition, scanning the radar screen for an aircraft that turned color, identifying its need for action, is another unit task. Similarly, in the text (unaided) condition, the subtasks of scanning a single text window or radar screen area constitute unit tasks as well. Finally, in the text condition, selecting the next part of the screen to scan is the top-level unit task. Those five unit tasks define the structure of the ACT-R model. The procedural knowledge required to solve them is described in detail in the following subsections.

Another design pattern that appears in countless ACT-R models (e.g., cognitive arithmetic, alphabet arithmetic, instance-based problem solving, etc.) deals with the trade-off between trying to retrieve an answer from memory, which tends to be fastest but most error-prone, and attempting to re-derive it using backup methods such as computation or perceptual scanning. In this simulation, this problem appears in many instances, such as identifying the position of an aircraft from its identifier when scanning a text window or deciding whether an aircraft has been processed when scanning it on the radar screen. Both of these questions could be answered[1] either by attempting to retrieve a related memory (respectively of scanning or processing that aircraft) or searching the proper screen area (respectively the radar screen or a text window) for the information. Although

---

[1]There might be cases when the information is not present on the screen, such as when a text message pertaining to an aircraft has scrolled off the top of the window or when an aircraft mentioned in a message has exited the radar screen, but the display changes slowly enough that those cases are relatively rare.

ACT-R provides the capacity for the model to decide between each course of action based on their expected cost (in terms of time to perform the action) and probability of success (in providing the needed information), this requires learning from experience with the system, which was not the focus of the Phase I modeling effort (but was highlighted in the Phase II model as is seen in a later section). Instead as is often the case, retrieval from memory is preferred over explicit scanning because of its relatively low cost. Only if that retrieval fails, either because the chunk encoding the information was not present in memory or because its activation had decayed below the retrieval threshold, will the strategy of explicit scanning be selected. This pattern of attempting to retrieve information from memory and only when it fails from the environment is a pervasive one in ACT-R models, and one that is transparently supported by the architecture. As the information is re-created from the environment or explicit computation, the activation of the chunk encoding it will gradually rise with practice until it can retrieved directly. This process of transition from explicit methods to a reliance on memory is a pervasive aspect of human cognition that ACT-R can account for in a direct, straightforward manner through its activation calculus.

Finally, a key aspect of our methodology that is also pervasive in ACT-R modeling (Anderson & Lebiere, 1998) is the use of Monte Carlo simulations to reproduce not only the aggregate subject data, such as the mean performance or response time, but also the variation that is a fundamental part of human cognition. In that view, the model does not represent an ideal or even average subject, but instead each model run is meant to be equivalent to a subject run in all its variability and unpredictiveness. For that to happen, it is essential that the model not be merely a deterministic symbolic system, but be able to exhibit meaningful nondeterminism. To that end, randomness is incorporated in every part of ACT-R's subsymbolic level, including chunk activations that control their probability and latency of retrieval, production utilities that control their probability of selection, and production efforts that control the time they spent executing.

Moreover, as has been found in other ACT-R models (e.g., Gonzalez, Lerch, & Lebiere, 2003; Lebiere & West, 1999), that randomness is amplified in the interaction of the model with a dynamic environment: Even small differences in the timing of execution might mean missing a critical deadline, which results in an airplane going on hold (with the resulting 50-point penalty), requires immediate attention, might cause another missed deadline, and so on. The magnitude of the sensitivity to random fluctuations was brought to our attention when an early, noise-free version of the model was run in real time against the simulation. Although both the model and simulation were deterministic and the only source of randomness was small subsecond variations in synchronization between the two systems, performance varied by as much as 100 points in the same condition.

To model the variations as well as the mean of subject performance, the model was always run as many times as there were subject runs. For that to be a practical strategy of model development, it is essential that the model run very fast—ideally significantly faster than real time. Our model ran up to five times real time, with the speed limitation being due entirely to the communication bottleneck between model and simulation rather than the computational requirements of ACT-R, which can run at several hundred times real time. This speed made it possible to run a full batch of 48 scenarios in about an hour and a half, enabling a relatively quick cycle of model development. One source of variation in subject performance that we could not exploit is individual differences. ACT-R has been able to provide a fine-grained account of individual differences in working memory performance through continuous variations in the value of the architectural parameter W controlling spreading activation (Lovett, Reder, & Lebiere, 1997). An obvious way to account for individual differences in this task would be to include variations of the effort production parameter controlling the speed of execution of the model in a manner consistent with the slow man–fast man distinction of Card, Moran, and Newell (1983). However, for the sake of simplicity and the avoidance of arbitrary degrees of freedom, we left the parameters unchanged. Generally, all parameters controlling the model were left at their default values established either by the architecture or existing models. The rate of base-level decay d was 0.5 and the level of activation noise was 0.25, both of which have been consistently used in many ACT-R models. The retrieval threshold was 0.0 and the latency factor was 1.0, both values being architectural defaults. The effort for productions that do not involve any perceptual or motor actions was left at the architectural default of 50 msec. Two parameters were roughly estimated: The effort for perceptual productions was set at 500 msec and the effort for productions involving actions (typically move the mouse to a target and click) was set at 1 sec.

Model

Six chunk types are defined using the chunk-type command. They consist of the name of the chunk type and the associated slots. One chunk type rule holds the basic content of the instructions to define each category of event by relating a specific action (e.g., contact) to the color used for that event in the aided condition (e.g., yellow) and the amount of penalty points associated with failing to act on it in a timely fashion (e.g., 50). Five chunks of that type are defined using the add-dm command to encode that information for all five event types. The initial base-level activation of those chunks is set by the command sdp to reflect the level of practice at that point in the simulation (i.e., 120 references over the last hour [3,600 seconds]), and to reflect the instruction study phase as well as the first block of practice. These history parameters determine the activation of those chunks according to the base-level learning equation, which in turn determines how fast and reliably they can be retrieved. These chunks are only used in the aided (color-coded) condition to map color of aircraft to required action. All other chunks defined by the add-dm command are simply symbols used in other chunks (which the system would define by default) and the initial goals for the color and text condition. The model tests the type of scenario obtained from the simulation to decide which of these two chunks to set as the initial goal. The other five chunk types that are defined correspond to the goals used for the five unit tasks that compose this task. Those goal types are color-goal, text-goal, scan-text, scan-screen, and process. They and their associated procedural knowledge are described in detail in the rest of this section. The productions that apply to each goal type are listed in a table using an informal English description meant to capture their function without obscure syntactic details. Production names are in bold, words in italics correspond to production variables, and words in bold within the production text correspond to specific chunks (constants). The order in which the productions are listed correspond to their order of priority in the conflict resolution process, with the earlier productions being favored and the later productions only allowed to fire if the preceding ones cannot match.

Table 4.1 presents the productions for the top-level unit task color-goal. The production color-target-detection detects a colored aircraft on the ra-

TABLE 4.1
Productions Applicable to the Unit Task Color-Goal

Subgoal-next
    IF the *goal* is of type color-goal
        and a *subgoal* to process a colored aircraft was formulated previously
    THEN push that *subgoal*

Color-target-detection
    IF the *goal* is of type color-goal
        and a colored *aircraft* is present on the screen
    THEN note that *aircraft*

Color-target-acquisition
    IF the *goal* is of type color-goal and a colored *aircraft* has been detected
    THEN note its *color*

Color-action
    IF the *goal* is of type color-goal and an *aircraft* and its *color* have been identified
        and a *rule* chunk can be retrieved linking *color* to *action*
    THEN push *subgoal* to process *action* on *aircraft* at current *position*

Wait
    IF the goal is of type color-goal
    THEN do nothing

---

dar screen and notes the aircraft identity in the goal. The production color-target-acquisition notes the aircraft color in the goal, and the production color-action retrieves from memory the chunk linking that color to the required action and pushes a subgoal to process that action on the aircraft. If none of these productions can apply, the production wait fires, essentially filling the 50 msec of this production cycle before the next cycle of detection can take place. These productions would provide a perfectly functional treatment of the color-goal unit task, but there is one additional production called *subgoal-next*, which has to do with onset detection. If an aircraft turns color while a subgoal to process another aircraft is the current goal, the model detects that aircraft while it processes the subgoal and creates a prospective subgoal to process that new aircraft. That subgoal is returned to the parent color-goal when the process subgoal is completed, and the production subgoal-next immediately pushes it without having to fire the productions to detect the aircraft, map its color to the action, and create a new subgoal. This treatment is consistent with subject awareness of event onset and predicts the right slope for the time to handle an aircraft as a function of intervening events.

Table 4.2 presents the productions for the top-level unit task text-goal. The text condition is more complex than the color condition because relevant events are much harder to detect and that is reflected in its unit task structure. Unlike color-goal, the text-goal unit task does not directly detect aircraft that require action and subgoal any process goal, but instead directs attention to specific areas of the screen in which to perform that detection. There are four screen areas to be scanned: the three text message windows, left for incoming aircraft, right for exiting aircraft and low for speed changes, which are scanned by the unit task scan-text, and the radar screen area between the green and yellow lines for exiting aircraft, which are scanned by the unit task scan-screen. The latter is necessary because the

TABLE 4.2
Productions Applicable to the Unit Task Text-Goal

Between-left
    IF the *goal* is of type text-goal and the last area scanned was **between**
    THEN push a subgoal to scan the text area **left** starting at the **bottom**
Left-right
    IF the *goal* is of type text-goal and the last area scanned was **left**
    THEN push a subgoal to scan the text area **right** starting at the **bottom**
Right-low
    IF the *goal* is of type text-goal and the last area scanned was **right**
    THEN push a subgoal to scan the text area **low** starting at the **bottom**
Low-between
    IF the *goal* is of type text-goal and the last area scanned was **low**
    THEN push a subgoal to scan the screen area **between**

---

central controller has to initiate the transfer of exiting aircraft to other controllers, whereas all other actions are taken in response to a text message. There are four productions that implement a sequential scan of the four areas by pushing a subgoal to scan each area given the previous one. This solution was chosen for its simplicity and systematicity,[2] but others are possible, such as a random scan or a scan based on the probabilities of finding a new event in each of the four areas—a strategy that might be optimal and for which ACT-R's utility learning mechanism would be well suited. However, the available data were inconclusive on that aspect of subject behavior, and finer-grained data such as eye movements would be needed to precisely determine subjects' strategies in that regard. Note that this systematic scan only happens when no event onset was detected in another window when scanning the present window.

Table 4.3 presents the productions for the unit task scan-text responsible for scanning a text window. As initialized by the text-goal productions described previously, scan-text goals start scanning at the bottom of the screen. This is contrary to the usual top–down scanning pattern, but new messages appear at the bottom of the screen and it is therefore the best place to look for them. Subjects probably took some time to learn this scanning pattern, but they are expected by that time in the simulation to have adopted the more efficient strategy. Again more detailed data such as eye movements and data from earlier trials would be needed to conclusively answer the questions regarding the subjects' scanning strategies. The production find-flush-message scans upward from the current position (initially bottom) to find the next message that is flush against the left side of the window, indicating a message from an aircraft or another controller requesting action. If no such message can be found, the production no-flush-message pops the goal, which returns control to the text-goal unit task. If a message is found requesting action, the model then tries to determine whether that action has already been completed. The production memory-for-message searches declarative memory for a chunk recording the completion of a process goal for the task and aircraft indicated by the message. Recall that when completed goals are popped, they become permanent declarative memory chunks that can be retrieved later. However, retrieval of a chunk is subject to its activation reaching threshold, and failure to retrieve a trace of past execution is no guarantee that it did not happen. Therefore, if memory retrieval fails the production, message-reply scans down the text window from the current message for an indented message containing the acknowledgment message that would have resulted from taking that action. If either a memory or message indicating completion of the action is found,

---

[2]Indeed the author significantly improved his personal performance by adopting that method.

TABLE 4.3
Productions Applicable to the Unit Task Scan-Text

Detect-onset-text
    IF the *goal* is of type scan-text and the area scanned is *window*
      and a message onset is detected in area *next* which is not *window*
    THEN make a note to scan text area *next*
Focus-onset-text
    IF the *goal* is of type scan-text,, no aircraft is selected and onset was detected in area
      next
    THEN focus on a *subgoal* to scan text area *next* starting at **bottom**
Find-flush-message
    IF the *goal* is of type scan-text of area *window* and no aircraft is currently selected
      and *message* is the next flush message in *window* going up from current position
    THEN note the *task, aircraft* and *controller* in *message*
No-flush-message
    IF the *goal* is of type scan-text and no aircraft is currently selected
    THEN pop the current goal
Memory-for-message
    IF the *goal* is of type scan-text with current task *task* and aircraft *aircraft*
      and there is a *chunk* for processing task *task* on aircraft *aircraft*
    THEN pop *goal*
Message-reply
    IF the *goal* is of type scan-text of area *window* with current aircraft *aircraft*
      and *message* is the next indented message in *window* containing *aircraft* going down from
        current position
    THEN pop *goal*
Subgoal-message-task
    IF the *goal* is of type scan-text with task *task*, aircraft *aircraft* and controller *controller*
    THEN clear *goal* and
      push *subgoal* to process task *task* on aircraft *aircraft* with controller *controller*

---

the goal is popped because under the bottom–up scanning strategy finding a message that had been attended to suggests that no unattended message older than the current message will be found. As we discuss shortly, this is not an ironclad guarantee, and it may be a natural source of skipped messages that result in violations. If no indication that the action requested by the message has taken place, the production subgoal-message-task pushes a subgoal to perform that action and clears the goal to allow further scanning to take place when that unit task is completed. Note that the strategy of first trying to retrieve a piece of information from memory and then resorting to an explicit strategy to reconstruct that information if the retrieval fails is a general design pattern in ACT-R (e.g., Lebiere, 1998), which is naturally supported by the architecture's conflict resolution mechanism. Because memory retrieval usually takes much less effort than implementing a complicated strategy, the utility learning mechanism will tend to assign a higher priority to the retrieval strategy, which is then attempted first. Again, because learning was not the focus of this model and training data were not available, this learning mechanism was not activated, and instead the production ordering was relied on to indicate priority.

Again this production set would provide a perfectly adequate implementation of the scan-text unit task. However, it would result in a systematic pattern of execution by exhaustively scanning a text window to find and process all unattended events and then move on to the next area, and so on. Although it might result in the right aggregate performance (and indeed did in the first version of the model, as is elaborated in the discussion section), its deliberate character would prevent it to display the subjects' ability to promptly respond to a new event as indicated by the sharply decreasing curve of number and average time of responses as a function of intervening events. The model needs to be able to focus on newly occurring events. The production detect-onset-text provides that capacity by detecting the onset of a new message in other text windows and record in the current goal to focus attention to that window as soon as the current message has been processed. The production focus-onset-text accomplishes that by focusing on a new goal to scan the text window in which the new message has appeared.

This onset detection mechanism has a number of interesting attributes. First of all, the ability to detect the onset of a new event is time limited (fixed at 1 second in our model). Although the onset detection productions have the highest priority in their unit task, if the model is otherwise busy during that limited time window (such as by an event-processing subgoal), it might miss the event onset and fail to record it. Second, only one event onset can be stored in the current goal, and subsequent ones are not recorded. An alternative would be to have the most recent onset overwrite the older ones, but again finer-grained data would be needed to shed light on that question. Third, the new goal to scan the text window in which the event onset appeared replaces the current goal rather than being a subgoal. This is consistent with viewing the goal stack as a limited memory and not relying on it to provide a perfect memory of past situations. However, it also means that messages further up in the current window might not be processed because of the distraction of shifting to a new text window, constituting a natural source of errors. Indeed it suggests a rational analysis (Anderson, 1990) of onset detections: Although they provide the ability to opportunistically respond to newly occurring events and emergency situations, they distract from the task at hand and might be detrimental to its performance. An onset detection mechanism along the lines of the one described here was subsequently added to ACT-R/PM (Byrne & Anderson, 2001), but much remains to be done to determine the proper treatment of onset detection in an integrated architecture such as ACT-R.

Table 4.4 presents the productions for the unit task scan-screen responsible for scanning the radar screen—more specifically, the area between the

TABLE 4.4
Productions Applicable to the Unit Task Scan-Screen

Detect-onset-screen
  IF the *goal* is of type scan-screen and no onset has been detected
    and a message onset is detected in area *next*
  THEN make a note to scan text area *next*

Focus-onset-screen
  IF the *goal* is of type scan-screen, no aircraft selected and onset was detected in area *next*
  THEN focus on a *subgoal* to scan text area *next* starting at **bottom**

Detect-red
  IF the *goal* is of type scan-screen and no aircraft is selected
    and a colored *aircraft* is present
  THEN note *position* and *controller* associated with *aircraft*
    and push subgoals to process both tasks for *aircraft* in *position* with *controller*

Scan-for-transfer
  IF the *goal* is of type scan-screen and no aircraft is currently selected
    and *aircraft* is outgoing in the **between** area
  THEN note *aircraft* with its *position* and associated *controller*

Scan-done
  IF the *goal* is of type scan-screen and no aircraft is currently selected
  THEN pop *goal*

Memory-for-transfer
  IF the *goal* is of type scan-screen with current *aircraft* and *controller*
    and there is a *chunk* for processing *aircraft* with *controller*
  THEN clear the *goal*

Trace-of-transfer
  IF the *goal* is of type scan-screen with current *aircraft* and *controller*
    and there is an indented message for *aircraft* in text area **right**
  THEN clear the *goal*

Subgoal-transfer
  IF the *goal* is of type scan-screen with current *aircraft* in *position* with *controller*
  THEN clear *goal*
    and push *subgoal* to process **transfer** on *aircraft* in *position* with *controller*

green and yellow lines in which exiting aircraft that need to be transferred can be detected. Because of the similarity between the two unit tasks, both of which consist of scanning a screen area to detect events that require actions, the set of productions for the unit task scan-screen is quite similar to those for the unit task scan-text. Scan-for-transfer scans the radar area for exiting aircraft, and memory-for-transfer and trace-of-transfer search in declarative memory and the top right text window, respectively, if the aircraft has already been transferred. If not, subgoal-transfer pushes a subgoal to transfer the aircraft. If no more exiting aircraft can be detected, scan-done pops the goal. The message onset detection productions detect-onset-screen and focus-onset-screen are similar to their counterpart in unit task scan-text.

There are noteworthy differences as well. First, the model does not assume any specific scan ordering, but instead detects exiting aircraft in an arbitrary order. Unlike the text window scanning, for which a natural ordering existed, any order in scanning the between radar screen area (e.g., clockwise, counterclockwise, starting at any corner, etc.) seems equally valid and indeed subject protocols indicated widely different strategies. Again more precise data such as eye movements would be needed to determine the answer.

Second, the model avoided focusing on the same aircraft twice in the same unit task by using an attended feature similar to the one existing in ACT-R/PM. This application actually suggests a possible answer to a long-standing question in ACT-R/PM regarding the duration of the attended feature tag: Unit tasks provide natural boundaries to reset attended tags. Third, there is an additional detection production detect-red that detects a red aircraft indicating holding violation in a manner similar to the color detection productions in the unit task color-goal. When a holding aircraft is detected, detect-red pushes two subgoals for that aircraft corresponding to the two actions that can be performed depending on the direction of the aircraft: accept and welcome for incoming aircraft and transfer and contact for outgoing aircraft. That pipelining of actions certainly leads to more duplicated or incorrect messages than necessary, but a more precise treatment would require a complex reasoning process that would best be implemented as a separate unit task. Subjects caught in a holding violation might not want to spend the time on such a process and might resort to this shotgun approach, and this would have significantly increased the model complexity as well. Nonetheless, further analysis of subjects' strategy choice in the case of holding infractions would be needed to sort out the matter, and too little data were available because of the relative rarity of that condition.

Table 4.5 presents the productions for the unit task process responsible for actually processing an action request through a sequence of button clicks and mouse selections. This unit task is common to the color and text condition because, although the information available will vary between conditions, the basic logic of the unit task remains unchanged. The first action to perform is to click the button on the right side of the screen corresponding to the requested action. The production answer-speed-request determines whether the aircraft is blocked and pushes the corresponding button. The production answer-other-requests pushes the corresponding button for all other actions because no action-specific decision is necessary. The next action is to select the aircraft. However, in some conditions (e.g., responding to a text message), the location of the aircraft is not yet known, and the aircraft has to be located first. The production memory-for-position attempts to extract the aircraft position from an existing process chunk. If that fails, the productions find-position-inner, find-position-between, and find-position-outer scan the radar screen area corresponding to the action requested (e.g., the outer area for accepting incoming aircraft) to find the

TABLE 4.5
Productions Applicable to the Unit Task Process

Next-target

    IF the *goal* is of type process and the display condition is **color**
      and an *aircraft* of *color* is detected
      and there is a *rule* associating *color* with *action*
    THEN note *position* of *aircraft* and
      create a *subgoal* to process *action* on *aircraft* in *position*

Answer-speed-request

    IF the *goal* is of type process with action **speed-change** for *aircraft* in *position*
      and step **select**
    THEN determine if *aircraft* is blocked
      and push button corresponding to accept–reject decision
      and note that the step is now **target**

Answer-other-requests

    IF the *goal* is of type process with *action* and step **select**
    THEN push button corresponding to *action* and note that the step is now **target**

Memory-for-position

    IF the *goal* is of type process with *aircraft* and no known position
      and there is a *chunk* for processing *aircraft* in *position*
    THEN note *position*

Find-position-inner

    IF the *goal* is of type process with action **speed-change** for *aircraft* and no position
      and the location of *aircraft* in screen area **inner** is found to be *position*
    THEN note *position*

Find-position-between

    IF the *goal* is of type process with action **contact** for *aircraft* with *controller*
      and no known position
      and the location of *aircraft* in screen area **between** on *controller* side is *position*
    THEN note *position*

Find-position-outer

    IF the *goal* is of type process with *aircraft* and no known position
      and the location of *aircraft* in screen area **outer** is found to be *position*
    THEN note *position*

Click-target

    IF the *goal* is of type process with *aircraft* in *position* and step **target**
    THEN select *aircraft* in *position* and update step to **controller**

Skip-speed-change-controller

    IF the *goal* is of type process with action **speed-change** and step **controller**
    THEN update step to **send**

Skip-welcome-controller

    IF the *goal* is of type process with action **welcome** and step **controller**
    THEN update step to **send**

Click-controller

    IF the *goal* is of type process with *aircraft* step **controller**
    THEN select *controller* associated with *aircraft* and update step to **send**

Click-send

    IF the *goal* is of type process with step **send**
    THEN push button **send** and pop *goal*

aircraft position. This is another instance of the retrieve-versus-compute design pattern encountered in the two previous unit tasks. Once its position is determined, the target can then be selected by production click-target. The production click-controller then selects the external controller associated to the aircraft unless preempted by productions skip-speed-change-controller and skip-welcome-controller that explicitly skip that step for the speed change and welcome actions, respectively. The click-send production then clicks the send button and pops the goal, which becomes a memory chunk encoding the processing of this task. As in previous unit tasks, there is an additional production to detect the onset of an event—in this case, the appearance of a colored aircraft on the radar screen—and it creates a subgoal to process that aircraft when the current goal is completed. That subgoal is then returned to the parent goal and pushed by the production subgoal-next in the color-goal unit task.

The final part of the model concerns the code at the top of the model that is used to compute the workload estimates. Although ACT-R has traditionally shied away from such meta-awareness measures and concentrated on matching directly measurable data such as external actions, response times, and eye movements, it is by no means incapable of doing so. For the purpose of this model, we proposed a measure of cognitive workload in ACT-R grounded in the central concept of unit task. *Workload* is defined as the ratio of time spent in critical unit tasks to the total time spent on task. *Critical unit tasks* are defined as tasks that involve actions, such as the process goal that involves handling an event with three or four mouse clicks, or tasks that involve some type of pressure, such as the scanning goal described earlier that results from an onset detection (i.e., carries an expectation of a new event that needs to be handled promptly). The ratio is scaled to fit the particular measurement scale used in the self-assessment report.

Finally, two specific considerations need to be discussed. First is the decision not to use ACT-R/PM. That decision was primarily driven by practical considerations, including the tight development schedule for Phase I and the fact that ACT-R/PM at the time only ran on the Macintosh, whereas the D-OMAR simulation only ran on Windows. Although the model is at a slightly higher degree of abstraction than ACT-R/PM (e.g., it performs a search of a list of messages in a single production), it operates in substantially similar ways, and an ACT-R/PM version could be developed fairly straightforwardly by expanding those specific productions that currently call the interface code directly. This would allow us to replace the only two parameters that we estimated—the average perception and action times—with more accurate ACT-R/PM predictions. However, it is an open question whether a higher degree of fidelity at the perceptual and motor levels would necessarily lead to a better model of the relatively higher level data (e.g., total penalty points) presented here. Yet that question of the right level of analysis is a fundamental one that an ACT-R/PM version of this model would allow us to pursue.

The second consideration is the inclusion on the Web site and CD-ROM of the complete text of the model. The first thing to point out is that the entire code of the model of a relatively complex task can indeed be included in a dozen fairly sparse pages. This is a reflection of the architecture's ability to generate complex behavior from a comparatively simple model. More fundamentally, providing the running code of our models has been an increasingly important practice in the ACT-R community. For example, the code from all the models described in our book (Anderson & Lebiere, 1998) is available on our Web site (http://act.psy.cmu.edu) and can even be run directly on the Web without having to download and install ACT-R. A point-and-click Web interface enables visitors to easily change the model parameters and rerun the model to determine whether its predictions are overly sensitive to the values of the parameters. Moreover, modelers are encouraged to adopt, if not pieces of models directly (which has been done; e.g., Byrne & Anderson, 2001), certainly the design patterns used in other models, as we have attempted to do in this case. The goal of this openness is both to facilitate model development and increase the constraints on the resulting models to increase their predictiveness and generality.

EXPERIMENT 1 RESULTS

Because the variability in performance between runs, even of the same subject, is a fundamental characteristic of this task, we ran as many model runs as there were subject runs. Figure 4.2 compares the mean performance in terms of penalty points for subjects and model for color (left three bars) and text (right three bars) condition by increasing workload level. The model matches the data quite well, including the strong effects of color-versus-text condition and of workload for the unaided (text) condition.

Because ACT-R includes stochasticity in chunk retrieval, production selection, and perceptual/motor actions, and because that stochasticity is amplified by the interaction with a highly dynamic simulation, it can reproduce a large part of the variability in human performance as indicated by Fig. 4.3, which plots the individual subject and model runs for the two conditions that generated a significant percentage of errors (text condition in medium and high workload). The range of performance in the medium workload condition is almost perfectly reproduced other than for two outliers, and a significant portion of the range in the high condition is also reproduced, albeit shifted slightly too upward. It should be noted that each model run is the result of an identical model that only differs from another in its run-time stochasticity. The model neither learns from trial to trial nor is modified to take into account individual differences.

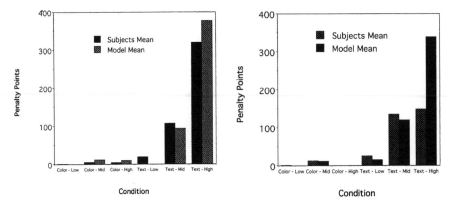

FIG. 4.2.   Mean performance for subjects versus model on tuneup (left) and
flyoff (right).

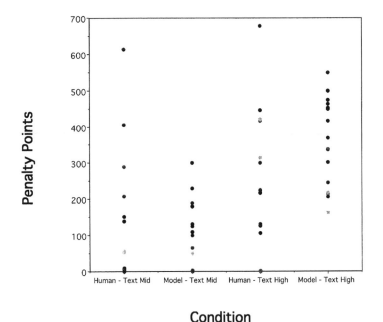

FIG. 4.3.   Performance for each subject versus model run.

The model reproduces not only the subject performance in terms of total penalty points, but also matches well to the detailed subject profile in
terms of penalties accumulated under eight different error categories as
plotted in Fig. 4.4. The model also fits the mean response times (RT) for
each condition as reported in chapter 8. The differences in RT between
conditions are primarily a function of the time taken by the perceptual

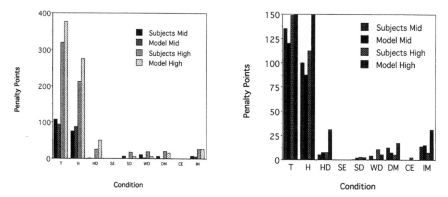

FIG. 4.4.   Penalty points for subjects versus model runs for each error category.

processes of scanning radar screen and text windows. A more detailed analysis is presented in Fig. 4.5, which plots the detailed pattern of latencies to perform a required action for each condition and number of intervening events (i.e., number of planes requiring action between the time of a given plane requiring action and the time the action is actually performed). The model accurately predicts the degradation of RT as more events compete for attention, including the somewhat counterintuitive exponential (note that RT is plotted on a log scale) increase in RT as a function of number of events rather than a more straightforwardly linear increase.

In a crucial test of the model's multitasking abilities, it also closely reproduces the probability of response to a required action in terms of number of intervening events (plotted in Fig. 4.6) before the action can be performed, a sensitive measure of the ability to detect and process events immediately after they occur.

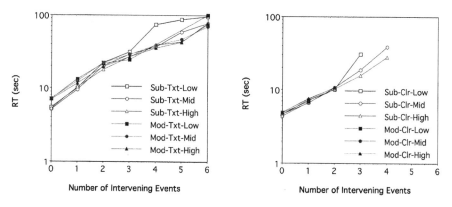

FIG. 4.5.   Response time for subjects versus model runs as a function of intervening events.

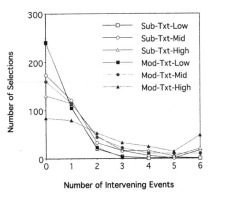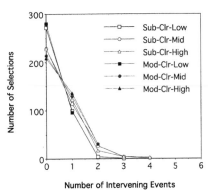

FIG. 4.6.   Number of selections for subjects versus model runs as a function of intervening events.

That multitasking capacity results from the model's ability to detect event onsets and set the next goal to process those events. Thus, despite ACT-R's strong goal-directed behavior, as indicated by its structure pictured in Fig. 4.1, it can exhibit the proper level of multitasking abilities without requiring any alteration to its basic control structure. Interestingly, a version of the model that ignores event onsets and stays with a systematic scanning strategy actually performs quite well, but provides a different multitasking profile.

Finally, the model reproduces the subjects' answers to the self-reporting workload test administered after each trial. Because ACT-R does not have any built-in concept of workload, we simply defined the workload of an ACT-R model as the scaled ratio between the time spent in critical unit tasks to the total time on task. The critical unit tasks in which the model feels "pressured" or "busy" are defined as the process goals, in which the model is busy performing a stream of actions, and the scan-text goals that are the result of an onset detection, in which the model feels pressured to find and process a new event requiring action. As shown in Fig. 4.7, that simple definition captures the main workload effects, specifically effects of display condition and of schedule speed. The latter effect results from reducing the total time to execute the task (i.e., the denominator) while keeping the total number of events (roughly corresponding to the numerator) constant, thereby increasing the ratio. The former effect results from adding to the process tasks the message scanning tasks resulting from onset detection in the text condition, thus increasing the numerator while keeping the denominator constant, thereby increasing the ratio as well. Another quantitative effect that is reproduced is the higher rate of impact of schedule speed in the text condition (and the related fact that workload in the slowest text condition is higher than workload in the fastest color condition). This is

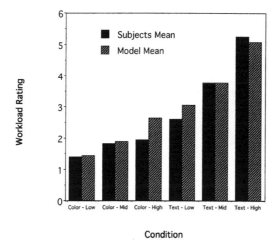

FIG. 4.7.   Mean workload for subjects versus model for each condition.

primarily a result of task embedding (i.e., the fact that a process task can be and often is a subgoal of another critical unit task—scanning a message window following the detection of an onset in that window), thus making the time spent in the inner critical task count twice.

In summary, the advantages of this model are that it is relatively simple, requires almost no parameter tuning or knowledge engineering, provides a close fit to both the mean and variance of a wide range of subject performance measures as well as workload estimates, and suggests a straightforward account of multitasking behavior within the existing constraints of the ACT-R architecture.

EXPERIMENT 2 MODEL

Initial Model

The methodology adopted in creating the Experiment 1 model was to not try to reverse-engineer subjects' procedures through a cognitive task analysis (CTA) or similar methods, but instead to simply develop a model that was simple and arose naturally from the architecture. At the basic cognitive level, it meant relying on architectural mechanisms like chunk creation to seamlessly accomplish functions like episodic memory for past actions and aircraft positions. At the higher, structural level, it meant leveraging the close relation between the architectural concept of goal and the HCI concept of unit task to structure the model around a modular set of goals and the knowledge needed to solve them. We follow this methodology again in the development of the Experiment 2 model.

At the structural level, this new model involved the removal of three unit tasks from the original model and the addition of one. The unit tasks removed were related to the text condition, which was not used in this model. They were the high-level unit task that handles the allocation of attention to various screen areas and the specialized unit tasks to scan text windows and the radar screen. Because of unit task modularity, they did not need to be removed and simply could have been ignored, never being called on, but we took them out for reasons of simplicity. The two remaining unit tasks are the high-level unit task for scanning the radar screen and identifying color-coded aircraft and the low-level unit task responsible for producing the sequence of actions needed to process an aircraft. The new unit task being added is inserted between the two. It involves a decision goal that is called by the high-level goal when a magenta aircraft is identified as requesting an altitude change. This goal involves deciding which action needs to be performed on the aircraft and then calls the process goal to perform it. This new unit task involves eight new productions that can apply to goals of the decision type, one being the crux of the decision engine while the others handle relatively straightforward stimuli input and feedback processing. The new model has 19 production rules distributed over the three goal types of color, decision, and process.

At the cognitive level, categorization is handled by relying on basic architectural mechanisms. Although the concept of categorization evokes the idea of production rules, the basic mechanism on which the initial model relies is memory. Before rules can be formulated, the knowledge must reside in the system on which to base those rules. Thus, this model relies on the same basic mechanism as the Experiment 1 model—that is, ACT-R's automatic creation of memory chunks encoding past goals (in this case, goals of the new decision type). When a decision is made and the feedback is processed, the decision goal is popped and becomes a long-term memory chunk. Future decisions can then be made from retrieving past decision chunks.

This model can be characterized as an instance-based model (e.g., Logan, 1988). Those models are characterized by an initial reliance on a general-purpose strategy (e.g., relying on external aids, performing a computation procedure, or, as in this case, simply guessing). As that strategy is exercised, knowledge from past decision-making instances builds into long-term memory and can gradually be used as the basis for making decisions. This gradual switch from general procedures to specific expertise is a hallmark of human cognition. In ACT-R, that approach has been applied with great success to a broad array of domains, including control problems (i.e., the Sugar Factory; Lebiere, Wallach, & Taatgen, 1998; Wallach & Lebiere,

2002; the Transportation Task; Wallach & Lebiere, 2002), game playing (i.e., Paper Rock Scissors; Lebiere & West, 1999; West & Lebiere, 2001; Backgammon; Sanner, Anderson, Lebiere, & Lovett, 2000; and 2×2 Games; Bracht, Lebiere, & Wallach, 1998; Lebiere, Wallach, & West, 2000), decision making (i.e., real-time dynamic decision making; Lerch, Gonzalez, & Lebiere, 1999; Gonzalez, Lerch, & Lebiere, 2003), and multiperson decision-making tasks (Lebiere & Shang, 2002). One argument often raised about the general instance-based approach is that it has so many degrees of freedom in representation and parameters that it can be applied to produce anything. Although such objections are often disingenuous (and are often leveled at the practice of cognitive modeling in general; e.g., see Roberts & Pashler, 2000), the ACT-R models listed earlier model a significant number of tasks over a broad range of domains while adopting consistent representations and parameter values. The ability to apply the same mechanisms across a wide range of tasks illustrates the major integrative advantage of cognitive architectures.

We now examine the model in detail (see Table 4.6). As previously mentioned, the production rules in the two remaining unit tasks from the Experiment 1 model are essentially unchanged. Exceptions involve a single production in each task that interacts with the new decision goal. In the top-level color goal, a new production color-magenta-action detects the magenta color associated with a plane requesting an altitude change and then pushes a goal to make a decision on whether to accept or reject the request (instead of directly processing the plane). In the low-level process goal, a new production answer-altitude-requests detects that the request is for an altitude change and presses the button (accept or reject altitude change) corresponding to the decision. Because this is the only request for which the button to select is not uniquely determined by the request, but is instead a function of a decision made, a different production is thus required.

All other productions apply to the decision goal. The order in which the productions are listed represent their utility ranking, and thus usually the order in which they fire to solve a given goal. The first three productions, target-fuel, target-turbulence, and target-size, encode the characteristics of the aircraft (i.e., its fuel, turbulence, and size respectively) by moving attention to the various pieces of information near the aircraft. The production remember-decision is the key production for this goal because it is primarily responsible for the decision making. It attempts to make a decision by retrieving a past decision for an aircraft sharing the characteristics of the current one. If it is successful in retrieving such a chunk, it simply makes the decision that was correct for that chunk. If no chunk can be retrieved, however, a backup production called guess-decision makes a decision by simply guessing randomly. Once a decision has been made, the production subgoal-process pushes a subgoal to process the aircraft with that decision.

After the process subgoal has been completed, the decision goal is resumed. The production wait-for-feedback waits for the feedback to appear. Once feedback is available, indicating either a correct or incorrect decision, the production feedback can fire. If the feedback indicates an incorrect decision, the decision is changed to the correct one. In either case, the goal is then popped, creating a declarative memory chunk (or reinforcing an identical one) holding the correct decision for an aircraft with these characteristics. That chunk can then potentially be retrieved as a basis for future decisions.

The effort parameters for these productions were set in accordance with the parameters for productions in the Experiment 1 model and with similar parameters in other ACT-R models. By default, all productions took 50 msec to fire. The three encoding productions (target-fuel, target-turbulence, and target-size) were assigned a latency of 200 msec. Because those items are in direct proximity to the aircraft and in predictable locations, that is directly compatible with the 185 msec estimate for small shifts of attention, such as when scanning menu items using the perceptual/motor layers (Byrne & Anderson, 1998). The feedback production latency was set

TABLE 4.6
Production Rules for Decision Goal and Related Goals

Color-Magenta-Action (**color** unit task)
    IF the *goal* is to detect a color aircraft at *position* and its *color* is **magenta**
    THEN push a *goal* to make a decision for *aircraft* at *position*
Target-fuel/turbulence/size (three separate productions)
    IF the *goal* is to make a decision for *aircraft* and no fuel/turbulence/size is known
    THEN encode the *fuel/turbulence/size* of *aircraft* in the *goal*
Remember-decision
    IF the *goal* is to make a decision for *aircraft* of *fuel, turbulence* and *size*
      AND there is a memory of a decision for an aircraft of *fuel, turbulence* and *size*
    THEN select decision
Guess-decision
    IF the *goal* is to make a decision for *aircraft* of *fuel, turbulence* and *size*
    THEN randomly decide between **accept-altitude** and **reject-altitude**
Subgoal-process
    IF the *goal* is to make a decision for *aircraft* at *position*
    THEN push the *goal* to process decision for *aircraft* at *position*
Feedback
    IF the *goal* is to make a decision and *feedback* is available
    THEN update decision according to *feedback* and pop the *goal*
Wait-for-feedback
    IF the *goal* is to make a decision and a *decision* has been made
    THEN wait for feedback
Answer-altitude-requests (**process** unit task)
    IF the *goal* is to process an altitude request *action* and the *step* is **select**
    THEN push the *button* corresponding to the *action* and change the *step* to **target**

---

to 500 msec in accordance with the color-detection productions in the color goal because both represent the detection of an unscheduled event such as the change of color of an aircraft or the appearance of the feedback icon. The wait-for-feedback production latency was set to 1 second, as for the wait production in the Experiment 1 model, representing the coarseness of the general alertness loop. The answer-altitude-requests production latency was also set to 1 second, as for all other action productions, representing the average action time factoring for an averaging of Fitt's law mouse movements, action preparation, and clicking movement. As in the Experiment 1 model, the latency times were not fixed, but instead varied according to a uniform distribution of $+/- 25\%$ around the mean. In summary, those parameters were not estimated to fit the data, but instead generalized directly from the Experiment 1 model and other architectural guidelines.

The critical step in the decision goal is the attempt to retrieve a past decision to provide the basis for the current one. That step is described schematically in Fig. 4.8. On top is the current goal, with each square representing one slot of the goal. After the first three encoding productions have fired, the goal contains the actual size, fuel, and turbulence of the current aircraft with no decision currently made. At the bottom is one of possibly many decision chunks in declarative memory. Note incidentally that those chunks have the same structure as the current decision goal: Because past goals become chunks when they are popped, the correspondence between structures is logical and allows for a direct correspondence in matching. One could request that the chunk retrieved from memory match exactly the characteristics of the current aircraft in the goal. This would correspond to the exact (symbolic) match process in ACT–R.

However, this would be undesirable for a number of reasons. First, at the start, the knowledge base is still sparse and activations are weak: Requiring the retrieval of an exact match would severely limit the probability of successful retrievals and reduce the decision to random guessing. Second, retrieving items that do not perfectly match allow for the model to generalize to new instances that have never been seen before—an essential characteristic in the real world where characteristics are not binary and the same situation is never seen exactly again. Finally, it makes the process more robust

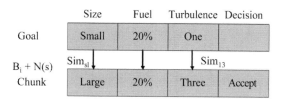

FIG. 4.8. Partial matching of decision chunks.

by preventing a single specific instance for exerting excessive influence (e.g., if it happens to be wrong) by letting all neighboring instances participate in the retrieval process rather than limit it to the one that happens to match exactly. This process of generalizing to similar stimuli directly produces the patterns observed for central versus peripheral stimuli.

In the training phase, only eight decision chunks are created in memory because that is the number of unique stimuli. For each new round of stimuli, the goal being popped is identical to an existing chunk in memory and is thus merged with it, resulting in a strengthening of the existing chunk through the base-level learning equation. As displayed in Table 4.6, the activation of the chunk is determined by its base-level activation B_i, with noise of amplitude s added. Over time the base-level activation of decision chunks increases, making it increasingly likely that their activation will be higher than the retrieval threshold τ and retrieval will be successful. If the memory chunk does not match the retrieval pattern perfectly, its match score will equal its activation decreased by the similarity between desired retrieval pattern and actual chunk value, scaled by the mismatch penalty MP. This partial matching process will apply for all slots specified in the retrieval pattern (e.g., in the case illustrated earlier, the similarity between large and small, Sim_{sb}, and between turbulence level 1 and 3, Sim_{13}, both apply additively to the match score). Partial matches are less likely to be the most active and to be retrieved. However, if the initial activation was high enough to overcome the mismatches and/or the activation of the perfectly matching chunk was sufficiently low, they have a chance to win the activation race and be the retrieved chunk.

Just as for productions, parameters involved for declarative memory were set using constraints from the architecture and other models. The latency factor F scaling retrieval latency was left at the architectural default of 1.0. The decay rate d in the base-level learning equation was also left at its architectural default of 0.5 used in almost all ACT-R models. The mismatch penalty MP scaling the similarity decrements in the partial matching equation was left at its default value of 1.5. The activation noise s controlling the stochasticity of memory retrieval was left at its default value of 0.25 used in many ACT-R models. The only architectural parameter that does not have a consensus default value is the retrieval threshold τ, which was coarsely estimated at -1.0. As Anderson et al. (1998) observed, the value of the retrieval threshold seems to vary with the average activation level and cannot seem to be fixed at this time. However, the value used here is well within the range of values for that parameter used in other models. As for chunk-specific parameters, the prior values for the activations of the color-action mapping chunks were left at their values set in the Experiment 1 model. The only additional parameters to be specified were the similarities between the quantities used in the stimuli (i.e., the fuel, size, and turbulence). Similarities between quantities are typically set according to regular scales, usually linear or exponential (e.g., Lebiere, 1998; Wallach & Lebiere, 2003). In the initial model, we set the similarities to decrease linearly as a function of distance on each scale, reaching minimal values for the extreme items of the scale.

Further Refinements

Based on the results of the first model (see next section), we implemented three changes and a significant addition to the model. The first change was primarily in reaction to the fact that, although the response time for the secondary task (transferring planes) was about right (as was to be expected because that task and that part of the model were essentially unchanged since the first experiment), the response time for the primary task (authorizing altitude changes) was significantly too high. A possible reason is that, although the altitude change task was clearly presented as the primary task, we did not provide a priority ordering among the various tasks. We made that choice partly for consistency with the Experiment 1 model and partly for simplicity, but it was clear that subjects gave higher priority to the primary task. Therefore, we modified the production ordering to give priority to the magenta aircraft over others when multiple planes request action at the same time. As expected, the response time for the primary task decreased significantly (by about 1 second), bringing it significantly closer to the subject data.

The second change concerned the similarities between stimuli components. One consequence of the linear similarities is that extrapolated stimuli had the same error rate as their trained neighbors because the translation in stimuli values simply added a constant value to the mismatch penalty for all training chunks, leaving the probability of retrieving them unchanged. Although linear similarities are often used for their simplicity, exponentially decreasing similarities have also been used and correspond more closely to human similarity metrics on domains like numbers (e.g., Whalen, 1996). Therefore, we changed the similarity scale between stimuli components to decrease exponentially with distance. That distribution has one parameter, which is the rate of the exponential decrease. It was fixed to leave the similarities between training stimuli unchanged, therefore affecting only the similarities to extrapolated stimuli. The result of a switch to an exponential similarity function is to decrease the similarity between close stimuli and increase the similarity between distant stimuli. This leads to an increase in probability of extrapolated error because distant instances, which are not likely to generalize well, are now more likely to be retrieved and generate the incorrect response.

The third change concerned the workload definition. Although the workload formula based solely on time on task captured the main effects, it did it so weakly that the match to the data is quite poor. There is just not enough difference in time spent in critical unit tasks between the various conditions and blocks to reproduce the size of the effects in the data. However, one measure of performance is strongly correlated with the observed changes in workload: the percentage of errors in altitude change decisions. Therefore, we added the time- and success-based (in terms of number of errors) measures of effort, still divided by total time on task, with the same multiplicative factor as in Experiment 1. One basic question was how to combine effort and success given that they involved two separate scales. To bridge the gap, we assigned to the goal of making an altitude decision the value G from the production utility function, which is its intended semantic in terms of time worth devoting to the task. Thus, we multiplied the number of errors by the value of G, which was set to 15 seconds, added it to the time spent on critical unit tasks (in this case, the decision and process goals), and divided by the total time on task. The result is a computational workload measure that closely captures the human data.

The main addition originated from the recognition that, although the instance-based model did an excellent job at capturing human performance for problem type 6, it could not learn fast enough to capture the steep learning curve for problem type 1. Therefore, although memory is still the primary foundation for categorization as is confirmed by the problem type 6 data, an additional mechanism, rule learning, must be introduced to account for the problem type 1 data. Category rule learning can certainly be thought of as a conscious process where explicit rules can be formulated, represented as chunks in declarative memory, and then iteratively tested, modified, and rejected or accepted. Yet that process is fraught with degrees of freedom. In effect, a great number of different algorithms can be implemented (Anderson & Betz, 2001), individual differences are paramount, and the architecture provides little constraint on the process. Therefore, we tried a different approach to provide for the learning of general rules while preserving strong architectural constraints.

To accomplish those ends, we represented categorization rules as production rules. Specifically, we created one production rule for each possible single-dimensional categorization rule—six production rules. Those productions could have been created through the process of production compilation (Taatgen & Anderson, 2002), but we wanted to avoid the complexity of the underlying process of explicitly formulating those rules. Those six production rules now compete with the remember-decision and guess-decision rules. The basis of the competition is the subsymbolic utility learning mechanism, which tracks the effectiveness of those rules at producing the correct answer and successfully solving the decision goal. For problem type 6, the single-dimensional production rules do no better than the random rule and worse than the remember rule, and therefore they are weeded out. For problem type 3, no single-dimensional rule can provide perfect categorization, but some can do significantly better than the random rule and even the remember rule until enough instances have been learned. In that case, the rule first predominates until it is replaced by the retrieve production. For problem type 1, one of the six rules can provide perfect performance, and its utility will quickly become dominant, leading to the nearly uniform use of that rule. The only parameters of the utility learning process are the value of the goal, G, which has previously been fixed at 15, and the value of the utility noise parameter, which is left at the default value of 1.0. A process of categorization rule learning has been added while preserving strong architectural constraints and avoiding arbitrary degrees of freedom.

EXPERIMENT 2 RESULTS

Original Results

The most important quantitative results are the percentages of error committed in the primary category task presented in Fig. 4.9. As for other following data figures, the left plot is for problem type 1, the central plot is for problem type 3, and the right plot is for problem type 6. The fit to problem type 6 is excellent. This is consistent with the fact that no useful (linear) rule exists for problem type 6, and an instance-based strategy like the one used in the model is likely to be the most effective for that problem type. For problem type 3, the model captures the shape of the curve, but is consistently slower than human subjects at learning the category by an approximately constant factor. The fit to problem type 1 is the worst, with the model only starting to significantly learn the category in Block 4 while humans have already significantly mastered it by Block 2. Although instance-based learning is more efficient on problem type 1 than 6 because a neighboring instance retrieved through partial matching is more likely to be of the right category, it is not nearly enough to match the human subjects.

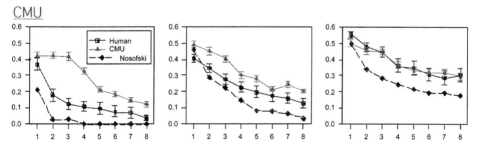

FIG. 4.9.   Error probabilities in primary task.

CMU

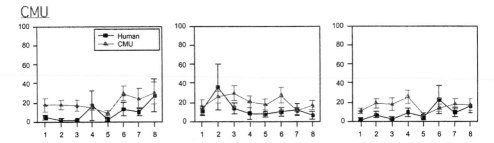

FIG. 4.10. Penalty points in secondary task.

This suggests that a more efficient strategy exists for learning problem type 1 (and probably problem type 3).

Figure 4.10 presents in the same format the penalty points for the secondary task, processing the aircraft moving between controller airspaces. Although errors on the secondary task are too few to generate significant numbers of penalty points, the model generally produces similar levels and patterns. The main sources of errors in the secondary task are the lack of time to accomplish the task in a timely manner and commission errors when retrieving color-action mapping chunks. Those two sources of errors are fundamentally the same as for the primary task. Therefore, the two error measures are not independent, but instead constrain each other through the same architectural mechanisms. They cannot be adjusted independently, but instead provide converging evidence on model performance.

Figure 4.11 presents the response time data for the secondary task. Because the response time to the secondary time is primarily determined by the latency of the processing steps, and those parameters were left unchanged from the Experiment 1 model, this is a direct prediction of the original model. No significant speedup with practice or any significant effect of primary task category is predicted in line with the human data.

Figure 4.12 presents the response time data for the primary task. The model consistently overestimates the amount of time required by the pri-

CMU

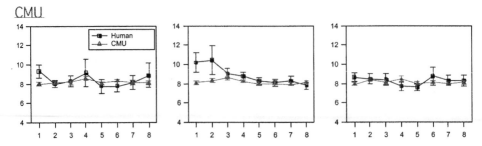

FIG. 4.11. Response time for secondary task.

CMU

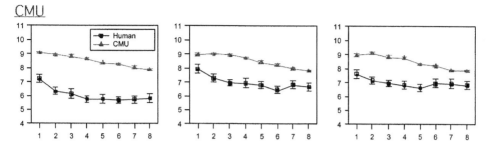

FIG. 4.12.   Response time for primary task.

mary time. In particular, response time for the primary task is larger than for the secondary task because the primary task involves an additional decision step that requires significant time. However, this does not take into account the fact that the primary task, as indicated by its name, carries a higher priority than the secondary task; when primary and secondary tasks conflict, the former is likely to take precedence. In the initial model, we did not implement any specific precedence scheme, which might have led to this overestimate of primary task response time.

A speedup with practice of about 1 second is predicted in all conditions, consistent with the data. This results from the increasing success and speed of retrievals. Initially, retrieval of previous instances is more likely to fail, which takes longer than successful retrievals. In addition, over time the activation of chunks representing previous instances increases with rehearsal, which, according to the retrieval latency equation, decreases the retrieval time. Both factors contribute to the speedup. However, the speedup seems to take place somewhat later than for the subjects. Also the model does not predict the shorter response time for problem type 1 observed for the subjects. This confirms the conclusion reached from the error rate data that rule learning might be involved for problem type 1, which would also decrease the response time in addition to increasing accuracy.

Figure 4.13 presents the workload ratings for the various conditions. No change was made to the definition of workload used for Experiment 1, which was a scaled ratio of time spent in critical goals to total time on task. The critical goals are the process goals, as in Experiment 1, and the new decision goals. Because no change was made to the definition or parameters, this is a direct prediction from the Experiment 1 model. Although it does a pretty good job at predicting base workload, such as in Blocks 4 and 8 of problem type 1 and Block 8 of Categories 3 and 6, it fails to reproduce the full range of the problem type and practice effects observed in the rest of the human data. The model in fact exhibits slight effects of problem type and practice. However, because they only reflect the response time decrease observed for the primary task (specifically the decision goal), they

CMU

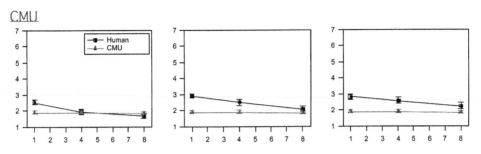

FIG. 4.13.   Workload ratings.

are insufficient in capturing the significant effects in the human data. Because the human data do not indicate a sizable difference in response time, but significant effects of problem type and practice on response accuracy that mirror the effects observed in the workload data, it seems reasonable that the subjects' workload self-assessments reflect not only considerations of time, but success as well.

Figure 4.14 presents error percentage data for the primary task in the transfer condition. The data presented represent the percentage of errors in the primary task for the last block (8) of the training phase, the instances of the transfer phase that were seen in the training phase (Trained), and the instances of the transfer phase that were seen in the training phase (Extrapolated). We focus on the data points for the transfer phase. The most important thing about the transfer phase is that it is handled exactly the same as the training phase (i.e., every stimulus is answered by attempting to retrieve a similar instance from declarative memory). No new procedure, with the attending degrees of freedom that it would introduce, is used for the transfer phase. The match to the trained examples is excellent.

For the extrapolated examples, the model predicts a similar error percentage to the trained examples, with the minor variations in the results due to the stochastic nature of the model runs. This results because of the form of

CMU

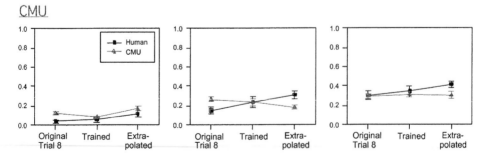

FIG. 4.14.   Error probability in transfer condition.

the partial matching equation used. An extrapolated stimulus will have an additional activation penalty subtracted from its match score compared with the neighboring trained stimulus. However, because the similarity function used in the original model is linear, the same penalty will apply to all chunks, and the probability of retrieving any given chunk will be unchanged (other than for their probability of reaching the retrieval threshold, but the chunks are active enough that this is not a factor). This is a direct consequence of using a linear similarity metric. Other forms of similarity functions (e.g., ratio or exponential as in other ACT-R models) have decreasing penalties with distance and would show the proper increase in error for extrapolated instances. The aggregation over broad categories of stimuli, such as trained, extrapolated, and equidistant, might obscure more specific results of the model. Figure 4.15 presents a comparison of human data and model results on the training phase for all individual stimuli.

Each individual point in the graph corresponds to a single stimulus (modulo category-preserving transformations) plotted by problem type. The X axis is the decision probability for the stimulus (accept, but it could equally well be decline) in human data, and the Y axis is the same for model results. Thus, a perfect fit would have all data points on the $x = y$ diagonal. The more points deviate from that line, the poorer the fit. Quantitative fits by categories are given at the top of the figure. Again an equation of $y = 0 + 1x$ with $R^2 = 1.0$ would indicate a perfect fit. The linear regression curves actually displayed are not quite that perfect, but all have a small intercept (absolute value of 0.05 or lower) and a slope roughly between 0.8 and 1.0. The underestimate of the slope for problem type 3 and especially problem type 1 is con-

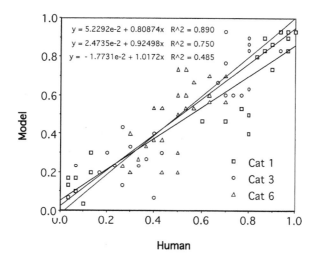

FIG. 4.15. Single-stimulus human and model comparison in transfer phase.

sistent with the larger consistency values for the model in the previous figure, especially for problem type 1, where the model is slower at learning the correct categorization values and therefore produces more extreme values. The $R \wedge 2$ correlations are generally high, indicating a good fit, although interestingly and somewhat surprisingly, $R \wedge 2$ is best for problem type 1 (0.890) and worse for problem type 6 (0.485), which is the opposite of the results for the aggregate error percentages presented previously, where the best fits were for problem type 6 and the worse for problem type 1. This primarily results from the characteristics of the categories. Problem type 1 is easier to classify and thus produces more extreme probability values, which makes larger correlation values more likely. Conversely, problem type 6 is harder to classify, with lots of mixed probabilities toward 0.5, which reduces possible correlations. Thus, $R \wedge 2$ correlation is actually a misleading indicator of model fit, in this case primarily reflecting characteristics of the task. A better measure of fit is Root Mean Square Error (RMSE), which measures the deviation between data and predictions. RMSE is 14.1% for problem type 1, 13.4% for problem type 3, and 12.5% for problem type 6, which correctly indicates a better fit for problem type 6 and a worse fit for problem type 1. Similar results can be plotted for transfer stimuli only, with similar fits and actually a slightly smaller RMSE for problem type 6.

FINAL RESULTS

As described in the modeling section, the main change between original and final model is the introduction of six production rules representing all possible single-dimensional categorization rules to compete with the retrieval and random strategies on the basis of learned production utility. The principal goal was to allow faster learning of problem type 1. Figure 4.16 presents the learning curves of error percentages on the primary task for the three categories for the original and revised model. One can see that the final results are significantly improved over the original ones. For problem type 6, no significant change occurs, and the excellent fit to human data of the original model is preserved. Because no single-dimensional rule can do better than 50% correct (i.e., chance), they are initially indistinguishable of the random production and then are quickly discarded in favor of the retrieval production rule. For problem type 3, the best a single-dimensional rule can do is to be successful 75% of the time, which is initially significantly better than the random and retrieval strategies and will boost performance to the subject level. Most significant, for problem type 1, a perfect single-dimensional rule exists and is quickly identified. Because of randomness in the utility computations, other rules, especially the retrieval rule, still occasionally fire depending on their utility level, generating less than perfect model performance (about 10% errors) similar to humans.

CMU $G^2 = 7.23(46.61)(49.69)$

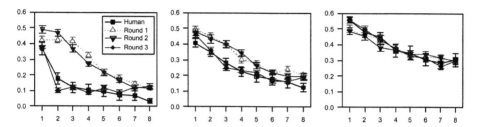

FIG. 4.16. Error probabilities in primary task.

Figure 4.17 presents the response time for the primary task in the final model. Prioritizing the primary task over the secondary task has led to a decrease in the primary task response time—much closer to subjects' RT for Categories 3 and 6, but still about 1 second too high for problem type 1.

Interestingly, the response time for the secondary task has not significantly increased because a better prioritization resulted in better performance overall as confirmed by Fig. 4.18, which presents the penalty points for the secondary task. A better prioritization scheme for the primary task has not only lowered response times, but also reduced error rates for the secondary task on a par with human level. As we have seen many times, components and parameters of the model have an influence on multiple data measures and cannot be optimized separately.

Figure 4.19 presents the workload ratings for the final model. By adding a success-based component to the workload formula, the model can now capture practice and problem type effects in the workload measure. Although workload levels seem a bit too high by about a constant factor, both the size of reduction with practice and the increase with problem type difficulty are about the right size. This is notable because the size of the success factor in the workload equation was not a free parameter, but instead was determined by the same G factor as weighing cost and success in the utility equation.

CMU SSE = 30.72(32.36)(88.67)

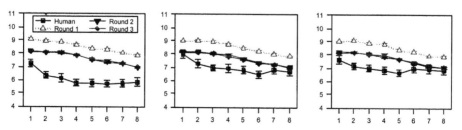

FIG. 4.17. Response time for primary task.

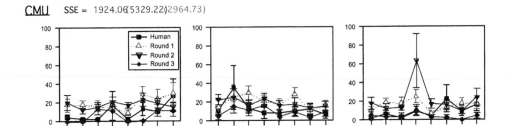

FIG. 4.18. Error probabilities in secondary task.

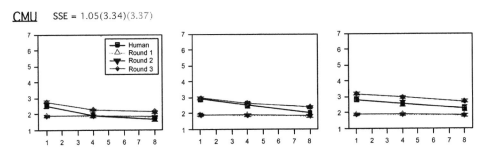

FIG. 4.19. Workload ratings.

Figure 4.20 presents the performance in the transfer task. Changing the similarity function to exponential similarities that exhibit sharper initial differences and then gradually flattening similarities similar to those obtained in human rating studies (e.g., Whalen, 1996) increases errors for extrapolated items because it reduces the relative probability of retrieving neighboring items. Because the change in similarity functions preserved the similarities between trained items, it did not change performance in the training task, and it also fixed the single parameter in determining the exponential function. Therefore, the size of the increase in errors for extrap-

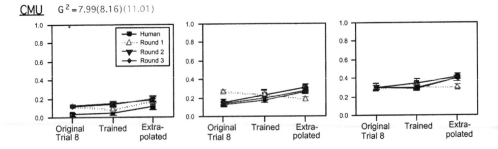

FIG. 4.20. Performance in transfer task.

olated items was not optimized, but instead a direct prediction of the shift to an exponential similarity function.

DISCUSSION AND CONCLUSION

Parameterization

Roberts and Pashler (2000) suggested that the behavior of cognitive models should be studied over their entire range of possible parameters to determine not only what data models can account for, but also what data they cannot account for. It is of course an open question what the model parameters are. Real-valued architectural and knowledge parameters seem to qualify, but they do not really constitute degrees of freedom if they are treated as constants set by the architecture or other models. However, Baker, Corbett, and Koedinger (2003) suggested that every knowledge structure, such as each chunk and production rule, should be counted as a free parameter. Our view is that, as long as the knowledge structures are specified by modelers, there will be a possibility of exploiting degrees of freedom in model specification, which need not be the case. Our methodology in developing our model has been to aim for the simplest, most natural way to solve the problem in the ACT-R architecture and explicitly mention when we revised that model and why. Moreover, Anderson, Bothell, Douglas, and Haimson (2003) and Taatgen (2003) used the production compilation mechanism to automatically encode instructions whose interpretation would then be compiled into the production rules executed by the model. Because task-specific declarative knowledge is the result of a direct encoding of instructions given to subjects and task-specific production rules are the product of an architectural compilation mechanism (and a general-purpose interpretation mechanism), one can argue that no degrees of freedom exist in the creation of their model. Although we did not follow that methodology here, we tried to avoid endowing the model with any expert knowledge that would clearly go beyond the instructions received.

Nonetheless, examining the influence of real-valued parameters on the model results is a valid and often worthwhile exercise in which we have engaged regularly (e.g., Lebiere, 1998; Lebiere & Wallach, 2001). In this section, we describe the impact of variations of three architectural parameters directly involved in the declarative memory retrieval process central to the instance-based categorization strategy. Those parameters are the retrieval threshold RT, which determines when a chunk is active enough to be retrieved; the activation noise S, which controls the stochasticity of the chunk activations and therefore of the retrieval process; and the mismatch penalty

MP, which scales the activation penalty for mismatches and thus controls the degree of retrieval generalization. The key measure of performance as a function of parameter variation is the probability of categorization errors for the primary task for all training blocks (a block here corresponds to a single presentation of all instances; i.e., half a block as described previously). Figure 4.21 presents the probability of categorization errors as a function of the retrieval threshold.

As expected, performance is worse for relatively high-retrieval thresholds (0.0 and −0.5), which delay retrieval from memory longer. Yet one would assume that the lower the retrieval threshold, the easier the access to memory, and therefore the better the performance. Yet that is counting without the possibility of errors of commission in memory retrieval (i.e., the possibility of retrieving an incorrect instance chunk because it is active and can overcome mismatch penalties). Thus, an overly low retrieval threshold leads to a process where a few chunks are retrieved quickly, build up more strength through rehearsal, and intrude on other retrievals, leading to a permanently high number of errors. That is the pattern displayed for retrieval threshold values of −1.5 and lower. One is better off delaying retrieval until all instances have had some time to establish their activation and will not be so easily invaded by overactive neighbors. Somewhat surprisingly (and satisfyingly), the retrieval threshold value of −1.0 that was chosen to correspond to the human learning curve, especially for problem type 6, also turns out to be optimal in terms of providing the best long-term performance (i.e., lowest number of errors). This echoes the conclusion reached in Lebiere (1998) regarding the influence of various parameters

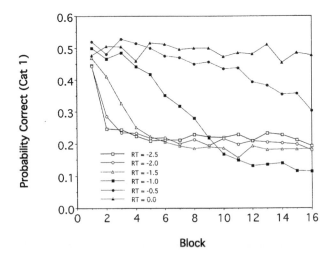

FIG. 4.21. Probability of categorization errors for various retrieval thresholds (RT).

on the learning of arithmetic facts through years of study and experience. This suggests that perhaps the human cognitive architecture is even more flexible than previously thought in adapting its mechanisms to provide optimum long-term performance.

Figure 4.22 presents the variations in performance as a function of the activation noise S. Different noise values seem to provide the best performance at different stages of training. For instance, a high noise value (e.g., 0.5) is best in the first handful of blocks because it increases the probability of retrieving anything rather than deciding randomly, whereas a low noise value (e.g., 0.1) is best after a lot of training (i.e., 12 blocks) because it reduces the probability that stochastic activation variations will lead to an error of commission. Intermediate values, such as the default value of 0.25, provide the best performance for intermediate amounts of training. This suggests that a truly optimal architecture would start with a high noise associated to new knowledge structures that would gradually decrease with practice. Lebiere (1998) suggested that it would produce a power law of practice for the reduction of commission errors. It is also similar to the technique of simulated annealing used in connectionist algorithms such as the Boltzmann Machine (Ackley, Hinton, & Sejnowski, 1985).

Finally, Fig. 4.23 presents the probability of errors as a function of the mismatch penalty MP.

A similar pattern to the previous two figures emerges. Overly lax mismatch penalties (e.g., 0.5) lead to a permanently high percentage of errors. However, different values provide the best performance for different amounts of training. The default value of 1.5 provides the fastest initial

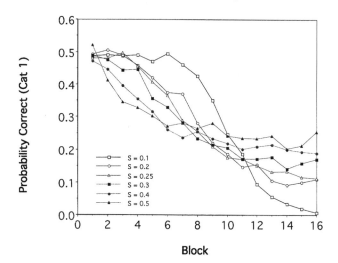

FIG. 4.22.   Probability of categorization errors for various activation noise (S).

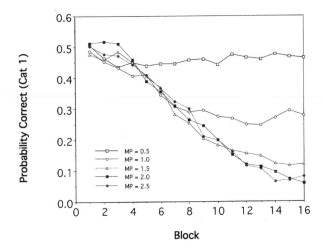

FIG. 4.23. Probability of categorization errors for various mismatch penalties (MP).

learning among *MP* values that trend toward perfect performance, thereby striking the best balance between the need for initial generalization and later precision in memory retrieval.

Implications for ACT-R Modeling

As mentioned previously, it has generally been the long-term approach of the ACT-R modeling community to view the various models developed in the architecture as compatible pieces of human knowledge and skills that could ultimately be integrated back into a whole individual. This presents constraints and opportunities that provide strong guidance to the enterprise of developing models within the framework of a unified theory of cognition. One opportunity is the potential ability of reusing previous models, and therefore be able to build increasingly complex models out of model libraries in a manner similar to software engineering practices. One constraint is the need to be compatible, in both parameters and knowledge representation, with previously developed models. As previously discussed, we leveraged this methodology in developing this model, and its parameters and representations do reflect the consensus of the ACT-R community. In turn this model suggests some new guidelines, practices, and extensions for future models.

One such guideline is the adoption of exponentially decreasing similarity metrics for continuous quantities. Past models have not been strongly sensitive to the specific shape of the similarity function as long as it remained monotonically decreasing with distance, but the generalization test of Experiment 2 provided a strong constraint in that regard, which seems retrospectively quite natural. Exponentially decreasing similarities will generally result in the accuracy of partial matching to decrease with the distance from known instances—a result that intuitively seems to hold in general fashion.

Another implication lies in the use of unit tasks and their applications. The concept of unit task is crucial to the functional organization of our model, but it is also relevant in other dimensions. One suggestion is that the attended tags associated with perceptual scanning should expire at the end of the associated unit task, which would provide a more natural limit on the growth of those tags than artificial upper bounds. Another implication of unit tasks is on their use in determining cognitive workload—a methodology that could be applied to any other model and provide a connection with a large human factors literature in which that concept plays a fundamental role.

A final general recommendation would concern the cognitive modeling enterprise in general. Although quantitatively fitting model to data is a central tenet of the field, there is such a thing as too much of a good thing. The dangers of overfitting model to data are well known to machine learning practitioners, and most of them might be applicable to model development. Given the pervasive variability of human behavior and the need for the efficient, affordable development of cognitive models, it might well be worth adopting the 80/20 rule as a guiding principle of cognitive modeling.

SUMMARY OF QUESTIONS AND ANSWERS

This section presents the ACT-R architecture of cognition, the methodology used in developing models, and its account of individual differences, cognitive workload, multitasking, and categorization.

1. How Is Cognition Represented in Your System?

Cognition is represented in terms of a computational architecture that implements a unified theory of cognition (Newell, 1990). Although unified, the architecture is highly modular and includes separate modules for procedural skill, long-term declarative memory, the current context (a.k.a. goal), and perceptual-motor systems including visual, manual, auditory, and speech (Anderson et al., in press).[3] The latter modules communicate

---

[3]As described previously, for practical reasons we used a previous version of the architecture without perceptual-motor modules. Instead we estimated compatible latency parameters for the production rules corresponding to perceptual-motor actions.

through limited buffers with the central production system. All modules operate in parallel, but are internally serial as is their communication through the buffer system. The central production system represents procedural skill in the form of production rules. Knowledge in declarative memory (as well as in the other modules and buffers) is represented in the form of structured chunks. Rules and chunks, as well as the operations of the other modules, are strongly limited in their complexity (i.e., the "Atomic Components of Thought"; Anderson & Lebiere, 1998). Although rules and chunks are represented symbolically to capture the sequential, structured nature of cognition, their characteristics are determined by associated subsymbolic quantities that endow them with soft qualities such as adaptivity, similarity-based generalization, and stochasticity. Production rules are selected according to their utility and chunks are retrieved from memory according to their activation, both of which reflect the history of those structures. All components of the model, including rules, chunks, and their subsymbolic parameters, are learnable by the architecture.

2. What Is Your Modeling Methodology?

Our modeling methodology is based on emphasizing the power and constraints of the ACT-R architecture. The basic methodology is to create the most natural and effective model of the task given the architecture (i.e., a model that respects rather than fights the constraints of the architecture and naturally leverages its mechanisms). The model relies naturally on fundamental features of the architecture, such as memory, for a broad range of purposes from incidental learning to concept formation. The central organizing construct to guide structured cognition is the concept of *goal*. Goals correspond well to the concept of unit task in human–computer interaction (Card, Moran, & Newell, 1983). Complex models are organized around a set of goal types, each with the skills needed to solve them in the form of production rules. Being able to add and remove goal types modularly provides both a tractable way to author complex models as well as a theory of skill compositionality.

3. What Role Does Parameter Tuning Play?

Parameter tuning plays a limited role in ACT-R model development. Some degree of parameter flexibility is required of any cognitive model because of the variety of ways that cognition can be applied to solve a task and the differences between individuals. However, parameter tuning must be limited and principled to address concerns that models can account for anything (Roberts & Pashler, 2000) and provide actual predictiveness. Architectural parameters should be fixed across models (modulo individual differences) because they represent a cognitive constant. Parameters associated with knowledge structures should be learned or set according to reasonable principles (again allowing for individual differences). Knowledge structures constituting the model (i.e., chunks and productions) can be viewed as parameters (Baker, Corbett, & Koedinger, 2003). Therefore, as described previously, they should also be learned or set to reflect the natural way for the architecture to solve the problem rather than specially engineered to fit the data.

4. What Is Your Account of Individual Differences?

The ACT-R architecture provides a number of accounts of individual differences. The first source of variation in individual differences is simply noise, especially when interacting with a complex dynamic environment as demonstrated in our results for Experiment 1. Stochasticity is a component of every subsymbolic mechanism, including activation, utility, and latency computations, which in turn determine every cognitive step including production rule firing and memory retrieval. The second source of individual differences are changes in architectural parameters that account for variations in fundamental abilities such as working memory (Lovett, Reder, & Lebiere, 1999), psychomotor speed, and emotions (Ritter et al., 2003). Once estimated, an individual's parameters can be applied to a model of any task to obtain predictions of that individual performance on that particular task. The final source of individual differences is variations in knowledge structures (chunks and production rules) and their associated parameters. Because those variations can be extremely complex and task-specific, it is the hardest source of individual differences for which to derive a consistent account.

5. What Is Your Account of Cognitive Workload?

Cognitive workload is defined as a function of the operations of the architecture. Certain goals (unit tasks) involving external manipulations and interruptions are defined as critical. The measure of cognitive workload is the ratio of time spent solving those goals to the total time on task. A similar but finer-grained measure of workload focused on atomic cognitive, perceptual, and motor actions might be defined in a manner similar to the BOLD response in fMRI experiments, but the data in this task did not address this level of detail. A single measure of workload is provided, but it could easily be defined in a modality-specific way by directly exploiting the modular nature of the architecture, basically defining a workload dimension per module in line with workload theories such as multiple resource theory (Wickens, 1992). Mechanisms by which subjects estimate workload are not specified, but could originate in a mechanism for aggregate retrievals of past goals called *blending* (Lebiere, 1999). In this model, our assumption was that performance determined workload, but the model could be augmented to allow workload to determine strategy and thus performance.

6. What Is Your Account of Multitasking?

Structured cognition in ACT-R is organized around the concept of goal. However, production rules can match inputs from any number of modules, especially perceptual buffers, to provide reactive as well as goal-driven behavior. Detection of a perceptual event can lead to a cognitively controlled goal switching. After the external event has been handled, the goal can be switched back to the original one or cognition can continue on another path. Switching back and forth between goals can be accomplished simply by retrieving previous goals from memory. Multiple tasks can be accomplished concurrently by combining their goal representations through extensive training (e.g., Byrne, & Anderson, 1998). However, the architecture imposes constraints on multitasking: The former solution requires lengthy and uncertain goal retrievals, whereas the latter leads to a slowdown in cognitive operations because of a diffusion in spreading activation.

7. What Is Your Account of Categorization?

Categorization is not a primitive function of the architecture, but rather depends on more basic mechanisms. The initial basis of categorization is memory—specifically, the identification of a stimulus by the retrieval of a similar instance from declarative memory. Similarity-based partial matching provides generalization and the gradual emergence of soft categories. Explicit categorization rules can also be formulated, which are in turn compiled into production rules.[4] Production utility learning can then be used to select between competing categorization rules and instances. Therefore, although categorization is not an ACT-R primitive, architectural constraints provide limits on categorization performance through underlying mechanisms like memory decay and stochasticity.

---

[4]For the sake of simplicity and efficiency, in this model we did not use the production compilation mechanism, but instead directly encoded the kind of production rules that would be created.

ACKNOWLEDGMENTS

The author would like to thank John R. Anderson for many helpful suggestions during the course of the project, Dan Bothell for supporting the integration for Experiment 1, and Eric Biefeld for supporting the integration for Experiment 2. This project was supported by grants N 00014-00-1-0380 and N 00014-01-1-0129 from the Office of Naval Research.

REFERENCES

Ackley, D. H., Hinton, G. E., & Sejnowski, T. J. (1985). A learning algorithm for Boltzmann machines. *Cognitive Science, 9,* 147–169.

Anderson, J. R. (1990). *The adaptive character of thought.* Hillsdale, NJ: Lawrence Erlbaum Associates.

Anderson, J. R., & Betz, J. (2001). A hybrid model of categorization. *Psychonomic Bulletin and Review, 8,* 629–647.

Anderson, J. R., Bothell, D., Byrne, M. D., Douglass, S., Lebiere, C., & Qim, Y. (in press). An integrated theory of the mind. *Psychological Review.*

Anderson, J. R., Bothell, D. J., Douglass, S. A., & Haimson, C. (2003). Learning a complex dynamic skill. In *Proceedings of the 2003 ACT-R Workshop,* Pittsburgh, PA.

Anderson, J. R., Bothell, D., Lebiere, C., & Matessa, M. (1998). An integrated theory of list memory. *Journal of Memory and Language, 38,* 341–380.

Anderson, J. R., & Lebiere, C. (1998). *The atomic components of thought.* Mahwah, NJ: Lawrence Erlbaum Associates.

Anderson, J. R., Matessa, M., & Lebiere, C. (1997). ACT-R: A theory of higher level cognition and its relation to visual attention. *Human Computer Interaction, 12*(4), 439–462.

Anderson, J. R., & Schooler, L. J. (1991). Reflections of the environment in memory. *Psychological Science, 2,* 396–408.

Baker, R. S., Corbett, A. T., & Koedinger, K. R. (2003). Statistical techniques for comparing ACT-R models of cognitive performance. In *Proceedings of the 2003 ACT-R Workshop,* Pittsburgh, PA.

Bracht, J., Lebiere, C., & Wallach, D. (1998, June). *On the need of cognitive game theory: ACT-R in experimental games with unique mixed strategy equilibria.* Paper presented at the Joint Meetings of the Public Choice Society and the Economic Science Association, New Orleans, LA.

Byrne, M. D., & Anderson, J. R. (1998). Perception and action. In J. R. Anderson & C. Lebiere (Eds.), *The atomic components of thought* (pp. 167–200). Mahwah, NJ: Lawrence Erlbaum Associates.

Byrne, M. D., & Anderson, J. R. (2001). Serial modules in parallel: The psychological refractory period and perfect time-sharing. *Psychological Review, 108,* 847–869.

Card, S. K., Moran, T. P., & Newell, A. (1983). *The psychology of human–computer interaction.* Hillsdale, NJ: Lawrence Erlbaum Associates.

Corbett, A. T, Anderson, J. R., & O'Brien, A. T. (1995). Student modeling in the ACT programming tutor. In P. Nichols, S. Chipman, & B. Brennan (Eds.), *Cognitively diagnostic assessment* (pp. 19–41). Hillsdale, NJ: Lawrence Erlbaum Associates.

Gonzalez, C., Lerch, F. J., & Lebiere, C. (2003). Instance-based learning in real-time dynamic decision making. *Cognitive Science, 27*(4), 591–635.

Lebiere, C. (1998). *The dynamics of cognition: An ACT-R model of cognitive arithmetic.* Unpublished doctoral dissertation (CMU Computer Science Dept. Technical Report CMU-CS-98-186).

Lebiere, C. (1999). The dynamics of cognitive arithmetic: Special issue on cognitive modelling and cognitive architectures. *Journal of the German Cognitive Science Society, 8*(1), 5–19.

Lebiere, C., & Shang, J. (2002, June 21–23). Modeling group decision making in the ACT-R cognitive architecture. In *Proceedings of the 2002 Computational Social and Organizational Science (CASOS)*, Pittsburgh, PA.

Lebiere, C., & Wallach, D. (2001). Sequence learning in the ACT-R cognitive architecture: Empirical analysis of a hybrid model. In R. Sun & L. Giles (Eds.), *Sequence learning: Paradigms, algorithms, and applications* (pp. 189–212). Springer Lecture Notes in Computer Science/Lecture Notes in Artificial Intelligence, Berlin, Germany.

Lebiere, C., Wallach, D., & Taatgen, N. (1998). Implicit and explicit learning in Act-R. In F. E. Ritter & R. Young (Eds.), *Proceedings of the 2nd European conference on cognitive modeling* (pp. 183–189). Nottingham: Nottingham University Press.

Lebiere, C., Wallach, D., & West, R. L. (2000). A memory-based account of the prisoner's dilemma and other 2 × 2 games. In *Proceedings of International Conference on Cognitive Modeling 2000* (pp. 185–193). Netherlands: Universal Press.

Lebiere, C., & West, R. L. (1999). A dynamic ACT-R model of simple games. In *Proceedings of the 21st Conference of the Cognitive Science Society* (pp. 296–301). Mahwah, NJ: Lawrence Erlbaum Associates.

Lee, F. J., & Anderson, J. R. (2001). Does learning of a complex task have to be complex? A study in learning decomposition. *Cognitive Psychology, 42*(3), 267–316.

Lerch, F. J., Gonzalez, C., & Lebiere, C. (1999). Learning under high cognitive workload. In *Proceedings of the 21st Conference of the Cognitive Science Society* (pp. 302–307). Mahwah, NJ: Lawrence Erlbaum Associates.

Logan, G. D. (1988). Toward an instance theory of automatization. *Psychological Review, 95*, 492–527.

Lovett, M. C., Reder, L. M., & Lebiere, C. (1997). Modeling individual differences in a digit working memory task. In *Proceedings of the 19th Conference of the Cognitive Science Society* (pp. 460–465). Mahwah, NJ: Lawrence Erlbaum Associates.

Lovett, M. C., Reder, L. M., & Lebiere, C. (1999). Modeling working memory in a unified architecture: An ACT-R perspective. In A. Miyake & P. Shah (Eds.), *Models of working memory: Mechanisms of active maintenance and executive control.* New York: Cambridge University Press.

Newell, A. (1990). *Unified theories of cognition.* Cambridge, MA: Cambridge University Press.

Newell, A., & Rosenbloom, P. S. (1981). Mechanisms of skill acquisition and the power law of practice. In J. R. Anderson (Ed.), *Cognitive skills and their acquisition* (pp. 1–56). Hillsdale, NJ: Lawrence Erlbaum Associates.

Ritter, F. E., Reifers, A., Klein, L. C., Quigley, K., & Schoelles, M. (2003). *Using cognitive modeling to study behavior moderators: Pre-task appraisal and anxiety.* Proceedings of the 2003 ACT-R Workshop. Pittsburgh, PA.

Roberts, S., & Pashler, H. (2000). How persuasive is a good fit? A comment on theory testing. *Psychological Review, 107*, 358–367.

Rubin, D. C., & Wenzel, A. E. (1990). One hundred years of forgetting: A quantitative description of retention. *Psychological Review, 103*, 734–760.

Sanner, S., Anderson, J. R., Lebiere, C., & Lovett, M. C. (2000). Achieving efficient and cognitively plausible learning in backgammon. In *Proceedings of the 17th International Conference on Machine Learning.* San Francisco: Morgan Kaufmann.

Taatgen, N. A. (2003). Variability of behavior in complex skill acquisition. In *Proceedings of the 2003 ACT-R Workshop*, Pittsburgh, PA.

Taatgen, N. A., & Anderson, J. R. (2002). Why do children learn to say "broke"? A model of learning the past tense without feedback. *Cognition, 86*(2), 123–155.

Wallach, D., & Lebiere, C. (2002). *On the role of instances in complex skill acquisition.* Proceedings of the 43rd Conference of the German Psychological Association, Berlin, Germany.

Wallach, D., & Lebiere, C. (2003). Conscious and unconscious knowledge: Mapping to the symbolic and subsymbolic levels of a hybrid architecture. In L. Jimenez (Ed.), *Attention and implicit learning* (pp. 112–143). Amsterdam, Netherlands: John Benjamins Publishing Company.

West, R. L., & Lebiere, C. (2001). Simple games as dynamic, coupled systems: Randomness and other emergent properties. *Journal of Cognitive Systems Research, 1*(4), 221–239.

Whalen, J. (1996). *The influence of the semantic representations of numerals on arithmetic fact retrieval.* Unpublished dissertation.

Wickens, C. D. (1992). *Engineering psychology and human performance.* New York: HarperCollins.

Chapter 5

A COGNET/iGEN Cognitive Model That Mimics Human Performance and Learning in a Simulated Work Environment

Wayne Zachary
Joan Ryder
James Stokes
Floyd Glenn
Jean-Christophe Le Mentec
Thomas Santarelli
CHI Systems, Inc.

COGNET is an executable cognitive architecture (see Pew & Mavor, 1998), although unlike most analogous systems it was created for engineering purposes (i.e., as a vehicle for creating practical applications), rather than as a platform for generating and/or testing psychological theory. Originally created as an engine to embed user models into intelligent interfaces (Zachary, Ryder, Ross, & Weiland, 1992), the system has been generalized and extended over time to create a flexible framework for building cognitive agents for use in intelligent training, decision support, and human performance modeling (see Zachary, Ryder, Santarelli, & Weiland, 2000). iGEN is an integrated software development environment that supports the authoring, editing, debugging, and integrating of COGNET models (Zachary & LeMentec, 1999). After describing the COGNET/iGEN framework, this chapter presents the results of its application to the AMBR modeling problems.

BACKGROUND: THEORIES, MODELS, AND TOOLS

Before discussing either COGNET or the AMBR model in more detail, it is useful to situate COGNET in the broader framework of cognitive modeling/simulation research. This provides a frame of reference used to describe COGNET and the design decisions it embodies plus, at various points in the chapter, comparing the COGNET approach with that of other approaches. This background begins by contrasting the notion of theory and model. *Theory* can be defined as a body of general principles and/or abstractions, formal or otherwise, about the world (both phenomenal and epistemic). Theory formation, then, is a process of creating such abstractions and principles without any inherent linkage to any specific purpose. It is simply the construction of a narrative on the universe. In contrast, a *model* can be defined as a specific representation of some set of phenomena[1] that attempts to re-create or predict some aspect of those phenomena for a specific purpose. Model building is thus viewed as an inherently purposive process—one undertaken to support a specific end or answer a specific question, such as "How should this device be engineered?" or "How might this building aesthetically change the neighborhood?" or even "How predictive or parsimonious is a specific psychological theory?" Thus, representing a city as a point in a directed graph model may be completely adequate for the purpose of calculating the optimal travel time of a multicity trip (as in the so-called *traveling salesman* problem), but completely inadequate for the purposes of actually traveling to that city (for which a different type of model—the road map—would be better) and vice versa.

When viewed in this way, models are all simplifying representations of the phenomena they address. Why? If they did not somehow simplify the phenomena, the purposes might just as well be addressed by experimentation—interaction with the phenomena directly. This leads to the proposition that all models are as-if models filled with simplifying assumptions (which in the best case are all explicit and deliberate). That is, they attempt to predict or re-create the first-order phenomenon as if it were equivalent to the simplified representation inherent in the model. Divergences between the model and the denotata of the model help identify the benefits or limitations of such simplifications given the purpose of the model. In this way, model building can be used as a way to wield Occam's Razor—one should not increase, beyond what is necessary, the number of entities required to explain anything—by providing a link between the level of parsimony of a representation and its usefulness.

Yet the fact that models are inherently simplifying, as-if representations means that the phenomena they represent are always more complex than the models. When a model is used to embody a theory, there is a tension between modeling in the purposive sense (which strives for parsimony) and

---

[1]The term *phenomena* is somewhat misused in the following discussions, in that it is intended to include physically sense-able information (the usual denotation), but also epistemic information such as knowledge and feelings, which rely on consciousness rather than sensation. The reasons for this should be obvious. The model being presented here is both phenomenological (predicting behavior) and epistemological (predicting knowledge use).

theory development (which strives for completeness). This can create a kind of slippery slope, where additional detail is added to the model (or, better put, simplifications are removed) because the process creates a more direct correspondence with the phenomena being modeled. The result, however, can be a representation that is called a model but has no specific purpose and may not stand up to Occam's Razor when it is used for a specific purpose. For example, a model of the unique cellular physiology of the heart muscle may be more complete in many senses than a model that represents the heart as a pair of interconnected pumps, yet for the purpose of predicting the rate and quantity of flow of blood to the lungs the latter may be a much more effective and parsimonious representation. The conclusions at the end of this chapter return to these notions.

COGNET RESEARCH FOUNDATIONS

COGNET (e.g., Zachary et al., 1992; Zachary, Ryder, & Hicinbothom, 1998) is a conceptual model of human information processing that is based on an explicit decomposition as expressed in the metaphorical Eq. 1, which is analogous to the equation used by Card, Moran, and Newell (1983) to decompose human–computer interaction. The focus of Eq. 1 is *competence*, in the sense used by linguists—that is, the ability of a person to construct appropriate behaviors in a specific context unburdened by various constraining factors of performance or pragmatics.

$$\text{Individual Competence} = \text{processing mechanisms} \\ + \text{internal expertise} + \text{external context} \tag{1}$$

In Eq. 1, competent problem solving emerges from the manipulation of a body of internal expertise by a set of (presumably biological) internal information-processing mechanisms as required by the features of and interactions with the external context of the behavior. The effect of the external situation is critically important in this equation. It provides the details and data from which the work goals are identified and activated, and in pursuit of which expertise is activated, retrieved, and manipulated. The relationships in Eq. 1 indicate how human information processing could be decomposed (and represented) if one wanted to capture and predict, under essentially perfect circumstances, the kinds of problem-solving situations for which a person was competent. The COGNET Eq. 1 formed the basis for a software system that modeled and simulated highly cognitive processes primarily for the purposes of providing embedded decision support and embedded training. However, when simulating human behavior, the constraining effects of performance limitations and pragmatics must be considered to generate realistic *performance.* These performance factors include constraints of timing—the fact that processing mechanisms can require nonzero amounts of time to accomplish various functions—and accuracy—the fact that these mechanisms can function in a way that may sometimes deviate from the ideal. These effects are seen in Eq. 2, which further constrains the competence model to create a human performance framework.

$$\text{Individual Performance} = \text{processing mechanisms}$$
$$+ \text{ internal expertise} + \text{external context} + \text{time} + \text{accuracy} \qquad (2)$$

The performance variant of COGNET expressed in Eq. 2 provided the basis for the AMBR work and is described in this chapter.

ARCHITECTURE AND PRINCIPLES OF OPERATION

The COGNET information-processing mechanisms can be defined in terms of their structure (i.e., what the mechanisms are and how they are interconnected) and function (i.e., what they do and the principles by which they operate). The overall architecture of the COGNET processing mechanism follows a well-established breakdown along the lines established by Broadbent (1958), Card et al. (1983), and Newell (1990), among others. It postulates fully parallel perceptual, motor, and cognitive subsystems, with the cognitive and perceptual subsystems sharing independent access to a memory structure. The memory construct in the underlying COGNET framework is a long-term working memory (LTWM) structure (e.g., Ericsson & Kinsch, 1995), which subsumes operations that have been ascribed in the literature to short-term, long-term, and working memory. COGNET does not presume that short- and long-term memory differences do not exist, but merely that cognitive processes can be modeled without these distinctions. Ideally, analysis of the resulting models can shed light on when and where such constructs are needed to achieve specific modeling goals.

Two major types of components were added to represent performance constraints: sensorimotor resources (which enable the simulation of time/accuracy constraints on physical interaction with the environment) and metacognitive components (which enable more realistic management of both cognitive and sensorimotor resources). The resulting processing mechanisms and their architectural integration are shown in Fig. 5.1. The principles of operation are provided as an appendix to this chapter.

Several features of the architecture and principles of operation are particularly relevant to the work reported here.

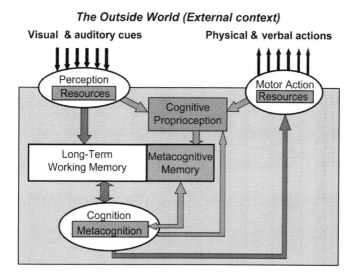

FIG. 5.1. COGNET processing mechanisms and architecture.

Emergent Attention and Multitasking

COGNET/iGEN represents attention and multitasking via a weak concurrence construct, which allows cognitive attention to focus on only one high-level goal at a time, but to maintain many threads of goal-pursuing activity simultaneously (e.g., as interrupted or pending lines of reasoning). Any high-level thread can interrupt any other at any time through a pandemonium-like (Selfridge, 1959) competition process. Competition for the focus of attention is based on context cues provided by the changing contents of LTWM. Thus, attention emerges from the lower level properties of the processing mechanisms, rather than from any explicit attention model or executive control mechanism.

Metacognition

COGNET/iGEN is unique among cognitive architectures in having metacognitive functionality (see Zachary, Le Mentec, & Glenn, 2000; Zachary & Le Mentec, 2000), which provides the system with a symbolic representation of the state of the three primary processing systems via a metacognitive memory. The contents of the metacognitive memory are populated by an internal mechanism called *cognitive proprioception*. Metacognition also includes representation of pervasive and/or underlying internal states (such as fatigue or specific beliefs or attitudes) that can affect the way in which goal-oriented processing occurs. The cognitive processor can also execute separate metacognitive processes that use information in metacognitive memory (and other metacognitive knowledge) to affect the execution or application of other procedural or declarative knowledge.

Flexible Knowledge Granularity

The architectural mechanisms in Fig. 5.1 make use of application/domain-specific knowledge and expertise. The representation of expertise is flexible and not tied to any specific level of architectural granularity (e.g., to atomic cognitive processes). COGNET provides different notations to represent declarative knowledge (a blackboard-like representation), procedural knowledge (a GOMS-like conditional goal-subgoal–operator hierarchy notation), and perceptual knowledge (a rule-like notation). Procedural and declarative knowledge are defined top–down, with the level of grain and stopping condition for goal decomposition left to the model developer. The guiding assumption is to use the least granularity needed to achieve the modeling goal. Perceptual knowledge granularity is constrained by declarative memory definitions and constraints in the external world.

Temporal Granularity

The complex work environments, which COGNET seeks to address, unfold over periods of time ranging from seconds to hours. This places them in what Newell (1990) called the *rational band* and the upper portions of the *cognitive band* of temporal granularity. COGNET focuses on this range of granularity, deliberately avoiding organic constructs that operate at coarser and (particularly) finer levels of granularity.

Embodiment

COGNET explicitly considers the physical mechanisms that link perceptual/action processes to the external environment. These physical mechanisms force COGNET to be an embodied cognition system (e.g., Gray, 2000) in which the interaction with the external environment affects internal processes in a fundamental and ongoing way. However, the time granularity of the overall system (seconds to hours) is to some degree inconsistent with the time granularity at which many of the effects of embodiment occur (microseconds to seconds). Thus, COGNET has adopted a granularity-neutral stance with regard to embodiment, allowing the model builder to incorporate constraints and features of the physical systems to the degree necessary and appropriate for the specific application. The flexible granularity means, for example, that there are no fixed models of body features. This is in contrast to systems such as EPIC (e.g., Kieras & Meyer, 1995), which adopt a fixed (and relatively fine) granularity for the structure and processes of the embodiments of the system.

Expert-Oriented Knowledge Structure

COGNET focuses on expert-level competence and performance in complex environments, and thus on representation of internal knowledge in a manner as similar as possible to that used by human experts. In turn this has led to the utilization of cognitive theories of expertise (e.g., Chi, Glaser, & Farr, 1988; Ericcson & Smith, 1991; VanLehn, 1996) and the use of highly structured knowledge representations that reflected the efficiency and parsimony of expert decision processes, particularly in real-time contexts. In particular, the COGNET representation focuses on highly compiled procedural knowledge that minimizes the need to search complex knowledge spaces and on the use of context cues (based on internal models of the external situation) to allow these compiled knowledge structures to be activated on a just-in-time basis.

These theories meshed with the notions of recognition-primed decision making, first suggested by Klein (1989), and the artificial intelligence (AI) concept of case-based reasoning (Kolodner, 1988). Although deriving from different bodies of data, both of these suggested that context cues, based on internal models of the external situation, allowed these compiled knowledge structures to be activated on a just-in-time basis in real-time settings.

REPRESENTATION OF KNOWLEDGE

The representation of knowledge (internal expertise) that is processed and manipulated by the information-processing mechanisms is largely defined by the architecture and principles of operation of those information-processing mechanisms. COGNET decomposes internal information into five basic types of expertise:

- *declarative expertise*—units of knowledge that contain state/attribute information about (i.e., describe) the external environment, the problem/situation being addressed by the system, and the problem-solving process;
- *procedural expertise*—units of knowledge that define teleological states (e.g., goals) and information manipulations (e.g., inferences, physical actions) that can achieve those states;

- *action expertise*—the units of knowledge that define transactions of the motor system that can be used to implement intended effects/actions in the external environment;
- *perceptual expertise*—the units of knowledge that define processing operations to generate/transform internal information in response to information that is sensed from the external environment; and
- *metacognitive expertise*—the units of knowledge used to control the selection and execution of procedural knowledge and to maintain awareness of the state of cognitive processing and declared resources.

In terms of the COGNET architecture:

- declarative knowledge, including declarative metacognitive knowledge, is maintained in memory and modified by both perceptual and cognitive processes;
- procedural knowledge is executed by the cognitive process, and both manipulates information in (declarative) memory (excluding the metacognitive portions) and sends intended actions to the motor system;
- action knowledge is processed by the action/motor system and manipulates the external environment;
- perceptual knowledge is executed by the perceptual process as information is sensed in the external environment. As the perceptual knowledge is executed, it manipulates information in the (declarative) memory; and
- metacognitive procedural knowledge is executed by the cognitive process and manipulates declarative memory (including the metacognitive portions).

The overall strategy for representation of each of these types of expertise is driven by the focus of the overall COGNET system as discussed earlier—on expert-level performance in complex, real-time environments. Theories of expertise and skill acquisition clearly point to the fact that experts rely, within their domain of expertise, on rich and highly compiled knowledge structures that have chunked many lower level productions into contingent structures that minimize the search of the knowledge space. In this view, specific desired end states, often called *goals*, are matched at a high level with features of the situation to call up a prepackaged, albeit abstract, strategy. The strategy is then instantiated in terms of the specific details of the problem/situation and executed.

This view has implications for the representation of both declarative and procedural knowledge. For declarative knowledge, it implies that there needs to be some hierarchy of abstraction in representation of the declarative information to support the pattern-matching and instantiation processes, which work at differing levels of abstraction. This was accomplished by adapting and substantially extending the hierarchical knowledge representation called the *blackboard representation* (cf. Nii, 1986a, 1986b). The blackboard representation was originally developed to capture the multiple levels of declarative information used by humans in the process of understanding spoken language in a speech understanding system called *Hearsay* (Erman et al., 1980). Although it was later widely used in AI (see Carver & Lesser, 1994), others have demonstrated its ability to capture the kinds of declarative expertise used by people in complex tasks (e.g., B. Hayes-Roth, 1985).

For procedural knowledge, the focus on modeling expert or near-expert cognition has also led to adoption of knowledge representation structures oriented to reasoning strategies typically involved in highly skilled performance. Specifically, procedural knowledge is represented in highly compiled goal/subgoal hierarchies called *cognitive tasks*, which have a structure analogous to the notation called Goals-Operators-Methods-Selection rules (GOMS), first developed by Card et al. (1983) as a way to capture procedural knowledge underlying human–computer interaction skills. The hierarchy incorporates contingencies in the way the knowledge can be instantiated via branches in the goal decomposition tree, which specify the problem conditions under which an instance of the overall strategy should apply to one branch (or subtree) instead of another. Within each branch, as in GOMS, there are lower level operators, but in COGNET all information manipulated within a procedure must be explicitly retrieved from declarative memory, and all new or modified information must be explicitly posted (back) to declarative memory.

The requirements for the representation of perceptual knowledge were that this type of knowledge be self-activated and essentially unitary in nature. The basic framework for this was first established by Reiger (1977) as a spontaneous computation knowledge source, to which the term *demon* was applied. This representation has been subsequently evolved and applied by others, and it formed the basis for the definition of the unit of perceptual knowledge in COGNET, which is termed the *perceptual demon*.

A more complete set of details on the COGNET knowledge representation formalism can be found in Zachary, Ryder, and Hicinbothom (1998).

REPRESENTATION OF HUMAN PERFORMANCE

There are three primary mechanisms in COGNET that enable the representation and simulation of the time/accuracy aspects of sensory and motor system performance. First, COGNET allows the creation of specific resources in each of the processing systems, but with particular emphasis on the motor-action and perceptual system. These specific resources can be defined at a level of granularity that is appropriate for the purposes of the specific model being built. The resources can have attributes that allow them to be controlled. For example, eyes may have a point of gaze attribute, by which the eyes can be directed; that is, a deliberate eye movement can be represented as replacing a current point of gaze with a new one. These attributes may also deal with the status of the resources, such as the current business of a hand or current use of the voice to complete an utterance. The ability to define resources allows COGNET models to be constrained with human-like limitations.

Second, permitting multiple, parallel execution threads in each of the three subsystems of the architecture (cognitive, sensoriperceptual, and motor) allows independent processing activities to be executed in association with the different resources that could now be defined within a given subsystem. For example, the motor system could control separate action processes associated with a right hand, left hand, and voice, or the perceptual system could receive sensory inputs from separate visual and auditory processes. COGNET allows activity threads in the sensorimotor subsystems to operate either in parallel with cognitive processes or linked with them. This allows, for example, a cognitive process to directly control an ongoing motor process or initiate it for ballistic execution and then proceed in parallel.

The third mechanism for representation of performance is the ability to define time to be consumed (independently) on any execution thread. This enables a thread of activity (and any associated resources) to become engaged in processes that occur over a period of time. The time consumption is typically controlled by micromodels (see Glenn, 1989), which are closed-form approximations of the time and/or accuracy constraints of specific physical resources in specific types of contexts (e.g., accuracy of reading characters of text; time to fingertip-touch an object within the current reach envelope, etc.) and which originated with the Human Operator Simulator (HOS) system (e.g., Wherry, 1969). Micromodels allow existing experimental data and empirical relationships to be encapsulated and reused, but do not force any specific level of representation of body features. The micromodel construct also enables the representation of moderators such as stress and fatigue (based on invocation context), as well as individual differences in performance.

LEARNING APPROACH AND MECHANISMS

As part of the AMBR Experiment 2 effort, a learning capability was added to the COGNET/iGEN system, which previously had no such facility. Although the learning task addressed in AMBR was a specific type of category learning, learning was implemented as a general capability to learn the conditions under which each of a disjunctive set of goals or actions should be taken—in other words, the ability to learn when to undertake different goals or actions. This approach was both general and consistent with the overall emphasis in COGNET/iGEN on procedural knowledge and multitasking. It was found that integrating this learning capability required other, deeper extensions to the system—most notably the creation for the first time of an explicit short-term memory model and development of memory-performance moderators. These extensions, in turn, enabled the representation of memory decay, rehearsal, and proactive interference needed to model human learning performance. The manner in which the architectural changes were implemented allows future evolution of memory (including memory moderation) mechanisms and of learning mechanisms in COGNET/iGEN. Creating this learning capability required three types of extensions.

1. Competence Level Architectural Extensions

COGNET/iGEN is a principled system, and the behavior of the component mechanisms and their architectural relationships are governed by explicit principles of operation. The preexisting system made no allowance for learning of any kind. Thus, to create the competence or underlying ability to learn, a learning mechanism had to be created and integrated into the system. As shown in Fig. 5.2, the mechanism was integrated as a general

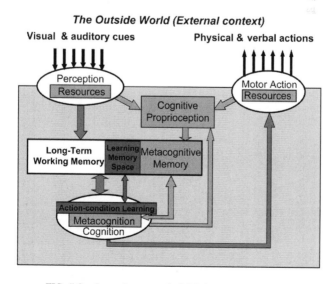

FIG. 5.2. Learning-extended COGNET architecture.

subcomponent of the cognitive process. Although the Shepard learning paradigm (Shepard, Hovland, & Jenkins, 1961) focuses on category learning, it was felt that the operationalization within the AMBR environment was one of learning the (boundaries) in a space of conditions that differentiated various action (or subgoal) options. Thus, the learning mechanism was created and integrated with the capability to learn the conditions (categories) under which different action options could be taken. Although in general learning could apply to any information in memory, the learning mechanism was initially implemented with access to only a subset of long-term memory, called the *learning memory space*, which segmented the previously undifferentiated LTWM into a short-term memory component separate from the remainder of LTWM.

2. Performance Level Architectural Extensions

Additional extensions were required to constrain the behavior of the learning competence to reflect the learning performance of people. In particular, human learning performance is highly constrained by limitations on memory. Thus, it was necessary to add the ability to constrain memory processes by bandwidth and recall limitations that were collectively termed *memory moderators*.

3. Knowledge Representation Extensions

The preexisting COGNET knowledge representational formalism did not allow for knowledge components (specifically conditional expressions) that could be learned by a model, nor for goal structures with open (i.e., initially null but subsequently) action conditions. However, these proved to require only simple extensions. The existing structure to represent a disjunctive goal set (i.e., to apply only one of a set of subgoals to a situational instance) was generalized to allow the condition set for each of the subgoals in the disjunction to be learned (rather than simply remembered as prior knowledge). The knowledge representation also did not support description of the metacognitive strategies that might control learning. This extension had to be added to COGNET/iGEN as well.

REPRESENTATION OF SUBJECTIVE WORKLOAD

As part of the AMBR experiments, the model was also required to provide assessments of various subjective aspects of task performance centering around the construct of subjective workload as measured by the Task Load Index (TLX) scales (Hart & Staveland, 1988). The modeling requirement was approached with the goal of implementing a subjective workload model that added no new features, constructs, or parameters to the existing COGNET/ iGEN architecture. This approach clearly affected the implementation of the subjective workload model if only as a decision criterion. That is, if multiple possible methods of modeling the process of responding to an existing TLX index probe were suggested by the literature, the one that could most directly be implemented using existing COGNET/iGEN constructs (or that required the fewest extensions) was chosen. Of all the models developed for AMBR, the COGNET model was unique in that it provided independently generated self-assessments on all six of the component scales that make up TLX.[2] The TLX self-assessments were generated as introspective, retrospective accounts by the model once a simulation run was completed. This introspective, retrospective self-assessment was modeled in four stages:

1. the six component TLX measures were conceptually mapped onto the internal architecture of COGNET;

2. the conceptual mapping was used to operationalize each measure in terms of specific aspects of metacognitive self-awareness (regardless of whether they existed within COGNET);

3. those that did not already exist were then implemented and integrated into the COGNET metacognitive mechanisms. This resulted in the ability of the model to introspect and create a post hoc report of its own workload on the six measures involved; and

4. because the scale of introspective process was not necessarily the same as that used by the measurement instrument (i.e., the TLX quasi-interval scales), the measures generated by the model were calibrated to those specific measurement scales using statistical regression based on data from human subjects not involved in the AMBR model comparison.

TLX consists of six scales subjectively defined as follows:

- Physical demand—"how physically demanding was the task"
- Mental demand—"how mentally demanding was the task"
- Temporal demand—"how hurried or rushed was the pace of the task"
- Performance—"how successful were you in accomplishing what you were asked to do"
- Effort—"how hard did you have to work to accomplish your level of performance"
- Frustration—"how insecure, discouraged, irritated, and annoyed were you"

---

[2]The development of the TLX self-assessment measures is discussed in more detail in Zachary, Le Mentec, and Iordanov (2001).

The scales are measured on a Likert-like scale divided into 10 intervals in Experiment 1 and 7 intervals in Experiment 2 and measured as 21 discrete values (integers 0–10 inclusive, plus all intermediate half-values). Thus, the model had to produce estimates of these same variables on this same scale. The general theoretical framework for this process was one of relating each measure to the self-awareness of various aspects of the processing within the COGNET representation as described earlier. The analysis of each measure in terms of COGNET constructs is given next.

Physical Demand

This construct was based on self-awareness of the overall level of activity of the motor system. The AMBR model did not declare and monitor individual motor resources (e.g., separate hands, eye resources, etc.), but rather directed action to the motor system on these channels using different *perform action* operations and micromodels. The awareness of physical workload is thus accomplished in two stages. First, the system had to be aware of (and collect) the total time spent in each kind of action (e.g., move mouse, move eyes, give verbal message). Second, weights had to be assigned to discriminate eye-movement actions from manual actions, which involve greater conscious control. The physical workload value could then be calculated as the weighted sum of the action times across all actions normalized to the length of the scenario.

Mental Demand

This construct was based on the self-awareness of the cognitive complexity of the various tasks being executed and their relative frequency. Mental workload was estimated separately for each cognitive task in the model. Because tasks can be carried out in many different ways, the average complexity of each task during the execution of a scenario is calculated as the average number of goals and method calls during task execution[3] (including the number of goals and method calls within the higher level methods called). The task complexity was then multiplied by the number of times the task was performed in the scenario. This weighted complexity was summed across all tasks and normalized to the length of the scenario.

---

[3]Following R. Wood (1986) and D. Woods (1988), one measure of task complexity is the number and complexity of components. Because goals and methods are the elements of iGEN task models that contain cognitive operations, these elements were counted in the mental demand measure.

Temporal Demand

This concept was ultimately represented in terms of a complementary construct—the sense of idleness or momentary sense of "nothing to do now." It was felt that the more frequently the model had such an awareness, the less time-pressure it would feel and vice versa. This sense would occur, in model terms, when the model was aware that it had no queued tasks, was scanning the screen for new tracks needing attention, and was finding none. Thus, a self-awareness capability for this nothing to do state was needed, and its negative value used to measure temporal workload normalized to the length of the scenario.[4] This use of negative value is analogous to the well-known use of regret to measure (negative) utility in decision theory.

Performance

A similar approach was selected to relate this measure to COGNET constructs. The model does not have any awareness of how well it is doing or how it is performing on a positive side, but it does have an awareness of when it makes errors of omission or commission because it attempts to correct those errors when it becomes aware of them. Thus, the more errors the model is aware of, the worse its perceived performance would be; when it is aware of no errors, its self-perception of its performance would be very high (regardless of whether it would be so empirically). The performance measure was ultimately assigned as the negative value of the count of perceived errors during a scenario, normalized to the length of the scenario. Although it might have seemed easier, for example, to simply count the number of tracks handled per unit time, such an approach would rely on the content of the task or work being done. The approach used in the AMBR model, however, makes no such reliance and is thus in principle more generalizable.

Effort

The concept of *effort* as defined for the human subjects seems to refer to the total amount of time they spent working in the scenario, possibly excluding or discounting the visual effort of scanning the display. (It was assumed that a scenario in which no tracks appeared would be said to have involved no effort, although visual scanning would still occur.) In COGNET, there can

---

[4]This conceptualization for temporal demand was one of several possible. In another conceptualization, for example, it could be argued that periods of idleness could be outweighed by periods of high demand. In the end, the conceptualization was selected by Occam's razor, in that it was simple and more parsimonious (i.e., did not require consideration of the level of effort when there was something to do and did yield an excellent fit with the data).

be multiple threads proceeding in parallel (e.g., hands, voice, and eyes), all with different and potentially overlapping action start and end times. Because of this parallelism, it would be incorrect to simply sum all work times. Alternatively, the total time in which some motor actions were occurring could be collected as the total amount of busy time in the problem. Thus, the reporting of effort required an awareness of the states when some activity was occurring on any motor channel, which was then divided by scenario total time to yield a measure of the proportion of time spent working the problem, and finally to report effort involved in the scenario.

Frustration

The approach selected for this ill-defined concept was based on an awareness of the times that a cognitive task was interrupted by another one. Although the nature of the AMBR tasks is such that interruption is minimized, there were still opportunities for this to occur, primarily with visual and/or purely interpretative tasks. Thus, frustration was simply reported as the number of cognitive task interruptions divided by the length of the scenario.

The preceding analysis was used to design specific computational operationalizations of the measures within the COGNET cognitive architecture. In this operationalization process, effort was made to (re-) use various aspects of self-awareness that had already been implemented within the COGNET software. Developing this functionality involved relatively few extensions of the existing metacognitive software.

The measure values resulting from these operationalizations were then calibrated to the 21-point scale imposed by TLX using a simple linear regression process in which, for a given set of scenarios, the model-produced measures were regressed onto human subject TLX data. (These were different subjects and scenarios than those used in the model comparison process.)

MULTITASKING ATC MODEL (EXPERIMENT 1)

Experiment 1 examined multiple-task management in the context of a simplified air traffic control (ATC) task (described in chap. 2) using the AMBR testbed (described in chap. 3) under two display conditions—aided (color) and unaided (text). The goal of the COGNET/iGEN model was to perform the ATC task in a human-like manner, generating performance measures, response times, and posttask subjective workload assessments within ranges documented for human subjects.

Model-Development Approach

The model was developed in five stages. The first was a cognitive task analysis (CTA) of the ATC process (as represented by the AMBR testbed). The CTA is discussed in more detail later in the chapter. The CTA was required because the AMBR moderator provided only subject performance data as a common starting point to various model-development teams, and additional insights were needed on the strategies and elements of knowledge used in performing the ATC task. Such information is typically obtained through a CTA. Zachary et al. (1998) detailed the general CTA process used to develop COGNET models. Three subjects for the CTA were drawn from the same general population used for the AMBR human subjects (under-30 individuals with substantial computer game-playing experience), trained on the ATC testbed, and used in the CTA process. The general strategy of the CTA process is to have subjects work scenarios in the work environment (here the ATC testbed), record their behaviors, and then have them participate in a question-answering verbal protocol during a replay of their actions in the scenario. When appropriate, the replay was stopped to enable extended discussions of strategy, procedures, knowledge, and so on.

The second step was development of a baseline competence model encompassing the knowledge required to do the more complex job (the text-only version of the ATC task). The initial baseline model was a competence model in that it contained all the knowledge needed to perform the job. However, it was characterized by the fact that at this early stage there were no errors, the visual search heuristic was exhaustive, and each individual task was performed properly, but without a realistic temporal priority scheme. This competence model, while representing the baseline knowledge required to "do the job," did not perform the tasks in a realistic order, nor did it generate realistic response times.

The third step involved refining the competence model into a realistic performance model yielding human-like response time and accuracy behavior. Refinement of the model into a performance model involved fine-tuning the task strategy, tuning the micromodels using the human subject tuning data, and adding features to the model to induce realistic errors. First, the visual search strategy was modified from an exhaustive search through all display regions to a search until first match. The revised (i.e., performance) models incorporated a visual scan strategy that searched regions in order of importance and, when something to do was found, stopped the search and performed the action. This change produced a more realistic task performance ordering in that it more closely matched the strategy employed by test subjects. The second component of performance involved refinement of response times generated by the model. Model response time data were compared to tuning subject response times, and the basic operation times in the micromodels were adjusted up or down to tune the micromodels. This was repeated until the model produced response times in the range of the times produced by the tuning subjects.

Once the model produced good performance and response time measures, the fourth step was to split the model into two versions—one for the text condition and one for the color condition. The second and third steps focused on modeling the more complex text-only condition, with the rationale (supported by the CTA data) that the color condition was a simpler derivative model. In the end, creating the model of the performance-aiding or color version of the ATC task involved changing only a single cognitive task—the "Update situation awareness" task. In the fifth and final step, the model was expanded to perform the workload estimation introspective task.

Model Organization

Cognitive Task Analysis. Analysis revealed that multitasking during ATC task performance is typically quite shallow even in the unaided condition. This is largely because the lowest level physical or interactional work tasks (i.e., accept an incoming aircraft into the airspace, welcome a new aircraft once it has been accepted into the airspace, etc.) were all designed in the AMBR testbed to be uninterruptible (although manually cancelable). Thus, the control actions needed to execute any such unit task were essentially ballistic. The sequence of control decision—click message, load arguments, click send—could not be interrupted to begin or resume a different task or task instance. Only the work tasks that involved no workstation interaction could be interrupted, such as scanning the screen for a track needing some action. This meant that, in general, where multitasking did occur, the interleaving of activities was also brief. For example, if while scanning for transfer candidates a new text message appeared, subjects would usually check it immediately. If it required attention, subjects would terminate scanning and process the message to completion. If it did not require attention, subjects would immediately return to scanning. Similarly, having remembered to check on an upcoming transfer event, subjects would quickly shift attention to check the threshold proximity of a transfer candidate previously observed. Subjects would then either immediately return to the interrupted activity or process the candidate to completion. In general, only a single activity was suspended at any one time, then quickly resumed or dropped altogether. The fact that only a single response message can be constructed at a time, within the ATC task, probably limits the need/utility of interleaving more than two activities.

Although all three subjects' behavior could be described in terms of shallow multitasking and generally characterized as before, subjects' task conceptualization and activity patterns were considerably varied in detail. At the highest level, subjects varied in their perception of the focus of activity or in the ordering of cycled subtasks. Individuals also varied in their adoption of specific low-level strategies for dealing with particular situations encountered in the ATC task. In fact details of task strategy varied not only from individual to individual, but also for individual subjects over time as experience supported the discovery of new solutions to specific problems. The COGNET ATC model was developed at a level of detail appropriate to the common strategies and task organization observed and documented during CTA. In the model descriptions that follow, the CTA results that drove specific design decisions are so noted.

Cognitive Model as Air Traffic Controller. The COGNET model of the air traffic controller and the model's relationship to the simulated ATC environment is pictured in Fig. 5.1. The ATC simulator executes as a separate software entity, passing information to the model, which also executes as an independent component (typically on a different machine, but not necessarily so). The model has access to the visual cues provided by the ATC displays through an application programming interface, which is used to create a middleware layer of software (called a *shell*), which allows the expertise model and execution engine to interact with an external context. The shell provides:

- inputs to sensation—capturing the events or processes within the ATC displays and translating them into cues that will become accessible to the COGNET sensory system; and
- outputs to the environment—translating actions taken by the model, such as hand movements, into software events or processes within the ATC simulation. For example, a hand movement to depress a button is translated into a message to depress the button electronically at a specific time.

The model consists of the shell, the ATC domain knowledge and expertise as coded in the COGNET description language, and the BATON engine that emulates the architecture in Fig. 5.1 and follows the COGNET principles of operation. Before execution, BATON loads in the domain knowledge (procedural, perceptual, and action) and initializes its declarative memory with information that a person would have at the start of an ATC scenario. Once the execution begins, the three information-processing subsystems (cognitive, perceptual, and motor) begin to operate in parallel. Cues from the environment are registered by the perceptual subsystem via the shell, and appropriate perceptual knowledge elements (i.e., the perceptual demons) are activated and executed by the perceptual sub-system within BATON. This results in symbolic information about the external environment being posted on the blackboard structure that represents declarative memory.

The changing patterns of information in declarative memory result in the activation (or deactivation) of various chunks of procedural knowledge (i.e., the cognitive tasks). The active cognitive tasks constantly compete for the focus of execution attention in the cognitive processor. This competition emerges from the application of metacognitive knowledge components associated with each cognitive task, such as the trigger (which defines the contexts under which the cognitive task is activated) and the priority (which defines the task's momentary importance relative to other tasks). Any cognitive task may, while being executed, modify the contents of declarative memory, thus further driving the dynamics underlying multi-tasking attention. At various points in time, the motor system may be invoked by a cognitive task, defining specific actions to be taken. The action processes, which reside entirely within the shell, generate events in the environment that implement the requested action.

The information-processing mechanisms provided by BATON are common to all COGNET models and were described earlier. The unique aspects of the ATC COGNET model are the various components of expertise incorporated within it, as well as the translation functions provided by the shell. The remainder of this section describes these, preceded by a brief review of the model-building process.

Model Structure and Processing Flow.   Figure 5.3 shows a conceptual overview of the AMBR COGNET model and the flow of information from the initial cue (stimulus) to the physical reaction (response). Information in the environment, specifically on the ATC displays, is sensed (via the shell) and registered on a special panel of the declarative memory. Termed the *raw display elements* panel, this portion of declarative memory is more properly a short-term visual information store (see Card et al., 1983) where sensory information is maintained while perceptual processing occurs. It was clear from the CTA that the perception of visual information is driven by a volitional scanning process, in which the eyes are moved in a planned and controlled manner looking for specific types of information. In the model, the scanning of the display is directed by the cognitive process, in which the perceptual process is directed to focus on specific display segments, called *panes*, in sequence, seeking a particular type of information from each pane. While focusing on a given pane, the perceptual processing extracts the relevant information from the visual information store (i.e., the *raw display elements*) and then posts it in symbolic form in declarative memory as *perceived display elements*. The declarative memory also contains the mental

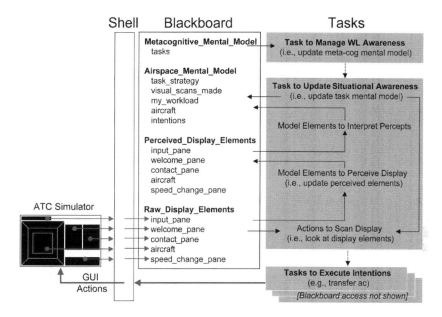

FIG. 5.3. Model structure and process flow.

model of the airspace, which is constructed through the combined activities of several different chunks of procedural knowledge.

The CTA on which the model was based showed two levels of cognitive processing. The procedural knowledge for the model was represented in a set of procedural knowledge chunks or cognitive tasks (see Table 5.1), each of which contributed to cognitive processing at either the strategic or interactive level. In general, the strategic tasks contain procedural knowledge that builds and updates the understanding of the situation in the airspace and identifies system interactions that need to be accomplished. New or revised facts about the situation are placed in declarative form and posted in declarative memory as they are created, as are newly identified system interactions that are needed based on the current (i.e., newly updated) situational understanding. The interactive tasks contain the procedural knowledge needed to undertake and complete, for each different type of system interaction, an instance of that system interaction type. *Update situational awareness*, which represents the strategies for scanning the display regions and determining what needs to be done, is an example of a strategic task. *Accept incoming aircraft*, which performs the procedures associated with accepting an inbound aircraft, is an example of an interaction task. Micromodels model the timing of the various visuomotor actions within the interaction tasks.

Activation and execution of an interaction task (instance) is triggered by the posting of needed system interactions of the corresponding type in de-

TABLE 5.1
Procedural Knowledge in COGNET ATC Model

Cognitive Task Name/Goal	Type	Description
Adjust task strategy	Strategic	Maintains self-awareness of changes in task load
Update situational awareness	Strategic	Maintains situational awareness of ATC task elements
Accept incoming aircraft	Interaction	Accepts incoming aircraft
Welcome incoming aircraft	Interaction	Welcomes incoming aircraft
Respond to speed increase request	Interaction	Responds to speed change requests
Transfer outgoing aircraft	Interaction	Transfers outgoing aircraft
Order aircraft to contact ATC	Interaction	Orders aircraft to contact ATC
Get aircraft out of holding	Interaction	Responds to red tracks to get them out of holding

clarative memory. The strategic *update situational awareness* task is triggered whenever the simulated person has no specific interactive tasks waiting to be accomplished.

Scan Process. The visual scanning part of the model is based on CTA data and incorporates two simplifying assumptions: (a) changes in the display (but not the quantity or type of change) could be consistently perceived with a single glance, and (b) the mental model that supports the visual scanning process is not degraded in the AMBR task by forgetting.

The second assumption was, in part, a function of the complexity of the scenarios, in that the CTA subjects never showed errors or problems associated with forgetting elements of the overall situation. It is also an assumption that has been used in most other COGNET/iGEN models of human–computer interactive work (e.g., Zachary et al., 1998), without any loss in predictive validity of the resulting models, as was the case here. In fact this assumption is not as bold as it might first seem, given the focus in COGNET/iGEN on skilled performance. People working in complex environments who achieve skilled levels of performance develop/learn strategies that take into account the inherent and evident factors that limit their own performance. In cognitive work, one such factor is the limited or unreliable nature of memory; as a result, skilled strategies rarely rely heavily on memory (i.e., most are memory independent). Perhaps a better way to view this phenomenon is from the perspective of learning processes; strategies that rely strongly on memory and reliable rapid recall of large numbers of dynamic items (visual or otherwise) are unlikely to work sufficiently well to enable development of a high level of skill, whereas those lacking such a reliance are more likely to result in successful performance and ultimately skill development. Seamster, Redding, Cannon, Ryder, and Purcell (1993), for example, presented a model of commercial en route air traffic controllers that demonstrates how this works. Instead of focusing on trying to keep track of the large number of air tracks in their airspace, skilled controllers instead learn to identify and focus only on potential conflicting tracks—a strategy that reduces the number of items that must be remembered at any one time to a small (and manageable) set. Doane and colleagues (Doane, Sohn, & Jodlowski, 2004; Sohn & Doane, 2003, in press) showed similar effects in other domains. Flach and Hoffman (2003) discussed the issue of cognitive limitations at a more general level and further argued for the irrelevance of limiting factors (such as memory limits) in understanding human cognitive skill. Thus, although COGNET supports the ability to incorporate memory moderators such as decay, neither the source data nor the model results argued in favor of including such features into the model of the ATC task.[5]

Scanning is a volitional process in the ATC model, controlled by strategic procedural knowledge. The overall scanning strategy developed from the CTA and incorporated in the model was to scan the display, region by region, for the visual indicators of something to do. Those display regions that had not changed from the last visual scan were ignored. (This uses the first assumption—that the presence of change can be directly perceived without a detailed subprocess of item-by-item comparisons.) For display panes consisting of text lists, the model scans the list and compares what it sees to its mental model of what it has (previously) read to distinguish things it has done from things it still needs to do. The scanning heuristic represented in the version of the model that deals with the unaided or text-only display is purposefully different from the scanning heuristic represented in the version of the model that operates the aided or color-coded version of the ATC display. Although the text model has goals mapped to scanning each of the various ATC display components (e.g., radar display, accept text pane, speed change text pane), the color model has the singular goal of scanning the radar display for color changes. This difference between the two models is consistent with the results of the CTA, which revealed two fundamentally different approaches for visually scanning under the two display conditions.

Memory/Mental Model Structure. In the ATC model, one panel of declarative memory functions as a visual information store, in which sensed information is temporarily stored during perceptual processing. The units of

---

[5]Interestingly enough, the one aspect of the AMBR model where such memory moderation features were needed was in the representation of the learning strategy (discussed later). The learning task was designed to emulate classical psychological experiments involving learning of arbitrary meaningless symbol sets (i.e., Shepard et al., 1961). Thus, the task was designed to force people to rely heavily on their (inherently limited) memory, although it is highly arguable how often such memorization-like tasks actually arise in naturalistic work settings or everyday experience.

perceptual knowledge (i.e., the perceptual demons in the COGNET expertise model) transform these to a symbolic form accessible to various procedural knowledge components on ATC. This perceptually processed or perceived information on external cues is organized within the *perceived ATC display* panel in declarative memory. Background (i.e., nondynamic) concepts about the organization of the airspace are maintained in the *ATC task concepts* panel. The most important panel in declarative memory is the *airspace mental model* panel. The contents of this panel are constantly and dynamically constructed through the execution of the various procedural knowledge chunks. It is through the contents of this panel that the controller maintains situation awareness, which is central to both understanding what needs to be done and planning for and doing it. Figure 5.4 depicts the organization of information in declarative memory.

The metacognitive portion of declarative memory has a more predefined structure corresponding to specific kinds of self-awareness the system has. It consists of two panels. The *metacognition* panel contains self-awareness on the cognitive processing—specifically, on the processing status of

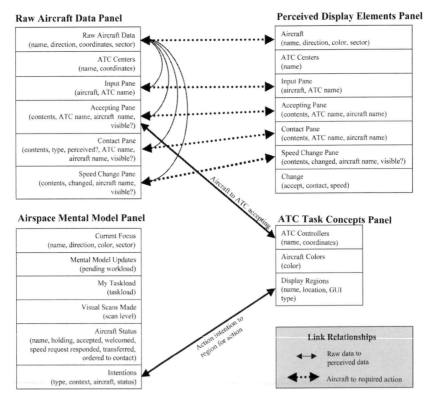

FIG. 5.4.   ATC-model standard blackboard structure.

each instance of each cognitive task used to work in this domain. The information, placed in declarative memory through a cognitive proprioception process described earlier, includes task start time, task (trigger) context, interruption and resumption information, task priority, as well as workload measures. The *self* panel stores information used for introspection and self-awareness of the ATC task. This includes information for use in task load determination, a representation of expertise level, and actions taken by the model in the situated environment.

Procedural Knowledge and Multitasking Attention. The procedural knowledge within the COGNET ATC model consists of a number of chunks (i.e., cognitive tasks) that focus either on ATC strategy or ATC system interactions. Strategic cognitive tasks contain the knowledge that the person uses to determine "what to do" and subsequently create intentions to do it by posting those intentions as elements on the declarative memory blackboard. The procedural knowledge used to carry out the intentions is contained in the interaction-oriented cognitive tasks. The activation and ultimate execution of these interaction-oriented cognitive tasks are triggered by the presence of unaccomplished intentions in declarative memory. Table 5.1 lists the strategic and interaction tasks in the ATC model. In all cases, the name of the cognitive task is the high-level goal around which its component procedural and metacognitive knowledge is organized.

Strategic Knowledge. The *update situational awareness* (SA) cognitive task represents the central strategic activity of visually inspecting the radar display to identify something to do. The knowledge in this cognitive task serves two functions. First, it builds and maintains situation awareness by maintaining the mental model of the air traffic situation in the mental model portion of declarative memory. Second, it uses the airspace mental model to form intentions for future actions in the ATC work domain. The mental model is thus the link between strategic and interaction-focused cognitive activity.

The update SA cognitive task directs the scanning precedence of display regions implicitly through its goal structure, which (as in all COGNET cognitive tasks) is organized as a hierarchy. Within the top level of this hierarchy for the text model, the following sequence of goals is pursued: (a) scan for red tracks; (b) scan for transfer candidates; (c) back check accept pane for accept, contact, and welcome candidates (in that order); (d) back check speed change pane; and (e) update mental model.

Each goal chunks the procedure for identifying a specific kind of need for action (e.g., welcoming an incoming track into the airspace). The sequence, however, represents the (learned) importance of the different classes of action, so more important or critical types of action needs are considered before less important ones in each scan/update cycle. Each goal in the sequence is associated with a precondition, which in essence represents the reasoning used to determine whether an action of that type is needed. If satisfied, the chunk is activated and executed, carrying out the reasoning needed to identify specifically what action is needed and to post it as an intention on the mental model. If any goal that is executed leads to one or more planned actions being created, the remaining display regions are not scanned during that instance of task execution. Thus, each scan cycle results in either something to do (one or more planned actions posted to the mental model) or nothing to do (no intentions posted).

Interaction and Action Times. The strategic knowledge in the model creates and prioritizes intentions to act. The actual implementations of these intentions, as embodied interactions with the outside environment (i.e., the ATC testbed), involves different chunks of knowledge. These are the interaction tasks in Table 5.1—the various cognitive tasks that contain the human–computer-interaction-oriented procedural knowledge for interacting with the ATC simulator. The COGNET ATC model is capable of two types of external interactions: those that represent visual scanning behaviors (such as seek transfer candidate) and those that represent human–computer interactions with the ATC simulator console (such as press accept button). Each of the respective interaction tasks encodes a chunk of knowledge that interrelates motor-system invocations (represented as perform-action operators) with the procedural logic required to perform the corresponding procedure.

Because the ATC model is a performance model, the various interactions with the external environment need to consume time equivalent to that used by people in undertaking the same activities. In COGNET, this time consumption process is modeled in a two-level structure. The amount of time to be required by an action is estimated through a parameterized model of the class of action involved—called a *micromodel.* The micromodel estimate is then used in a spend-time operator, which causes that amount of time to be consumed along that processing thread—for example, the visual or motor process.

As noted earlier, the COGNET micromodel construct is granularity-neutral and does not imply or require any predetermined level of representation. Rather, it allows the modeler to define and employ an appropriate level of detail given the desired characteristics of the prediction and purpose of the model. Table 5.2 lists the various perform-action operators contained in the ATC model, along with the approach used to determine the performance time of each.[6]

---

[6]The micromodels used in this model reflect an initial set of working assumptions based on both the literature and empirical data. The limited time frame of the AMBR modeling effort precluded development of more sophisticated models. Additional modeling efforts could easily improve these first-order estimates.

TABLE 5.2
Action Types and Micromodels

Action	Micromodel Time Prediction (ms)[7]
GUI-OBJECT-SELECT	Fixed charge given dynamic task load level high 580, med 600, low 650
GUI-BUTTON-PUSH	Fixed charge given dynamic task load level high 580, med 600, low 650
Back check accept pane for accept candidates	200 * number of items in accept pane
Back check accept pane for welcome candidates	200 * number of items in accept pane
Back check speed change pane	300 * number of items in speed change request pane
Scan display for any red tracks	300 * number of red tracks on display
Scan display for transfer candidates	200 * the number of perimeters that are searched until candidate found (4 max)
Back check contact pane for contact candidates	300 * number of items in contact pane
Look at pane	Fixed charge given dynamic task load level high 580, med 600, low 650
Look at button	Fixed charge given dynamic task load level high 580, med 600, low 650
Look at aircraft	Fixed charge given dynamic task load level high 580, med 600, low 650
Look at aircraft	Fixed charge given dynamic task load level high 580, med 600, low 650
Look for collision conflicts	300–500, depending on context

Errors. Error is an important differentiator between competence and performance. There is no inherent source of error in COGNET. Rather, specific sources of error (e.g., forgetting, manual inaccuracy, etc.) must be identified and incorporated into the model, along with appropriate error recovery knowledge that could be used to detect when an error has been made and determine how to correct it. Here again the CTA was invaluable, revealing at least four different types of errors (Table 5.3), which could in principle combine in complex ways. Unfortunately, there were no data that allowed these possible sources of error to be related to the categories of observed error types and human subject performance measures. As a result, there was no clear way to model this relationship between underlying errors

---

[7]Initial values for each parameter were estimated based on micromodels in the Human Operator Simulator (HOS) work (Glenn et al., 1992; Lane et al., 1981) and the model human processor (Card, Moran, & Newell, 1984) and adjusted using the tuning data from Experiment 1. The values were adjusted again for Experiment 2 and were slightly higher. Because the parameters were estimates of times within a task context rather than elementary cognitive operations, it was expected that the times might vary due to the task contexts being different.

TABLE 5.3
Error Types in ATC Task Performance

Type	Example
Cognitive	Misprocess an aircraft name
Mental	Misremember the status of an aircraft and repeat an action
Perceptual	Misperceive an aircraft name and perform action on incorrect track
Motor	Press the wrong button

and surface errors/performance results. Moreover, the time taken to handle/correct errors affected aggregate response times in an indeterminate manner, further muddying the modeling problem.

In the absence of either a theoretical or an empirical relationship between underlying error sources and the observed data, it was decided to make some simplifying assumptions. The first was that the sources of error integrated into the model would be those that did not require significant amounts of error-recovery logic. Second, after analyzing the subject data, it was decided to generate errors at the motor level by assigning a probability to the inducement of such errors and stochastically inducing this error type based on the dynamic task load. Specifically, when the error probability was met for a given AC that was required to be transferred, the model would incorrectly press the "contact" button instead of the "transfer" button. The result is that the track eventually turns red because of the incorrect actions being applied. The components of the model that respond to a track turning red are used to recover from this error (i.e., task "get aircraft out of holding"). Moreover, this error inducement was capable of affecting multiple performance score components, such as total score, holding delays, duplicated messages, and incorrect messages.

Workload Self-Assessment. The workload model is described in detail in Zachary, Le Mentec, and Iordanov (2001) and summarized in Table 5.4. In Table 5.4, the first column identifies a component measure calculated by the model, the second column identifies the computational formula for that measure, and the third column describes how the terms in the formula are operationalized in the COGNET architecture.

The workload self-assessment process added no parameters to the model or underlying architecture. However, because the measurement scale of modeled processes was not the same as that used by the measurement instrument (i.e., the TLX quasi-interval scales), the measures generated by the model had to be calibrated to those specific measurement scales. This was done with a statistical regression using data from human subjects in the model-development training set. This calibration process added two regression values (slope and intercept) for each of the six TLX measures. The cal-

TABLE 5.4
Experiment 1 Workload Self-Assessment Model

Measure	Computational Formula	Operationalization
Physical	$(\sum_{all\ i} k_i \bullet action\text{-}time_i)/T_S$	Where i is an action type, k_i is the weight of that action type, and *action-time*$_i$ is a function that collects total time spent taking that action during a scenario by instrumenting the action mechanism
Mental	$(\sum_{all\ i} DPC_i \bullet DTT_i)/T_S$	Where i is a cognitive task, and DPC_i and DTT_i are available through metacognitive self-awareness
Temporal	$-(\sum_{all\ i} nothing\text{-}to\text{-}do_i)/T_S$	Where *nothing-to-do$_i$* is a cognitive operator that returns a value of one *iff* the visual scan task has been completed and the model found nothing to do
Perform	$-(\sum_{all\ i} error\text{-}detected_i)/T_S$	Where *error detected$_i$* is a cognitive operator that returns a value of one *iff* a cognitive task found that the model had made an error and was about to try to correct it (if correctable)
Effort	$(\sum_{all\ i} time\text{-}spent\text{-}in\text{-}work_i)/T_S$	Where i is an increment in time, and *time spent in work$_i$* is a function measuring the time within that increment in which motor activity is occurring on any execution thread
Frustrate	$(\sum_{all\ i} DTI_i)/T_S$	Where DTI_i is available through metacognitive self-awareness as a measure of the number of times cognitive task i was interrupted during the scenario

ibration formula used in Experiment 1 can be found in Zachary, Santarelli, Ryder, Stokes, and Scolaro (2000).

Experiment 1 Results

The AMBR ATC task includes three workload conditions (low, medium, and high aircraft density) and two aiding conditions (aided and unaided). Four different scenarios were available for each of the resulting six conditions. The results reported here derive from 16 human subjects, each of whom performed the ATC task under all six conditions, and from four model executions for each condition. The different scenarios were assigned to human subjects to prevent them from learning to anticipate the course of problem development. For comparability, the models (for aided and unaided performance) were executed once with each of the four scenarios under each of the six conditions. The human means represent the averages of the 16 subjects for each condition. The model results are the mean of the four separate scenario run results for each condition. With the exception of error generation, the COGNET/iGEN models are nonstochastic and produce similar results across executions. However, minor timing variations between scenarios can account for fairly visible result differences, as in a case where one scenario produces events that require subject response slightly closer together in time than a similar scenario and are specifically related to events associated with large penalty errors.

Accuracy.   Figure 5.5 presents the mean penalty totals for both human subject trials and model executions for all six conditions. As might be expected, the point scores for the unaided conditions are substantially greater. In the unaided cases, the number of penalty points also increases sharply from the low to high aircraft track density workload conditions. In the aided case, however, the penalty scores are low overall and do not present the same trend of penalties increasing with workload. As shown in the figure, the COGNET/iGEN model was assessed no penalty points at all for any of the three aided conditions. This pattern is consistent with the details of the human subjects' results where 10 out of the 16 subjects also accrued zero penalty points for the aided condition. In general terms, the model produced results similar to those of the human subjects within a single standard error of the human mean for most conditions (the figures for Experiment 1 include error bars showing the standard error of the mean confidence intervals for the human subjects).

Response Time.   The ATC task consists of a series of actions triggered by aircraft states in the task environment. In the unaided cases, these states

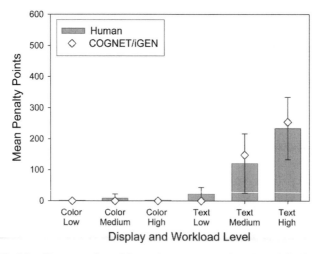

FIG. 5.5.   Human and model penalty scores as a function of display and workload.

might be recognized either in the messages shown in text displays or the current position of the various aircraft symbols. In the aided cases, these states could be determined directly from the color of the aircraft symbols. *Response time* was defined as the time interval between the presentation of the context trigger and the completion of the response input. In some instances, the triggering event was followed immediately by subject or model response, but often other events and actions intervened, especially in high aircraft density (high-workload) conditions. As a result, there was considerable variability in response time for the various events, in many cases conditioned by the response priorities driving the subject's or model's decision of when to attend to the triggering event. Figure 5.6 presents the mean response times for both human subject trials and model executions for all six conditions. Both human and model results show response time increasing as aircraft density (workload) increases within both the aided and unaided conditions. Both also show a substantially steeper increase in the unaided case.

Subjective Workload. A subjective workload rating was obtained from each human subject for each of the NASA-TLX measures—mental demand, physical demand, temporal demand, performance, effort, and frustration—for each of the conditions. The human results, as seen in Figs. 5.7 through 5.12, show that, with the single exception of physical workload, the participants rated workload higher, at least on average, for all unaided conditions than for aided conditions. The model results, presented in the same figures, do not follow this general pattern. With the single exception of the performance measure, the model results indicate that the high track den-

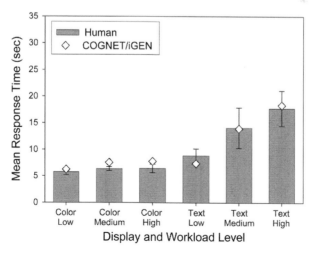

FIG. 5.6. Human and model mean response times as a function of display and workload.

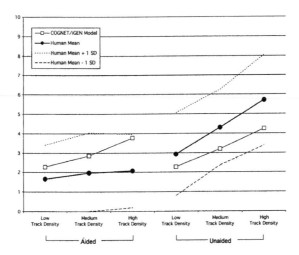

FIG. 5.7.   Mental workload.

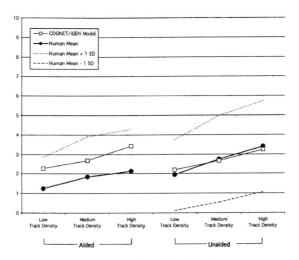

FIG. 5.8.   Physical workload.

sity aided condition is of higher subjective workload than the low track density unaided condition. A similar and probably related pattern can be seen for response time in Fig. 5.6. The model is clearly not capturing the difference in cost between the scanning/processing of symbols and the scanning/processing of text. Because there is no explicit reading model in the COGNET/iGEN ATC model, it is understandable that both response time and subjective mental workload would diverge from the human pattern. The strong occurrence of the same pattern in subjective physical workload is less easily explained.

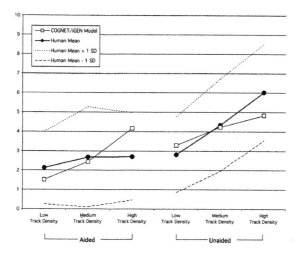

FIG. 5.9.   Temporal workload.

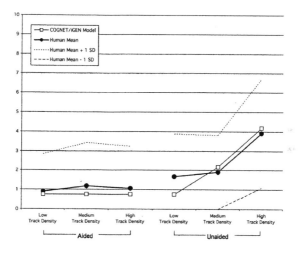

FIG. 5.10.   Performance.

Overall, there is a distinct tendency for the workload ratings of the human subjects to increase more sharply over the unaided conditions than the aided, although this pattern is not present in the model results, again possibly related to the issue of modeling the reading process. Despite these differences, however, the model results are within a single standard deviation of the human mean in every case. Additionally, with the exception of a single case discussed later, the results follow the general trend of increasing subjective workload within the aided condition as well as within the unaided condition. That is, higher track density maps to higher subjective

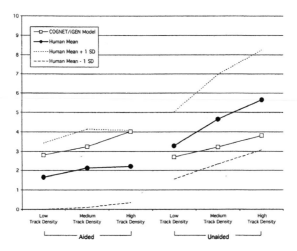

FIG. 5.11.   Effort.

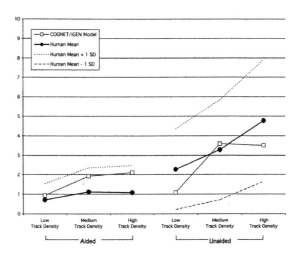

FIG. 5.12.   Frustration.

workload for both human subjects and the COGNET/iGEN models developed for the aided and unaided conditions.

In several cases, the human results present a departure from the pattern of higher workload rating paralleling higher track density. In the aided condition, both the measure of performance and measure of frustration are rated lower for the high-density scenarios than for the medium-density scenarios. This pattern accurately tracks the penalty point pattern noted earlier and is best understood as a reflection of a small number of specific individual task executions. For the model, a similar departure from the

TABLE 5.5
Percent of Human Subject Variance (R^2) Accounted for by AMBR
Experiment 1 Model Predictions and Associated Significance

Workload Measure	R^2 value	Significance
Physical	36%	$p \sim .2$ (=.205)
Mental	38%	$p < .2$
Temporal	68%	$p < .05$
Performance	98%	$p < .0005$
Effort	13%	No significance
Frustration	53%	$p \sim .1$ (=.103)

general pattern appears in the case of the frustration measure for unaided performance, shown in the right half of Fig. 5.12. Although the human mean shows relative levels of frustration that correspond to the relative levels of track density, the model results indicate a frustration level for the medium-track density that is greater than that for either the low- or high-density conditions. This case is discussed in a later section.

It should be noted that the COGNET/iGEN model was the only AMBR model that produced a separate response for each of the six TLX measures as done by the human subjects. Statistically, the Experiment 1 model-generated workload assessments predicted the human values well in the Experiment 1 training data set, yielding r-squared statistics and significance values as shown in Table 5.5. Significance was computed via the F statistic using (1,4) degrees of freedom, reflecting the one variable in the regression equation and the six data points used in the estimation process.[8] As shown in Table 5.5, the models for temporal and performance are highly significant. The model for frustration, with a $p \sim .1$, shows a strong association (only 1 in 10 chance of being by chance alone), but is not significant at the conventional .05 or less level. Similarly, the models for physical and mental workload show moderately strong association, with $p \sim .2$ (1 in 5 chance of being by chance alone). The model for effort is not better than chance alone. As with many aspects of the AMBR Experiment 1, the small n for this analysis is clearly creating a difficult situation in which to establish statistical validity. This can be seen in the workload models for Experiment 2, in which the same models led to generally smaller R^2 values, but showed greater significance because of a much larger sample size.

Figure 5.13 shows the overall workload (averaged across the six individual scales) for COGNET/iGEN compared with humans. Using aggregate workload ratings, the COGNET/iGEN model produces the same pattern of ratings as the human subjects, in that subjective workload increases with

---

[8]See embedded documentation for the LINEST function in Microsoft Excel for Macintosh, 2001.

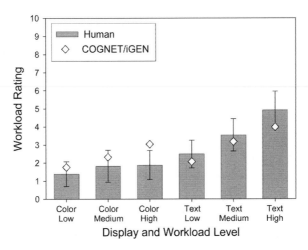

FIG. 5.13.   Human and model subjective workload as a function of display and workload condition.

workload and the color condition is viewed as less demanding than the text condition. The model tended to underestimate the difference in subjective workload between color and text conditions when compared with human subjects.

CATEGORY LEARNING MODEL (EXPERIMENT 2)

Experiment 2 added a category learning component to the ATC task in Experiment 1. As chapter 2 describes, the learning task was the primary task in Experiment 2 and the ATC task was secondary.

Category Learning or Action-Condition Learning?

The research reported here added a learning capability to the COGNET/iGEN system, which previously had no such facility. Despite the limitations of the Shepard paradigm, which motivated the larger project, learning was implemented as a general capability to learn the conditions under which each of a disjunctive set of goals or actions should be taken—in other words, the ability to learn when to undertake different goals or actions. This approach was both general and consistent with the overall emphasis in COGNET/iGEN on procedural knowledge and multitasking. It was found that integrating this learning capability required other, deeper level extensions to the system—most notably the creation for the first time of an explicit short-term memory model and development of memory-performance moderators. These extensions, in turn, enabled the representation of memory decay, rehearsal, and proactive interference needed to model human learning performance. The manner in which the architectural changes were implemented allows future evolution of memory (and memory moderation) mechanisms and of learning mechanisms in COGNET/iGEN.

Organization of Learning Model

The Experiment 2 learning task required subjects and models to learn when to accept/reject aircraft requests for altitude change based on aircraft size, amount of fuel remaining, and turbulence (see chap. 2, this volume). In general, Experiment 2 model development proceeded as reported for Experiment 1, with a CTA leading first to a competence model and then to a performance model of the learning task.

Learning Task Strategy. To study learning strategies, a simple system was developed for presenting the learning task independently from the ATC task and testbed. Using this learning task presentation software, a limited CTA was conducted collecting performance data with concurrent verbal strategy self-reporting. Based on this limited CTA in combination with information gathered during human subject experiments as reported by BBN and a review of the category learning literature, a learning task strategy was developed. A key simplification strategy observed during CTA was a subject's decision to cast all categorization hypotheses in terms of which stimuli to accept (e.g., "Accept requests from any small aircraft"). That is, the subject intentionally avoided the formulation of rules based on the identification of which stimuli to reject, including general acceptance rules with explicit rejection exceptions. Some more general effects that were clear in the CTA results included the fact that learning mechanisms were differentially based on rule complexity, with single-dimension rules being tried first, followed by two-dimension rules, then three-dimension rules (three-dimension rules specify unique individual stimulus instances).

To think about and represent category rules, a notation was developed in which each rule (determining request acceptance) is represented as a parameter triplet, written in parentheses, specifying a value for each dimension as follows: *size, turbulence, fuel remaining.* The following examples present the full compliment of parameter values used outside of the transfer task:

(Small Aircraft, Low Turbulence, 20% Fuel Remaining)
(Large Aircraft, High Turbulence, 40% Fuel Remaining)

Written in a more compact, encoded form, these example rules appear as follows:

(S,1,20)
(L,3,40)

Using "x" as a wild card, more general rules can be constructed:

(S,x,x)—a single dimension rule that could be stated as "Accept request from any small aircraft."

(S,1,x)—a two-dimension rule that could be stated as "Accept request from any aircraft that is small and encountering low turbulence."

(S,1,40)—a three-dimension rule that could be stated as "Accept request from any aircraft that is small, encountering low turbulence, and has 40% fuel remaining."

A categorization hypothesis consists of one or more rules for accepting altitude change requests:

(L,x,x)—hypothesis with a single one-dimension rule
((L,1,x) (S,3,x))—hypothesis with a pair of two-dimension rules

As all rules specify request acceptance, at any point in time, the categorization hypothesis may contain rules that overlap (no conflict resolution between rules is required). Requests are rejected if no rule specifies that they be accepted.

With this scheme, the model would begin with a single one-dimensional guess. Using the assumption that size is a good first guess (as a primary dimension of interest), the model would begin with (L,x,x) or (S,x,x). Trial results either:

- confirm the rules requiring no change (rules gave correct answer),
- disconfirm one or more rules and require that they be narrowed or removed (rules produced an incorrect "ACCEPT" answer), or
- are unaccounted for in the current set of rules (rules produced an incorrect "REJECT" answer) and require the addition of a new rule.

In this process, rules are specialized after "ACCEPT" errors because the rule set is too broad. For example, if a rule (L,x,x) incorrectly accepts the stimulus (L,3,40), the rule would be specialized to one of the form (L,1,x) and ultimately, if appropriate, to the form (L,1,20). In general, this process of rule specialization seems to be consistent with observed attempts to find the most powerful rule possible for a given set of stimuli as well as with the need to remember generalities when detailed memory is of necessity incomplete. New rules are generated based on "REJECT" errors because the rule set is too narrow. For example, after a rule (S,1,x) incorrectly rejects the stimulus (L,3,40), a new rule is generated (L,x,x) yielding two rules in the rule set.

From the human perspective, some dimensions are more important than others, with reference to the altitude change decision. For example, aircraft size may be the primary consideration for a decision, and turbulence may be a secondary consideration. This is termed *dimension bias* or a priority among dimensions. In general terms, the initial bias selection would be based on a fixed or random guess, whereas later bias selections would be based on explicit strategy changes.

The approach described thus far accounts for learning competence. However, learning performance is constrained by memory and other performance constraints. Thus, in addition to the learning competence, additional architectural constructs had to be implemented to represent learning performance, the most important of which was memory.

Approach to Memory Moderation. A memory moderation model was adapted from the Human Operator Simulator (HOS) work (Glenn, Schwartz, & Ross, 1992; Lane, Strieb, Glenn, & Wherry, 1981). The term *memory moderation* was used to include various memory-related factors, such as memory load, decay, opportunities for rehearsal, and interference. The model was a two-stage memory model incorporating a short-term memory (STM) with exponential decay and a long-term memory (LTM) with no decay, adapted from the model of Waugh and Norman (1965). Rules are maintained in STM by rehearsal and converted to LTM with a probability based on memory load and integration decay.

On each trial, the subject attempts to retain some number (1–4) of rules in memory. For simplicity, it is assumed that each stimulus (and feedback) occurs at a regular time interval T. During that time, the subject rehearses the rules to maintain them in the STM, and each rehearsal provides an opportunity for conversion to LTM. The number of slots (nonwild-card values) for a particular rule as n (n varies from 1–3). The memory load is based on the total number of dimension values specified in all rules being remembered (varies from 1–12 because up to four rules can be retained and each can have up to three values). There is no decay from LTM, but the hypothesis can be fully purged from both LTM and STM by volitional deletion on determination that it is inconsistent with the outcome of a trial. The probability of recalling a hypothesis from STM from one trial to the next is determined by the number of slots that constitute the hypothesis and the amount of rehearsal that is permitted by the memory load of the total stack of rules being maintained. The probability of recall for a rule with n slots is P(short-term) = p^n, where p is a learning parameter. N is the total number of slots for all the rules in the rule set (hypothesis). M is the total number of slots that can be rehearsed in the time interval between two stimulus presentations. Note if t is the time to rehearse an individual slot, then $M = T/t$. Each rule can be rehearsed on average once every N slots or every Nt seconds. The probability that a rule can be rehearsed after each such interval is:

$$\mathrm{PR}(N \text{ slot interval}) = p^n \, e^{-aN}$$

where a is a decay rate constant.

On average, there will be M/N such rehearsals and recall attempts for each rule between each stimulus, so the probability of recall across the interval between two stimuli is:

$$\mathrm{Pr}(\text{interstimuli}) = (p^n \, e^{-aNt})^{M/N}$$

and the probability of forgetting is:

$$\mathrm{Pf}\,(\text{interstimuli}) = 1 - (p^n \, e^{-aNt})^{M/N}$$

The probability of a rule transferring to long-term memory on each rehearsal (and also on original formulation) is defined as q. The probability of conversion to long-term between two feedback events is then:

$$\mathrm{Pc}(\text{long-term}) = 1 - (1 - q)^{M/N} \text{ or } \mathrm{Pc}(\text{long-term})$$
$$= 1 - r^{1/N} \text{ where } r = (1 - q)^M$$

This approach to memory moderation allows problem types to be distinguished by number of opportunities for easily learned solutions—one-dimension rules or two-dimension rules in combination, thus providing performance as expected from humans.

Learning Mechanism.   The learning task strategy and memory model described earlier were integrated to produce a computational learning mechanism within the COGNET/iGEN cognitive architecture. The learning engine is based on an explicit model for hypothesis generation and testing (similar to the RULEX model of Nosofsky, Palmeri, & McKinley [1994]) to describe concept learning behavior as it occurs in a complex task environment.

This approach was pursued to determine how effectively complex concept learning could be described by a deliberate symbolic learning process as contrasted with the primarily passive processes described by connectionist models.

The learning mechanism was developed as a subcomponent of the cognitive system. It receives stimuli, provides a classification in return, and then receives a positive or negative feedback on its classification. The components of the learning mechanism (see Fig. 5.14) include:

- learning memory divided into short and long term that contains classification rules,
- memory moderator that memorizes or forgets rules,
- learning engine that uses the current rule set (categorization hypothesis) to generate classifications and new rules or modify existing ones after receiving feedback, and
- metacognitive strategy that influences the learning engine.

As described previously, the knowledge used for classification is represented by a set of rules (triplets) for deciding to accept altitude change requests. Within the particular constraints of the classification problem (four cases of acceptance and four cases of rejection), at most four accept rules are sufficient to specify all possible classifications. Wild cards are used to specify more general rules. For example, (S,x,x) indicates a rule where size = S and turbulence and fuel remaining are unspecified. As each dimension has two possible values, such a rule describes four cases of acceptance and is sufficient by itself to classify all possible combinations of stimuli. Cases where a single rule is sufficient for classification correspond to the Type I classification problem. Type III problems require at least two rules to account for all possibilities. For example, (S,1,x) and (L,3,x) belong in that type. Problem Type III demands that all dimensions be specified and therefore requires at least four rules with no wild card. This representation implicitly makes the Type I case easier to find and remember than Type III, which should in turn be easier than Type VI. When being asked to classify a

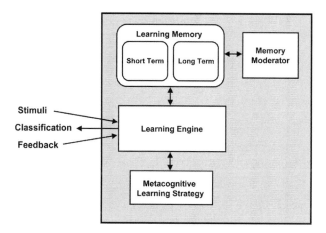

FIG. 5.14. The COGNET/iGEN learning mechanism.

new triplet of stimulus values, if one of the current rules can match the stimulus, then the result will be to accept and reject otherwise.

The learning engine is responsible for the creation, modification, and deletion of the classification rules. It is based on the following principles of operation:

- Remove invalid rules—if there is a rule with no wild card that matches the stimulus and the feedback is negative.
- Specialize rules—if the feedback is negative and there is a rule with a wild card that matches the stimulus, then replace the wild card with the opposite value of the stimulus for this dimension.
- Create new simple rules (with two wild cards)—if the feedback is positive and if no rules currently cover the stimulus.

One important aspect of the principles of operation of the learning engine is that most of them are dependent on the order in which the dimensions are evaluated. For example, considering size then turbulence and fuel (STF) does not provide the same result as considering fuel then size and turbulence (FST). The "create rule" principle produces (S,x,x) in the first case and (x,x,20) in the second. The order in which the dimensions are evaluated as a strategy is explicitly designated. In this study with three dimensions, six different strategies are possible. In general, no particular strategy is better than another, but for a specific classification problem some strategies may be more efficient than others. For example, the strategy STF will immediately find the correct classification rule for a problem of type (S,x,x), but will struggle for a problem of type (x,x,20).

To remedy this problem, a meta-strategy was used to switch from one strategy to another: Anytime a strategy encounters N cases of negative feedback, another strategy is selected. To add a stochastic effect to the meta-strategy, N is randomly chosen each time between 1 and 3. Switching strategies might help some cases find the correct classification more rapidly, but it may also be disruptive because no particular strategy is allowed to run for an extended period.

Memory moderation was incorporated into the learning mechanism by applying the memory moderation algorithm on each trial prior to determining the classification response. First, forgetting from STM is applied, then transfer to LTM determined, then the classification response determined from all rules in LTM or STM.

The values for the parameters in the memory moderation algorithm were determined by using an initial value based on the Human Operator Simulator (HOS) work (Glenn et al., 1992; Lane et al., 1981) and then adjusting those values based on some trial-and-error experimentation after the learning mechanism was integrated into the COGNET architecture.

The value of T (the length of the intertrial interval) was determined from the task environment simulation to be 50 sec. The initial and final values for the learning parameters were:

a = STM decay parameter (initial value = .0003) (final value = 0.0015)

q_s = base probability for single-slot LTM conversion (initial and final value = .03)

b = LTM decay parameter (initial value = .2) (final value = 0.15)

t = time required to rehearse a single hypothesis slot (initial and final value = 0.5 secs)

Using this memory moderation model, it takes more time to learn three-dimension rules than one- or two-dimension rules because problem types are distinguished by the number of opportunities for simple solutions—one-dimension rules or two-dimension rules in combination. Consequently, Type I and III problems are learned more easily than Type VI because one- and two-dimension rules dominate while three-dimension rules are more likely to be discarded.

Transfer Task Modeling. To handle the transfer task, the model was implemented to map new stimulus values onto known values and use the same mechanisms as in the learning task. New values were mapped to the most similar existing ones. Extrapolated stimuli were mapped 100% of the time to the nearest end value. Equidistant stimuli were mapped (arbitrarily) to the closest lower value.

Following the initial Experiment 2 model runs, the human data for the transfer task were made available. Analysis of these data indicated that performance was degraded overall due to the appearance of unfamiliar stimuli, and that the degradation was greater for untrained than trained stimuli. Thus, the revised Experiment 2 model incorporated a confusion factor (which could also be interpreted as a lack of confidence or cognitive bias effect) into the model. This was accomplished by reversing the trained response on a percentage of the transfer trials.

The algorithm used was the following:

When 0 errors in preceding trial block:
   Trained stimuli → use trained response 94% of time
   Untrained stimuli → use trained response 88% of time
When > 0 errors in preceding trial block:
   Trained stimuli → use trained response 76% of time
   Untrained stimuli → use trained response 64% of time

Learning and Response Time.   Model tuning involved refinements to response times on both the primary and secondary tasks and to probability of errors on the secondary tasks to make the model performance more consistent with the tuning subject performance. Accomplishing these changes involved considering the effect of the primary task on the secondary task. Time consumption for motor actions and scanning behavior in the Experiment 1 version of the AMBR model was accomplished using micromodels. Additional time consumption was added for rule application in the learning task. A workload coefficient was calculated based on perceived workload (across all tasks) and used as a scaling factor for secondary task response times. Probability of error on the secondary task was also adjusted based on perceived workload. Response times for the primary task were adjusted by including two time charges:

- a response time charge based on number of strategy changes, and
- a response time charge for processing feedback based on whether the response was correct or incorrect.

After initial model results were reviewed, a practice effect (Lane, 1987) was added to the motor and scanning micromodels to account for a slight but steady decrease in time needed over trial blocks as a result of practice. The log of current scenario time, in seconds, multiplied by the log of trial number was computed [$\log(t)*\log(\text{trialNum})$] and then scaled to approximate human secondary task performance [$-x/95$] and subtracted from action/scanning component of response time.

Experiment 2 Workload Model

In Experiment 2, there were three workload-related changes from Experiment 1:

- At the most superficial level, the moderator had changed the workload reporting scale from a 10-point to a 7-point scale.
- In addition, the nonlearning (i.e., secondary) tasks had been changed to create a single set of tasks that were different from either the unaided or aided tasks performed in Experiment 1.
- At a deeper level, the introduction of a learning task had required addition of a learning mechanism into COGNET.

The change in workload reporting scales required a simple recalibration of the mapping from model self-reports to the TLX reporting scales. This was done using the same statistical process used in Experiment 1. The change in tasks was analyzed as not relevant to the Experiment 1 workload model. That is, it was concluded that the Experiment 1 workload model should still be valid even with the changes to the ATC tasks, including the new learning (altitude change request) task.

The addition of a learning mechanism to the architecture, however, was more problematic. At the procedural level, the learning mechanism operated by developing a strategy for guessing at rules and then applying the strategy to produce and apply rules. A rule would be used until it led to an incorrect guess. After a number of incorrect guesses applying rules with a given strategy, the model would revise its strategy and begin again. The rules and past guesses were stored in a decaying memory. Thus, learning difficulties could be introspected as strategy changes. However, the number of strategy changes is directly related to the number of erroneous guesses because it is only after a number of incorrect guesses that the strategy changes. Of course the number of correct guesses is clearly related to the number of incorrect guesses as well (as the two sum to 16 in each trial). Given these relationships, it seemed that the number of incorrect guesses was the most clear aspect of the learning mechanism to incorporate into the workload self-assessment model for two reasons: (a) determinism rather than randomness, and (b) clearer conceptual link to workload. Thus, the Experiment 1 workload was modified in only one way—by adding to each self-assessment rule an added factor of the number of incorrect guesses in the just completed trial. With the Experiment 1 workload model adjusted in this single way, a new set of model predictions was generated and calibrated to the (new) 7-point rating scale.

The calibration coefficients in that adjusted model are given in Table 5.6. In Table 5.6, the terms in capital letters (e.g., PHYSICAL) refer to the component measures from the Experiment 1 workload model (Table 5.1). The term PT refers to the number of incorrect guesses that the model made during the just-completed trial.

TABLE 5.6
Calibration Formulae for the Experiment 2
Workload Model Measures

Calibration Formula
Physical demand = $-10.5*\text{PHYSICAL} - .036* \text{PT} - 10.478$
Mental demand = $.08*\text{MENTAL} + .126*\text{PT} + 2.308$
Temporal demand = $-1.57* \text{TEMPORAL} + .036* \text{PT} - 1.567$
Performance = $-87*\text{PERFORM} + .42 * \text{PT} + 1.91$
Effort = $.04*\text{EFFORT} + .16* \text{PT} + 2.1$
Frustration = $-.7*\text{FRUSTRATE} + .17*\text{PT} + 1.985$

Experiment 2 Results

In the category learning experiment, modeling teams were provided with human learning data to reference in developing their models and generating predications for transfer of learning to a new condition. Following initial model results and transfer predictions, human transfer performance data were provided, and the models were revised. The discussion of initial and revised model results refers to these two versions of the model.

The Experiment 2 independent variables of Problem Type (I, III, and VI) and workload (low-, medium-, and high-aircraft density) result in nine conditions run as a between-subjects design. Ten subjects were run in each of the nine conditions, for 90 subjects. The model also ran 90 times to provide equivalent performance data with reference to the full set of stimulus presentation sequences used in the human-subject runs.

Initial Experiment 2 model run results indicated the need for revisions, specifically in the output format of workload results and in the modeling of response time and the transfer task. Results were generated again after revisions, and initial and revised model results are discussed next.

Category Learning. As shown in Fig. 5.15, probability of error decreased over trials (trial effect) and was higher in the more difficult learning conditions (category effect) for both humans and model. In addition to providing a good fit to the human means, the model's solutions and intermediate results resemble human rule formulations. Problem Type III was typically solved with either two 2-dimensional rules or one 2-dimensional rule and two rote cases (3-dimensional rules). Problem Type VI could only be solved by four rote cases and often was not solved by the end of eight blocks of trials. A typical model output at the end of the session was a near solution, with three rote cases and one higher level rule.

No changes were made for the revised model runs, so the differences seen in the figure are due to random variation. In both initial and revised

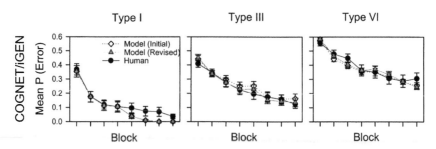

FIG. 5.15.   Human category learning data for Type I, III, and VI problems and initial and revised model data.

cases, there were significant category and trial effects for both the model and humans.

Learning Response Time. Human subjects showed both a category and trial effect in response time to the category learning task, whereas the initial model runs only showed a category effect and no decrease over trials. Introducing a practice effect in the revised model produced a trial effect in the results as shown in Fig. 5.16.

ATC Response Time. As for learning response time, the initial model runs did not show the trial effect for the ATC handoff task found for humans. A practice effect was introduced in the revised model. As Fig. 5.17 shows, the response times on the secondary task for the revised model were similar to those of humans, including a trial effect.

ATC Penalty Points. For the secondary task—the ATC handoff task—neither the humans nor the revised model showed any significant effects. As Fig. 5.18 shows, although there was some variability in the functions, there were no significant differences in secondary task due to the difficulty of the primary task. Initial and revised model run results were similar as no changes were made to the ATC task model.

Transfer Task. The initial model configuration predicted better transfer performance than humans actually exhibited, as indicated in Fig. 5.19. The difference was greater on the extrapolated stimuli than the original eight or trained stimuli. A reduction in model error for *trained* and *extrapolated* cases is possibly related to cases of late solution by the model. If the model achieved a solution within Block 8, then the model would improve

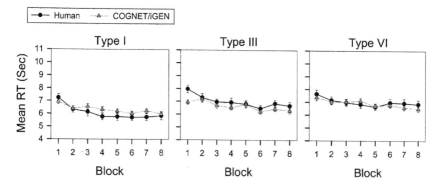

FIG. 5.16. Human and revised model response times on the category learning task as a function of category learning problem type.

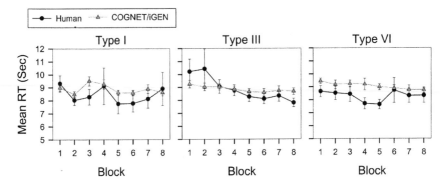

FIG. 5.17. Human and revised model response times to the handoff task as a function of category learning problem type.

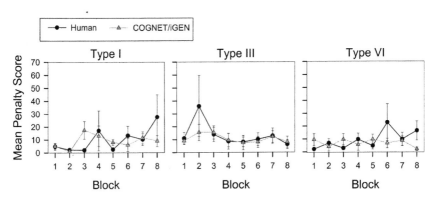

FIG. 5.18. Human and revised model penalty scores on the handoff task as a function of category learning problem type.

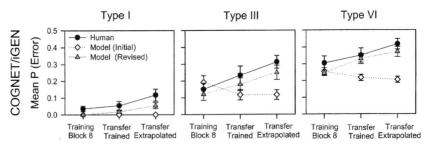

FIG. 5.19. Human data, initial model predictions, and revised model data for Block 8 learning data, trained, and extrapolated transfer test stimuli.

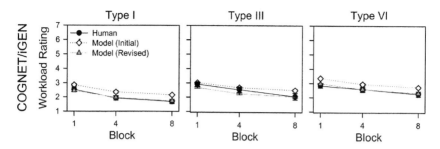

FIG. 5.20. Observed and predicted subjective workload ratings administered after Blocks 1, 4, and 8.

its performance (lower probability of error) in the transfer block. As humans exhibit some kind of interference or decay in both the *trained* and *extrapolated* cases, the initial Experiment 2 model was subsequently revised as noted earlier.

The addition of the confusion factor in the revised model degraded transfer task performance in a human-like manner. The results from the revised model runs show both humans and model with significant category and trial effects, but no significant interaction.

Subjective Workload. Initial Experiment 2 runs showed workload ratings by the model that were consistently higher than those recorded for human subjects. This pattern was analyzed and determined to result from a mismatch in output format (1-based instead of the 0-based results expected by the moderator). The unit error noted in the initial results was corrected, and the appropriate 0-based values were output for analysis during the Experiment 2 revised model runs.

In the revised model runs (with the output unit error corrected), the model provided workload rating trends similar to humans. Both humans and the model showed significant trial and category effects, but no significant interaction (Fig. 5.20). As in Experiment 1, the COGNET/iGEN model was the only AMBR model that produced a separate response for each of the six TLX measures as human subjects did. Statistically, the Experiment 2 model-generated workload assessments predicted the human values well, yielding r-squared statistics and significance as shown in Table 5.7. In this case, the F statistic was calculated with (2,24) degrees of freedom, reflecting the two variables in the regression equation and the 27 data points used.[9] The F tests show that all measures except physical demand were significant at less than the 1% level. The lack of significance for the

---

[9]See embedded documentation for the LINEST function in Microsoft Excel for Macintosh, 2001.

TABLE 5.7
Percent of Experiment 2 Human Subject Variance (R^2)
Accounted for by AMBR Experiment 2 Workload
Model and Associated Significance

Workload Measure	R^2 value	Significance
Mental demand	28%	$p < .025$
Physical demand	15%	$p < .2$
Temporal demand	30%	$p < .025$
Performance	58%	$p < .001$
Effort	41%	$p < .005$
Frustration	65%	$p < .001$

physical demand measure is, in some sense, reassuring. This is because the human subject data showed reporting behaviors that were contrary to the instructions. Specifically, the human subjects reported an increase in physical workload within a given scenario when only the complexity of the learning task changed. In such cases, the physical workload of screen scanning and keyboard/mouse manipulation was identical, only the difficulty of the learning (a nonphysical work activity) increased. This suggests that there was some bleed through of the perceived increased cognitive workload to the self-report of physical workload—an effect contrary to the explicit instructions, which the model did not replicate.

DISCUSSION AND CONCLUSION

Individual Differences and Psychological Models

Clearly, the COGNET/iGEN model is a model of an individual. The BATON engine, which executes the model, represents the information-processing mechanisms that are posited to be possessed by all (developmentally normal) people. However, although COGNET/iGEN represents these internal mechanisms as a least common denominator of human cognition, the other component of the model—the expertise model—represents a distinct collection of problem-solving strategies, one of many that could be used. The specific strategies that were built into the expertise models were extracted from a CTA of several in-house subjects as discussed earlier. The behavior produced by these subjects also appeared to be similar to that of subjects in the tuning and comparison data sets. Thus, the COGNET/iGEN model is also a model of an individual applying a specific expert-level strategy.

As a model of a single individual, it should be treated the same as the data for any of the individual human subjects. Having defined the COGNET/ iGEN model in this way, the difficult philosophical issue that remains is determining to what the model's behavior should be compared and how the comparison should be conducted. If the purpose of comparison is determining whether the model produces human (-like) behavior, then a pure Turing test approach would suffice. This could be done by simply having outside (human) observers review the behaviors (e.g., through re-plays) of human and model and determine whether it is possible to differentiate one from another. In AMBR, however, the criterion was stronger than simple face validity (i.e., did the model behavior appear to be human?). The AMBR comparison sought to establish the degree to which each model statistically corresponded to a given reference sample of human subject data.

In principle, a statistical comparison of individual behavior to populational means of various measures could add substantial rigor to the comparison process. However, in retrospect, it also introduced an additional strong assumption that may have, in the end, only muddied the issue. The parametric statistical comparison approach assumes that the observed (human) behavior on a given measure was generated through a shared/common human cognitive and behavioral process, which varied across the population from which the sample was drawn only in specific parameter values and in randomly distributed noise/error. A model that had a significant fit to the human data could then be viewed as having correctly represented the underlying process.

Different data from both of the AMBR experiments, however, cast serious doubt on this underlying assumption. The data from the AMBR human subjects suggested that there were categorical differences in strategy within the populations of subjects, resulting in significant differences in behavior (subjects may have represented different levels of expertise or different expert approaches). Thus, the observed variation in human behavior on any measure is likely not just the result of normally distributed noise. This further suggests that comparing any single individual (or any model) to a mean of the subject sample would produce an inappropriate comparison based on an inappropriate pooling of variance across behaviors generated with different strategies (see also the discussion in Estes, 2002, on the dangers of group means not preserving individual functions). Without subjects trained to the same form of expertise represented in the model, the approach to statistical comparison must remain murky. In the end, there may be no easy solution to this problem other than the simpler Turing test strategy suggested earlier, which clearly lacks the rigor desired. Accordingly, an important conclusion is that development of better methods to compare and assess the behavior of cognitive models with regard to human behavior is a substantial and largely unexplored research problem.

An examination of two AMBR examples is instructive with regard to this issue. First, the Experiment 2 category learning model, despite its incorporation of a stochastic strategy switching mechanism, represents a single hypothesize-and-test strategy for category learning (distinct from strategies that encode exceptions, for example). Extensive in-house testing of the model, independent of the larger ATC task context, indicates that the model strategy rarely, if ever, reaches a solution by the end of a Problem Type VI scenario. Individual human subjects also vary from this pattern, with several individuals arriving at a solution well before the end of the eight trial blocks. At least some humans are employing strategies that are more efficient than that represented in the model. The comparison of means in Fig. 5.15 gives no indication that the model is failing to capture specific types of individual performance.

The Experiment 1 subjective workload results provide a reverse example, with comparison to the human mean suggesting that the model is not producing human-like results. In Fig. 5.12, the model results seem counterintuitive, with frustration decreasing when workload increases in the unaided context. The human results, however, were highly variable in regard to frustration; as a result, the mean is somewhat deceptive. Table 5.8 presents the differences in reported frustration level, across the three track density conditions for unaided performance, as a series of paired cases. Row 1 indicates, for example, that 5 of the 16 human subjects rated the medium density condition as more frustrating than the low, as well as the high as more frustrating than the medium—the same pattern seen in the human mean. Although the patterns of relative frustration across the track density conditions are weighted in the direction of this pattern, there are fairly dis-

TABLE 5.8
Frustration Level Comparison by Track Density
in Unaided Condition

Low To Medium	Medium To High	
Track Density	Track Density	Number of Subjects
1. Increase in frustration	Increase in frustration	5
2. Increase in frustration	No difference in frustration	1
3. Increase in frustration	Decrease in frustration	2
4. No difference in frustration	Increase in frustration	4
5. No difference in frustration	No difference in frustration	3
6. No difference in frustration	Decrease in frustration	0
7. Decrease in frustration	Increase in frustration	1
8. Decrease in frustration	No difference in frustration	0
9. Decrease in frustration	Decrease in frustration	0

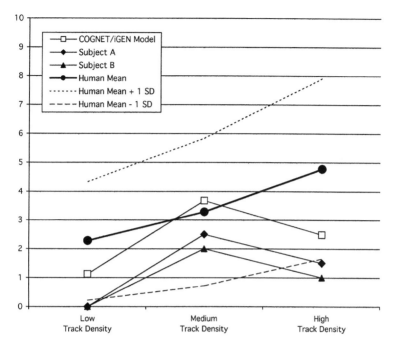

FIG. 5.21. Frustration: Model and individual human subjects.

tinct departures. Row 3 indicates that the pattern generated by the model was similar to that produced by two of the human subjects. (Row 7 presents a similar, although reverse, departure from the pattern of the mean.) Figure 5.21 presents a comparison of the results for the two subjects cited in Row 3 and a single model run—one of four identically patterned model run results. The similarity here may well derive from similarities in strategy between the task performance of these particular human subjects and the COGNET/iGEN model, but there is no way to determine this with the available data.

Another conclusion that can be drawn from such data is that there cannot be a single cognitive model that represents the variability within a population of people. Different strategies seems to abound—for learning, assessing workload, performing different aspects of the work task—and furthermore seem to be distributed at least somewhat randomly across individuals. Even if each variation in strategy could be separately represented, their independent distribution would give rise to a combinatoric set of possible model variations, each of which could have a slightly different behavioral outcome. In engineering applications of human behavioral representations, such as simulation-based design evaluation, this raises an important question as to how a representative test population could be generated. Future research is needed to address this question.

Boundaries to Rationality

Evaluation of the results of the AMBR models illustrates some boundaries to our ability to represent human behavior. One case in point is the transfer task in the initial results of Experiment 2. No modeling team was able to account for the drop on performance for stimuli that had been learned (i.e., responded to correctly) by the last block of the learning. No account of category learning predicted the drop. Thus, some factor involved in human performance was not reflected in any model. Our second iteration of the Experiment 2 model added a confusion factor to handle this decrement. Although in hindsight such a factor makes sense and improves model performance, it was not predicted a priori from either the operation of the cognitive mechanism or from a rational analysis of the task. It may be that special strategies for accomplishing tasks with arbitrary information (e.g., mnemonics and rehearsal) were invoked by subjects rather than the general strategies for learning in skilled everyday activities (see also Ericsson & Delaney, 1999, for a discussion of working memory in the performance of laboratory tasks). In turn these strategies may have been interrupted in the transfer task, in that subjects may have thought the "rules of the game" had changed and required a new strategy.

The subjective workload results illustrate another case in which a model based on rational principles was not able to predict human behavior. Of the six measures in the TLX scale, a rational analysis would suggest that, although mental demand, performance, effort, and frustration would be affected by addition of the learning task, physical demand and temporal demand would not because the physical work involved and the time it required were totally independent of the learning aspects of the task. However, human subjects were varying their report of these factors according to differences in learning condition. Again, although the model could be successfully modified to account for the human data, this was based on evaluating human performance not on rational a priori analysis.

Benefits and Limits to the COGNET/iGEN Approach

COGNET was created as a general model that could be used for building specific models (or model instances) of human cognition and/or behavior for a range of specific purposes (which has grown over time). These purposes include design/analysis of person–machine interfaces and human work tasks, performance diagnosis in intelligent training systems, decision and performance support in real-time computer-based work environments, and simulation of human behavior and performance, the purpose in this project. As new COGNET model instances have been built, a deliberate effort has been made to identify features that are common to most/all model instances and to retain these within the architecture while maintaining customization affordances for more detailed architectural features that may be needed (only) for certain types of model instances. This process has been motivated by theory ideally in the sense noted initially: to identify useful simplifying assumptions and boundary conditions of the known assumptions.

In specific, the COGNET cognitive architecture is based on the modified stage theory of human information processing. COGNET incorporates distinct but interdependent declarative and procedural knowledge representations. On the procedural side, it supports hierarchical goal/subgoal/operation procedural knowledge structures, integration of cognitive and behavioral operations, and context-sensitive modification of strategies based on declarative knowledge content. On the declarative side, it allows the notion of mental model or other domain-specific expert constructs to be incorporated. Attention management is an emergent property of the architecture and principles of operation, supporting multitasking easily and naturally. More recent COGNET developments provide metacognition mechanisms and allow a model to be aware of its own processes and states. This cognitive proprioception allows decision making and performance to be modified based on the state of cognitive processing. These mechanisms were used in our ATC model to drive task load-based strategies and error generation.

COGNET provides a surprisingly simple core architecture. Representations of process or structure limitations, such as memory capacity, decay, recall constraints, visual regions and their acuity constraints, and so on, are not included in the core architecture, although the iGEN implementation is extensible and allows such representations to be added. The principles of operation that describe the functionality of the core architecture are derived from macrotheories of expertise, including Klein's recognition primed decision theory and Ericcson and Kintsch's long-term working memory model. As noted earlier, both here and in other applications, COGNET/iGEN has been able to produce highly realistic representations of human behavior in contexts as simple as the AMBR testbed or as complex as that of advanced Navy command and control. Although some might suggest that the lack of such subprocess models makes COGNET/iGEN a framework in search of a theory, the authors actually see the results as leading to a quite different conclusion. The lack of embedded theories of processing limits or other subprocesses makes COGNET/iGEN a simpler and more parsimonious model than other models that incorporate these components, but has not prevented COGNET/iGEN from producing high-quality (and, in many AMBR cases, the best-fitting) behavioral predictions. Thus, it can be concluded that, for the purposes of human behavioral representation, such architectural features are not necessary and do not pass the test of Occam's razor.

COGNET does place substantial emphasis on the representation of knowledge, both procedural and declarative. It provides no standard or atomic level of representation, allowing adaptation to the modeling goal. Yet the representational forms, like the architectural principles of operation, are targeted toward the forms of expert knowledge typically used in generating skilled performance (rather than novice performance).

Summary of Model Comparisons

COGNET/iGEN was created for engineering purposes. Although internal mechanisms provide a least common denominator of human cognition, they are embedded in a system that provides the kind of flexibility required for developing practical applications. Based on this underlying approach, the COGNET/iGEN AMBR models have produced results that correspond well to human experimental data involving relatively abstract and non-naturalistic tasks. When comparing results to human mean values, the COGNET/iGEN models frequently present the most human-like results of any of the models developed, including cases of initial model runs. Given the general similarity of the results produced by all of the models, it is possible that a Turing test would judge the behavior of all of the models to be indistinguishable from human behavior. However, it is difficult to imagine a human observer reviewing some of the behavior, particularly in the categorization task. In this context, human expertise may only be recognizable to another human on the basis of the final result, itself highly variable, and not on the basis of intermediate results or observable processes.

SUMMARY OF QUESTIONS AND ANSWERS

1. How Is Cognition Represented in Your System?

Cognition in COGNET/iGEN is separated into underlying mechanisms, domain/task strategies and expertise, and the dynamics of the external (work) environment. Underlying mechanisms include a cognitive processor and long-term working memory (LTWM), which operate in a way consistent with explicit principles of operation as defined in the appendix. Domain/task strategies and expertise are represented in an expertise model, which explicitly represents the structure/organization of LTWM within the strategy being modeled, and a procedural knowledge model, which explicitly represents the work strategy in terms of a collection of highly compiled (i.e., chunked) goal-action sets called *cognitive tasks*. Each such cognitive task consists of a pattern of memory contents that will lead to its activation and a body to be executed as a means of accomplishing the goal. The body is a hierarchy of conjunctive and disjunctive goals and subgoals, similar to a

GOMS model, but is instantiated and executed in terms of the current contents of LTWM. The cognitive processor executes a current cognitive task one subgoal at a time by carrying out the sequence of primitive operators (described earlier) within its body.

Cognitive operations are generally represented at what Newell (1990) defined as the "rational band" and the upper portions of the "cognitive band," but there is no requirement or limitation to do so. Rather, the primitive cognitive action is not limited to any specific level of granularity, either across the model as a whole or even within different components (e.g., cognitive tasks).

There is no general learning mechanism (other than a constrained mechanism implemented for AMBR Experiment 2), although a typical model will learn during its execution in the sense that it may form detailed, abstract, and often predictive internal or mental models of the problem at hand and use it to accomplish its work goals.

2. What Is Your Modeling Methodology?

A COGNET/iGEN model is assumed to represent an expert or near-expert strategy in a recurring type of problem area, and thus model development focuses on capturing such strategies from human experts. A range of development methods have been published, including a CTA-based method (Zachary et al., 1998), which combines in situ task performance with thinking-aloud data elicitation in an immediate replay of the task performance. The data arising from this process are systematically analyzed and aggregated to product the various components of an expertise model. Models are built in a top–down manner, which allows the level of granularity in the representation to be matched to that used in the strategy being modeled. The flexible granularity of the system, as described previously, enables this top–down process.

Models are authored in a graphical environment that allows easy access to different components of the expertise models in different windows, provides graphical icons for most expertise primitives, and allows outline-based management of expertise models for enhanced management of model complexity. The graphical environment also includes debugging, syntax/semantic checking, and execution tracing.

Models are typically validated in a Turing test-like manner by allowing domain experts (different than those used to create the model) to view model performance and compare/differentiate it from human performance.

3. What Role Does Parameter Tuning Play?

There are no organic parameters in the core or baseline COGNET/iGEN system. Three specific parameters were incorporated into the short-term memory model created as part of the learning mechanism in the extended version of the system created for AMBR Experiment 2. These parameters are readily interpretable as representations of short- and long-term memory decay and probability of fixation of single elements of information into long-term memory. The model predictions are moderately sensitive to specific values of these parameters. Initial values for these parameters were taken from the prior HOS system and tuned to the sample or tuning data provided in Experiment 2. Additional parameters were included within the AMBR expertise models via micromodels primarily to add variability in performance. Such parameters are estimated through analysis of the work/task environment, either dynamically (e.g., calculation of reach distances for use as parameters in Fitts law) or a priori (e.g., via a CTA such as that used to insert mental operators into an Keystroke Level Model; see Card, Moran, & Newell, 1980). Micromodel parameters are typically highly interpretable in terms of the underlying component model they implement. The learning mechanism within COGNET/iGEN has been used only in AMBR, but it is expected that any future use would be consistent with its use in AMBR. Micromodels are adapted to the specific work environment being modeled, but are typically used in a highly consistent way.

4. What Is Your Account of Individual Differences?

COGNET/iGEN presumes that in naturalistic settings, differences arising from domain knowledge and task strategy overwhelm any differences arising from individual differences in the cognitive system. Thus, the primary source of variability in COGNET/iGEN (and the only source in the baseline system) is in differences in the knowledge and strategy, which are encoded in the expertise model component of a COGNET/iGEN model. Within a given expertise model, individual variability (whether intra- or interindividual) is captured by micromodel subcomponents. Such micromodels compartmentalize and introduce model variability arising from sensorimotor mechanisms (e.g., reach/read errors), from situational moderators (e.g., effects of stress, workload, fatigue), as well as from individual differences in these two categories (e.g., differences in keystroke accuracy, differing sensitivities to workload).

5. What Is Your Account of Cognitive Workload?

Cognitive workload is defined as the (subjective) perception of the effect on the internal information-processing mechanisms of applying a specific work/task strategy and body of domain knowledge under a specific set of problem conditions. It is computed via an implicit process called *cognitive proprioception*, which perceives various kinds of activity of the cognitive, perceptual, and motor mechanisms in the COGNET/iGEN system. Cognitive proprioception makes the results of these self-perceptive processes available to the rest of the system via a metacognitive memory, which can be used to affect strategy selection. This was the case in all AMBR models. The COGNET/iGEN cognitive proprioception provides a range of low-level sensations of internal processes. In the AMBR models, these were combined into six individual dimensions reflecting the form of introspection sought on each of the six TLX workload scales.

6. What Is Your Account of Multitasking?

Multitasking is organic to COGNET/iGEN and is the main motivation for its initial development. COGNET/iGEN incorporates strong concurrence (i.e., simultaneous execution in simulation time) across the motor, perceptual, and cognitive systems. Within the cognitive system, units of procedural knowledge reflecting procedural expertise and strategy in a given task/domain are subject to weak concurrence. This allows multiple units to be activated and in various states of execution simultaneously, but with only one unit actually being executed by the cognitive process at a time. Other units may be interrupted, suspended awaiting some future knowledge state, or activated but awaiting an opportunity to begin execution. Interrupted cognitive activities that are resumed can be adapted to changes in the current context by metacognitive resumption strategies. More important, changes in memory caused by introduction of newly perceived information can lead to interruption of the currently executing cognitive unit by another. Thus, multitasking is pervasive and fully organic to the system, with no explicit multitasking mechanism required. It should be noted, however, that the ways in which the AMBR task environment was defined (e.g., uninterruptibility of unit tasks) forced a sequential process onto the work to be done and rendered most of these mechanisms irrelevant in AMBR.

7. What Is Your Account of Categorization?

Although categorization was the motivation of the AMBR Experiment 2 model, the learning task was expressed not as one of categorization, but rather as one of learning the boundary conditions on (disjunctive) action options, and this is how it was implemented in the COGNET/iGEN Experiment 2 system extensions. A boundary condition is learned by developing a hypothesis about a plausible condition given an action opportunity, testing the hypothesis via a trial action, and processing the (successful or unsuccessful) results. A learning strategy is used to create new hypotheses based on past results and accept certain hypotheses as assumed correct. The mechanism is sufficiently general to utilize learning strategies based on rules or instances, although the strategy used in AMBR Experiment 2 was based on rules. Because the task was designed to be only minimally meaningful to the subjects (or models) in AMBR, factors related to memory of present and past hypotheses were key in determining model performance. Thus, the limits in memory provided strong limits to learning speed and power. It would be expected, however, that such learning of boundary conditions on procedures in a naturalistic setting would lead to development of learning strategies that would circumvent such limits (see Ericsson & Delaney, 1999).

ACKNOWLEDGMENTS

The work reported here was funded by the Air Force Research Laboratory (AFRL) under contracts F33615-99-C-6007, F33615-99-C-6002 (through a subcontract to BBNT), and F33615-01-C-6078, for which we are grateful. The authors wish to thank Kevin Gluck and Mike Young from AFRL, Harold Hawkins from the Office of Naval Research (ONR), Ruth Willis from the Naval Research Laboratory (NRL), Wayne Gray from Rensselaer Polytechnic Institute, all the members of the AMBR evaluation teams, and all the members of the other modeling teams for their inputs and support during the development of the AMBR COGNET/iGEN models. The AMBR team meetings at the start and finish of each experiment were exciting events in which everyone learned from everyone else, and their absence at the conclusion of the project will be sorely missed. We also wish to thank all the people at CHI Systems who worked on the AMBR model development efforts, particularly Daniel Scolaro, Vassil Iordanov, and Larry Rosenzweig, and all who assisted with manuscript preparation, particularly Glenna Taylor and Christine Volk.

APPENDIX: COGNET PRINCIPLES OF OPERATION (COGNITIVE SUBSYSTEM)

COGNET/iGEN™ is a principled system in that its internal operation is governed by explicit principles that have evolved over time (and continue to do so). Although there are principles of operation for each of the three subsystems—cognitive, perceptual, and motor—only the cognitive subsystem principles are listed here. More complete discussion of the principles and their implications for the behavior of the iGEN™ software is contained within the iGEN™ documentation.

1. *Attention Focus*—At any point, the cognitive process executes, at most, one given rich procedural chunk—a cognitive task.

2. *Pattern-Based Attention Demand*—Each cognitive task is associated with one or more patterns of information in memory that trigger its activation as relevant to the current context. When such a triggering pattern is recognized, the cognitive task become active and vies for attention.

3. *Attention Capture*—Each cognitive task can estimate its own relative priority when triggered and while activated. Once activated, a cognitive task will capture the focus of attention if its priority exceeds all other active tasks.

4. *Task Interruption*—An executing cognitive task that loses the focus of attention through attention capture has been interrupted and continues to compete for attention.

5. *Cognitive Process Modification*—Cognitive operators within cognitive tasks can change the state of memory.

6. *Perceptual Process Modification*—Self-activating perceptual knowledge sources called *perceptual demons* can change the state of memory when executed by the perceptual process.

7. *Multiple-Task Instances*—A cognitive task may be activated for execution in the context of a specific piece of knowledge in memory. Such a cognitive task may have multiple active instances, each instance reflecting a unique knowledge context called a *scope*. Multiple cognitive task instances compete for attention as if they were separate cognitive tasks.

8. *Task Suspension*—A cognitive task may relinquish attention based on the knowledge contained in it and the state of memory. On such suspension, all remaining active cognitive tasks vie for attention, and the suspended cognitive task sets a resumption condition that determines when it is reactivated and resumes competing for attention.

REFERENCES

Broadbent, D. (1958). *Perception and communications.* New York: Pergamon.

Card, S., Moran, T., & Newell, A. (1980). The Keystroke-Level Model for user performance time with interactive systems. *Communications of the ACM, 23,* 396–410.

Card, S., Moran, T., & Newell, A. (1983). *The psychology of human–computer interaction.* Hillsdale, NJ: Lawrence Erlbaum Associates.

Carver, N., & Lesser, V. (1994). Evolution of blackboard control architectures. *Expert Systems with Applications, 7*(1), 1–30.

Chi, M., Glaser, R., & Farr, M. (1988). *The nature of expertise.* Hillsdale, NJ: Lawrence Erlbaum Associates.

Doane, S. M., Sohn, Y. W., & Jodlowski, M. (2004). Pilot ability to anticipate the consequences of flight actions as a function of expertise. *Human Factors, 46*(1), 92–103.

Ericsson, K., & Delaney, P. (1999). Long-term working memory as an alternative to capacity models of working memory in everyday skilled performance. In A. Miyake & P. Shah (Eds.), *Models of working memory* (pp. 257–297). Cambridge, England: Cambridge University Press.

Ericsson, K., & Kinsch, W. (1995). Long-term working memory. *Psychological Review, 102*(2), 211–245.

Ericcson, K., & Smith, J. (Ed.). (1991). *Toward a general theory of expertise: Prospects and limits.* Cambridge, England: Cambridge University Press.

Erman, D., Hayes-Roth, F., Lesser, V., & Reddy, D. (1980). The HEARSAY-II speech understanding system: Integrating knowledge to resolve uncertainty. *ACM Computing Survey, 12,* 213–253.

Estes, W. (2002). Traps in the route to models of memory and decision. *Psychonomic Bulletin & Review, 9*(1), 3–25.

Flach, J., & Hoffman, R. (2003). The limitations of limitations. *IEEE Intelligent Systems, 18*(1), 94–96.

Glenn, F. (1989). The case for micro-models. In *Proceedings of Human Factors Society 33rd annual meeting,* HFES, Santa Monica, CA.

Glenn, F., Schwartz, S., & Ross, L. (1992). *Development of a Human Operator Simulator Version V (HOS-V): Design and implementation* (Research Note 92-PERI-POX). Alexandria, VA: Army Research Institute.

Gray, W. D. (2000). The nature and processing of errors in interactive behavior. *Cognitive Science, 24,* 205–248.

Hart, S., & Staveland, L. (1988). Development of NASA-TLX (Task Load Index): Results of empirical and theoretical research. In P. Hancock & N. Meshkati (Eds.), *Human mental workload* (pp. 139–183). Amsterdam: North-Holland.

Hayes-Roth, B. (1985). A blackboard architecture for control. *Artificial Intelligence, 26,* 251–321.

Kieras, D., & Meyer, D. (1995). *An overview of the EPIC architecture for cognition and performance with application to human-computer interaction* (EPIC Tech. Rep. No. 5). Ann Arbor, MI: University of Michigan.

Klein, G. (1989). Recognition-primed decisions. In W. B. Rouse (Ed.), *Advances in man-machine systems research* (Vol. 5, pp. 47–92). Greenwich, CT: JAI Press.

Kolodner, J. (1988). *Proceedings of the case-based reasoning workshop.* San Mateo, CA: Morgan Koffman.

Lane, N. (1987). *Skill acquisition rates and patterns: Issues and training implications.* New York: Springer-Verlag.

Lane, N., Strieb, M., Glenn, F., & Wherry, R. (1981). The Human Operator Simulator: An overview. In J. Moraal & K.-F. Kraiss (Eds.), *Manned systems design: Methods, equipment, and applications* (pp. 121–152). New York: Plenum.

Newell, A. (1990). *Unified theories of cognition.* Cambridge, MA: Harvard University Press.

Nii, P. (1986a). Blackboard systems: The blackboard model of problem solving and the evolution of blackboard architectures, Part One. *AI Magazine, 7*(2), 38–53.

Nii, P. (1986b). Blackboard systems: The blackboard model of problem solving and the evolution of blackboard architectures, Part Two. *AI Magazine, 7*(3), 82–106.

Nosofsky, R. M., Palmeri, T. J., & McKinley, S. C. (1994). Rule plus exception model of classification learning. *Psychological Review, 101,* 53–79.

Pew, R., & Mavor, A. (1998). *Modeling human and organizational behavior.* Washington, DC: National Academy Press.

Reiger, C. (1977). Spontaneous computation in cognitive models. *Cognitive Science, 1*(3), 315–354.

Seamster, T. L., Redding, R. E., Cannon, J. R., Ryder, J. M., & Purcell, J. A. (1993). Cognitive task analysis of expertise in air traffic control. *International Journal of Aviation Psychology, 3*(4), 257–283.

Selfridge, O. (1959). Pandemonium: A paradigm for learning. In *Proceedings of the Symposium on the Mechanization of Thought Processes* (pp. 511–529). London: H. M. Stationery Office.

Shepard, R. N., Hovland, C. L., & Jenkins, H. M. (1961). Learning and memorization of classifications. *Psychological Monographs, 75*(13, Whole No. 517).

Sohn, Y. W., & Doane, S. M. (2003). Roles of working memory capacity and long-term working memory skill in complex task performance. *Memory and Cognition, 31*(3), 458–466.

Sohn, Y. W., & Doane, S. M. (in press). Memory processes of flight situation awareness: Interactive roles of working memory capacity, long-term working memory, and expertise. *Human Factors.*

VanLehn, K. (1996). Cognitive skill acquisition. *Annual Review of Psychology, 47,* 513–539.

Waugh, N. C., & Norman, D. A. (1965). Primary memory. *Psychological Review, 72,* 89–104.

Wherry, R. (1969). The development of sophisticated models of man-machine system performance. In *Symposium on Applied Models of Man-Machine Systems Performance* (Report No. NR-69H-591). Columbus, OH: North American Aviation.

Wood, R. E. (1986). Task complexity: Definition of the construct. *Organizational Behavior and Human Decision Processes, 37,* 60–82.

Woods, D. (1988). *Coping with complexity: The psychology of human behaviour in complex systems. Tasks, errors, and mental models.* New York: Taylor & Francis.

Zachary, W., & Le Mentec, J.-C. (1999). A framework for developing intelligent agents based on human information processing architecture. In *Proceedings of the IASTED International Conference on Artificial Intelligence and Soft Computing* (pp. 427–431). Anaheim: IASTED/Acta Press.

Zachary, W., & Le Mentec, J.-C. (2000). Incorporating metacognitive capabilities in synthetic cognition systems. In *Proceedings of the Ninth Conference on Computer Generated Forces and Behavioral Representation* (pp. 513–521). Orlando: Institute for Simulation and Training.

Zachary, W., Le Mentec, J.-C., & Glenn, F. (2000). *Developing computational models of metacognition in support of manning reduction technology* (Tech. Rep. 000115.9705). Lower Gwynedd, PA: CHI Systems.

Zachary, W., Le Mentec, J.-C., & Iordanov, V. (2001). Generating subjective workload self-assessment from a cognitive model. In *Proceedings of the Fourth International Conference on Cognitive Modeling,* Fairfax, VA.

Zachary, W., Ryder, J., & Hicinbothom, J. (1998). Cognitive task analysis and modeling of decision making in complex environments. In J. Cannon-Bowers & E. Salas (Eds.), *Making decisions under stress* (pp. 315–344). Washington, DC: American Psychological Association.

Zachary, W., Ryder, J., Hicinbothom, J., Santarelli, T., Scolaro, J., Szczepkowksi, M., & Cannon-Bowers, J. (1998). Simulating behavior of tactical operators and teams using COGNET/GINA. In *Proceedings of the Seventh Conference on Computer Generated Forces and Behavioral Representation.* Orlando, FL: Institute for Simulation and Training.

Zachary, W., Ryder, J., Ross, L., & Weiland, M. (1992). Intelligent computer-human interaction in real-time, multi-tasking process control and monitoring systems. In M. Helander & M. Nagamachi (Eds.), *Human factors in design for manufacturability* (pp. 377–401). New York: Taylor & Francis.

Zachary, W., Ryder, J., Santarelli, T., & Weiland, M. (2000). Applications for executable cognitive models: A case study approach. In *Proceedings of the Human Factor & Ergonomics Society 44th annual meeting.* Santa Monica, CA: HFES.

Zachary, W., Santarelli, T., Ryder, J., Stokes, J., & Scolaro, D. (2000). *Developing a multi-tasking cognitive agent using the COGNET/iGEN integrative architecture* (Tech. Rep. 001004.9915). Spring House, PA: CHI Systems.

Chapter 6

Distributed Cognition and Situated Behavior

Robert G. Eggleston
Air Force Research Laboratory

Katherine L. McCreight
N-Space Analysis

Michael J. Young
Air Force Research Laboratory

Computer simulations of humans and machines interacting in work situations are increasingly being used in a variety of ways. They are beginning to take on a larger role in the exploration and evaluation of new operational concepts in business and business markets; to help develop and hone human skills under complex, extreme, and hazardous work situations; and to investigate the design implications of advanced technologies and their interactions with humans in complex, often open-ended work situations. To support these advances in computer simulations, corresponding advances are needed in modeling the work knowledge, skills, and abilities of software actors who serve as human surrogates in these increasingly complex simulated environments.

We have recently embarked on a research and development program to address the growing need to improve the ability to rapidly produce human-like software agents that can make intelligent adjustments in the evolving and complex work situation. Our system, known as the Distributed Cognition (DCOG) framework, takes the position that cognitive abilities are distributed throughout the mind. One of the main tenets of the DCOG design philosophy is that cognition is best modeled by a distributed, state change system. This stands in contrast to a classical information-processing metaphor that treats information as distinct from the structural architecture of the mind system. In the information-processing view, information is considered to enter the system and is subsequently processed and transformed to produce the output. In contrast, according to the state change view, mind states give rise to information based on energetic stimulation from other local mind regions and the external environment. Complex adaptive behavior arises from the coordination of a variety of mind regions that operate under local control.

In this chapter, we introduce the DCOG research program by describing two related behavioral models that are able to perform complex work in a simulated world. The models were developed as part of the Air Force Research Laboratory's project on Agent-Based Modeling and Human Representation (AMBR).

We begin with a general sketch of the DCOG modeling paradigm, which includes a brief discussion of our theory of cognition. The original DCOG model, DCOG-1, is described next. The presentation covers a description of the model components, operation, and performance in a simulated air traffic management work domain. Comments on model behavior, parameters, parameter tuning, and design methods are included. This is followed by a similar discussion of the second model, DCOG-2, that emphasizes associative learning and adaptive learning strategies. We conclude the chapter with a general discussion that contains a brief outline of future research and a summary of basic features of the DCOG models.

THE DCOG FRAMEWORK

DCOG is a framework for the design and development of software actors that emulate skillful human behavior and performance. It involves the coordination of sensory, perceptual, cognitive, and motor resources that are organized as a complex dynamical system. We speculate that the architecture of the mind consists of an integration of a system of systems. As a minimum, we postulate that there is a system which is organized to provide behavior from a sensory point of view, a second system that provides behavior from a perceptual point of view, and two other systems that provide behavior from a cognitive and motor point of view, respectively. All of these systems are integrated, under distributed control, to yield the range of skills and adaptive abilities of human behavior.

We refer to this system of systems view as a *mind system*. It treats sensory-, perceptual-, cognitive-, and motor-guided behavior as high-level functional properties of the mind. Because our treatment of each of these systems is not fully developed here, we often speak of them as functional mind regions or centers because they have not yet been developed as full-fledged interactive systems.

Many human work tasks of interest involve a combination of perceptual and cognitive processing. This is certainly true for the air traffic management task used in this study. Given this nature of many complex work tasks, we have elected to emphasize perceptual and cognitive aspects of the mind system in our initial DCOG development work. For the initial research, we concentrated on the development of a basic distributed control architecture to effect control for the entire mind system and placed major emphasis on modeling the cognitive region. We then developed a perception-oriented mind region and included a learning structure that integrated perception with cognition, which supported flexible and adaptive mental behavior. Although neither implementation fully reflects the envisioned DCOG architecture, they are able to illustrate some important aspects of our theory in its current state of development.

In this section, we provide a general overview of the current DCOG research. We focus on three major characteristics of the mind system and show how specific software implementations begin to supply these desired factors. The three main characteristics are outlined in the first column of Table 6.1 in terms of defining properties of the mind system. Entries in Columns 2 and 3 indicate in general terms how these characteristics are implemented in the DCOG-1 and DCOG-2 models, respectively.

Our goal for the DCOG architecture is to develop a system in which both knowledge and control are distributed within an associative, state change framework (Goals 1 and 2 in Table 6.1). We believe this architecture will enable the modeling of flexible, adaptive behavior in complex cognitive tasks (Goal 3 in Table 6.1). Adaptive behavior includes both differences

TABLE 6.1
Characteristics of the DCOG Architecture

Research Goal	DCOG-1	DCOG-2
1. Control		
a. Distributed	Four agents	Six agents
	Broadcast messages	Messages and procedures
b. State change	—	—
2. Memory/knowledge		
a. Distributed	Agent-specific knowledge	Agent-specific knowledge
b. Associative	—	Associative categorization
1. Perceptual objects	—	Perceptual memory
2. Symbolic objects	—	Symbolic memory
3. Flexible/adaptive behavior		
a. Individual differences, expertise	Variable: **process-two** (influences work processing pattern)	Personality variables for decision-making mode **patience** **tolerance**
b. Strategy shifts, work-centered behavior	Variable: **worry-factor** (influences work processing pattern)	Meta-cognitive measures: hypothesis evaluation mode shifting

across individuals and the different strategies that may be chosen by one individual at different times. As Table 6.1 shows, the current models are only partial implementations of this framework. The state change aspect of the framework is only implemented implicitly in the current DCOG models. Near the end of the chapter, we discuss our plans for making this feature explicit in future models. Each current implementation of the DCOG framework is discussed in turn.

Architecturally, the main feature of the proposed DCOG framework is the distribution of both knowledge and control among agents representing various mind regions. DCOG-1 takes the first step in this direction, distributing control among four independent agents. Distributed control is also effected through message posting. All agents are able to attend to messages created by the simulation or other agents; messages are not sent to specific destinations. The code for each agent determines which messages it will process. Because messages are broadcast in this manner, we do not have one agent directly supervising the activity of another agent. (The second model, DCOG-2, relies somewhat more on procedural control; see the DCOG-2 Model Section.)

Knowledge is partially distributed in DCOG-1. Some knowledge is shared among agents, through global data structures and broadcast messages, whereas other knowledge is distributed among the agents. For example, all agents are able to access a plane data structure, which contains information about the aircraft's current location, heading, and color. However, some data structures are specific to individual agents; this represents knowledge held by that agent alone. For example, the schema agent contains an inbound aircraft schema, which encodes the sequence of events required to process the aircraft. Additionally, only one agent, radar agent, pays direct attention to the radar screen on the air traffic control (ATC) console; the other agents rely on information created by the radar agent.

Another goal of the DCOG architecture is to implement knowledge as an associative system. However, to meet the time line established for the initial AMBR comparison study, we deferred incorporating associative coding into the architecture until later in the AMBR project. For the first implementation, DCOG-1, knowledge was coded procedurally. For example, when working with an inbound aircraft, the schema agent first identifies the current state of the aircraft based on the plane data structure and the system-provided messages and radar states (e.g., the aircraft is inbound from the north, the nose of the aircraft has touched the border, and the aircraft has not yet been welcomed). The schema agent then consults the inbound aircraft schema to determine the next appropriate step (e.g., welcome).

The DCOG-1 code includes two variables that address individual differences in behavior. The process-two variable models the difference between subject behavior that prefers to maintain vigilance, checking the radar screen after each action, and subject behavior that stresses getting the task done fast, processing two aircraft before returning to a scan of the radar screen. In other words, the actor either alternates information collection (eye scans) and aircraft servicing actions or elects to service multiple aircraft in a batch before systematically rescanning the work field. The worry-factor variable tracks the number of aircraft about to need service. It serves to invoke a directed gaze procedure that acts as a short cut in evaluating the state of the work field in terms of aircraft service needs. Rather than systematically scanning the entire field, the actor uses memory to guide a directed gaze at a known impending service event to more rapidly initiate aircraft service activity. This procedure tends to be invoked when the actor is anticipating that many aircraft service events are likely to occur in a small time window. Process-two and worry-factor work together to increase attention to areas in which the subject anticipates a number of required actions in the near future. Individual difference variables play a minor role in DCOG-1; individual differences are addressed in a more comprehensive way in DCOG-2.

The DCOG-2 implementation builds on the distributed control established in DCOG-1 and adds both associative memory and more flexible, adaptive behavior. Associative memory guides learning and decision making in the altitude request task, allowing both emergent decision making based on direct associations (perceptual objects) and deductive decision making based on symbol-mediated associations. For example, if the quality, small aircraft is consistently associated with reject, the model learns to reject altitude requests from small aircraft: The concept {reject —— small aircraft} emerges from the structure of association links. This may be regarded as a form of perceptual learning. However, the model learns more complex concepts like {reject —— (small aircraft AND low turbulence) } by forming symbolic nodes to represent the complex condition (small aircraft AND low turbulence) and associating these nodes with accept or reject. The symbolic node and concomitant associations form a model of hypothesis formation.

Flexible, adaptive behavior emerges from the interaction of personality variables in DCOG-2. We assume that human subjects vary in their preferred mode of decision making (e.g., emergent vs. deductive). We also assume that subjects monitor their performance and may shift to a different strategy if the original strategy fails to yield a successful categorization. We assume that subjects differ in their patience in seeking a correct categorization and in their tolerance of exceptions to a generalization. The DCOG-2 code provides personality variables to model individual differences in decision-making mode, patience, and tolerance, as well as measures to model subjects' metacognitive awareness of the effectiveness of their decisions. These measures include the overall proportion of correct answers, as well as evaluation of the predictive value of specific hypotheses. The model begins by reasoning in the preferred mode, monitors its own performance, and shifts strategy when the proportion of failures exceeds the model's patience and tolerance values.

For the DCOG-2 implementation, we created a set of models with varying personality traits and aggregated them to create the overall results. To determine the appropriate mix of model personalities, we examined individual human subject results and attempted to model the individuals' preferred decision-making modes. The personality variables offer interesting ways to approach expert–novice differences in terms of reliance on hypothesis formation versus emergent recognition of patterns. We hope to explore these possibilities in future research. No attempt was made to distinguish expert decision making within DCOG-2 because all human subjects were assumed to have similar levels of expertise.

Our emphasis on strategic behavior reflects our goal to model work-centered behavior. Following the methods of cognitive systems engineering (Rasmussen, 1983, 1986; Rasmussen et al., 1994; Vicente, 1999), we analyze the task in terms of features of the work domain, control tasks, and work strategies.

Rasmussen defined a *strategy* as a category of procedures (see Vicente, 1999). From this view, the notion of a strategy is taken to be a structural concept. It is a mode or frame that identifies a "way to think" about the task that guides or shapes goal-directed activity. This structural definition of strategy is in contrast to other definitions that either define it as an end state to be achieved (goal or intention) or a process or procedure that leads to the desired end state. The structural definition of strategy emphasizes the idea that a goal-driven problem can be framed in different ways, and that the frame both guides and focuses activity without invoking a fixed process or procedure. In this sense, a strategy operates at a higher cognitive level than a simple goal-driven process, setting a way to view the problem situation as a whole. As a result, a strategy does not constrain actor behavior to follow a fixed goal-driven process.

A person may have knowledge of several strategies that are applicable to any given task. As the situation in which a task is embedded changes, an expert may notice when it is advisable to shift from one strategic frame to another. For example, in a study of air traffic controllers, Sperandio (1978) discovered shifts in structural strategies as a function of mental workload induced by the density of aircraft that defined the airspace situation.

We identified three structural strategies or thinking frames for the overall ATC task situation: one where the actor had a sense of staying ahead, another where she or he was falling behind, and a third involving full stop recovery that would be used after feeling overwhelmed and out of control.

For the ATC task specified for this experiment, the staying ahead strategy was sufficient to guide work behavior. The staying ahead situation was therefore the only one implemented for both DCOG-1 and DCOG-2. However, the categorization subtask provided enough difficulty to induce strategy shifting with respect to that particular task. Accordingly, strategy shifting is an important part of the DCOG-2 model described later.

Our ultimate goal is to develop the DCOG architecture as a system of systems within a state change computational framework, in which knowledge and behavior are both modeled as changes in the states of different mind systems. Because the current model implementation does not yet fully conform to this view, except analogically, we defer discussion of the state change architecture until later.

DCOG-1 MODEL IMPLEMENTATION

We now turn attention to a more detailed discussion of the DCOG-1 and DCOG-2 implementations. The initial implementation of the DCOG framework involved the creation of a behavior model of an actor intended to work in a simulated air traffic management environment. We implemented the DCOG actor as a network of four software agents, as indicated earlier, that contain different knowledge forms and exercise local processing that sets up a coordinated behavior flow. It is able to successfully accomplish multitasking work in terms of managing the flow of aircraft in and out of the designated airspace under different density conditions, and in a manner that is similar in behavior and outcome performance as that shown by humans who accomplished the same work in a simulated microworld.

We had modest goals for our first actor-level behavior model. The basic goal was to demonstrate the employment of strategic thinking in a distributed control and distributed knowledge architecture (Goals 1a and 2a in Table 6.1). We also wanted to develop a strategy-guided, flexible, and adaptable model of cognitive behavior (Goal 3b) while supporting individual differences in performance (Goal 3a). DCOG-1 achieves distributed control and incorporates strategic features that enable some flexible behavior.

We begin the discussion with an overview of the air traffic management work environment. The model, known as the DCOG-1 actor, was tasked with managing air traffic flow for an airspace sector. This involves handling both arriving and exiting aircraft, as well as responding to requests from aircraft within the sector. Both the air traffic environment and the air traffic management workstation are provided by a discrete event simulation. The workstation consisted of a radar display that depicted a central airspace region and smaller portions of the four (north, south, east, and west) adjacent regions and three message displays. Aircraft icons represented airplanes transiting through the airspace. The ATC manager had to accept airplanes into its sector when requested by an adjacent ATC manager. It was also standard practice to welcome the airplane into the sector by calling the aircraft commander. For outbound traffic leaving the central sector, the ATC manager must ask the gaining center for permission to hand off control of the aircraft to it. Once granted, the manager must also contact the aircraft commander to give it permission to proceed. Messages for accepting and welcoming an aircraft and transferring and contacting outbound aircraft are posted on the separate message panels. While inside the sector, an aircraft may request permission to change speed. The ATC manager accepts this request if there is no traffic directly in front of the requesting airplane; otherwise the request is denied.

Work in this environment is complex for several reasons. First, many aircraft may simultaneously be in or approaching a service state. In what order should they be serviced? Second, there are limited time windows for servicing. For example, an outgoing aircraft cannot be serviced for a transfer until its nose touches the inner marker approaching the gaining sector, and the contact service must be complete before the outer maker is reached. Penalty points are accrued if the aircraft must wait at the border. Third, there is a possibility for negative transfer across the response procedure used for a welcome service event as opposed to the accept, transfer, and contact events. A four-step response is required in the latter cases, whereas only a three-step response is involved for the former subtask. Negative transfer comes into play because the three-step procedure completely overlaps elements of the longer four-step one. A more detailed description of the work environment, penalty point scheme for aircraft delays and other factors, and the level of human training is provided in chapter 2.

The DCOG-1 actor served as the ATC manager for the center airspace sector. The model had to interact with the simulation and operate the workstation console in the same manner as the human participants in the AMBR study. To accomplish the ATC work, the DCOG-1 model had to collect information from the work environment, detect aircraft service conditions, decide how to best provide service over the set of aircraft, and perform service in the environment one aircraft at a time. Our primary design task, therefore, was to create a cognitive architecture for the DCOG-1 actor.

For our design, we focused on crafting an internal cognitive process distributed among separate agents that comprised the DCOG-1 actor. These agents operate in parallel and encompass different kinds of knowledge. They communicate via messages and shared data structures. Shared data structures represent the current state of the system, while messages call attention to significant changes in the system. Messages also serve to coordinate the interactions of the agents.

Some messages are generated from the input to the system, whereas other messages are created by the agents, representing their own internal processing capability. Messages are not directed to any one agent, but are visible to all agents; an agent notices a message if the agent has an appropriate with-signal command (see How DCOG-1 Senses the Simulation World section).

In addition to messages, the DCOG-1 model uses globally accessible data structures to share information among agents. These include structures that represent information about aircraft, panel messages from the simulation environment, and learned aircraft processing procedures. The dynamic interplay of these agents provides a way to model human memory, task awareness, and strategic thinking in the process of achieving ATC work.

We sketch the model in terms of its implementation, noting psychological attributes along the way. First, the individual model components are described. We then show the model in action as a whole by way of walking through a single thread of work. In describing the specifics of the model components, we consider these questions:

- How does DCOG-1 sense the simulated world?
- How does DCOG-1 form, store, update, and use knowledge?
- How does DCOG-1 think strategically?
- How does DCOG-1 develop responses to the simulated world?

How Does DCOG-1 Sense the Simulated World?

The DCOG model was developed using the Distributed Operator Model Architecture (DOMAR), which is an agent system development tool written on top (as macroextensions) of Lisp (cf. http://omar.bbn.com/ for a full description of the DOMAR system). This system was used to create the ATC task and environment. The DOMAR system implements agents as separate threads of execution within a Lisp image. Computational primitives are provided to create, destroy, and communicate among agents. The signal-event form is used to send messages to other agents. The with-signal form enables an agent to "hear" messages that match the antecedent clause of the form. When a with-signal is triggered, the "hearing" agent then executes the behavior described in the rest of the clause.

The signal-event-external and with-signal-external forms are used to communicate externally. They work in a similar manner to the internal forms, but in addition they wrap the message in a manner that allows it to be exported (or imported) via a socket or high-level architecture federation.

The DCOG-1 model uses four agents: radar agent, schema agent, exec agent, and action agent. The agents differ in which messages they attend to, what knowledge they maintain, and what actions they take.

DCOG-1 uses a radar agent to collect environmental information and store it in a manner accessible to the other agents. Radar agent "listens" for messages from the ATC simulation. It responds to system messages such as *init-ac, update-ac,* and *communication-event,* which communicate information about the position and velocity of the aircraft on the ATC radar screen and the messages appearing on the three message panels of the ATC console. Radar agent stores this information in two data structures, plane and mess, that represent aircraft and message information. These are scenario (global) variables and can be accessed by the other DCOG agents.

How Does DCOG-1 Store, Update, and Use Knowledge?

Each of the four agents in DCOG-1 contains a local memory. Interactions across the agents account for the use of memory in performing the traffic management work. The radar agent provides two memory functions. First, the raw data items (e.g., ac name, ac color) made available from the simulation are stored in the manner of an iconic memory. Second, based on prior learning, work-relevant concepts are continuously formed and stored as the simulated world is updated. Simple work-relevant concepts are represented as memory elements, such as ac-velocity, ac-leaving, and ac-arriving. These knowledge elements are computed for each update cycle by the radar agent and encoded in a data structure that is accessible to schema agent and exec agent.

We provide the schema agent with schema data structures that represent symbolic knowledge about the work domain. This models the knowledge a human actor would have acquired during training and general experience with that work domain. A basic structure is provided for the knowledge of the five elemental work tasks (accept ac, welcome ac, transfer ac, contact ac, and speed request). The general form of the knowledge expression for an accept task is: <center X> accepting <aircraft Y>. The schema agent fills in the two variables based on knowledge broadcast by the radar agent. A separate specific schema form is made for each aircraft service condition.

The exec agent contains knowledge about how to process each elemental task and knowledge about the global work situation. Each procedural step that needs to be executed to operate the workstation to service an elemental event is encoded as a separate knowledge element. To provide a welcome service, for example, requires the actor to complete three steps: select welcome button, select desired ac, and select send button. Each of these expressions represents a unit of knowledge—a high-level concept. Internal processes in the exec agent allow it to form the action steps appropriate for any selected service to be provided. The exec agent also includes work knowledge that is relevant to organizing the work pattern over all air traffic defining a current situation. We assume that human subjects learn the advantage of sorting aircraft in terms of severity of action condition; this knowledge is modeled in exec agent by a procedure that sorts aircraft into three groups. Each aircraft in or near a service condition is placed on one of three stacks expressing overdue service, new service need, and anticipated service need, respectively. Aircraft are ordered in terms of service severity on each stack.

The action agent contains knowledge about how to interact with the simulated workstation. It is responsible for achieving actor behavior in the external world. Its knowledge includes expressions for operating the workstation to implement each specific response procedure. Expressions are of the form: GUI-button-push <welcome AC>.

In summary, each agent contains data structures that emulate knowledge states. Selected knowledge states are activated by signals gathered from the simulation and other agents in the network. The centers differ in the forms of knowledge that they contain and in their special processing capabilities.

How Does DCOG-1 Think Strategically?

One of our goals for the DCOG framework is to develop models in which cognition is situated in the work environment. We discuss the strategic properties of DCOG-1 in this context.

By nature, work is goal directed. Individual actors may approach work in different ways. In particular, highly skilled actors differ from less skilled actors in their approach to work. We are interested in modeling the work behavior of such experts. It has been suggested by Rasmussen et al. (1994) that experts approach work by employing a strategy. A strategy is different from a detailed plan for working or from a specified step-by-step work procedure. Rather a strategy reflects an interpretation of the evolving work situation relative to a guiding framework. The framework acts as an organization structure for action taking. As a result, it is less rigid than a plan or procedure, and thus it is more amenable to supporting flexible and adaptive behavior. Experts may make a shift in strategy based on how well the actor believes work is progressing. If a significant change in the environment occurs, such as a rapid influx of several aircraft, the expert may believe service delays are unavoidable without a change in strategy. Experts may have learned several appropriate strategies that can be flexibly deployed based on the external environmental situation relative to the actor's internal cognitive environment situation (cf. Sperandio, 1978).

In the DCOG framework, we model a strategy as an implicit organizing state that spans the activities of several local agents. An interaction across distributed processes and knowledge sources gives rise to the basic work strategy in a manner that supports adaptive adjustments to local conditions.

The DCOG architecture can support a variety of global work strategies. Our analysis of the ATC work led us to consider three work strategies based on the subject's sense of workload and task success: staying-ahead, falling-behind, and recovery. We subsequently determined that only one work strategy, staying-ahead, was needed to model the behavior of the skill level of human participants in the AMBR study (see DCOG-1 Model Evaluation section).

Within the staying-ahead strategy, the DCOG-1 model invokes a process-one strategy to guide the interaction between eye movements and service activities. Recall that the radar agent uses eye movements to acquire data from the environment, whereas the exec and schema agents determine the actions necessary to service air traffic. According to the process-one strategy, a new situational update is interspersed between the servicing of each aircraft. The model scans the environment, determines the work situation, selects the most appropriate elemental task event to service, initiates service, and then starts another eye movement scan of the environment.

This work process is under distributed control across the schema and exec agents using data provided by the radar agent. Both the schema and exec agents can issue an eye movement command. Because of other processing internal to the schema agent and the exec agent, the strategy can be applied in a flexible manner, creating temporary shifts in processing behavior.

We model temporary shifts in processing behavior through two variables—worry-factor and process-two. The worry-factor variable models the shift in behavior of a human agent who anticipates having to complete several actions in the near future: The subject begins to pay more attention to the anticipated action items. In the current experiment, anticipated work occurs when an aircraft approaches a border: The agent knows the aircraft will soon need to be transferred, but the agent cannot complete this work until the aircraft actually reaches the border. Worry-factor encodes a subject's reaction to having a large number of aircraft about to need service. When the model is not worried, it routinely scans the radar screen and message panels for new situations. When the number of aircraft about to need service exceeds the worry-factor value, a directed gaze procedure is invoked, and the model starts watching for the indications that the aircraft are ready to be serviced. The model pays more attention to the specific sectors of the radar screen and the specific message panels that will indicate the changes, and, consequently, it pays less attention to information accruing in other areas. For example, if the model has noticed a large number of inbound aircraft, it will start watching the inbound panel for accept queries instead of scanning the entire screen.

The process-two variable is designed to model the varied reactions of human agents to situations in which several aircraft are in need of service. The variable was not exploited in the current experiment, but was held constant. However, we mention it here as an example of the type of variation possible in the DCOG system. When process-two is true, the model acts on two serviceable aircraft before conducting another scan of the environment; this reflects a human agent who is concerned with quickly clearing the list of serviceable aircraft. When process-two is false, the model checks the environment after each action; this reflects a human agent who is more concerned with monitoring developing situations. This strategic variation could model intrinsic variation across subjects or strategic shifts by one subject. For the AMBR experiment, we have maintained process-two as false for the main aircraft processing procedure. Thus, all of our DCOG-1 actors share the preference to process one aircraft and then make a routine scan as the basic strategy.

The worry-factor and process-two variables provide a relatively simple means for the DCOG actor to make flexible adjustments in deploying the implicit work strategy. These features also provide a limited means to model individual differences in work behavior. Our second DCOG model takes up the issues of strategy shifting and individual differences in greater detail (see DCOG-2 Model section).

How Does DCOG-1 Respond to the World?

The exec agent has procedures that encode the order of tasks for processing an aircraft. This represents knowledge that a human actor would have gained from prior experience. The agent uses this knowledge to choose an action message, which is then picked up and acted on by the action agent.

DCOG-1 Work Thread Walk Through

A flavor of the behavior of the DCOG-1 model is perhaps best gained by inspecting a process sequence for selecting and processing an airplane for servicing. Here we present a brief process walk through of the model as a way to provide more detailed information about its behavior. It illustrates the two eye movement patterns available to the actor and other information about global work knowledge not covered previously.

The actor initiates coordinated behavior with an eye scan under the control of the schema agent. The eye scan simulates the pickup of information from the environment that has been stored in the radar agent. (The radar agent updates its image of the environment every five ticks of simulation time.) The eye scan pattern concentrates on the four boundary zones around the airspace sector being worked by the DCOG-1 actor. One boundary region is covered in each scan element. This approximates a parafoveal field of view for each eye fixation for the viewing conditions used in the AMBR study. The raw data contained in these regions and the conceptual knowledge formed by the radar agent are sorted and stored by aircraft trouble regions (identified as arriving-east, leaving-east, arriving-north, leaving-north, arriving-west, leaving-west, arriving-south, and leaving-south). Eye scanning continues to the three message panels, each serving as a point of fixation, and the latest message posted to the panel is made available. Messages that signal a simulation world state are separated by an indentation pattern from messages that provide feedback on service actions taken by the actor. The data structure in the radar agent encodes knowledge about the aircraft (ac name, position, velocity, and display color), the message text strings (e.g., accepting VIR199?), the panel on which the message appears, and the speaker of the message (i.e., the sending ATC center). At the completion of a regular eye scan, the schema agent broadcasts a scan-complete-event message, which triggers processing by the exec agent. The exec agent determines the highest priority aircraft, takes appropriate action, and calls on schema agent to conduct another scan.

The sequence of events required to successfully process an inbound aircraft is shown in Table 6.2, where the actions of the system and the DCOG actor are represented by the messages posted to the inbound panel of the workstation. The schema agent associates arriving-<direction> knowledge with the aircraft-name knowledge (VIR199) contained in the radar agent and uses it to develop the accepting VIR199 schema.

The sequence of events required to successfully process an outbound aircraft is shown in Table 6.3, where the actions of the system and the DCOG-1 model are represented by the messages posted to the outbound panel and also the location of the aircraft on the radar screen.

In this case, the nose-touch border concept is simulated as being derived from the radar screen by the radar agent, whereas the outbound text mes-

TABLE 6.2
Event Sequence for Inbound Aircraft

System	DCOG-1 Actor
Inbound panel	**Inbound panel**
Accept VIR199?	
	Accepting VIR199

TABLE 6.3
Event Sequence for Outbound Aircraft

System		DCOG-1 Actor
Radar screen	*Outbound panel*	*Outbound panel*
Nose touches border		
		EAST accept UAL244?
	EAST accepting UAL244	

sages are read directly from the environment by the radar agent. The <center>accept<aircraft> schema is populated with data made available by the radar agent. The exec agent forms the procedure for accomplishing this elemental task and triggers the action agent to complete the task in the simulated world (see Table 6.4).

Information about the set of tasks required to process inbound, outbound, or speed request aircraft is contained both in the schema created by schema agent and in the procedures used by exec agent.

For each aircraft being processed, schema agent creates a schema data structure with a set of variables representing each step of the process. Schema agent updates these variables as information from the environment (mediated by radar agent) shows the aircraft progressing. A panel message indicating a speed request causes schema agent to create a speed schema for the relevant aircraft; speed schema contain information about the processing of a speed request.

Exec agent uses the schema variables to determine the next appropriate action. Exec agent also updates the schema variables to reflect its actions.

The variables within the schema data structure are not temporally ordered. Exec agent's determination of the next action in the sequence is based on procedural definitions such as: If an outbound aircraft's nose has touched the border and it has not yet been transferred, then transfer it.

The schema also includes variables that echo the plane data structure variables for the aircraft color, sector, and the distance variables, which measure distance to the border. Various pieces of knowledge about the work domain and elemental task are distributed across the agents. The local controls and internal processing provided by each agent establish an implicit coordination structure that results in the outcome behavior.

To provide more insight into this work thread example and global traffic management work, in general, we need to provide more detail about aircraft condition variables and the way the model processes speed requests.

TABLE 6.4
Inbound Process and System Messages

System	DCOG-1 Actor
Communication-event:	
speaker EAST	
message accept VIR199?	
Panel inbound	
	GUI-button-push accepting AC
	GUI-object-select VIR199
	GUI-object-select EAST
	GUI-button-push send

Some aircraft are in a nonactionable condition: The model cannot process the aircraft until the system accomplishes some action. We use the terms *actionable* and *nonactionable* to describe aircraft that are ready to be processed and aircraft that cannot currently be processed. (In the code, nonactionable aircraft are labeled *waiting*—an unfortunate term because it is not the aircraft, but the model that is waiting.) We keep track of the aircraft's status with the schema variable waiting. When a plane's position or a panel message indicates that the plane has become actionable, schema agent updates the schema, setting the variable waiting to nil.

When creating schema for outbound aircraft, schema agent sets the variable waiting to true because the model is waiting for the aircraft's nose to touch the border. When updating the outbound schema, if a certain variable has a value of less than one, we know that the plane has touched the border. Hence, schema agent knows to set the schema variable nose-touched to true, and, at the same time, schema agent sets the schema variable waiting to nil because the model is no longer waiting for the system to do something.

When creating schema for inbound aircraft, schema agent sets the variable waiting to true because the model is waiting for the system to post an accept query (e.g., Accept VIR199?). During subsequent processing, schema agent checks messages and updates schema. When the system posts the Accept? Message, schema agent knows to change the schema variable accept to true and the variable waiting to nil.

Waiting also occurs when the model has transferred an outbound aircraft to an ATC, but the ATC has not yet responded with a panel message accepting the aircraft, and when the model has accepted an inbound aircraft, but the aircraft has not yet said hello.

The wait variable and related processes provided the DCOG-1 actor with the knowledge it needs to anticipate service events. As DCOG-1 executes its basic work strategy, it analyzes aircraft, selects the most likely next service event, and prepares itself for the anticipated event when there are no other aircraft currently in a service condition.

The speed request subtask addresses aircraft inside the DCOG-1 actor's sector. Knowledge about speed request, like other elemental tasks, is also encoded as a schema in the schema agent. The speed scheme structure contains the message keywords *asked, accepted,* and *rejected,* as well as the control keyword *fulfilled.* Thus, it contains work-relevant knowledge and control knowledge in the same structure. A scenario variable, speed-schema-list, keeps track of the schema. This list is indexed by a string including the aircraft name and the suffix *speed-script.* This list is only accessed when the exec agent determines that no higher priority actions are needed.

When processing a speed request, the exec agent must first calculate whether any aircraft are in the way. A subprocedure scrolls through the list of visible aircraft, adding any obstructing aircraft to a trouble list. If the subprocedure detects any obstructing aircraft, the exec agent denies the speed request; otherwise the request is accepted. The keyword *accepted* or *rejected* is set to true, as well as the keyword *fulfilled*, and the message is broadcast, which signals the action agent to push the appropriate buttons.

DCOG-1 MODEL EVALUATION

The DCOG-1 model was included in the AMBR model comparison study. Both human participants and computational behavioral models performed air traffic management work. The study included the full factorial combination of two display and three workload conditions. The workstation configuration described earlier served as the baseline display and is referred to as the *text condition*. The alternative condition provided color coding of aircraft icons on the radar panel of the workstation. This was intended to make the task easier by providing enhanced support for perceptual-based performance. Traffic density was used as a workload variable, which determined the number and relative concurrency of service events that needed to be processed. The three workload levels consisted of 12 (low), 16 (medium), and 20 (high) service events per session. Each model development team submitted their model to a study moderator who, in turn, ran the models and defined, collected, and analyzed the performance data for both model and human participants. A complete description of the experimental design and data analysis for AMBR is presented in chapter 2.

In preparation for this evaluation, each model team was given the opportunity to calibrate their model to the human subject pool. We were provided access to the data produced by subjects during their familiarization and training exercises with the air traffic management simulation work. Based on these data, we tuned the modeling timing so that error performance (in terms of penalty points) was roughly in line with that of the human subjects. At this stage in the DCOG system development, we have not yet established a principled way to integrate timing into the structure of the model. Rather, for DCOG-1, we used normal code processing time and two wait states as a crude method for modeling the temporal dynamics of work. A fixed, short wait state was used when delayed aircraft were processed two at a time between routine eye scans. A global wait state was included in the exec agent, and it served as the variable that was used to provide rough calibration with human performance.

The performance data are presented in Figs. 6.1 and 6.2 for all six conditions. Figure 6.1 displays group mean error performance in terms of penalty point score, while Fig. 6.2 shows group mean response time performance. As can be seen, the performance of the DCOG-1 model was inversely related to

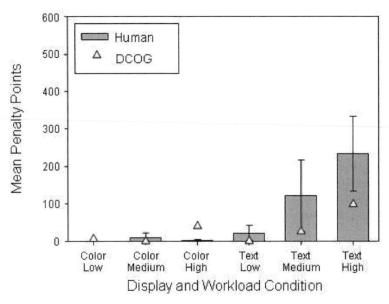

FIG. 6.1.   Observed and DCOG-1 predicted mean penalty point scores as a function of display and workload. Human data are based on 16 participants. DCOG-1 model data are based on a single trial. All data were collected by the AMBR study director.

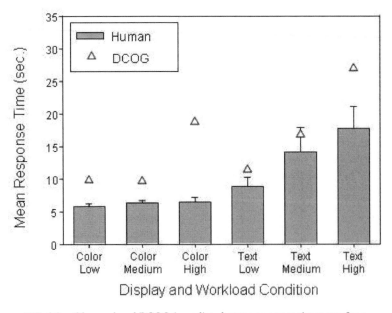

FIG. 6.2.   Observed and DCOG-1 predicted mean response times as a function of display and workload. Human data are based on 16 participants. DCOG-1 data are based on a single trial. All data were collected by the AMBR study director.

workload, for both time and penalty points. This correlated with the human subject performance in the text condition: Higher workload led to increased penalty points and increased time expenditure. However, the DCOG-1 model was not as sensitive to workload as the human subjects in terms of errors, and it was more sensitive to workload in terms of time expended based on visual inspection of the data. This led the DCOG-1 model to be low in errors and high in response time in the text/high-workload condition.

In the color condition, human subject behavior was flattened: There was little response to workload in either penalty points or time expended. It appears that the color condition provides enough supporting information to the subjects so as to minimize the strain imposed by higher workload. The flattening of human performance in the color condition causes the DCOG-1 results to be too high in the color/high-workload condition for both penalty points and time expended.

Although the DCOG-1 model shows an appropriate qualitative response to workload, obviously the model needs to be refined in terms of sensitivity to make it more closely parallel human subject behavior.

In addition to the performance measures just discussed, we also analyzed the behavioral process of the DCOG-1 model in comparison with the human subjects. In particular, we were interested in the actors' cognitive strategies: Did they use a strategy? Did they shift strategy? Alternatively, did they follow a fixed procedure or set of procedures? Did they use a combination of a strategy, rules, and opportunistic methods? Although the human subject data did not afford detailed strategy analysis, we were able to infer some information about how subjects prioritized their actions, and this indicated some basic strategy information. On this qualitative measure, the DCOG-1 model's performance paralleled the human data.

We were able to visually inspect event data logs from the AMBR study. By making some calculations by hand, we could construct an event prioritization representation of the work process flow. An Event Prioritization Timeline is established by cross-correlating two time series. As shown in Fig. 6.3, one time series is ordered in terms of the onset time of a service event (i.e.,

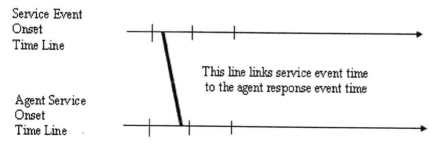

FIG. 6.3. Description of the Event Prioritization Time method for qualitatively assessing task behavior.

accept, welcome, transfer, contact, speed request). Another time series is ordered in terms of actor service onset time. A line drawn between a specific service event onset and actor service onset to that event provides a visual representation of how the actor prioritized subtask work relative to the event forcing function. Note that, although we are discussing the times at which events and reactions occur, our focus here is on event prioritization and not process time modeling.

What can this event prioritization analysis tell us about the work process? As work difficulty increases, we would expect to see a longer lag between event onset and event processing. Hence, the relation line should tilt more away from vertical. With service event onsets on the top timeline and agent service onsets on the bottom timeline, a delayed reaction is reflected as a tilt to the bottom right. The amount of tilt is an indication of the priority given by the agent to a service event. If the actor maintains the original sequence of events in processing, the lines will not cross. Crossing lines indicate a situation in which an actor delays processing one event while processing another event with a more recent onset. If the actor falls behind, lines will cross more and tilt more to the bottom right. In contrast, if a line tilts to the bottom left, this indicates that the actor anticipated the event and started work processing based on this anticipation. Anticipation may also lead to line crossing as anticipated events are taken out of sequence compared with other events.

This qualitative evaluation method is illustrated in Fig. 6.4. The top time series is for a human subject in the text/high-workload condition. The bottom series is for the subject in a color/high-workload condition. Solid lines are used to highlight the most prominent delays in processing or to highlight processing anticipations. First, inspect the bottom series. It shows the

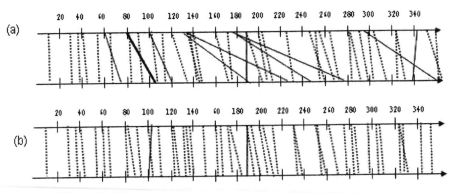

FIG. 6.4.   Example of the Event Prioritization Time method using data from a human participant in the AMBR study.

subject was able to keep up with the pacing function and in two instances actually had time to anticipate work. Interestingly, it appears that fixation on the first anticipated service event caused the subject not to notice another event that actually reached a service onset state slightly prior to the anticipated one, leading to line crossing in the diagram. Also, near the end of the run (about 320 seconds), two events occurred nearly simultaneously, but they were not processed as a pair. These variations in behavior did not in any way degrade outcome performance. In fact given the processing time available before a penalty was imposed, it is reasonable to believe that an expert performer would show some line crossovers in this representation.

The top series shows a combination of delayed servicing and a few instances of anticipation. The data indicate that the actor was basically able to keep up through the first 80 seconds of the session, but was making some response delays. During the middle of the run, response to four items was significantly delayed, and there was one long delay later. Overall, all of the lines tend to tilt more to the bottom right, indicating higher mental workload. The response delays add further evidence for higher workload. It is interesting to see response delays in the same regions where response anticipation also occurred. This suggests that actor used a strategy: Some services were being allowed to slip more than others. This would be quite rational behavior given that the penalty cost of some types of service were lower than for others. Thus, the Event Prioritization representation seems to provide a means to gain a deeper understanding of work behavior.

Figure 6.5 illustrates DCOG's work processing for the most challenging condition, text/high-workload, compared with human performance in the same condition. You will note that the lines on the DCOG strip tilt more to the bottom right, indicating its slower average processing time. Yet its delay pattern is in general similar in both number and magnitude to that of the human subject. We inspected several examples of the Event Prioritization graphs, and they all indicated behavior that was similar to that of the human subjects. Thus, this behavioral process analysis strengthens the view that the DCOG-1 model behaved cognitively in a human-like manner.

What about strategic thinking and shifts in strategy? Based on our examination of Event Prioritization graphs and raw data logs, there was clear evidence for work patterns like that shown in Fig. 6.5 for human subjects under the text/high-workload condition. In general, this work pattern reflects a basic process-one strategy (i.e., cyclically scan the field, select and service an aircraft, repeat the cycle). This is consistent with the basic work strategy used by the DCOG-1 model.

We manually sifted through the human data attempting to find evidence for the use of more sophisticated strategies. Based on an examination of all of the text/high-workload condition data, there was slight evidence of the use of more complex strategies on occasion, but the analysis is not conclusive. For example, subject t17ma appeared to deliberately de-

DCOG- txt 6

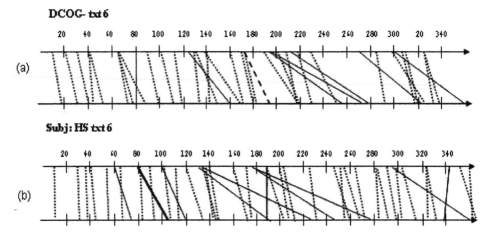

(a)

Subj: HS txt 6

(b)

FIG. 6.5.   Example of the Event Prioritization Time method comparing (a) DCOG-1 model behavior with (b) human behavior with the AMBR task.

lay processing welcome events under the high-workload text condition. Four welcome events with dispersed onset service demand times were processed as a group at the end of the session. This is a rational strategy given the instructions and low-cost penalty associated with this type of event, especially if the actor is in a perceived state of "falling behind" (perhaps due to excessive mental workload). A second subject, t10kr, delayed the processing of a speed request event until the end of the session. There was a slight hint that several other subjects gave less weight to speed requests by delaying response to them, but the number of events of this type was too small to reveal a consistent pattern. This would also be rational given the high penalty cost of making an error, but the low cost of not responding at all. A subject might tend to wait until there was a lull in the action before addressing speed requests. In its current form, the DCOG-1 model did not have the ability to engage in any of these more sophisticated work strategies. (Although DCOG-1 contains two variables, worry-factor and process-two, that could in principle be used to endow the model with individualistic characteristics, these variables were held constant during this experiment. We address strategy shifting in greater detail in our second model, DCOG-2.)

In general, DCOG-1 was successful in demonstrating how a distributed model of the mind was able to accomplish complex, human-like work. In this model, various forms of knowledge were encoded, and cognition involved a coordination of distributed mind processes that used and associated the available knowledge. The model incorporates a simple form of strategic thinking as a guide for shaping effective behavior, and cognitive resources are deployed in a flexible manner.

The second round of the AMBR study used the same simulated work environment, but with a modification that required the models to demonstrate real-time learning as part of air traffic management. This provided an opportunity to study strategic behavior more thoroughly. For this round, we developed an advanced version of the DCOG model with an emphasis on flexible, adaptive behavior. This new model, called DCOG-2, is described in the next section.

DCOG-2 MODEL IMPLEMENTATION

DCOG-2 supports a wider range of mental behavior than the original model. It focuses on mental activities involved in learning a solution to a categorization problem embedded in the air traffic management work domain. Learning is a general psychological construct, and it may involve the deployment of many functional processes used to acquire knowledge and solve a problem. DCOG-2 provides an amalgamation of learning methods based on the employment of a feature-based associative memory capability spread over mind regions. As noted in Table 6.1, DCOG-2 builds on the distributed knowledge and control established in DCOG-1, adding associative memory and more detailed modeling of individual differences and strategy shifting. Here we describe these new features of the DCOG system. We begin with a brief description of the modified air traffic management work and an overview of the DCOG-2 model. The majority of the discussion is devoted to strategic thinking in the subtask that involves real-time learning as a component of the AMBR task work. Initially, the learning aspects of the model are discussed in terms of strategies. Associative memory is central to all forms of learning and thus underlies each strategy. Accordingly, we then deepen the discussion by inspecting the associative memory properties of the DCOG-2 model. As with DCOG-1, we also address personality factors, model calibration, and its performance both during the air traffic management task and on a subsequent transfer of training task.

The original AMBR work domain was changed to include a modified altitude request task. The new version of the task required the actor to learn which requests to accept or reject. As a result, the new task was a form of category learning. This was one of five subtasks that had to be completed and integrated into an overall organization of work activities, just as in the original air traffic management simulation. The modified altitude request task required the actor to evaluate the state of three binary factors (fuel remaining—40% or 20%, aircraft size—L or S, and local turbulence—low = 1 or high = 3) and determine whether the altitude request should be accepted or rejected. The correct category, accept or reject, had to be learned over a series of trials that contained performance feedback information. Loosely speaking, actors had to discover a rule that could be applied to the three-factor exemplars that would discriminate items to be accepted from those to be rejected. Three different levels of problem complexity or learning difficulty were employed. Difficulty was established in a way that replicated category problem Types I, III, and VI of the classic Shepard, Hovland, and Jenkins (1961) learning task.

Category learning problems for the altitude request task varied in terms of difficulty. Three difficulty levels were used in the AMBR task. Recall that three parameters are provided when an altitude request is made: fuel remaining (40, 20), aircraft size (L, S), and weather turbulence (3, 1). The solution to a Type I problem requires the discovery of a simple one-parameter rule, such as accept large (L) aircraft. Any of the three dimensions could carry the correct concept. A Type III problem involves the conjunction of three parameters to a varying extent. The majority of cases may be handled with a single, complex rule, but some exception applies. Thus, for example, a correct concept might be: large aircraft unless high altitude and low turbulence, except when small aircraft and high altitude and high turbulence. For Type VI problems, no compact generalization applies to all instances. In other words, each exemplar represents a specific case. For all three types of learning problems, half of the exemplars support an accept response while half support a reject response. That is, the concept is correctly reflected in half of the presentations. It should be clear that, for humans, Type I problems are easier than Type III, and these are easier than Type VI. A more detailed description of the air traffic management simulation environment and the different types of categorization problems is presented in chapter 2.

The original DCOG-1 model was written in Allegro Lisp. This model was rewritten in Java 1.3 and served as the basis for the DCOG-2 model. The structure of the new code varies somewhat from the original, mainly to better ensure a consistent temporal interface with an outside event-based simulation and to support associative behavior.

A new agent was added to the DCOG architecture to provide a learning capability. Named the altitude request task (ART) agent, this agent implements an associational memory that handles all learning for the model. It is able to learn using both features and symbols by an associative linking process. We assume this learning agent spans several mind centers. In particular, it at least covers a perceptually based memory center (or system) and a symbolically based memory center. A feature is taken to be a discrete perceptible element, such as an S or L in a visually presented exemplar. A feature is a sensory-based representation that is assumed to be generated by the perceptual center or system. A set of co-occurring (within a space-time window) features defines an image. A symbol is a different type of representation. It is an abstract representation based on the preexistence of a language-based processing ability. For example, S may be symbolized abstractly as "standing for small aircraft." An entire exemplar may be symbolized as an instance of an abstract concept. It is assumed that symbols are generated by a cognitive system or center that utilizes language processing.

To facilitate development, major effort in the design of the associative agent was focused on supporting a complex, activation-based feature and symbol learning capability for handling the altitude request task. A more primitive feature-based associative memory capability supported the air traffic management portion of the model; this was named the *association agent.*

In addition to these changes, the former exec and schema agents were combined into one ATC agent, which prioritizes the aircraft, selects the next appropriate processing action, and makes this information available to the action agent. The model also includes a radar agent and a report agent, which reports workload measures.

DCOG-2 development focused on the associative memory component. Consequently, some of the distributed control features of DCOG-1 were implemented in a simpler, procedural manner. The ATC agent, for example, explicitly posts required actions on an activity queue instead of simply broadcasting a message. In addition, when the next priority aircraft involves an altitude request, the ATC agent calls on the ART agent directly to determine whether to accept or reject the request. The next generation of DCOG models will integrate the distributed control and associated memory components of the two models.

As described earlier, the model was set to operate according to the process-one strategy. The strategy for the new model differs only in that now the altitude request task is designated a priority task to be completed within a fixed time window once an attitude service request is made by the simulation. This change is consistent with changes in instructions given to human participants and the change in penalty score formula used in the second experiment. Thus, the model cycles between eye scans, picking up events that needed to be serviced, selecting one to service (using cognitive properties to determine prioritization), and continuing until the service task is completed. When performing the altitude request subtask, the model attempts to learn the correct answer over a series of exemplars (one per trial) and bases its response on its current best guess. As part of the model enhancement, a primitive associative strength mechanism is applied to the standard air traffic management portion of the work. Strength values are associated with schema data structures for the original subtasks and influence the process of ordering elemental subtasks and the use of routine and direct gaze eye scan patterns. This appears to cause little or no change in the model's overall behavior. The remainder of the discussion focuses on the associative agent and real-time learning.

Our discussion is divided into three sections. The first section addresses the question, How does DCOG-2 learn? We introduce the various learning strategies employed by the model, and we explain how these strategies are implemented within the associative memory. The associative memory includes both symbolic and perceptual nodes, and can thus support both emergent categories and hypothesis formation. Certain strategies also incorporate a procedure for evaluating hypotheses.

The second section discusses how the model can shift among learning strategies depending on perceived success. The third section explains how personality factors influence learning, in the choice of initial learning strategy and in the decision to shift strategies, and in the evaluation of hypotheses.

How Does DCOG-2 Learn?

DCOG-2 employs five learning modes, each of which may be regarded as a basic learning strategy. The model may also shift between learning modes, and in this way it can form more complex learning strategies that reflect individualistic, flexible, and adaptive work behavior.

We label the five modes *emergent, rote, deductive, inductive,* and *abductive.* Each of these modes may be deployed by DCOG-2 against all three types of category learning problems. The model starts with an initial learning strategy and then self-organizes its learning behavior as it gains experience over a set of exemplars. One or more learning strategies may be invoked in this process.

The emergent mode is largely an expression of latent learning. This mode operates by storing feature-based knowledge about each presented exemplar and its association with response category features. For example, each level of the three binary factors may be regarded as a feature of a three-element exemplar, such as 20, L, 3. This represents knowledge about an aircraft's states and the weather situation. For this example, the aircraft has 20% fuel remaining, it is a (L) large plane, and the weather turbulence is (3) high. Accept and reject represents response category knowledge formed on the basis of performance feedback. In the emergent mode, these categories are also treated as features, and associations are implicitly formed between them and the features of each exemplar based on the capabilities of the associative agent. Thus, over time, strength builds up such that some exemplars are more strongly associated with one response category relative to the other, achieving category learning. This may be regarded as a form of perceptual learning.

The rote mode expresses learning as pure memorization. DCOG-2 forms an abstract symbol that stands for each exemplar bound to the appropriate response category. There are four exemplars each in the accept and reject categories for each type of challenge problem provided in the AMBR study. Thus, the rote learning process must be able to both form and support recall of the exemplar-category knowledge over a set of eight different exemplars.

The deductive, inductive, and abductive strategy modes all deploy some type of hypothesis testing as the basis for learning. In general, the goal of learning in these modes is to find an explanation that is as simple as possible to account for sorting the eight exemplars per challenge problem type into the accept and reject categories. This goal is pursued in DCOG-2 by first collecting exemplar and response category information as feature- and symbol-based knowledge facts and then by reasoning over them. In effect, this amounts to forming a hypothesis for future use and updating the hypothesis as new knowledge is formed. A hypothesis confirmed by evidence reflects a consolidation of latent knowledge into a learned form. Because all of these learning forms involve evaluation of evidence, we refer to them collectively as the *evaluative type* or *evaluative strategy*.

To perform reasoning by the hypothesis testing strategy, the model exploits knowledge about the three binary factors. Each factor may be regarded as a dimension. Further, if an exemplar classified as accept contains the feature L and another exemplar also classified as accept contains the complement feature S, this dimension is not useful for discriminating among the other remaining exemplars. It can be eliminated for consideration as a candidate element of an abstract generalization for inclusion in a future hypothesis formation cycle. Sometimes a one- or two-dimensional generational is completely successful in classifying the exemplars into accept and reject categories. Other times such a generalization may only be partially successful. When this occurs, a three-dimensional hypothesis is formed for the unique case.

In the deductive learning mode, the DCOG-2 actor begins by making a random one-parameter guess on the first two trials. Once feedback has been provided for two exemplars, this knowledge can be used as evidence from which a deduction can be formed. Hereafter the model uses the accumulating evidence deductively to form and test hypotheses. The inductive learning mode operates in the same manner except it begins making inferences after the first trial. That is, given information about the correct answer for a single exemplar results in sufficient knowledge being available to support an induction learning strategy in this context. The abductive mode can begin forming hypotheses immediately with the first trial because it exploits world knowledge in the hypothesis testing process. Because the exemplar items were formed artificially in the AMBR task, world knowledge is not valuable. In fact if used, it will likely induce poor performance. However, a human participant might try to rely on world knowledge during the transfer task when new exemplars are introduced, and answers are required without having the benefit of using feedback to improve performance.

All of the evaluative type learning methods start with a preference for a one-dimensional (1-d) or simple hypothesis. If the evidence does not support this form of hypothesis, more complex two- and three-dimensional hypotheses can be formed. It is in this way that more complex one- and two-dimensional hypotheses with exceptions can be formed.

The DCOG-2 actor also has the ability to dynamically shift among learning strategies. Shifts in strategy are motivated on the basis of self-awareness of performance and mediated by personality differences represented in the patience and tolerance (see How Personality Factors Influence Learning section). Given this ability to shift strategy and the various methods of learning, the DCOG-2 actor offers flexible and adaptive learning and behavioral patterns.

The behavior of these learning strategies can be better understood by a more microinspection of the associative agent. We need to discuss the model in terms of features, symbols, knowledge activation states, and associative memory states and other capabilities of the associative agent.

The associative agent functions as a memory system. We use the term *node* to represent a feature or symbol internal to the memory system. Nodes may be in either an active or inactive state. When nodes are co-active, they form a link. A trace memory of the link is stored as an associative strength. Prior associative links provide possible paths for the spreading of activation from a currently active node in a mind region to other nodes in memory.

Figure 6.6 presents the general arrangement. It depicts the relation between an actor and the outside world. The actor is represented in terms of

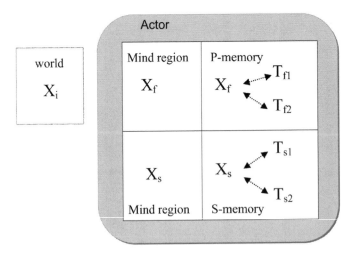

FIG. 6.6. A schematic depiction of features and symbols that are activated in the DCOG-2 mind model. The mind regions on the left represent new information in a sensory-based form (X_f) and in a language-based form (X_s). The arrows show spreading activation to other features and symbols in memory based on prior associations.

different mind regions. The regions in the left column of the actor process new information from the outside world. One region forms new sensory-based feature nodes. The other region forms new language-based symbol nodes. The mind regions in the right column represent long-term storage or memory of sense- and language-based information, respectively, as node networks. We use the terms *P-memory* and *S-memory* to distinguish these two different node networks.

As Fig. 6.6 shows, some pattern (x) in the external world acts as an energy source that triggers the formation of an image of the pattern. This image consists of a set of feature nodes. In the simple case, the world pattern maps to a single feature node in a mind region as shown. This feature node then triggers the perceptual memory of the feature X_f, which in turn spreads activation to other feature nodes T_1 and T_2 that have previously co-occurred with X_f in the past. The strength of activation of T_1 and T_2 is proportional to the stored associative strength that has built up over prior experiences. Associative links are bidirectional.

The same basic process occurs in another mind region based on language-based processing. In this region, the pattern in the external world triggers the formation of a new abstract symbol. The world object is treated as an abstract or symbolic feature, X_s, which in turn leaves a memory trace whose activation can spread to previously associated features T_{s1} and T_{s2}, as shown in Fig. 6.6. For example, in the altitude request task, a mind region generates a symbol such as 20L3 based on an exemplar. In S-memory, activation of this symbol results in the activation of other symbols (T_{s1} and T_{s2}) based on prior associations.

It is important to maintain the distinctions among the notions of an input feature, a new mind feature, a new mind symbol, and memories of them as we review the details of the learning modes. We use bold type to represent exemplars as input features: **20, L, 3**, where individual features are separated by commas. P-memory nodes are represented in normal text: 20, L, 3, with spaces between the letters. S-memory nodes are represented in italic type: *20, L, 3*.

Given these conventions, we can now more easily discuss learning strategies at the operational processing level of the DCOG model. Because of the similarity in operational mind activities for the inductive, abductive, and deductive modes, they can be lumped into a single evaluative-based learning category for the purposes of discussion. We use the deductive mode to represent this evaluative class of learning strategies. We begin with the simplest learning strategy.

The emergent strategy is based on the use of latent learning. The presentation of an exemplar followed by an accept or reject stimulus activates in memory associative links between individual exemplar features and the selected accept or reject feature (e.g., **20, L, 3** → 20, L, 3), and this is linked feature by feature to the accept and reject features (**A** = accept results in 20-

A, L-A, and 3-A associations in P-memory). After a series of exemplars and responses occur, activation in P-memory reflects the associative strength patterns, which can be used directly as the basis for making the response to the next exemplar. That is, pick the strongest associative link; if there is a tie, choose randomly among the tied features.

An example of the P-memory state after exposure to eight exemplars is shown in Table 6.5. Each feature of the altitude request exemplar is in a column, and the accept (A) and reject (R) responses define the rows. Cell entries are the activation levels. This example indicates that the model will always be successful if it accepts an exemplar that contains the fuel feature of 20 and always rejects the fuel feature of 40. In other words, it has learned a Type I concept. Because the solution for a Type I or simple challenge problem is always specialized to a single dimension, DCOG-2 can be completely successful in solving these problems by using the emergent mode exclusively. It is also able to find the central construct for Type III problems and thus performs fairly well on these problems. Yet it fails completely in the long run on Type VI problems.

The rote learning mode involves the creation of symbols of the type *xyz*. Symbols are abstractions that encode concepts and are needed to maintain this information in the S-memory region of the mind model. An S-memory region has the ability to associate an exemplar *as a symbol* with accept and reject categories as symbols (*xyz-A* and *xyz-R*). Therefore, S-memory has provisions for the direct storage and retrieval of specific cases to be learned. In other words, the rote mode expresses instance learning. Clearly, this mode can successfully solve Type I, Type II, and Type VI challenge problems. Errors in the mode derive from memory activation constraints.

The construct formed by the symbolic node (e.g., *xyz*), the accept or reject node, and the link between these nodes constitutes a hypothesis. In the rote mode, each hypothesis is completely specified by an exemplar and, hence, always correct. In the deductive mode, hypotheses may be formed involving one, two, or three dimensions and may be incorrect or subject to exceptions. For example, given the exemplar, **xyzA**, the model may hypothesize accept x by creating a symbolic node *x* and linking it to the node A. This hypothesis may be correct or it may be disproved in the face of further evidence (perhaps the correct generalization is accept z instead).

By far the evaluative type learning strategies that encode hypothesis testing represent the most complex kind of DCOG-2 learning at the opera-

TABLE 6.5
Latent Learning

	40	20	L	S	3	1
A	0	8	4	4	4	4
R	8	0	4	4	4	4

tional mind level. This general strategy involves hypothesis creation and hypothesis evaluation during the process of responding to each exemplar within the time period provided for the altitude request subtask. Because different hypotheses may complete against each other and because the available facts may be vague and unable to resolve the competition, the operational level of the model also uses a relative specificity memory element to evaluate the validity of a hypothesis. First, as feedback is received after a guess, associations between the target symbols (accept or reject) and any active symbols are strengthened. Next, a relative specificity calculation is performed to test the validity of the hypothesis. (This is considered to be part of the local capability of a mind region.) Symbols with low relative specificity are not used and discarded.

The s-region of the DCOG-2 model includes knowledge about binary dimensions. It knows that the elements of such a dimension are mutually exclusive. Access to this dimensional information guides the creation and selection of hypothesis in two ways. First, if the operational mind process creates a one-dimensional (1-d) hypothesis such as $A(x)$, it will simultaneously create the complementary hypothesis, $R(x_c)$. Second, if both members of a dimension are equally associated with accept, the model will recognize that the dimension is not able to discriminate between the two categories, accept and reject.

In addition, the s-region knowledge has been biased to favor a low-dimensional hypothesis over a high-dimensional one. In other words, it has a preference for a 1-d hypothesis (x) followed by a 2-d hypothesis (xy). This preference could be a personality variable, subject to individual differences, although it was held constant in DCOG-2.

The basic strategy of the hypothesis testing modes is to form a low-dimensional generalization over the set of exemplars for each type of challenge problem. When this strategy is not completely successful, the model may call on 3-d symbolic information to represent an exception to the general rule. This is accomplished by using a hypothesis evaluation process.

Several operational-level activities are involved in creating and evaluating a hypothesis. The process flow of these activities can best be appreciated by stepping through a sequence of events that includes external events from the environment and internal events (indented) within DCOG-2.

T1: input exemplar (e.g., **20L3**)

T2: spread activation from input features (20 L 3) to accept and reject mental features, proportionally to the strength of association (P-mem).

T3: spread activation from input features to any existing symbols (S-mem).

T3:   select among symbols. If more than one symbol is active, find the symbol with the highest number of input features (several may still exist) (S-mem).

T4:   spread activation from any active symbols to accept and reject (S-mem).

T5:   sum activation for accept; sum it for reject (S-mem). Choose the one with the highest activation level as the guess.

T6:   Feedback input (correct or incorrect).

T7:   Use feedback calculation ; if feedback = correct do nothing, else create a new symbol based on the input and associate with accept or reject (S-mem)

T8:   Make association in P-memory from input features to accept or reject.

T9:   Make association from accept or reject to any active symbols (S-mem).

T10: Symbol reduction. Calculate the relative specificity (described below) of each active symbol with respect to the current classification, accept or reject.

T11: next exemplar (presented on next altitude request service event)

The mental process is based on feature and symbol knowledge activation and residual associative formations among these elemental units of knowledge. This involves activities of various mind regions that have local processing capabilities. The activation-based memory process involved in both learning and behavioral decision making is depicted schematically in Fig. 6.7. The knowledge state at T0 indicates the stored associative links among exemplar features and additional links between some of these features and the abstract symbol (*20, 3*) stored in the S-memory region. For the given exemplar, **20, L, 3**, it can be seen that this exemplar would stimulate an accept response due only to the preexisting activation strengths with the accept and reject nodes.

Given this state, when the new exemplar arrives at T1 from the world, three feature images are formed in the mind, stimulating features in the P-memory region. (We do not explicitly model the formation of the feature images, but assume that this takes place in a separate mind region.) At T2, activation is spread from the activated feature nodes, in proportion to stored associative strength, to the accept and reject feature nodes. During the next time step, T3, spreading occurs to the target symbol in the s-memory region based on the prior stored associative strength. This node, in turn, spreads activation at time T4 to the accept node. Thus, both feature- and symbol-based knowledge can be brought to bear in forming the accept or reject decision based on prior learning when an evaluative strat-

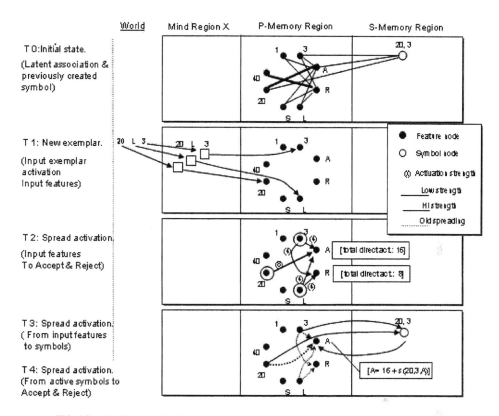

FIG. 6.7. A schematic depiction of an event trace in the DCOG-2 memory model. See text for details.

egy is used. It is in this way that tacit and emergent feature-based knowledge may influence deliberative symbol-based thinking in the process of demonstrating category learning in the AMBR task.

Relative specificity (RS) between exemplar symbols and accept or reject symbols is a key aspect of all of the evaluative learning strategy modes. A symbol is specific to, say, an accept action if the associations from that symbol tend to activate accept over reject in symbolic memory. Relative specificity measures the proportion of association strength for one target memory item over another. This is the most sophisticated aspect of the associative memory capability. It is defined as follows.

Let T and Tc stand for accept and reject in either order. Let alpha (α) represent a symbol. We use the notation S(a,b) to indicate the strength of an associative link between nodes a and b:

$$\text{If } S(\alpha, T) > S(\alpha, Tc),$$
then alpha is relatively specific (RS) for T.

The precise value for the relative specificity of alpha with respect to T is given by the proportion of association strength linking alpha to T versus Tc:

$$RS_{\alpha,T} = \frac{S(\alpha, T)}{S(\alpha, T) + S(\alpha, Tc)}$$

Note that if a symbol is consistently associated with T, then $RS_{\alpha,T} = 1$. If a symbol is associated evenly with T and Tc, then $RS_{\alpha,T} = \frac{1}{2}$. When α is relatively specific for T, then the value of $RS_{\alpha,T} > \frac{1}{2}$. Therefore, a hypothesis that encodes a category generalization with exceptions will, with a sufficient number of exemplars, be reflected in an RS value between 1 and $\frac{1}{2}$.

Based on this knowledge, the DCOG-2 model discards certain symbols that are no longer useful. We use a personality variable, n, to distinguish individual differences in hypothesis evaluation. When $RS_{\alpha,T} < n$, the model discards the symbol. A person who demands high success on nearly every trial will have an RS requirement near 1. A person who is more tolerant to being less successful on each trial will have an RS requirement close to $\frac{1}{2}$. (We assume that a value of $RS_{\alpha,T}$ at or below $\frac{1}{2}$ will always cause symbol discard.)

Relative specificity represents implicit knowledge contained in the DCOG-2 model. It is intended to correspond to a qualitative, conscious level understanding of feasible hypotheses as the learning opportunities accumulate. The feasible set varies based on personality factors. It is also influenced by a capacity limit that restricts the ability to recall past exemplar outcomes. For DCOG-2 this limit was set at three past outcomes that could be remembered. In future work, this variable could be adjusted to reflect individual differences based on findings from empirical research studies.

To complete this discussion of hypothesis testing by the model, we need to address how latent learning factors interact with hypothesis creation. If the other factors that select hypotheses provide for two or more potential hypotheses, emergent associations serve to guide the choice of a hypothesis. Given the currently active target (A or R) and the current input (xyz), the model checks the relative specificity of each individual input feature with respect to the target. It then chooses to create a symbol corresponding to the input feature with the highest RS. Thus, a model in deductive mode may behave in an emergent manner if the current set of hypotheses does not provide a basis for deductive reasoning about the input.

For example, given **xyzA**, check RS(x,A), RS(y,A), and RS(z,A). Suppose x has the highest RS: then create a symbol, *x*, and associate it with x and A. This new symbol inherits the associative strengths of the input feature nodes with respect to the target. This means that a hypothesis is stronger if it is created on the basis of an input feature that has frequently been associated with the target. In other words, the feature-based knowledge accumu-

TABLE 6.6
Associative Links in s-Memory

	X	X_c	Y	Y_c	Z	Z_c
A	1	0	1	0	1	0
R	1	0	0	1	1	0

lated in the p-region is made available to the symbol-based knowledge in the s-region of the mind model.

Consider the deductive mode. Given inputs **x y z A** and **x yc z R** over successive trials, the model develops associations.

For the most recent feedback, **x yc z R**, the possible hypotheses are

$$R(x \ yc \ z) \qquad R(x \ yc) \qquad R(x \ z) \qquad R(yc \ z)$$
$$R(x) \qquad R(yc) \qquad R(z)$$

Recall that 1-d hypotheses are preferred over 2- and 3-d options. This leaves

$$R(x) \qquad R(yc) \qquad R(z)$$

Now within this set, the input feature information has the following RS values for reject:

$$RS(x, R) = 1/2 \qquad RS(yc, R) = 1/1 = 1 \qquad RS(z, R) = 1/2$$

Accordingly, the model chooses to use the hypothesis R(yc). The model uses relative specificity to identify yc as the likely suspect in the rejection of the input **x yc z**. Therefore, it creates the symbol yc, linking it to the input feature node yc and the node reject. The association between yc and reject inherits the association strength established between yc and R from previous trials. In this case, the inherited value from the earlier trial, **xyzA**, is 0, and the feature knowledge does not change anything. In other situations, inherited feature knowledge can become quite important.

Changing Learning Strategy

The DCOG-2 actor may start out by using the emergent, rote, or any of the evaluative learning strategies. The selection of an initial learning mode may reflect an individual bias or preference on the part of a specific performer. In addition, these modes differ both in terms of the cognitive effort or mental workload they require and in terms of the degree of success they can achieve with the different types of classification problems. As a result, the

TABLE 6.7
Performance by Strategy and Category Type

Strategy	Type I	Type III	Type VI
Emergent	100%	75% (max)	Chance
Rote	100%	100%	100%
Deductive	100%	100%	100%

DCOG-2 actor may decide to shift to a different learning mode under certain conditions.

Table 6.7 shows the relative degree of success the emergent, rote, and deductive learning modes can have for the three types of classification problems. We use the deductive mode as the standard form of evaluative learning (i.e., hypothesis testing). As the table indicates, DCOG can always be successful using a deductive strategy or a rote strategy, but the emergent strategy performs progressively worse as problem difficulty increases. Thus, on performance grounds, the DCOG actor tends to shift out of the emergent strategy to a deductive strategy when performance is deemed to be unacceptable.

We may also anticipate shifting from a rote learning strategy to a deductive one. Rote learning is the most cognitively demanding; it imposes the highest level of mental workload. If the mental load is deemed to be excessive, then a shift to a deductive mode can be anticipated.

These types of shifts in learning strategy are supported in DCOG-2. In emergent mode, the model remembers the outcome of the past three classification opportunities (i.e., they are maintained in conscious awareness). If the feedback is not good (i.e., a high proportion of misses), then DCOG shifts from an emergent strategy to a deductive one. Success with rote learning may start slowly because the actor will have to make guesses for all new (not previously seen) exemplars. A shift to the deductive strategy will occur based on the model's failure rate relative to its patience with initial incorrect performance. (Memory constraints were not explicitly modeled; however, a model actor in rote mode with low patience performs as if there is insufficient memory to retain all eight exemplars. The model takes the need to create new symbols after patience is exceeded as evidence that the rote mode is failing and shifts into deductive mode.) In the deductive mode, the model tracks the number of rejected hypotheses. If, after patience is exceeded, the number of rejected hypotheses exceeds a threshold, the model shifts to emergent mode.

We should also note that it is reasonable to shift from a deductive learning strategy to a rote one for Type VI challenge problems. This shifting routine has not been explicitly implemented in the model because the deductive mode can emulate rote learning by creating 3-d symbols to represent exceptions to earlier hypotheses. During the course of a Type VI problem, a model in the deductive mode may accumulate an entire set of 3-d symbol exceptions to its initial, 1-d hypothesis. This constitutes an implicit shift to rote or instance learning.

How Personality Factors Influence Learning

Context plays an important role in the behavior of the DCOG-2 actor. The external context is established by the sequential presentation order of exemplars that constitute the altitude request challenge problem. This ordering interacts with the random and learning-based guesses made by the model, and it can influence shifting behavior in the use of learning strategies. Internal factors also provide context elements that influence behavior, performance, and learning mode shifting. We refer to these internal context variables as personality factors. These factors are intended to represent individual idiosyncrasies that might influence the behavior of two equally skilled persons. The variables serve to increase the range of flexible behavior the model can exhibit. This flexibility derives both from the application of these variables and their interaction with learning strategies.

The model contains three personality factors: preference, patience, and tolerance. The preference factor addresses both the range of freedom and any bias a person may have when trying to discover a concept or principle to apply to a set of data. In this work domain, the exemplars included data facts about items that were clearly located on three dimensions (fuel %, ac size, turbulence). As a result, a person could anticipate patterns involving one, two, or three dimensions. For this study, we held preference constant with a 1-d bias for the deductive mode, meaning that 1-d concepts would be explored as possibilities before moving to two and three dimensions. Preference only applies in the evaluative modes. In the rote mode an instance or case is equivalent to a 3-d concept, creating an implicit 3-d bias, whereas in the emergent mode no symbolic concepts are created.

Patience is a related personality factor. Although all performers would like to solve a challenging problem as quickly as possible, some may be more willing to experience a larger number of examples to ensure enough time has been provided for a pattern to be readily detectable. A patient person sticks with a basic strategy longer than a less patient person, perhaps refining it along the way. Hence, a patient individual is more influenced by long-term memory and processing capabilities. A less patient individual relies more on working memory and factors in the immediate environment. In general, the patience variable is a crude way to capture this flavor of personality influence on problem-solving behavior. It is used to govern the number of learning trials before evaluating success with a learning mode. It applies to all five modes.

Tolerance is a threshold setting for the relative specificity evaluation process, and thus it serves as an implicit personality variable relating to perfection in performance. A tolerant person continues to hold onto an incomplete or partially correct solution option, despite only moderate success, with the hope of improving on it. An intolerant person will readily give up on that concept and look for a better one even if it means shifting strategy. The tolerance threshold was a major factor in determining strategy shifts.

Both an instance-based memorization strategy (rote mode) and various forms of a hypothesis and test strategy (deductive mode) can be successful across all problem types. Latent learning (emergent mode), however, is reasonably successful with Type III problems and does not do well with Type VI, but this is not the whole story. There is also a difference in the cognitive effort or mental workload associated with each strategy as shown in Table 6.8. Workload is generally low in emergent mode, where there are no symbols to create and evaluate, and high in the rote mode, where a large number of 3-d symbols must be created regardless of category type. In the deductive mode, workload tends to be low in Type I and Type III categories, where the model needs to create primarily 1-d hypotheses. Yet workload tends to be high in Type VI categories, where the model needs to create multiple 3-d hypotheses.

The effectiveness of a particular mode should be considered in light of both performance and workload measures. If a high importance is assigned to workload, the emergent mode is the best choice for solving Type I categories because it yields high success in exchange for low workload, but a weaker choice for Type III categories, yielding only moderate success. If workload is less important, the deductive mode becomes a better choice for both Type I and Type III categories, generating high levels of success in both categories, although creating high-workload levels as well. Because the subject does not know what category type is present at the beginning of the exercise, it is not possible to specify one best strategy.

Within the AMBR study, category type was blocked over subjects. Had the category types not been blocked, the interaction of workload and performance would have become more important. We speculate on this inter-

TABLE 6.8
Workload by Strategy and Category Type

Strategy	Type I	Type III	Type VI
Emergent	Low	Low	Low
Rote	High	High	High
Deductive	Low	Low	High

action here as an example of the type of strategy shifting that should be modeled in more complex tasks.

There are several possible cognitive trade-offs. For example, a learner might use the emergent mode successfully for Type I problems, and thus be encouraged to apply it to other problem types. This mode still works reasonably well for Type III problems, but fails utterly for Type VI problems. The cost of waiting until Type VI problems to switch strategies might prove to be rather expensive. Activation must be shifted to another mode, and it may take time for the model to achieve success in the new mode. A deductive mode may be slightly more costly for simple problems, but overall it may be less expensive because any start-up costs associated with working in a new mode would be eliminated. Conversely, a learner who decides to start with a rote strategy for Type I problems pays a heavy cognitive price until more difficult problems are encountered. We may assume that an individual's preference for a particular strategy mode on a new task is shaped in part by such past experiences in using various strategies.

DCOG-2 Model Summary

The DCOG-2 model uses strategic thinking to guide learning and its deployment in completion of task work. Three main strategies, emergent, rote, and deductive, provide a range of reasoning approaches, with differences in both performance and workload depending on the categorization task. The model uses personality variables to provide individual variation in strategy selection and shifting. Within this strategic structure, the model employs an associative memory component with both perceptual and symbolic elements. The perceptual elements afford emergent categorization, whereas the symbolic elements model hypothesis formation. The model evaluates the ongoing success of its strategies and hypotheses, providing a level of metacognitive awareness.

DCOG-2 MODEL EVALUATION

The DCOG-2 model was included in a second AMBR model comparison study. Both human participants and computational behavioral models performed air traffic management work with the embedded learning task expressed as a modified altitude request task. The study included two parts. In Part 1, category learning was embedded as a subtask in the air traffic management work. Only the color condition from the original AMBR study was used. Part 2 was a transfer of learning task. The number of values on each dimension of the altitude request task was extended from two values to five. This expanded set of exemplars was presented one at a time, and the actor rendered a judgment as to whether it should be accepted or rejected. No augmented feedback was provided on these 25 trials. Hence, there was no new information available to aid additional learning. Ninety human subjects participated in the study. The experiment was blocked on the category problem type variable, therefore each category learning problem was accomplished by 30 subjects, with any one subject only experiencing one category problem type. Each model development team submitted models to handle each category problem type. A study moderator ran the models and defined, collected, and analyzed the performance data for both model and human participants.

In preparation for this evaluation, each model team was given the opportunity to calibrate their model to the human subject pool. We were provided access to aggregate data produced by subjects during the Part 1 task. This included performance scores on the ATC hand-off portion and learning curves based on blocks of 16 exemplars for the category learning portion. We were also provided with the extended dimensional values to be used in the transfer part of the study.

Our main aim for the DCOG-2 version of DCOG was to introduce a flexible, real-time learning component. Accordingly, we concentrate on this aspect of the model in this evaluation. (An evaluation of full task performance for four behavioral models and human subjects is provided in chap. 2.) As you may recall from the discussion of DCOG-1, we are most interested in evaluating the cognitive behavior of the model as distinct from only evaluating the model's task performance. We believe that a good way to approach an evaluation of cognitive behavior is to focus on the behavioral aspects of individual performers, rather than on summative performance at the aggregate group mean level. This belief stems from the hypothesis that equally skilled individuals deploy a common set of cognitive resources in different ways based on their history of experiences, their personality biases, and differences in constraints on these abilities. Thus, the analysis needs visibility into the behaviors of individual actors to gain a better understanding of aggregate outcome performance data. Given this orientation, we elected to produce 12 variants of the DCOG-2 model that reflected different learning tendencies and personal styles that could achieve comparable skill in the category learning task.

DCOG-2 actor models were formed by selecting values for three parameters: strategy mode, patience, and tolerance. A model was initialized to start in one of the five strategy modes described earlier. Strategy shifting was influenced by patience and tolerance values. Patience determined the number of exemplars tried before a strategy shift could occur. Tolerance determined how quickly an actor would abandon a strategy in favor of a shift to a new one. These variables interact, and, in some situations, patience can overrule tolerance. For example, suppose a subject begins in deductive mode and, based on the input **xyzA**, postulates accept x. The subject creates a symbol, x, linked to both the feature x and the node A. Next the subject gets the input **x y zc R**. This contradicts the initial hypothesis. If the subject has a low tolerance for error, we might expect the subject to shift modes at this point. However, it is possible that we are working with a Type III category, in which accept x is the correct basic generalization and xyzcR is an exception. The patience variable permits the subject to continue working with the initial hypothesis even after some contradictory evidence. If the hypothesis is generally correct, additional exemplars will improve the error ratio, and the tolerance variable may eventually be satisfied, allowing the subject to remain in deductive mode. The rate of concept learning within a particular mode is thus dependent on the values for patience and tolerance, as well as the order of presentation of exemplars.

The second factor in cognitive profile design and selection comes from the subjective data provided by the human subjects. During Part 1, subjects were asked four questions at selected times over blocks of eight trials: How did you decide to accept or reject an altitude request? Did your strategy change over the eight trials? Did you use a rule? If yes, I accepted an altitude request when. . . . We inspected these data to determine (a) learning strategy used, and (b) success in solving a problem. It also provided clues about when a correct solution was found, although the performance data may have shown some errors after this point. Among other things, the analysis revealed that some subjects believed they had correctly solved a problem when, in fact, the expressed concept and performance data indicate they had not. Use of the rote strategy was relatively easy to uncover, but latent learning (emergent mode) was difficult to uncover in any direct way, and detection of the evaluative modes fell in between. It often was not possible to make a reliable judgment about what strategy was used or how and when it may have been shifted. Nevertheless, the subjective data indicate that strategies were used and shifts in strategy were employed when deemed useful. Further, it also provided at least a rough guide to aid in designing the models.

A second analysis was performed on the individual subjective data to determine what proportion of the subjects actually solved the category learning problem and the individual rate of learning. We used this information to provide a rough guide for the learning rate and success level to be distributed over the 12 DCOG-2 model profiles. In other words, we did not attempt to accurately model either the group mean data or any specific individual learning data when setting the tolerance and patience variables or setting an initial learning strategy. Rather the human data were used only as a rough guide for setting these values. We elected to use 12 profiles, in part, to make the point that different cognitive styles in behavior can result in identical outcome performance from the same cognitive architecture. This is in keeping with our interest in gaining a better understanding of how equally qualified experts might use their cognitive resources in individualistic ways.

In general, the deductive mode profile was the one we used most frequently across all three problem categories because it could act in an emergent manner, a pure deductive reasoning manner, a rote memorization manner, or a combination of all three. Thus, with the use of suitable patience and tolerance values, this could have been the sole learning mode incorporated in the DCOG-2 model. However, we feel that an amalgamation of strategic learning modes and mode shifting better reflect the cognitive architecture of humans and the range of cognitive styles likely to have been used by the human participants in the AMBR study.

Altitude Request Task Performance

The outcome performance data for the category learning is shown in Fig. 6.8. The graphs compare DCOG-2 learning behavior with human subjects by type of learning problem. The proportion of exemplars classified incorrectly (error proportion) is shown as a function of learning epoch, expressed as a block number, where each block is comprised of 16 learning trials. Each curve reflects group mean data over 30 actors.

From visual inspection, it is clear that model learning is similar to that of humans for each of the three problem types. For Category I problems, DCOG-2 starts with more errors, but improves at about the human rate until Block 8. Terminal performance is slightly worse for the model relative to the human subjects. For Category III problems, DCOG-2 did not improve in performance at Block 4 while the humans did. Then DCOG's performance increased too fast relative to the human and ended with slightly better per-

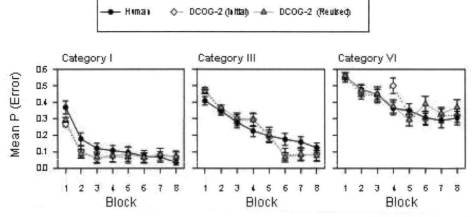

FIG. 6.8. Observed and DCOG-2 predicted (initial and revised) category learning data for Type I, III, and VI problems.

formance at the end. For Category VI problems, DCOG-2 essentially matched the human profile except at Block 4. At that point, the model regressed in learning while humans, on average, continued to improve.

The degraded DCOG-2 group mean performance at Block 4 is probably the result of two factors. As an expedient to dramatically reduce the amount of time required to produce the model data, the exemplar order used by a small subset of human subjects was used for all of the model runs. The presentation order of exemplars influences the rate of learning and the potential for strategy shifting as a random effect. As a result, DCOG's learning rate is expected to be more structured and localized at a point because the smoothing provided by the random factor is not able to occur as well for the model. Block 4 happened to be a point where several shifts in learning occurred. Normally the impact of the strategy shift would be smoothed over more trials when different exemplar presentation orders are used because some shifting would occur earlier or later in the block. We expect that if the full set of presentation orders were used, the Block 4 data points for Problems III and IV would better approach that of the human subjects.

Part 2 of the study involved a transfer of training task. The results of this part of the study are depicted graphically in Fig. 6.9. Classification errors (proportion) are shown as a function of exemplar classification. The exemplars presented on the transfer task were divided into the subset that was also presented during training in Part 1 of the study (trained) and the exemplar subset that was presented for the first time in Part 2 (extrapolated). There were eight trained exemplars and 17 extrapolated exemplars. Terminal learning performance from Part 1 is also provided as a reference (original trial). Separate plots are shown for the three types of category learning

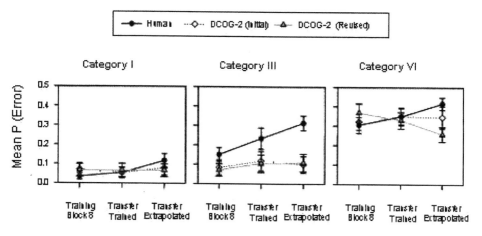

FIG. 6.9.   Observed and DCOG-2 predicted (initial and revised) transfer task results for Block 8 learning data, trained, and extrapolated transfer test stimuli.

problems. The graphs are based on group mean data (n = 30 subjects per category).

For Category I problems, DCOG-2's transfer of learning performance appears to be quite similar to that of human subjects. This is markedly less true for Category III problems. The model tended to perform too well, relative to humans, on both trained and extrapolated exemplars. Overperformance by the model on extrapolated exemplars is also seen for Category VI problems. Taken together, this suggests that DCOG-2 used knowledge from the original training in a more comprehensive and consistent manner than did the human subjects.

We are not surprised by this outcome. The solution to Category I problems is easily characterized in terms of a simple concept involving knowledge about a single dimension. Extrapolation from the values to be accepted and rejected is, in general, straightforward. More extreme new exemplars are grouped with their nearest originally trained neighbor. Only a mid-value exemplar presents a problem: Should the actor round up or down? As a result, one would expect humans to perform well on the new items and to be consistent in solving the problem for the new items. DCOG-2 shows the same attributes. The model takes a new exemplar, interpolates it to the form of the training set of exemplars, and makes its accept or reject decision accordingly. The model performance was about 6% to 8% better than human performance. This suggests that the added cognitive burden of matching new exemplars with similar old ones induces slightly more errors for the human subjects. DCOG did not suffer from this effect.

The situation is different for Category III and VI problems. For Category III problems, some of the difference between human and DCOG performance in the transfer task may simply reflect the difference in end-of-training learning state. Because DCOG had fewer errors at the end of initial training, the model had a head start in evaluating the transfer task exemplars. Another source of performance differences is the possible use of abductive reasoning by human subjects in novel situations.

In contrast to Category I problems, no simple concept subsumes the Category III problems. As a result, use of knowledge about the previously learned exemplars is problematic in terms of its value to aid the learner in how to best think about the newly seen extrapolated exemplars. We suspect that humans tend to turn to abductive logic under these conditions. That is, they appeal strongly to their rich world knowledge, past experience, and selected stored cases. DCOG-2 was not able to appeal to a similarly rich world knowledge base. Although DCOG-2 did support abductive reasoning, its world knowledge was impoverished and restricted to a few data facts relevant to items in the work domain. The model relies more on the initial learning experience within the task, which turns out to be the more appropriate response. If the human subjects did indeed turn to abductive reasoning when faced with the new task, we might expect the model to perform more consistently relative to the humans.

Comparable DCOG and human performance on the trained exemplars is not surprising for Category VI problems. Both DCOG and humans seem to move toward instance learning. Hence, they can respond to the trained items in the transfer task in a straightforward manner. Given comparable end-of-training performance, we would expect this to carry over to the trained exemplars in the transfer condition.

It is not clear why DCOG's performance on the extrapolated exemplars is better than that of the human subjects. Obviously, instance learning does not apply directly to the extrapolated exemplars. DCOG relates the extrapolated exemplars to known exemplars and uses the accept or reject values associated with those exemplars. Human subjects may have used some other method to evaluate extrapolated exemplars. Perhaps the human subjects' performance was reduced by the introduction of abductive reasoning in this novel situation. Another possibility is that the additional workload of dealing with the extrapolated exemplars interfered with the human subjects' memory for known exemplars.

Modeling teams were given an opportunity to make model modifications to improve transfer of learning performance. This was unexpected, and we did not have the resources to carefully revisit the model in this regard within the allowed time frame. However, we did make a small change to the model. We reasoned that subjects who did not successfully solve a learning problem might be less consistent in making responses on the transfer task. If they behaved more randomly, this might account for why humans made more errors on the transfer task than the DCOG-2 model, and that the mean error performance was worse than the DCOG-2 model. Based on this logic, we added code to identify solvers from nonsolvers. For the solver group, the original model code was used, which was biased toward making interpolations relative to the end-of-training learning state. For nonsolvers, the code was modified to eliminate this bias, and decisions were made solely on the basis of activation strength of the raw knowledge components available at the beginning of the transfer task. We expected this change to result in more varied (random-like) behavior for the nonsolver group.

The graph for the revised model is shown in Fig. 6.9. The data indicate that DCOG performance better matched human performance at the end of training. This may simply be a random fluctuation in DCOG performance induced by the interaction between the initial guess and the exemplar sequence. DCOG's improvement on the trained exemplars during the transfer task follows directly from the pervious result. Yet DCOG performance on the extrapolated items was surprising. It implies that the correct answer for new extrapolated items was correlated with end-state, feature-level knowledge of the DCOG model. Why this might be the case is not clear.

It is important to note that we chose not to simply manipulate a parameter to fit the DCOG model behavior to the human transfer data. This could have easily been done, but the data would not be particularly informative given our belief that humans revert to abductive reasoning when uncertainty is high. It remains a challenge to adequately address abductive reasoning in a computational model.

Subjective Workload Performance

The DCOG-2 model included provisions for calculating mental workload values. Human subjects provided subjective workload estimates using the NASA TLX workload index. Accordingly, cognitive properties of the DCOG-2 model were reviewed in an effort to locate potential measurable characteristics that could map to the six TLX scales.

The workload evaluation covers the complete air traffic management work. That is, it covers the four hand-off subtasks and the embedded category learning subtask. Based on a review of the model code, 11 cognitive

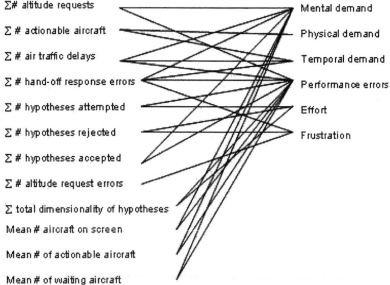

FIG. 6.10. A list of DCOG-2 variables used to predict subjective workload and their mapping to the TLX workload scales.

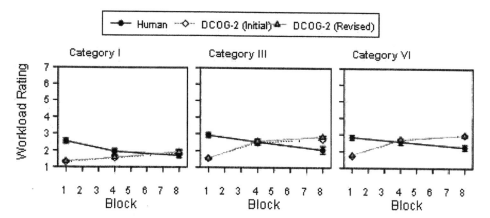

FIG. 6.11.   Observed and DCOG-2 predicted subjective workload ratings administered after Blocks 1, 4, and 8.

factors provided data that could be readily evaluated and linked to TLX workload scales. These factors and the mapping to the TLX scales are provided in Fig. 6.10. A single variable may be included in the calculation of several TLX scale values. Different weights are used to specify each variables contribution to each TLX scale.

Workload data from the AMBR study are presented for human subjects and the DCOG-2 model in Fig. 6.11. Workload ratings were administered after Blocks 1, 4, and 8. The graphs show mean composite ratings for human subjects, DCOG-2, and the revised model. The data are presented by category learning problem type.

The general trend of the DCOG-2 model data is that they underestimate subjective workload, relative to humans (early in the learning process), they nearly match the human data at Block 4, and they overestimate it at the end in Block 8.

Given the state of development of the DCOG architecture, we believe it is premature to identify factors that may correlate with subjective workload except in a tentative manner. Many properties of the architecture remain to be defined, and some current properties are artifacts of the current model instantiations. For example, the perception of time figures into different subscales of subjective workload. As indicated earlier, we do not yet handle time in the DCOG architecture in a principled manner. Thus, it is unlikely that current properties of the DCOG architecture can be used to provide a satisfactory picture of its metacognitive state. Given this situation, we think it is best to defer a more comprehensive discussion of the architecture in terms of subject workload until a later time. We have included the workload data mainly for the sake of completeness and to illustrate how properties of the operational level of the architecture could be mapped to the metacognitive variable of subjective workload.

We also hasten to point out that even if the DCOG architecture were stable, it would be a large undertaking to provide empirical justification for defining the mappings between individual DCOG model properties that are congruent with the mapping of cognitive properties of human subjects and their mapping, in turn, to the TLX scales. If this congruence is not formed, then the mapping is ad hoc.

In DCOG-2 as in DCOG-1, we were mainly concerned with demonstrating how a distributed modeling framework using a combination of abstract representational objects and associative weight strengths could achieve human-like cognitive behavior doing complex work. The results indicate that, at least to a first approximation, the model does emulate human learning behavior and performance. Yet it clearly deviated from human behavior on the transfer task. We believe this is likely due to the fact that inadequate world knowledge was available in the DCOG memory to support a suitable range of abductive and inductive behavior.

PLANS FOR FUTURE DEVELOPMENT OF THE DCOG ARCHITECTURE

We intend to eventually model the mind computationally as a state change system. This section presents an overview of the state change paradigm and our plans for extending the DCOG architecture.

The state change paradigm treats information and knowledge as properties of the mind system architecture. That is, information and knowledge constitute states of the substrate that are produced by local processes which are also part of the substrate (i.e., the mind substrate and stored knowledge are not separate items). Knowledge and knowledge formation are intrinsic properties of the mind system. The term *state change* is used to describe the system to emphasize the notion that the dynamics of the system necessarily change the active state of knowledge. Knowledge is latent when a state does not exist or is said to be inactive. Given a current stimulus situation, some knowledge is brought into an active state. State changes can be initiated from stimulation derived from both external and internal sources. A movement in the external environment, for example, may stimulate a state change in a specific mind region. A state in mind Region A may stimulate a change in mind Region B. Cognitive behavior of the mind as a whole involves the coordination of states and state changes across the set of mind regions.

The state change metaphor of mind has been proposed by several neurophysiologists (e.g., Damasio, 1989; Edelman, 1987, 1989; Engel et al., 1991; Hebb, 1949; Singer, 1993, 1995; von der Malsburg, 1987). Our version of a state change framework for computational modeling is perhaps most consistent with ideas from Damasio (1989), who emphasized the existence of a distributed set of neural work areas that incorporate local processes that follow a set of unified operating principles. It is also consistent with the theorizing of Maturana and Varela (1980), who proposed a structural coupling theory as a way to study and understand complex living organisms. Although it is more difficult to implement this framework computationally at the scale of complex human behavior than it is to implement an information-processing framework, the state change perspective appears to have greater potential in terms of current understanding of human neurophysiology.

We model a state change system by utilizing a software agent architecture. A software agent is an independent thread of execution that performs local processing. Multiple threads may operate in parallel. We form software agents into a state change mind system by applying a basic set of principles to capture the essence of a mind system. These principles are realized through various architectural features. As our framework matures, we expect to modify and extend these principles based on empirical findings. The framework is founded on four principles:

- Distributive knowledge and distributive control
- Multiple emergent forms of knowledge
- Broadcast signaling as the means of communication among mind centers
- Cognitive strategy as the foundation for complex purposeful behavior

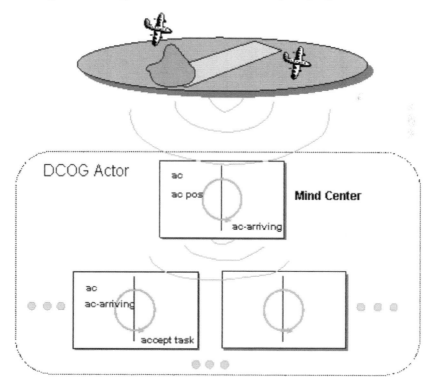

State Change Framework

FIG. 6.12.   A schematic representation of the DCOG mind model.

The first three of these principles are illustrated by the schematic depiction of the DCOG state change mind model shown in Fig. 6.12.

The principles are expressed as properties or characteristics of a mind model. We briefly discuss the embodiment of these principles in the context of a DCOG actor model that is situated in an environment. A DCOG actor is composed of several mind regions or centers, each of which has its own knowledge, knowledge forms, and processing capabilities. An energy pattern from the environment may stimulate one or more centers through specialized sensors. As shown in the figure, one mind center picks up stimulation from the world. This activates a pattern in the center that is locally processed as knowledge. Knowledge is a property of the processing state. In this instance, it constitutes an image of the environment or, more accurately, some aspects of the environment over some region. The mind center may also have other processing capabilities that create other knowledge and knowledge forms. Here knowledge in the initial mind center results from stimulation provided by the environment. It results in the activation of aircraft (ac) and aircraft position (ac pos) as local knowledge elements. We call this *feature-based knowledge.* Through other local processing, the center has the ability to perceive this information in another form, ac-arriving. Several different forms are possible across different centers. For example, the ac-arriving knowledge in the initial center may be a more abstract form of feature-based knowledge, while the same meaning may be conveyed in a *symbol-based knowledge* form in another center, such as the one on the left side of the figure. A third form of knowledge may be called *functional knowledge,* which is derived from its use potential relative to an actor's work situation. When this form of knowledge corresponds with feature-based images, it is called an *affordance* (Gibson, 1979). When it is based on symbolic information, it represents a kind of conceptual knowledge. Various forms and aggregations of knowledge may be developed from associations within local centers. In the figure, the knowledge items on the left side in a mind center represent states that have been stimulated from outside sources, whereas the knowledge items on the right have been formed internally from local capabilities. Each local mind center favors certain knowledge and knowledge forms, and the same knowledge may be available in several centers.

Each center broadcasts some of its states. These states act as stimulation for other centers and may induce coordinated knowledge states across them. Here broadcasts from the center at the top of the figure stimulate two other centers in the mind network. Each produces local knowledge, some of which is then broadcast to the network. Centers may be tuned for certain broadcast, and thus the broadcast may act like a trigger or control information for other centers. Therefore, knowledge may serve as a meaning structure as well as a control mechanism.

The dynamics of the system are carried by state changes. At any point in time, some knowledge states are active, whereas others are not. Some states serve as control signals and some do not. Specialization of knowledge forms and content across centers provide a method to achieve a coordinated flow of activity over the mind network. This results in the outcome behavior at the actor scale.

Mind centers are broad functional units. They are not intended to correspond directly with the functional descriptions of brain structures. Each center produces a form of awareness and understanding. We assume there is a center for the four high-level functions of sensory, perceptual, cognitive, and motor understanding. Each of these is regarded as a system, with the complete mind being a system of systems. These systems are governed by principles that yield a self-organizing macrosystem.

The state change framework supports highly flexible and adaptable behavior. Numerous patterns of activity can wash over the network in a manner that is associated with the external situation. Based on internal dynamics, patterns within and across the functional domains can form, and patterns of patterns can also form. Because some of these patterns encode the basis for generating symbolic objects, complex and original cognitive creation can be supported. These capabilities support highly flexible and adaptable behavior.

Mind patterns may encode a broad strategy for framing and hence organizing activity in the environment. A strategy acts as an activated conceptual framework or global way of thinking. Although two different strategies or guiding frameworks may be applicable for the same goal-directed task, what state elements constitute information and how it is viewed depend on the invoked strategy. There is a fundamental circularity here: A set of information elements may trigger a strategy (induce it into an active state). Alternatively, an active strategy may set expectancies for what patterns constitute information elements—the interpretation given to these elements in the context of the active strategy or frame. Thus, a strategy may serve to prime the recognition of functional meaning useful for task performance. Either the frame or the relevant information may be active first, and over time they will tend to achieve a coherent coupled state.

We propose the strategy-guiding principle as a means for an intelligent cognitive actor to achieve our asserted goal of cognition—to enhance the adaptive range of a living entity. We reason that the central purpose of a cognitive system is to extend the range of environments and environment states in which an actor may behave in a successful manner. The introduction of symbolic forms of knowledge and symbolic-based reasoning represents the highest known basis for extending flexibility and adaptability.

Our initial research with the DCOG framework reported here begins to show some of the characteristics of our state change theory. We used a simple associative weighting scheme based on feature activation to form both implicit and explicit concepts. Strategies served as high-order cognitive units that guided how the lower level feature and concept information were utilized in problem solving. These strategies, interacting with so-called *personality factors* of an actor, influenced the approach to problem solving. This demonstrated how different styles of work behavior could achieve comparable performance.

The DCOG framework shares characteristics with other paradigms for modeling cognition while it also has some unique features. We summarize here some similarities to an information-processing framework, a connectionist framework, and a self-organizing state change framework. The information-processing framework presents a functional model of mind that includes separate store and control structures. Data from the environment are transformed in various ways as they are processed, stored, recalled, and used in performing a task. In general, knowledge is encoded symbolically in modeling, which follows the information-processing framework. However, ACT-R (Anderson & Lebiere, 1998), perhaps the most accomplished cognitive architecture, which has its roots in the information-processing framework, is best classified as a hybrid architecture that represents knowledge both symbolically and subsymbolically (see chap. 4, this volume).

The connectionist approach attempts to model cognition in terms of neural networks. In part it represents an effort to avoid the brittleness of classical artificial intelligence (AI) approaches to modeling human intelligence. It is a subsymbolic approach in that symbols are not used to denote objects and relations. Instead knowledge is represented implicitly in the patterns of interaction among a network of common, nondescriptive computational units.

The concept of self-organization plays a prominent role in other approaches used to model cognition within a state change framework. For example, Kelso (1999) developed a research program around the notion of dynamic, self-organizing patterns. In this approach, high-level synergetic units are postulated to act as global parameters, called *collective variables*, that both organize and depend on lower order microfluctuations to achieve coordinated action patterns.

The DCOG framework resembles the state change framework developed by Kelso: DCOG also follows a layered approach, with the notion of a strategy serving as a higher order framing, guiding, and organizing construct. In some sense, a strategy is a cognitive-level Gestalt that operates interactively with lower level cognitive elements.

The DCOG approach takes a self-organizing position, like Kelso, but exploits the use of symbolic elements in the computational architecture, like the classic information-processing approach. The state change framework is in general consistent with the connectionist paradigm in its use of associative patterns. However, like classical AI, we use descriptive symbolic units instead of uniform, nondescriptive ones.

We further invoke separate functional mind systems or centers as using different types of symbolic information. As a result, we have interactions across symbol systems, as opposed to direct transformation of a symbol into another one. Our use of symbolic elements allows us to integrate implicit and explicit representations of abstract knowledge. We believe this will add considerably to the flexibility and adaptability of cognitive models produced within the DCOG framework.

Our long-term goal is to provide a state change architecture that has general features and thus can support the implementation of a wide range of behavioral models. We think that the various types of knowledge units—the symbolic and subsymbolic representations of knowledge units, the real-time associative-based formation of such units, and the strategy-based learning modes of knowing, thinking, and learning implemented so far—are amenable to the development of a stable, open cognitive architecture. We also believe this approach allows us to more rapidly produce software actors that can behave intelligently in complex, simulated worlds that require an actor to adjust to subtle shifts in a situation or reorganize thinking to meet new demands.

GENERAL DISCUSSION AND SUMMARY

In the last section, we briefly described the direction along which we plan to mature the DCOG framework. Although the DCOG-1 and DCOG-2 models cannot yet achieve the degree of desired robustness in terms of human-like flexibility and adaptability of behavior in accomplishing complex work, they were able to show these properties in the AMBR project. Complex work usually has some degree of openness, in the sense that novel situations can arise that cannot be fully anticipated. Humans are able to handle this openness by creatively formulating new and nonstandard methods to meet the exigencies of the moment. Models of human behavior must be able to do the same thing.

The ATC task is an example of complex work. The detailed traffic movement pattern, for example, is unpredictable from trial to trial. This openness is a major reason why flexible and adaptable behavior is valuable. As a result, we believe a model of cognition, and more generally a cognitive architecture, must be able to address variations in expert performance and understand features and symbols in terms of the local context. In other words, individual differences in behavioral strategy and the contextualization of meaning are general cognitive phenomena that need to be handled by any cognitive architecture. They indicate that cognitive behavior is situated. To address these important properties of cognition, we developed models of cognition in a distributed framework that emphasized multiple centers of local processing capability and control, each using and producing knowledge units. Some knowledge is used internally within a mind center, and other knowledge is broadcast for use elsewhere. The coordinated interplay across these regions accounts for flexible and adaptable behavior of the model at the scale of the actor. Taken as a whole, the DCOG modeling framework as developed is an example of a complex distributed system that utilizes abstraction in performing work.

In contrast with the classic information-processing framework, which emphasizes a transformation style process, the DCOG framework emphasizes an activation and association style of processing. Activation is assumed to select primitive (previously complied) knowledge units for a state of readiness of use. Association allows the system both to form new knowledge units and coordinate existing (active) ones into large operational units meaningful for the prevailing context. We may think of the most basic or distilled knowledge unit as a feature. Active association then generates local concepts, and broader coordination results in unitized concept sets.

We have shown a range of expressions of concepts in the DCOG system. Each concept represents a form of knowledge expressed at some level of aggregation, either explicitly or implicitly. For example, schema and procedural concepts are explicitly represented in the schema and exec agents. Smaller concepts like 20-L-3-accept are formed and activated in the associative memory agent. Still other forms of concept knowledge are encoded in an implicit manner. The activation pattern over a set of feature nodes, for example, defines concepts based on the activation strength profile. It reflects emergent concept formation. Perhaps one of the more interesting features of the DCOG system is the fact that both feature- and symbol-based concepts coexist in the same system, and they can interact to determine the knowledge state in an emergent context. This was demonstrated in the deductive learning mode when some uncertainty about what guess to make still existed based on symbol knowledge, and image-based feature knowledge (i.e., latent learning) was included in the process to aid the actor in formulating an answer.

The contextualization of meaning is another important characteristic that a mind model must address. The DCOG-2 model reveals how context may span the sequence of external events, internal task-related facts, and other internal states of knowledge. This distributed collection of states establishes an implicit meaning state that may significantly influence the observed behavior of the model. For example, the DCOG-2 model records the input feature stream and uses it to trigger different feature- and symbol-based knowledge forms. It also records knowledge about the success of concept learning performance over the last three learning events. These task-relevant bits of distributed knowledge interact with the nontask knowledge that expresses idiosyncratic characteristics of an actor in terms of the attributes of tolerance and patience. The event stream data, task-relevant, and nontask-specific knowledge mutually influence each other to establish the context in which the next guess is made and thereby impact learning and learning rate. Once learning is consolidated, however, some of these bits of knowledge are less dominant, and the model may appear to simply rely on a single fact or concept (e.g., it demonstrates instance learning). This suggests that context is dynamically changing, and the relative importance of different features of the model changes also. Perhaps this is one reason why it is exceedingly difficult to discover fundamental properties to be encoded into a mind model that attempts to predict human behavior under naturalistic work situations.

From a control perspective, the DCOG system employs a family of nested layers of control, each of which may involve distributed interaction across several mind centers. At the lowest level, activation and associative mechanisms serve to create a control system for memory formation and accumulation. At the next level, other variables such as relative specificity, patience, and tolerance serve to create a control system for learning strategy selection and shifting among alternative strategies. At the outermost level, the broadcasting of state information across the full collection of agents induces a flexible process-one control strategy that tends to result in a cycling between updating awareness of the environment situation and executing a single aircraft service decision. This process-one strategy prevailed for the entire ATC work task, but could have been modified based on changes in local conditions.

We suspect that the co-occurrence of multiple levels of nested control may be a defining property of a complex adaptive system, such as the human mind, providing a wide range of flexibility and adaptability in potential behavior. However, it is much too early in our research to make such claims. At this point, we only note that the control properties of the DCOG-2 model can be characterized in this manner.

We have demonstrated how the inclusion of a small set of variables in the DCOG mind model can contribute to different behavior processes that give rise to a comparable level of skill in category learning performance. This is consistent with the subject data, which indicated that the pool of subjects used different strategies to achieve comparable performance on the learning task. We believe it is important for a mind model to address individual differences. On the one hand, a mind model must be able to define fundamental properties of the architecture that apply to all humans. On the other hand, it must also be able to show how these same properties can be employed in flexible and adaptive ways to support individual differences in style of behavior. We have used the concept of a strategy as a high-level basis for guiding behavior. Given our distributed and nested control architecture, it has been possible to include variables that give rise to individual differences while yielding comparable performance. Again it is too early to suggest that the variables we have selected should be regarded as fundamental properties that must be included in an architecture of the mind that wishes to emulate a complex and sophisticated level of human cognitive behavior and perform- ance. Nevertheless, this is a challenge for the research community to address the issue of individual differences in a fundamental way.

Both DCOG-1 and DCOG-2 demonstrated qualitatively human-like be- havior and performance. Qualitative measures are, we believe, the most ap- propriate level of evaluation at this time given the state of maturity of the ar- chitecture. As indicated earlier, timing was not included in the models in a principled manner. Further, we have not yet fully implemented our envi- sioned feature-based memory system. Nor have we established principles that can be used to help determine what properties of a mind model are fundamental and what properties should be represented implicitly or ex- plicitly. These are difficult issues, and we have just started our journey to ad- dress them.

COMMON QUESTIONS

To facilitate comparison across the various computational cognitive systems described in this book, each modeling team was asked to provide answers to a set of common questions. We close with our answers to these questions.

How Is Cognition Represented in Your System?

Cognition is represented in terms of features and concepts. In DCOG-1, these knowledge elements are formed into knowledge schemas that exe- cute under distributed control. In DCOG-2, the associative weight across features serves to define implicit concepts and also provides a basis for the generation of explicit symbolic concepts. In addition, cognition is also rep- resented at the level of an organizing frame or strategy. One single strategy was implicit in the structure of DCOG-1; several strategies for decision mak- ing are explicitly available in DCOG-2.

What Is Your Modeling Methodology?

The DCOG-1 and DCOG-2 models represent incremental developments of a new architecture. There are fundamental differences between the two models, and some elements of the architecture are not fully specified (see Table 6.1 for a summary). Hence, there is no specific methodology for cre- ating DCOG models at this time.

What Role Does Parameter Tuning Play?

The model is not tuned via parameters. Parameters exist to model individual differences. We create individual model actors and aggregate their performance. We attempt to fit the model to the data by varying the number of individual models in each personality type to better match the distribution of human actors.

What Is Your Account of Individual Differences?

We propose that actors use a variety of reasoning modes for categorization, including emergent reasoning (latent, exemplar-based), rote reasoning (instance learning, requiring memorization of particular exemplars), and deductive reasoning (hypothesis creation and testing).

Actors differ in their preferred reasoning style, their patience in achieving an understanding of a category, and their tolerance of errors or exceptions. We create individual actor models, each with its own preferred reasoning style and its own numerical patience and tolerance values.

We assume that, although an actor has a preferred reasoning mode (strategies), all modes are available, and that actors shift modes when they perceive that the current mode is unsuccessful.

What Is Your Account of Cognitive Workload?

Workload measures are not fully integrated in the model at this time. Workload affects the model indirectly via time limitations on the number of actions that can be completed before penalties take effect. Workload affects the model explicitly, in that the model adjusts its scanning behavior when anticipating a large number of service events. In this situation, the model pays more attention to the problem areas.

Workload is explicitly measured as an aggregate of several factors, including external factors, such as number of aircraft and number of altitude requests, and internal factors, such as number and dimensionality of hypotheses under consideration. However, this workload measure is not used to directly affect the model's behavior.

What Is Your Account of Multitasking?

The DCOG-1 model is not under general control. Rather control is distributed across several agents representing various mind regions. The agents communicate by broadcasting messages and attending to messages created by the other agents and the simulation. A radar agent continually updates the interpretation of incoming visual information. Another agent maintains an associational memory structure for categorization decision-based information, whereas an executive agent determines appropriate actions. This distributed control leads to multitasking as part of the normal behavior of the model.

The DCOG-2 model relies on some procedural behavior. For example, the executive agent directly calls on the associative memory agent to categorize altitude requests. Operations are still concurrent, however, in that the associative memory agent maintains memory of feature and symbolic information independently of the executive agent.

What Is Your Account of Categorization?

Categorization in this model involves both perceptual features and abstract symbols. Feature-based categorization is based on associative knowledge derived from a series of exemplars; it is considered emergent or latent knowledge. Symbol-based categorization models hypothesis creation and testing. Symbols represent concepts; the creation of symbols and association links from symbols to features constitutes hypothesis formation. An observation of the proportion of links from the symbol to each category feature provides a means of hypothesis evaluation.

Individual actors may prefer to rely more on perceptual features or abstract symbols, although feature-based knowledge is always available to inform decision making. The extent to which the actor relies on features versus symbols depends, in part, on individual differences in preferred reasoning style, patience, and tolerance relative to success on the categorization task.

ACKNOWLEDGMENTS

We would like to express our sincere appreciation to Dr. Vincent Schmidt and Mr. Robin Snyder, Jr. Vince and Rob were instrumental in rehosting the DCOG-1 model in Java and made significant contributions to the Java implementation of DCOG-2. We would also like to thank the anonymous reviewers for their thoughtful comments.

REFERENCES

Anderson, J. A., & Lebiere, C. (1998). *The atomic components of thought.* Mahwah, NJ: Lawrence Erlbaum Associates.
Damasio, A. R. (1989). Time-locked multiregional retoactivation: A systems level proposal for the neural substrates of recall and recognition. *Cognition, 33,* 25–62.
Edelman, G. M. (1987). *Neural Darwinism.* New York: Basic Books.

Edelman, G. M. (1989). *The remembered present: A biological theory of consciousness.* New York: Basic Books.

Engel, A. K., Konig, P., Gray, C. M., & Singer, W. (1991). Stimulus-dependent neural oscillation in cat visual cortex: Inter-columnar interaction as determined by cross-correlation analysis. *European Journal of Neuroscience, 2,* 588–606.

Gibson, J. J. (1979). *The ecological approach to visual perception.* Boston: Houghton-Mifflin.

Hebb, D. O. (1949). *The organization of behavior.* New York: Wiley.

Kelso, J. A. S. (1999). *Dynamic patterns: The self-organization of brain and behavior.* Cambridge, MA: MIT Press.

Maturana, H. R., & Varela, F. (1980). *Autopoiesis and cognition: The realization of the living.* Dordrecht: Reidel.

Rasmussen, J. (1983). Skills, rules, knowledge: Signals, signs, and symbols and other distinctions in human performance models. *IEEE Transactions on Systems, Man, and Cybernetics, SMC-13*(3), 257–267.

Rasmussen, J. (1986). *Information processing and human-machine interaction: An approach to cognitive engineering.* New York: Elsevier Science Publishing.

Rasmussen, J., Pejtersen, A. M., & Goodstein, L. P. (1994). *Cognitive systems engineering.* New York: Wiley.

Shepard, R. N., Hovland, C. L., & Jenkins, H. M. (1961). Learning and memorization of classifications. *Psychological Monographs, 75*(13, Whole No. 517).

Singer, W. (1993). Synchronization of cortical activity and its putative role in information processing and learning. *Annual Review of Physiology, 55,* 349–374.

Singer, W. (1995). Development and plasticity of cortical processing architectures. *Science, 270,* 758–763.

Sperandio, J.-C. (1978). The regulation of working methods as a function of work-load among air traffic controllers. *Ergonomics, 21,* 195–202.

von der Malsburg, C. (1987). Synaptic plasticity as the basis of brain organization. In J.-P. Changeux & M. Konishi (Eds.), *The neural and molecular basis of learning* (pp. 411–432). New York: Wiley.

Vicente, K. (1999). *Cognitive work analysis: Towards safe productive and healthy computer based work.* Hillsdale, NJ: Lawrence Erlbaum Associates.

Chapter 7

Inheriting Constraint in Hybrid Cognitive Architectures: Applying the EASE Architecture to Performance and Learning in a Simplified Air Traffic Control Task

Ronald S. Chong
George Mason University

Robert E. Wray
Soar Technology, Inc.

This chapter describes the development and evaluation of models of behavior in the AMBR air traffic control (ATC) and category learning tasks, with an emphasis on modeling constraints derived from our methodology. Our overall modeling philosophy is driven by cognitive architectures as theories of human perception, cognition, and action. Architectures are critical to the development of broad, comprehensive theories Allen Newell (1990) called *unified theories of cognition* (UTCs). Cognitive architectures, as instantiations of UTCs, comprise a set of fixed (or slowly evolving) mechanisms and representations on which models of a wide range of behavior can be built.

We adopt, as constraints, several of Newell's principles and recommendations on the development and use of models and architectures. First is "listening to the architecture" or making a commitment to an architecture's mechanisms. When modeling a new behavior or phenomenon, one must use the existing mechanisms rather than introduce new mechanisms solely to address the requirements of the model or fit data. However, only when behavior cannot be plausibly implemented using an architecture's existing mechanisms should the set of mechanisms be amended, either by modifying existing mechanisms or adding new mechanisms. In this work, when considering architectural change, we followed an integrative approach, incorporating validated components from other architectures rather than modifying the architecture less conservatively. EASE, the architecture developed and used here, combines elements of ACT-R, Soar, and EPIC into one integrated hybrid architecture.

For architectures to have theoretical power, results and validations from previous model implementations must cumulate as constraints on future modeling efforts (Newell, 1990). This principle of cumulation as constraint led us to reuse existing models. For Experiment 2 (the category learning with ATC task), one previously developed model was reused, and another, not originally developed in an architectural theory, adapted to EASE. The principle of cumulation also applies to architecture mechanisms: EASE brings together theoretical strengths of several existing architectures, incorporating both the mechanisms and common parameter settings in an explicit attempt to inherit the validation and consequent constraint of multiple architectures. Cumulation reduces flexibility in creating models, but increases the predictive and theoretical power of architectural models.

Taking architectural constraint seriously during model creation and refinement leads to an emphasis of explanation over fitting. Freely changing architectural mechanisms, model knowledge, and model and architecture parameters may lead to better fits to the data, but not necessarily to an improved understanding of the underlying phenomena. We deliberately chose to minimize such changes, fixing model knowledge, parameter settings, and the architecture to the extent possible. The positive consequence of such constraint is clearly evident in the Experiment 2 Symbolic Concept Acquisition (SCA) model. Although the initial prediction of the aggregate human data was quite poor, we resisted abandoning the model or radically reformulating it or the architecture, choosing instead to perform a fine-grained analysis of the individual human data. This analysis revealed that the model did match the learning trajectories of some individual subjects, and that some subjects were considering factors that the task instructions directed them to ignore. Thus, the architectural constraint led to significantly broader understanding of the human behavior in the task.

In summary, the focus of this work was to understand architectural and task constraints and to develop plausible models that took these constraints into account.

SYSTEM-LEVEL ANALYSIS OF THE TASK

Like most complex tasks humans perform, the ATC and category learning tasks, as described in chapters 2 and 3, rely on multiple human systems—visual sensation and perception, memory, cognition, and action—and the interaction of such systems (e.g., eye–hand coordination).

Our first model development step was to assess the influence of each of these systems on task performance. This preliminary assessment is useful because it:

- informs the selection of a modeling framework or architecture,
- provides the modeler with a sense of the model's eventual complexity,
- helps identify existing empirical task-relevant behavioral data that can be modeled, and
- points to existing models that might be reused and further validated.

This evaluation step, based on a functional analysis of the task and empirical studies that show connections between systems and behavior, provides qualitative bounding constraints for the modeling effort.

The ATC task has a strong visual perceptual component.[1] In functional terms, the eyes are responsible for finding features in the world that will trigger task-relevant behavior. Eye scan patterns affect what can be seen and when it can be seen. Therefore, we hypothesized that perception must have a significant influence over task performance.

The memory system also plays a key role in this task. There is often a long delay between attending to a blip on the display and performing an action on it. For example, when handing off an aircraft, one of the important features to be remembered is what action was last performed on the aircraft. Another feature is blip location. The volatility of human memory in situations such as these is readily observed in subjects and reported by them. Memory effects influence the overall task performance.

Knowledge in the cognitive system is inherently related to performance because it provides the strategies and decision-making processes for the task. In addition, the cognitive system can have strategies for coping with the limitations of the perceptual and memory systems. For example, memory rehearsal can be used to enhance one's ability to recall an item. Although all subjects should have the same task knowledge (per the task instructions), they can also employ vastly different knowledge (e.g., preexisting heuristics; their own resolution of ambiguities in the task) and biases (driven by motivation, personality, etc.). Arguably the greatest source of within- and between-subject variability is due to the knowledge.

The contribution of the manual motor system (hand movements) to performance was expected to be insignificant for the ATC tasks. We came to this conclusion because, once a task action sequence is triggered, its constituent steps can (nominally) be performed ballistically without intervening reasoning, producing roughly the same execution times regardless of the task conditions.[2] Therefore, we could have represented motor behavior as a simple, constant-time process. However, because mouse movements influ-

---

[1]Throughout this chapter, we use the term *perception* to refer to the sensory, perceptual, *and* ocular motor function of the eye.

[2]When task action execution time was later analyzed, no significant effect of task condition (aided/unaided) or difficulty was found, confirming this assumption.

ence eye-scan patterns through the eye–hand coordination required to move the mouse, we modeled manual motor behavior.

Other human systems could be considered in this kind of analysis. For example, the influence of the motivational, emotional, and physiological (e.g., fatigue, stress, etc.) systems could have been assessed. We instead made the simplifying assumption that, on average, these systems had an insignificant effect on overall performance.

Taken together, this qualitative analysis suggested a significant influence of the perceptual, memory, cognitive, and motor systems on task performance—not only due to the individual systems, but also the interaction of those systems. From this we concluded that we should construct a model that not only captures the details of the individual systems, but also their interaction.

ARCHITECTURE

The preceding analysis indicated we should use an architecture that provides psychologically plausible implementations of perception, cognition, memory, and motor systems. EPIC-Soar (Chong & Laird, 1997), a combination of EPIC (Meyer & Kieras, 1997a, 1997b) and Soar (Newell, 1990; Rosenbloom, Laird, & Newell, 1993), provided all of these elements except for a straightforward account of memory effects (forgetting).

During the course of the AMBR project, EPIC-Soar was extended to include base-level learning—the fundamental memory mechanism in ACT-R (Anderson & Lebiere, 1998)—to provide a validated account of memory volatility and retention. With this addition, EPIC-Soar was renamed EASE, for Elements of ACT-R, Soar, and EPIC. EASE is a hybrid system incorporating both symbolic and subsymbolic representations and mechanisms. We briefly describe each of these architectures, in order of their integration into EASE, concentrating only on aspects relevant to AMBR.

Soar

Soar is a general architecture for building artificially intelligent systems and modeling human cognition and behavior (Newell, 1990; Rosenbloom, Laird, & Newell, 1993). Soar has been used to model central human capabilities such as learning, problem solving, planning, search, natural language, and HCI tasks.

Soar is a production system that has been significantly extended to include mechanisms and structures believed to be functionally necessary for producing intelligent behavior. The processing cycle consists of a search for operators, the selection of a best operator, and the application of the

. operator. Operators encode persistent actions in Soar and generally correspond in function to the productions of ACT-R and EPIC. Soar has two memory representations: Procedural memory is represented by production rules, and declarative memory is represented by attribute-value structures.

There are occasions when knowledge search is insufficient and does not lead to the selection or application of an operator. This situation is called an *impasse*. To resolve an impasse, Soar automatically creates a subgoal where processing focuses on selecting and applying operators to resolve the impasse so that processing toward the parent goal can resume.

Soar incorporates a single learning mechanism called *chunking*. Chunking compiles the results of problem solving in a subgoal into new production rules. When combined with various problem-solving methods, chunking has been found to be sufficient for a variety of learning (Chong, 1998; Lewis et al., 1990; Miller & Laird, 1996; Wray & Chong, 2003).

One weakness of Soar is the difficulty of producing memory effects such as forgetting. In humans, forgetting is the default, nondeliberate condition, whereas remembering requires an effortful process (e.g., rehearsals or the use of a reliable encoding) or multiple exposures of the stimuli. Soar's declarative memory system has exactly the opposite properties: Remembering is the default condition, whereas forgetting requires the deliberate act of removing items from memory. Although Soar's present memory mechanisms can account for some memory effects (Young & Lewis, 1999), the architecture does not require models to follow such accounts. Performance in the ATC task, based on the system-level analysis, appears to be strongly influenced by memory effects. Therefore, we chose to explore an architectural change to EPIC-Soar for producing such memory effects.

EPIC

In contrast to Soar, which is theoretically silent on the topics of perception and action, EPIC's perceptual and motor processes provide sophisticated accounts of the capabilities and constraints of these systems. EPIC (Executive Process-Interactive Control; Kieras & Meyer, 1997; Meyer & Kieras, 1997a, 1997b) is an architecture whose primary goal is to account for detailed human dual-task performance. It extends the work begun with the model human processor (MHP; Card, Moran, & Newell, 1983). Like MHP, EPIC consists of a collection of processors and memories. There are three classes of processors: perceptual, cognitive, and motor. However, the EPIC processors and memories are much more elaborate, each representing a synthesis of empirical evidence and theories. Unlike MHP, EPIC, being an architecture, can be programmed and executed.

EPIC includes three perceptual processors—visual, auditory, and tactile. These receive input from simulated physical sensors. The visual perceptual processor, which is of particular interest for the ATC task, represents the eye's retinal zones (bouquet, fovea, parafovea, periphery) and the constraint of feature availability as a function of retinal zone.

The output of perceptual processors is sent to the cognitive processor. The cognitive processor consists of working memory, long-term memory, production memory, and a multimatch, multifire production system. The cognitive processor performs task reasoning and initiates actions by sending output commands to the motor processors: ocular, vocal, and manual.

Similar to Soar, EPIC uses a memory system where persistence is the default. The cognitive processor has no learning mechanism. The merging of EPIC and Soar provided a system that gave good coverage of perception, cognitive, learning, and motor behavior. The missing component for the AMBR task was a plausible memory system.

ACT-R

ACT-R (Anderson & Lebiere, 1998; also see chap. 4, this volume) is a hybrid architecture that implements a theory of cognitive adaptation. ACT-R, at the symbolic level, like Soar and EPIC, is a production system representing procedural knowledge as production rules and declarative knowledge as attribute-value memory structures. ACT-R features many subsymbolic mechanisms that each address a specific form of cognitive adaptation. In general, these mechanisms modulate the availability of symbolic elements (declarative and procedural), as well as the time to retrieve these elements from memory.

One of these mechanisms is called *base-level learning*. It assigns each declarative memory element an *activation*. The activation learning mechanism varies the activation of each chunk as a function of its recency and frequency of use. When a memory element is created, it is assigned an initial level of activation. The activation begins to decay exponentially as a function of time. If the activation falls below the retrieval threshold, the memory element will not be retrievable and is effectively forgotten. As a consequence, the memory element is not available to satisfy the conditions of a production rule. A memory element's activation is boosted through several avenues: use (through task-related recall), spreading activation from associated memory elements, and activation noise. The decay process immediately resumes after an element's activation has been boosted.

EASE (Elements of ACT-R, Soar, and EPIC)

ACT-R, Soar, and EPIC provide unique strengths that EASE combines into one hybrid, integrated architecture. EPIC has perceptual and motor processors, but presently a nonlearning cognitive processor. Soar, in contrast, has no perceptual or motor processors, but is a learning cognitive architecture. ACT-R contains mechanisms for representing memory effects that exist in neither EPIC nor Soar. EASE (Fig. 7.1) is an integration of the sensory, perceptual, and motor processors of EPIC, one of the memory mechanisms of ACT-R, and the cognitive mechanisms of Soar.

In EASE, cognition (Soar) receives perceptual and motor processor messages (from EPIC) as input to its working memory and returns motor processor commands to the motor processors (EPIC) as output based on the processing of the inputs. EASE's version of ACT-R's base-level learning mechanism (Chong, 2003) is controlled by this activation equation:

$$A_i = \beta + \ln(\sum_j t_j^{-d}) + \varepsilon \tag{1}$$

The primary difference between Eq. 1 and the ACT-R activation and base-level learning equations in chapter 4 is that the spreading activation

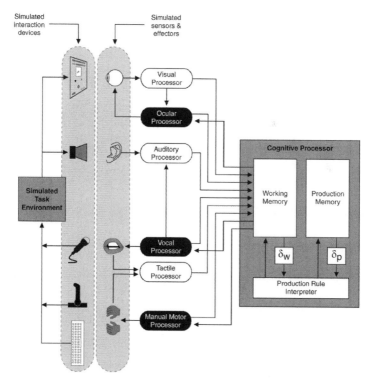

FIG. 7.1. Diagram of the EASE hybrid architecture. The sensory, perceptual, and motor processors are provided by EPIC; Soar provides the cognitive control and symbolic learning; the base-level learning mechanism of ACT-R provides subsymbolic modulation of declarative and procedural knowledge through the base-level learning mechanism, represented as δ_p and δ_w.

component is not used. (ACT-R's spreading activation and association mechanisms have not yet been incorporated into EASE.) The base-level learning mechanism is controlled by four free parameters, three of which are variables in the activation equation:

- *Base-level constant* (β): This value specifies the initial activation given to a newly created memory element. β in our model was set to 1.0, a value used in many ACT-R models.
- *Learning rate* (d): The rate of activation decay. The ACT-R default of 0.5 was used.
- *Transient noise* (ϵ): Noise is sampled from a zero-centered logistic distribution and added to an element's activation. A commonly used ACT-R value of 0.25 was used.
- *Retrieval threshold*: When activation falls below this value, the memory element cannot be retrieved and is effectively forgotten. The ACT-R default value of 0.0 was used.

These parameter values were not tuned to produce the fits presented later in the chapter. In accordance with our modeling philosophy, these ACT-R values, determined through successful modeling of a wide range of behavior, were used as a constraint on the model-building process.

EASE inherits the detailed predictions and theory embodied in the sensory, perceptual, and motor systems from EPIC; the cognitive problem solving, planning, and symbolic learning capabilities of Soar; and the constraints of human memory provided by the ACT-R mechanisms, as well as the reuse of default and commonly used free parameter values.

EXPERIMENT 1: MODELING BEHAVIOR IN THE SIMPLIFIED ATC TASK

This section presents the model for the ATC task by discussing three categories of knowledge—perceptual, declarative, and procedural—and the model results. Because we chose to model at the level of eyes, hands, and memory constraints, we present these aspects of the model in finer detail.

Perceptual Representations

The task environment simulator (as described in chap. 3) notifies EASE of the appearance, movement, and disappearance of blips; the appearance of messages; color change events; and the basic perceivable features of each screen object. These notifications enter the visual sensory and perceptual processors where a mental representation of the display is created, maintained, and sent to cognition.

The simulator sends the basic features of each blip: x and y (location), v_x and v_y (velocity components), blip name, and blip color. This basic feature set was elaborated with other features. One feature of particular importance is the DIRECTION a blip is traveling, derived from the velocity components and reported as NORTH, SOUTH, EAST, or WEST.

The task environment simulator also provides the basic features of messages: speaker, message, and panel. The speaker feature identifies the sender of the message. However, this feature was ignored on messages regarding incoming blips because it was not represented on the display, and hence not available to human subjects. The message feature is parsed and converted to a unique symbol that represents the semantic content of the message (e.g., "Accept NWA747?" becomes [ACCEPT?, NWA747]). The panel feature specifies the message history list (MHL) of the message (incoming, outgoing, or speed-request), effectively identifying the kind of message.

Perceptual Limitations. The EPIC visual sensory processor represents four concentric, circular retinal zones and the limitations of feature availability in those zones. In order of increasing eccentricity, they are the bouquet, fovea, parafovea, and periphery. Table 7.1 lists some of the perceptual features used in the model and indicates the retinal zones where the features are available. Perceptual events such as onsets, offsets, and color change events are available in all retinal zones. The assignment of features to retinal zones was based partly on previous modeling work in EPIC, but also on simplifying assumptions.

Declarative Representations

The model contains three classes of task-relevant declarative structures: feature memories, event memories, and derived memories. These classes are shown in Table 7.2. All memories are affected by base-level learning.

TABLE 7.1
Some of the Perceptual Features
and Associated Retinal Zones of Availability

Feature	*Retinal Zones of Availability*
Ident	Bouquet
Direction	Bouquet, fovea
Color	Bouquet, fovea, parafovea
Proximity	Bouquet, fovea, parafovea
In or out	Bouquet, fovea, parafovea
ATC	Bouquet, fovea, parafovea
Location	Bouquet, fovea, parafovea, periphery
Events (onset, color changes)	Bouquet, fovea, parafovea, periphery

TABLE 7.2
Task-Relevant Declarative Structures

Perceptual		Cognitive
Features Memories	*Events Memories*	*Derived Memories*
atc	blip-onset	anticipation
color	new-messages	expectation
direction		did-command
location		kbp
in-or-out		searched-blip
proximity		

Feature memories associate an aircraft's blip name (IDENT) with each of the blip's perceptual features. These associations are independent memories resulting in a distributed representation that allows the model to capture the fragmentary nature of recall. For example, it is possible to remember the location of blip, but fail to recall the direction the aircraft was traveling. Because feature memories require the IDENT feature, which is only available in the bouquet, these memories can be created only when a blip is fixated.

Event memories encode the occurrence of perceptual events, such as the onset of new blips and messages. If the model does not attend to the new object before the event memory fully decays, the model forgets about the onset. This sometimes leads to only partial exploration of new events, as can occur in humans.

Any memory that the model creates which does not encode perceptual features is a derived memory. Derived memories hold the products of reasoning. For example, the model creates anticipation and expectation memories to facilitate future performance.

Procedural Representations: An Overview

Having described the perceptual and declarative representations in the model, we now describe the procedural knowledge in the model. Figure 7.2 shows a flowchart of the model. The shaded areas define four classes of model activity. Each class is implemented with one or more Soar operators shown in the unshaded boxes. The activities are as follows:

• MONITOR-RADAR: This operator class scans the radar display. It consists of two operators: MONITOR-RADAR-SACCADE determines which blip to fixate and then saccades to that blip; MONITOR-RADAR-FIXATE represents fixations as the time for the model to encode information about the blip.

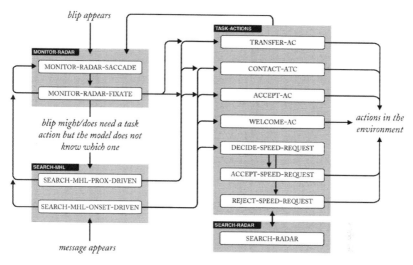

FIG. 7.2. Block diagram of the model for the unaided condition.

• SEARCH-MHL: This activity concerns reading the messages in the message history lists (MHL). It consists of two operators: SEARCH-MHL-PROXIMITY-DRIVEN initiates a search of the lists when an aircraft has been observed to be in close proximity to a border or is RED (in a hold pattern) and the model does not remember enough about the aircraft to determine what needs to be done to the blip; SEARCH-MHL-ONSET-DRIVEN reads new messages activated by their onset.

• TASK-ACTIONS: This activity consists of seven operators. Six of these operators perform the six different kinds of transactions in the task— TRANSFERRING-AC, CONTACT-ATC, ACCEPTING-AC, WELCOME-AC, ACCEPT-SPEED-REQUEST, and REJECT-SPEED-REQUEST. The seventh operator, DECIDE-SPEED-REQUEST, analyzes the display to determine whether a speed request should be allowed or denied.

• SEARCH-RADAR-DISPLAY: This activity consists of one operator. It searches the radar display for the blip when its location is unknown. A blip's location can be unknown because it has been forgotten or because the blip was never fixated. This operator is used only as a subgoal of one of the task-action operators when it cannot recall the location of a blip.

As presented in chapter 2, there were two task conditions: an aided condition, where the simulated task environment indicates (by blip colors) what task action is needed for each blip, and an unaided condition without this assistance. Because there were different task decompositions for each condition, we developed a model for each condition.

Procedural Details: Unaided Condition Model

Each operator (in the unshaded box in Fig. 7.2) is designed to capture a specific behavior necessary to perform the ATC task. Because we were building a detailed model of the task, we tried to identify and model the aspects of the behavior that might be observed in subjects.

Monitor-Radar-Saccade.   Some of the assumptions incorporated in this operator are: Saccades are influenced by both bottom–up (reactive and perceptually driven) and top–down processing (deliberate and goal-directed), scan patterns are neither random nor systematic, saccades tend to be to blips near the airspace border, saccades are biased toward "important" blips, and it is possible to forget which blips are important or unimportant.

The primary task of this operator is selecting which blip to fixate. That selection process captures the bottom–up and top–down influences on eye-scan patterns. It does so by assigning each blip two kinds of priorities—perception-based priority and knowledge-based priority—that represent a blip's bottom–up and top–down importance. These priorities are used by the operator to reason about which blip to fixate next.

The first kind of priority, perception-based priority (PBP), embodies the assumption that attention can be drawn to blips that are close to the airspace border, onset or change color, or not currently fixated. The perceptual system computes a "closeness to the airspace border" feature (which uses only a blip's LOCATION feature). This is illustrated by the regions and associated "closeness" values (or PBP) in Fig. 7.3.[3] For example, the PBP for FIN14 is 1 because it is far from the airspace border; JAL34 has a value of 6; TWA747 has a value of 7 because it is very close to the airspace border; AAL108 and SWA229 are special cases that indicate the onset or color of the blip, respectively; both are very salient features or events with demonstrated ability to capture attention. PBPs are continuously derived for each blip regardless of whether the blip is fixated. PBPs are a quick, approximate, but error-prone assessment of a blip's real priority.

Unlike perception-based priority, the second kind of priority, knowledge-based priority (KBP), is associated only to blips that have been fixated. KBP also differs from PBP because it is slower to compute, requiring deliberation—fixating the eye to a blip, consider the blip's absolute proximity (derived from the blip's LOCATION *and* DIRECTION features), recalling known facts about the blip and then creating a KBP derived memory. A KBP therefore yields an accurate assessment of the importance of saccading to the blip in the future. However, because it is a derived memory, it can be forgotten if unused.

---

[3]The absolute extent of each region in both Figs. 7.3 and 7.4 was arbitrarily chosen, although the relative size of each region was a deliberate choice.

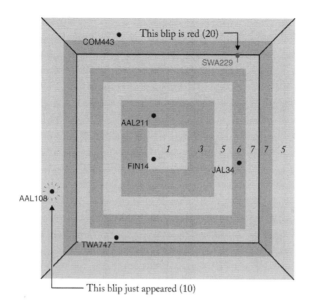

FIG. 7.3.   Perception-based priority regions and values (see text for details).

Figure 7.4 illustrates the different proximity regions that emerge when direction is considered.[4] The regions and values shown are specific to eastbound blips.[5] To compute a blip's KBP, the model first considers its absolute proximity and then what is known (what can be recalled) about the blip.

For example, according to Fig. 7.3, TWA747 would be assigned a greater PBP (7) than JAL34 (6). However, if the model were to fixate TWA747, it would find that, because it is eastbound, its absolute proximity is VERYFAR from the east border. This is sufficient to assign TWA747 a very low KBP (e.g., 2) because it will be some time before TWA747 can be handed off. If the model subsequently fixates the eastbound JAL34, it would find its absolute proximity is NEAR to the east border. Further, if the model could recall it had performed all the necessary hand-off actions for this blip, there would be no need to refixate the blip in the future, resulting in a very low KBP (e.g., 1). If, instead, the model were aware it had not completed the necessary hand-off actions, then JAL34 would be assigned a relatively high KBP (e.g., 6) to cause the model to revisit the blip. This illustrates how top–down influences—full consideration of a blip's features, available

---

[4]The absence in Fig. 7.3 and then presence in Fig. 7.4 of direction pointers is only to aid the description of the priority processes. The physical task display always includes direction pointers.

[5]When the model fixates a westbound (e.g., FIN14), northbound (e.g., AAL211), or southbound blip (e.g., SWA229), the absolute proximity arrangement in Fig. 7.4 would be the mirror image, rotated 90° clockwise or rotated 90° counterclockwise, respectively.

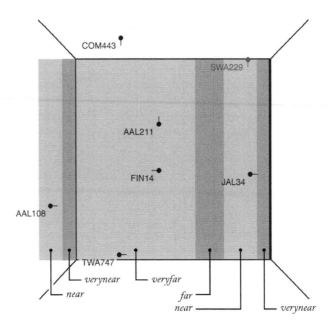

FIG. 7.4. Absolute proximity regions/values for eastbound blips AAL108, TWA747, and JAL34 (see text for details).

knowledge about the blip, and task goals—can significantly influence the derivation of this priority.

To generate a saccade using both kinds of priorities, the operator compares all blips in parallel fashion, preferring the blip with the highest KBP (top–down importance) if both blips have recallable KBP memories, the highest PBP (bottom–up importance) if neither have recallable KBP memories, or the highest priority (of either kind) otherwise. If this process yields a single "winning" blip, then the operator initiates a saccade to the blip. In the more typical case, where several blips have the highest priority, one is randomly chosen and a saccade is initiated.

The combination of perception- and knowledge-based priorities allows the model to balance the need to be both reactive to display events yet remain goal-directed. Although no systematic scan patterns are defined, some do occasionally emerge due to the distribution of blips and current task state. However, any patterns that do emerge can be broken by the onset of blips or messages, the need to perform a task action sequence, or the forgetting of KBPs for unimportant blips.

Monitor-Radar-Fixate.   When humans complete a saccade, there is a period of time where the eye will rest on the object. This brief dwell time is called a *fixation*. The purpose of the MONITOR-RADAR-FIXATE operator is to represent the processing that may comprise a fixation. This operator is based on the following assumptions: Derived memories are created during fixations, and fixations can be prematurely terminated by events in the environment.

In the model, fixations allow the internalization of blip features and the creation, rehearsal, or encoding of those features into task-specific representations (derived memories). After the ocular motor system has completed the saccade initiated by the MONITOR-RADAR-SACCADE operator, a blip's perceptual features pass through the visual sensory and perceptual processors and eventually arrive in cognition. The fixation operator is then initiated. Following the functional dependency graph illustrated in Fig. 7.5, the operator internalizes the blip's perceptual features and reasons about its higher level properties. For example, it is not possible to know the inbound or outbound status (IN-OR-OUT) of a blip or the ATC region to which it is headed (ATC) without first knowing both its LOCATION and DIRECTION. The layers of the dependency graph are processed serially, whereas the memories in layers are processed concurrently.

The top two levels (the rounded boxes) are perceptual features that get internalized into feature memories. The lower two levels (square-cornered boxes) are derived memories. The perceptual features COLOR and ATC are memorized, but are not a prerequisite to the creation of other memories. COLOR is needed to initiate corrective behaviors when a blip enters a hold pattern and turns red; ATC is used when composing most task actions. The DID-COMMAND memory is created when task actions are performed.

After creating feature memories, the operator creates two forms of prospective memory: anticipations and expectations. An anticipation memory is created for an outbound blip that will be transferable when it crosses the inner "transfer" border (see chaps. 2 and 3, this volume, for a complete description of the task and display). An expectation memory associates a

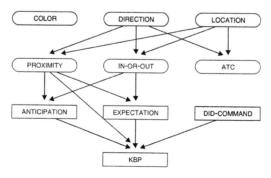

FIG. 7.5.   Functional dependency used by MONITOR-RADAR-FIXATE in the unaided condition. Rounded boxes are perceptual memories. Squared boxes are derived memories.

blip's IDENT with the expectation of the appearance of a relevant message. Both anticipation and expectation memories influence the model's eye-scan behavior through the knowledge-based priority memories, the last item in the functional dependency graph.

Generally, when a blip is fixated, the model steps through each level of the dependency, creating and rehearsing or inferring memory structures. However, this can be prematurely terminated once the operator has determined that an action is needed for the fixated blip. For example, if the fixated blip is red, the thinking operator will stop processing memories and reason about what corrective action should be taken to resolve the hold. The operator then terminates and activates the necessary task actions. Another situation where the operator will self-terminate is when it is observing a blip with an absolute proximity of VERYNEAR and the model does not know whether the blip has been sufficiently transacted to prevent a hold condition.

Search-MHL-Proximity-Driven. The purpose of the SEARCH-MHL-PROXIMITY-DRIVEN operator is to search a message history list (MHL), beginning at the bottom (new messages appear at the bottom of the MHL), looking for a target message that matches a pattern given as input to the operator. It is initiated by the MONITOR-RADAR-FIXATE operator. Some of the assumptions that constrain this operator are: list search is nonexhaustive, and "duplicate message" errors can occur from a nonexhaustive search.

As we see in Fig. 7.2, SEARCH-MHL-PROXIMITY-DRIVEN is activated when the fixated blip might need or definitely needs a task action. A fixated blip might need an action when the blip's absolute proximity is VERYNEAR (e.g., Fig. 7.4), but the model does not remember whether the blip had been fully transacted. A fixated blip definitely needs an action when the aircraft is RED and an action is needed to rectify the condition, but the model does not know what action is needed.[6] In these situations, the model needs to acquire more information to be able to continue. This information is available in the message history lists.

The model saccades to the last message of the appropriate list and searches back through the list looking for the most recent message that refers to the fixated blip's IDENT. If found, the model reads the entire message, determines what action is indicated, further deduces what action is needed, and initiates it. If no message is found, the operator will assume no transactions have been performed and will activate the first task action in the hand-off sequence—TRANSFERRING-AC.

---

[6]The particular case concerning red blips only applies to outbound blips. Red inbound blips are resolved by immediately performing an ACCEPTING-AC command. Outbound blips require two transactions. Therefore, when an outbound blip is red, there is no indication of which transaction was omitted.

Subjects rarely, if ever, exhaustively search the MHL, particularly when the list is long. Subjects may be satisficing. Because we did not have a model of satisficing behavior, we approximated the premature termination of search by hard coding a search depth limit of seven (7) messages—roughly one-third of the list capacity. If a target message is not found within the seven most recent messages, the search would terminate with a failure. One side effect of a limited search is errors in performance (e.g., duplicating a previously performed action).

Search-MHL-Onset-Driven. The previous operator is triggered to search the MHL based on the location of blips on the radar. This operator, SEARCH-MHL-ONSET-DRIVEN, is activated when a new message appears in the message history lists. One of the assumptions of this operator is that searching the MHL provides an opportunity to reconstruct or rehearse memories for completed actions.

When activated, this operator reads the new message to determine whether the message prompts an action. If it does (e.g., "ACCEPT AAL108?"), the action is performed. If not ("ACCEPTED AAL108"), the model rehearses (or re-creates) DID-COMMAND and/or EXPECTATION derived memories referred to in the message.

Task-Actions. There are seven task action operators that use the simulated mouse to compose messages to aircraft or controllers in adjacent airspaces. Before a mouse movement can be performed, the eye must either be at the destination or on its way to the destination location.[7] Therefore, the time to perform mouse movements is not just the time to move the mouse, but also the time to initiate the eye movements. These task operators are constrained by the following assumptions: eye–hand coordination is necessary to produce behavior, a memory of having done a command is created, and an expectation of a new message for the blip is created when appropriate. After completing each task action, the operator creates a DID-COMMAND memory, associating a blip's IDENT with the action just performed. After performing a TRANSFER-AIRCRAFT actions, the operator creates an expectation memory for the blip.

Search-Radar-Display. If a subject needs to perform a task action on a blip, but cannot recall the blip's location, he or she can search the display for the desired blip. The SEARCH-RADAR-DISPLAY operator produces this behavior. It is constrained by the assumptions that search is biased to relevant regions of the display, and that blips can be fixated more than once.

---

[7]This constraint is not architecturally enforced (i.e., it is possible to move the mouse to an object without looking at the object). To implement eye–hand coordination, we deliberately program the eye to move to the object before the mouse movement is initiated.

The operator records, as a derived memory (see "searched-blip" in Table 7.2), each blip that is fixated during the search. The operator does not produce saccades to blips that it remembers previously fixating. However, because the derived memories can be forgotten, refixations can occur. Additionally, the task action that is to be performed influences the blips that are considered. For example, if the model were trying to perform an ACCEPT-AC task action (an action required for incoming blips), the operator would only saccade to blips outside the center airspace.

Procedural Details: Aided Condition Model

We now discuss the model used for the aided condition. Although the unaided condition model could perform under the simpler aided condition, it would not take advantage of the aiding and would not produce behavior representative of subjects. Hence, a separate aided condition model, derived from the unaided condition model, was created.

The block diagram of the aided condition model is illustrated in Fig. 7.6. It differs in three ways from the unaided condition model. The first clear difference is that SEARCH-MHL-ONSET-DRIVEN is not used. Because blip color changes prompt task actions, there is no need to check for action-prompting messages. The SEARCH-MHL-PROXIMITY-DRIVEN operator is retained to assist handling blips that may enter a holding pattern and turn red. However, we expected that the task aiding makes it unlikely that a blip would ever enter a holding pattern. This expectation was verified by the data.

A second difference in the aided condition model is a much simpler method of generating saccades. The MONITOR-RADAR-SACCADE operator relies solely on perceptual (bottom–up) properties because the aided model

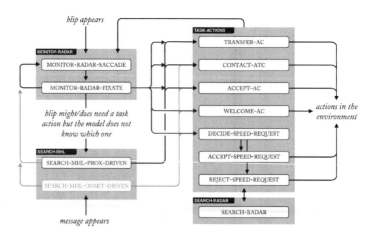

FIG. 7.6. Block diagram of the model for the aided condition.

only needs to be aware of color changes. Knowledge-based priorities are not used. Rather the perception-based priority (PBP) is elaborated with color-related priorities: CYAN (PBP = 8); MAGENTA (12); GREEN (14); ORANGE (16); YELLOW (18). A saccade is made to the blip with the highest PBP priority.

Because knowledge-based priorities are not used to generate saccades, MONITOR-RADAR-FIXATE no longer creates KBP memories or any of the derived memories and perceptual memories on which KBP memories depend. As a result, deliberation in the aided model is only two deep (Fig. 7.7).

Multitasking

When running, the model first selects one of the three operator classes—MONITOR-RADAR, SEARCH-MHL, and TASK-ACTIONS. It then executes an appropriate operator within the class. Due to the task's dynamic nature, there are often times when the preconditions of more than one operator class is satisfied. For example, the simultaneous onset of a new message and a new blip creates a competition between the MONITOR-RADAR and SEARCH-MHL operator classes. The model contains a set of arbitration rules, analogous to the executive process as formalized in Kieras and Meyer (1997), for deciding which operator class should be performed. The executive process arbitrates between-class competition by assigning highest priority to TASK-ACTIONS, intermediate priority to SEARCH-MHL, and lowest priority to MONITOR-RADAR. These priorities represent a "greedy" approach to maximize performance.

Additionally, operator competition is possible within an operator class. For example, two task actions could be simultaneously triggered (e.g., the presence of two or more nonwhite blips in the aided condition). Again the model encodes arbitration rules to choose which operator to perform. Resolution of within-class competition is similar to that used for between-class competition.

Modeling Subjective Workload

The AMBR models were required to report subjective workload. Although there are many ways to compute subjective workload, our measure is based on the realization that there is work to be done. Table 7.3 shows the factors that are used to trigger different kinds of realizations.

FIG. 7.7. Functional dependency used by MONITOR-RADAR-FIXATE in the aided condition.

TABLE 7.3
"Work to Be Done" and Associated Workload Values

Unaided Condition	Aided Condition	Work to Be Done	Workload Value
Anticipation	Orange	Transfer outgoing blip	3
Expectation of MHL message "<ident> accepted"	Yellow	Tell outgoing blip to contact ATC	4
MHL message "accept <ident>"	Green	Accept incoming blip	3
MHL message "<ident> says hello"	Cyan	Welcome incoming blip	1
MHL message requesting speed change	Magenta	Allow/deny speed change request	2
Red	Red	Varied	10

In the unaided-condition model, a realization occurs when the model creates anticipation and expectation memories, reads action-prompting messages, or fixates on a blip in a hold pattern. In the aided condition, blip color signals when task actions are needed; therefore, realizations are based on blip color.

Table 7.3 also shows the workload values associated with each kind of work. The values represent the importance or urgency of the tasks, relative to one another, as can be deduced from the task instruction and the penalty point schedule. These values are used in this workload equation:

$$w(t) = \alpha * \Sigma l_i / t, \text{ where } t = \text{\# of cognitive cycles}; \alpha = 100 \qquad (2)$$

This formulation captures two intuitive characteristics of workload: It is a function of the amount of work to be done per unit time and also the difficulty or urgency of the work to be done per unit time.

For each realization, i, the model records the associated workload value, l_i. At the end of a model run, the total workload, Σl_i, is divided by the duration of the scenario, t, measured in cognitive cycles (varies between 9,000 and 18,000 cycles) and multiplied by a scaling factor, α. The scaling factor was selected to provide the best fit to the empirical data. Although we prefer predictions over fitting, we knew of no preexisting work on model-generated subjective workload work from which to borrow ideas or parameters. Instead we developed our own model (Eq. 2) and fit the results to the data.

The procedure for computing workload under the aided and unaided conditions is the same. The primary distinction is that, in the former, a realization contributes only once to the cumulative workload score. By contrast, multiple realizations are possible or likely in the unaided condition due to the creation and re-creation of forgotten expectation and anticipation memories.

Forms of Stochasticity

Stochasticity is provided by the perceptual, memory, cognitive, and motor systems:

- At the perceptual level, the sizes of the foveal and parafoveal retinal zones are varied between saccades. This is done because there are no hard retinal zone boundaries in the human eye, so we vary the radii to soften the boundary between these zones. Additionally, other perceptual parameters (feature transduction times) are stochastically varied between trials as a normal characteristic of the perceptual processors.
- At the cognitive level, the duration of the cognitive cycle varies uniformly between 33 and 67 ms and changes between trials. Also there are times when the model randomly chooses an operator among a set of competing candidates.
- The activation equation (Eq. 1) includes a noise term.
- At the motor level, various performance parameters are stochastically varied between runs.

Because of this nondeterminism, we view each model run as representing an individual's performance on a single trial.

Run Time Environment

To generate the model data, we ran the entire simulation—the simulated task environment and model—on a 400 Mhz Pentium II laptop using the Linux operating system. Unfortunately, the simulation and model complexity were great enough to severely limit the number of complete model runs that could be collected in the 8 hours allotted for final data collection. Although the stochastic nature of the model ideally requires many more runs—preferably as many runs as there were human subjects—only two complete model runs were possible.

Experiment 1: Results

Due to the limited number of model runs, we focus on qualitative fits of the model to the data. Figure 7.8 shows the human and model results for penalty points by task difficulty and the distribution of penalty points by error type. In both measures, the model produces a good qualitative fit to the data. For penalty points (the top graph), the model produces the gross differences due to automation—penalty scores are lower for the aided condition than the unaided condition—and to task difficulty—essentially uni-

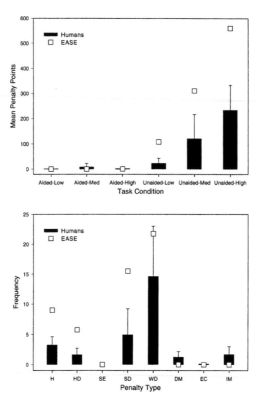

FIG. 7.8. Penalty point results. The top graph shows penalty points by task condition. The bottom graph show the frequency of penalty types: Hold (H), Hold delay (HD), Speed request response error (SE), Speed request response delay (SD), Welcome delay (WD), Duplicate messages (DM), Extra Clicks (EC), Incorrect message (IM). Error bars indicate 95% confidence intervals.

form scores for the aided condition, whereas penalty scores increase with task difficulty in the unaided conditions.

The model accounts for the automation effect simply because separate aided and unaided condition models are used. Task difficulty is manipulated by reducing the time available to do the same amount of work. The model's explanation for this effect is twofold. First, it is natural for performance to degrade with an increase in multiple-task demands (i.e., the increased likelihood that the model will need to serialize simultaneously triggered actions and thus incurring penalties as actions for some blips are deferred). Second, the base-level learning mechanism contributes to this effect because as task difficulty rises the model has less opportunity to maintain its task memories. The results are more blips entering hold patterns, important blips forgotten, message onsets forgotten, too much time spent reading the MHLs (because the model forgot what actions were performed), and longer delays in responding to requests. The fact that there is no task difficulty effect for the aided condition indicates that automation made the task very easy.

The distribution of penalty points by error type (the bottom graph of Fig. 7.8) is a prediction of the model; no tuning to match these data was performed during model development. The model produces a notable task-shedding effect—the high frequency of speed request and welcome delays. This effect is due solely to the multitask arbitration scheme described in this chapter. Speed requests and welcome actions incur the lowest penalty and can therefore be delayed or omitted if higher priority actions are pending. Additionally, delayed responses or deliberate omission of these actions does not produce "downstream" penalties. For example, if the model were to omit or delay accepting an incoming blip, the downstream consequence is that the blip might enter a hold pattern, resulting in a large increase in penalty points. No such costs are associated with delaying or omitting responses to speed change requests and welcome messages.

Figure 7.9 presents the reaction time and workload fit of the model. The model shows the same qualitative trends as the data for both measures. The model's explanation for reaction time is much the same as for the penalty point data. The main effect of automation on subjective workload arises from the working memory decay mechanism. The unaided condition is memory intensive and involves more activities (e.g., searching the MHLs) compared with the aided condition. There will be many occasions where the model, unable to maintain all the required memories, will "re-realize" work to be done—such as when anticipations and expectations were forgotten and re-created—thus increasing the workload. The effect of task difficulty on subjective workload is due, in part, to the inverse relationship of time and subjective workload in Eq. 2.

Critical Analysis of the ATC Model

The strengths of this model include its integration of components from the three ancestor architectures of EASE and the subsequent application of the model to produce task behavior at least qualitatively consistent with human performance. However, the model's fits and predictions, shown in Figs. 7.8 and 7.9, are based on only two model runs. With so little data, only qualitative statements can be made about the model fits and predictions. During the final model testing phase, prior to the data collection that produced these graphs, we recorded only penalty point data for multiple model runs per task condition. Table 7.4 shows a comparison of the individual human and model penalty point scores for the six task conditions. Although the model data are incomplete (in most conditions, there are less model runs than humans), they do show that individual model runs tend to fall within

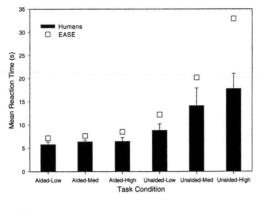

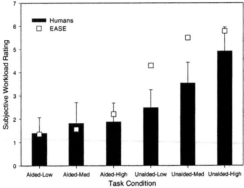

FIG. 7.9. The top graph shows mean reaction time by task condition. The bottom graph show the model's subjective workload rating by task condition. Error bars indicate 95% confidence intervals.

the range of performance for subjects. Quantitatively, the means compare quite well, particularly if outlier human and model trials are removed. (If those means were plotted on Fig. 7.8, only the unaided/high condition would fall outside the error bars.) Further, the functional characteristics of the task, combined with the model's explanations of various effects, suggest an interdependence of penalty points, subject workload, and reaction time.[8] Thus, improved quantitative matches for the fits and predictions of the other three task metrics could be expected.

---

[8]In the ATC task, high task difficulty is accomplished by requiring the same amount of work to be performed in less time. From the model's perspective, higher task loads afford less opportunity to reinforce memories necessary for perfect performance. The consequence is more recurring realizations of work to be done, thus increasing subjective workload. Additionally, the model will spend more time refreshing memories (e.g., searching a blip whose location was forgotten) on the critical path to producing a task action, thus increasing reaction time.

TABLE 7.4
Comparison of Individual Model and Human
Penalty Point Data by Task Condition

Task Condition	Human Data	Model Data
Aided/Low	0, 0, 0, 0, 0, 0, 0, 10	0, 0
	(*avg.* 1.25)	(*avg.* 0)
Aided/Med	0, 0, 0, 0, 0, 0, 10, 30	0, 0
	(*avg.* 5.00)	(*avg.* 0)
Aided/High	0, 0, 0, 0, 0, 0, 10, 24	0, 0
	(*avg.* 4.25)	(*avg.* 0)
Unaided/Low	0, 0, 0, 5, 10, 11, 60, 704	6, 50, 50
	(*avg.* 19.50)	(*avg.* 48.67)
Unaided/Med	0, 4, 6, 57, 140, 152, 208, 289	54, 63, 101, 101, 132, 149, 149,
	(*avg.* 106.87)	200, 213
		(*avg.* 129.11)
Unaided/High	106, 131, 131, 224, 417, 421, 446,	228, 294, 370, 381, 382, 623, 649,
	674	1050
	(*avg.* 318.75)	(*avg.* 497.125)

Note. These data were generated late in the model development phase, but before final data collection.

One lesson learned while developing the model was the importance of tools that make observable the model's covert and overt behavior and its internal state. These tools are useful for assessing the model's behavior, debugging the model, and demonstrating the model in presentations. One such tool was a graphical representation of the movement of the model's eye overlaid on the task environment. (This tool is included on the CD provided with this volume.) The tool allowed us to determine that the overall eye movements were reasonable. However, the model relies on many assumptions about eye movements, none of which can be substantiated given the data that were collected—only performance scores and a time-tagged trace of mouse clicks. Eye-tracking data would have been necessary for architectures and modeling approaches that emphasize peripheral constraints and the representation of eye and hand movements. The validity of many of the assumptions, as well as the behaviors and predictions produced due to these assumptions, could also be assessed. For instance, one could compare the number of times the message history lists were visited, how often subjects read new messages, the average depth of MHL searches, or the number of times subjects had to search for blips.

Relatedly, chapter 2 discussed subject self-reports of their eye-scan behavior. Roughly 75% responded "yes" to the posttest question, "Did you scan the screen in a consistent pattern?", with 50% of those respondents stating they used a clockwise scan pattern. These reports contradict the

nonsystematic scanning assumptions used in the saccade generation operator. In retrospect, this assumption was too strong and overlooked systematic
patterns subjects may have used. Eye-tracking data would be necessary to
determine whether the self-reported patterns were actually used and the extent to which they were used.

EXPERIMENT 2: INTRODUCTION

The focus of Experiment 2 was category learning in the context of the ATC
task used in Experiment 1. The task environment was extended to include a
category learning task. As described in chapter 2, the learning task is iso-
morphic to the study performed by Nosofsky, Gluck, Palmeri, McKinley,
and Glauthier (1994). Figure 7.10 shows a comparison of their data to the
AMBR learning task. A main effect of problem type was found in both
Nosofsky et al. (1994) and the AMBR data. However, the AMBR aggregate
learning rates are much slower.

Several task differences might account for the dissimilar learning performance results. The stimuli in the original study were composed of three
orthogonal features: shape (triangle or circle), size (small or large), and in-
terior (solid or dotted). In contrast, the instances used in the AMBR learning task consisted of contextually meaningful features, allowing subjects to
benefit or suffer from using domain knowledge (e.g., "small planes [SIZE =
S] should avoid high turbulence [TURB = 3] so their requests should be allowed [CATEGORY = ALLOW]"). In addition to feature contextuality, the features are also more similar relative to one another. All features were represented with alpha-numeric characters, and some features (e.g., S and 3, L
and 1) share similar shapes.

A second task difference is the presence of a secondary task. Whereas
subjects in Nosofsky et al. (1994) performed only a category learning task,
the AMBR subjects performed both category learning and performance
tasks. This may account for the learning difference (e.g., perhaps the sec-

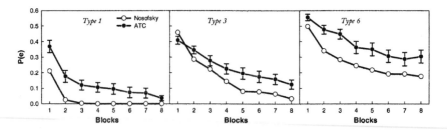

FIG. 7.10. A comparison of the learning trajectories for Nosofsky et al.
(1994) and the ATC study.

ondary task "consumes" limited cognitive "resources," slowing learning). As stated in chapter 2, Experiment 2 was designed to produce this kind of slowing. However, AMBR control subjects—those exposed to the full learning and performance scenarios, but who only performed the learning trials and ignored the ATC task—learned as slowly as noncontrols. This finding suggests that reduced learning performance of the ATC task may not be due to the existence of the secondary ATC task.

A third task difference that may contribute to the performance difference is that subjects in Nosofsky et al. (1994) were self-paced: A stimulus appeared, the subject made a classification, feedback was given, and the process repeated. Although not reported, an interstimulus time on the order of 5 seconds is a reasonable guess. In the AMBR learning task, 16 altitude requests (category learning stimuli) were presented over a 10-minute scenario, giving an average interstimulus time of 37 seconds—a sevenfold increase. Perhaps this differences in interstimulus time also contributes to the difference in learning rates.

Motivating an Architectural Approach for Modeling Category Learning

There are many existing models that fit the Nosofsky et al. (1994) or Shepard, Hovland, and Jenkins (1961) data: Nosofsky et al. presented the fits of four exemplar-based models; Nosofsky, Palmeri, and McKinley (1994) presented the fit of RULEX, a hypothesis-testing model; and Love and Medin (1998) reported the fit for SUSTAIN, a network model of human category learning.

Any of these models, by virtue of demonstrating good quantitative fits to the Nosofsky et al. (1994) data (and a number of other data sets), could have been recruited to the AMBR learning task. However, these models are all stand-alone models; they are purpose-built systems that perform only category learning and are not situated within a larger modeling framework of a cognitive architecture. When used appropriately, the architectural approach addresses some of the limitations of many stand-alone models (see also chap. 9):

- *No account of process:* Few of these models are process models. Process models are desirable because they declare the individual steps and mechanisms—perceptual, cognitive, and motor steps—that define behavior. Most cognitive architectures, being based on production systems, naturally accommodate process models of behavior.
- *Unable to make time predictions:* Human data collected for the ATC task included the time to respond to an altitude change request; in other words,

the time required to produce a category prediction. Response time predictions cannot be produced, in a principled way, by most stand-alone category learning models. However, production system-based architectures have a cycle-based means of accounting for time. Time predictions are a byproduct of model execution and a function of model complexity. If two models produce similar behavior (e.g., producing a category prediction), but one requires 100 cycles while the other requires 50 cycles, their time predictions will be different. Therefore, time predictions serve as a critical post hoc constraint in architecture-based models.

• *Human memory limitations ignored:* Few stand-alone learning models represent memory effects, such as forgetting. In some cases, memory effects have been simulated by imposing arbitrary constructs such as *capacity limits* or *probability of storage.* Architectures may include primitive mechanisms that influence properties of memory. For example, the base-level learning mechanism of EASE (inherited from ACT-R) modulates the availability of knowledge. Therefore, memory effects such as apparent capacity limits, apparent probability of storage, forgetting, and priming can emerge from primitive memory mechanisms.

• *Large number of free parameters:* Models often rely on free parameters to improve their fit to data. Free parameters are placeholders for details that are yet to be uncovered or implemented. All things being equal, one would prefer a model with the fewest free parameters. Stand-alone models often contain a large number of free parameters. For example, RULEX contains 10 free parameters that manipulate selection of a learning strategy, memory characteristics, and response error rates, among others. In contrast, the philosophical and theoretical pressures of architectural approaches encourage the parsimonious use of free parameters. Building models on a slowly evolving set of primitive mechanisms implies using a slowly evolving set of free parameters. Architectural mechanisms and their parameters are task-independent, and therefore must apply to all models regardless of the behavior under study. Finally, as architecture-based models are validated, an acceptable range of values for each free parameter is often identified, providing further constraints.

• *Insensitivity to interstimulus time:* Stand-alone models are usually insensitive to time. They would predict the same performance if learning trials occurred every 10 seconds or once per hour. The base-level learning mechanism in EASE is responsive to the recency and frequency of use of memories. Therefore, the availability of memories is affected by the timing of events in the environment or the use of memories within a model.

• *Isolated learning:* It is unclear how stand-alone models could be made to be sensitive to the presence and possible interference of a competing task. This makes them inappropriate for modeling or predicting the effect a secondary task may have on learning. Architectures allow individual models to be executed together. EASE models of category learning were first developed in isolation and then integrated with the ATC model developed for Experiment 1. The architecture thus provides an environment for composing behavior and exploring if and how multiple tasks interact. Although architectures do not guarantee that combined models will produce and explain all psychologically meaningful interactions, it does at least provide a framework and some constraints for this kind of exploration.

The remainder of this chapter presents the development of two architecture-based category learning models along with their fits and predictions. The first model is based on the reuse and extension of an existing Soar category learning model, Symbolic Concept Acquisition (SCA; Miller & Laird, 1996). The second is a new process model, RULEX-EM, inspired by RULEX; it incorporates both rule and exemplar representations as well as memory effects.

These models explore two alternate explanations for the learning differences depicted in Fig. 7.10: the role of contextually meaningful features and the influence of interstimulus time. The SCA model posits that performance differences derive from the use of additional but irrelevant information available in the AMBR task; this additional information decreases the learning rate in the model. The RULEX-EM model explores the interaction of memory effects and prediction strategies to produce learning rates sensitive to problem difficulty. Both models emphasize the reuse and extension of existing category learning models, which is a critical aspect of the UTC philosophy. The key point of difference between the models is the role that knowledge and architectural mechanisms play in producing behavior, resulting in contrasting explanations of the data.

EXPERIMENT 2: SYMBOLIC CONCEPT ACQUISITION (SCA)

Working within an architectural theory requires model reuse and cumulation (Newell, 1990). Symbolic Concept Acquisition (SCA) is an existing model of category learning in the Soar theory. We adopted SCA because the architectural philosophy dictates that we should seek to reuse existing models, and SCA is the only extant Soar category learning model. Although developed over a decade ago, we were able to reuse the model's code.

A second important component of the modeling philosophy is to work within the constraints of the architecture without introducing extra-architectural or new mechanisms. For example, because chunking is the Soar architecture's sole learning mechanism, we chose to limit ourselves to this mechanism alone for the SCA model. For this reason, the base-level learning mechanism in EASE was not used in the SCA model.

The original SCA model also included a production-based algorithm for simulating frequency effects. Because frequency effects are not an architectural component, we excised them from the model. Thus, an open question in Experiment 2 was to determine whether this existing model could produce results that quantitatively matched human learning within the constraints of the architecture, and thus without introducing extra-architectural (or new) mechanisms. We removed the frequency effects, but made no other changes to the model that would change the results reported by Miller and Laird (1996).

Description of SCA

Figure 7.11 presents a high-level representation of the SCA prediction and learning algorithm. The main body of the algorithm (Lines 2–4) consists of a search for a matching prediction rule. The same search loop is used for both prediction and learning. Prediction is performed when feedback is not available; when category feedback is available, the model will refine its concept representation via learning. In contrast to the RULEX-EM model presented next, SCA does not use an explicit category representation. Instead it focuses on the recall of prediction rules. Because all rules in Soar, including the prediction rules, are impenetrable, SCA models cannot report a category representation without additional introspection.

For prediction, SCA performs a specific-to-general search over previously learned prediction rules. As learning progresses, SCA learns more specific rules (i.e., rules that test more features). Thus, there may be rules at different levels of specificity. The algorithm first attempts to recall a prediction rule for all features (and feature values) in the instance (the condition in Line 2). If no matching rule is retrieved, SCA enters the search loop. The first step is to abstract (ignore) a feature in the instance representation (Line 3). Abstracting the feature enables the search for less specific prediction rules. Determining which feature to abstract can occur in a number of different ways; the next section presents some of these options. The retrieve-abstract loop repeats until a matching rule is found. SCA includes rules to guess randomly when all features have been abstracted, so a matching rule will always be found.

```
1.  instance = features and values /* from perception */
2.  while (no matching prediction rule for instance)
3.      abstract feature from instance
4.      remember most recently abstracted feature
5.  if (no feedback) return prediction else
6.      restore most recently abstracted feature to instance
7.      store new prediction rule for instance
```

FIG. 7.11.   A pseudocode representation of the SCA algorithm.

When learning, SCA searches for a matching prediction rule as before. When SCA retrieves a rule matching the current instance, the prediction rule is specialized (6) by adding the last feature abstracted from the instance (remembered at 4). SCA stores this specialized rule as a new prediction rule (7). Over multiple learning trials, learning results in a general-to-specific search over the feature space. That is, SCA generally learns rules sensitive to one feature, then to two, and so on. The concept representation becomes more specific as more features (and combinations of features) are incorporated into learned prediction rules.

Figure 7.12 presents an SCA learning example. The example assumes that the model has previously learned a prediction rule (3) that indicates an instance with a fuel percentage of 20 should be accepted. A new positive instance (S, 3, 20) is presented. For this example, assume the abstraction order is size, then turbulence, and then fuel. Because there are no matching prediction rules for all three features of the input instance, SCA abstracts size from the instance, leaving (3, 20). Again it looks for prediction rules for these features and, finding none, abstracts the turbulence value, leaving (20). Rule 3 matches this instance. SCA now specializes Rule 3, adding the last abstracted feature and value (turbulence 3). The new rule, Rule 4, indicates that (3, 20) instances should be accepted. Had the example instance been negative, SCA would have learned a prediction rule that indicated instances with fuel values of 20 should be denied. In this case, given the previously learned prediction rule (i.e., FUEL = 20 → ACCEPT), the model would have come to recognize that fuel values of 20 could not be used, by themselves, to make category predictions. This situation does not reflect a contradiction, but rather that this feature alone cannot be used to make correct predictions.

In summary, SCA is an incremental learner that creates rules in a general to specific manner with respect to instance features and values. Because it presented more examples, it acquires additional rules, gradually

Available prediction rules:
1. (null) ➡ accept
2. (null) ➡ reject
3. fuel 20 ➡ accept

New instance:
size S, turbulence 3, fuel 20
category accept
Abstraction order: size, turbulence, fuel

New Prediction Rule:
4. fuel 20, turbulence 3 ➡ accept

FIG. 7.12.   Example of an SCA learning trial.

(but not monotonically) improving its category prediction performance. With enough training, SCA will eventually learn a maximally specific rule (one that matches all the features of an exemplar) for each training instance. At this point, learning effectively ceases, and SCA can readily predict the category of each exemplar by the use of its specific prediction rule. This "saturated" state represents what happens to subjects who are overtrained in a concept learning task; they memorize each training instance and its category.

Initial "Out of the Box" SCA Model

We began applying SCA—without the simulated frequency effects, but otherwise as described by Miller and Laird (1996)—to determine how well this minimalist model represented the human data. We concentrated only on the Nosofsky et al. (1994) data initially and made no attempt to fit any ATC learning data in the first experiment. The goal was to assess the efficacy of the SCA model in capturing the ATC learning results without any re-engineering of the previous model for the new domain. Such reuse is necessary for the cumulation of results within an architectural theory.

The simulated frequency effects in the original SCA model were used to determine the abstraction order. Thus, having removed this aspect of the original model, we had to determine what abstraction order to use for the model. There were two obvious possibilities: random abstraction and systematic abstraction. With random abstraction order, the search over prediction rules is similar to a breadth-first search, generating many one-feature rules, then two-feature rules, and so on. With a systematic abstraction order, the search is more like a depth-first search over prediction rules, specializing rules with the most relevant (last abstracted) feature, to ones with the two most relevant features, and so on.

Examples of the progression of rule learning for the two types of abstraction orderings are shown in Fig. 7.13. The random approach is generally slower than the systematic approach because the depth of the search space over all prediction rules is relatively shallow, relative to its breadth, and all leaf nodes represent acceptable predictions (i.e., the experimental design assumed deterministic exemplars over all possible feature vectors). However, either resulted in significantly faster learning than found in Nosofsky et al. (1994) except for Type I, in which the random feature abstraction was slower than the human learning.

One missing element in the original SCA model was any kind of hypothesis testing or relevant feature recognition. This omission was especially problematic in Type I problems, when most subjects likely would quickly recognize the single-feature discrimination. To capture this kind of knowledge, we added a simple encoding of relevant feature detection. A feature

Random Abstraction Order	**Systematic Abstraction Order**
0. fuel 20 ➡ accept	0. turb 1 ➡ accept
1. size L ➡ reject	1. turb 3 ➡ reject
2. fuel 40 ➡ reject	2. turb 1, fuel 20 ➡ accept
3. turb 1 ➡ accept	3. turb 1 ➡ reject
4. size S ➡ accept	4. turb 1, fuel 40 ➡ reject
5. size L, turb 1 ➡ reject	5. turb 3 ➡ accept
6. turb 1 ➡ reject	6. turb 3, fuel 20 ➡ accept
7. size L ➡ accept	7. turb 1, fuel 40, size S ➡ reject
8. fuel 20, turb 1 ➡ accept	8. turb 3, fuel 40 ➡ reject
9. size S ➡ reject	9. turb 1, fuel 20, size S ➡ accept

FIG. 7.13.   Example progression of rule learning in random (left) and systematic (right) abstraction orderings.

can be considered relevant to the prediction when an ignored (i.e., abstracted) feature leads to an incorrect prediction. The SCA model notes this situation and considers the feature that was ignored a relevant feature and abstracts it last, rather than randomly, in the future. This relevant feature detection allows the model to learn Type 1 (single-dimension) categories more quickly. The chosen feature can change as the model is run so that a model attempting to learn a Type 6 category will continue to try different features as relevant.

Figure 7.14 illustrates the ATC+SCA model results (30 model runs per problem type). The results reflect a poor fit to the aggregate human data; the G^2 aggregate fit statistic (described in chap. 2) is 674. Although there is a category and block effect—duplicating the qualitative results of Miller (1993)—the SCA mean learning rate for each problem type was much faster than the mean of the human subjects.

SCA as a Model of an Individual

Given the constraints imposed by methodology and architecture, we turned to the human data to understand what humans were learning during task performance and provide guidance in adapting SCA to fit the human re-

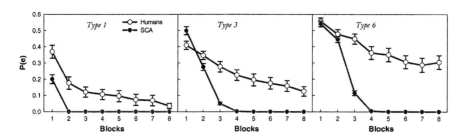

FIG. 7.14.   Initial SCA model results for the ATC learning task ($G^2 = 673.62$).

sults quantitatively. Other solutions might be to consider new learning algorithms; one is introduced in the next section. However, because we are embracing the constraints of an architectural approach, it was important to further explore the possibilities of explaining the results within the context of the existing architecture and category learning model.

The BBN analysis of initial results focused exclusively on aggregate data. We examined the learning trajectories of individual subjects to determine whether they corresponded qualitatively with the learning trajectories of individual model runs. Figure 7.15 plots the human individual data for Types 1, 3, and 6 category learning in the ATC task. These figures more effectively communicate the large variation in human subject learning trajectories. For example, for Type 1, four subjects failed to recognize the relevant feature by the end of the final block; the error of just these four subjects accounts for the error in Block 8; other subjects had learned the category. For Type 6, one subject learned the correct classifications by Block 2, while almost a third of the subjects were still performing at chance in the eighth block. Further, the trajectory of no individual human learner matched the shape of the aggregate human learning curve. This observation is important because it highlights the importance of our overall philosophy. Tuning the learning to match the aggregate learning might result in improved fits, but would not likely shed further light on human behavior because individual behavior is distinct from the aggregate in this task.

In the SCA model used to generate Fig. 7.14, the model knowledge is identical across all model runs, and there are no learning parameters other than this (constant) model knowledge. Hence, the initial SCA model is better viewed as an individual model rather than models of a population of subjects. Although SCA's learning rate appeared much too fast in comparison with the aggregate, the SCA results for the three problem types are within the bounds of the fastest and slowest human learners. Individual SCA learning curves also qualitatively matched the shape of some individual learning curves. SCA provided an exact fit to nine Type 1 subjects and to at least one subject for each type if the first block (essentially random guessing) is ignored. Thus, some SCA individual runs matched individual humans.

The limitations of creating models that match aggregate data alone are widely recognized (Estes, 2002). The analysis at the level of individual learners provided evidence that the SCA model might not be nearly as poor as one-dimensional comparisons to aggregate data suggested. This analysis provided the impetus to continue using SCA to model the ATC learning task. We now discuss improving the aggregate fit by introducing more complex feature mappings and simulating knowledge differences in subjects.

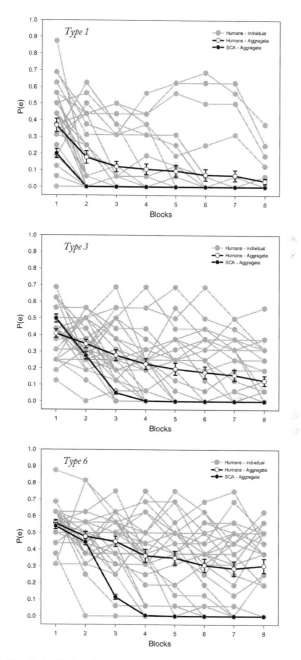

FIG. 7.15. Individual and aggregate human data compared with the aggregate SCA data.

More Complex Feature Mappings

One major difficulty in modeling learning experiments is that models tend to focus only on a restricted set of features—those to which the experiment instructed the subjects to attend. However, the brain interprets its environment, notices features, and learns continuously. Subjects (consciously or unconsciously) are likely detecting and possibly using all sorts of features aside from the ones instructed in the experiment.

The initial SCA model for the ATC task employed only three binary-valued features to represent the feature space for the learning task. Because SCA performs a refinement search over feature space when learning, its learning rate is sensitive to the number of features; they define the size of the search space. For the ATC experimental conditions (three features and two classifications), the size of search space is only 54 prediction rules. One of the reasons SCA learns so quickly is that the size of the search space is so trivial.

We empirically and mathematically explored the sensitivity of SCA to the number of binary-valued features. For example, for four features, the learning rate is not significantly affected, and the total search space remains modest (162 total rules). For six features, however, in the eighth block, probability of error is only slightly better than chance for Type 6. For six binary features, the total search space is 1,458 total rules; after 128 trials, less than 10% of the search space will have been explored. This analysis demonstrates that the introduction of additional features would slow the learning rate dramatically, and thus potentially improve the fit to the aggregate human data.

An obvious possible source of additional features is the additional information available on the screen. Within the immediate vicinity of the instance features to which subjects were instructed to attend are the iconic representation of the aircraft (pointed in one of four different compass directions), a text string representing the airline name, and a three-digit flight number. Subjects were given explicit instructions to ignore all but the instance values, but some human subjects reported that their hypotheses and learning were influenced by these additional factors in the posttest questionnaire. Table 7.5 lists the subjects that reported being influenced by additional stimuli. Further, because participants likely perceived this information, it is still possible that it influenced their categorization processes even if not reported (e.g., some subjects answered the question about strategy change with "my strategy did not change after I determined the pattern").

In addition to considering extra features, Table 7.5 also shows that subjects considered still other factors when performing the decision task. Some constructed new features from the combination of features (e.g., Subject 30's consideration of "all high" or "all low" inputs). Some may have considered the type of the values. For example, one subject reports aircraft with

TABLE 7.5
Human Subject Self-Reports of Their Learning Process

S#	*Responses Suggesting a Consideration of Factors Other Than Fuel, Turbulence, and Aircraft Size*
1	Other features: "... I thought it might be the direction, the area it was in, the location of nearby planes and the amount of fuel for the size of the plane ..."
19	Other features: "... I also took into consideration the direction the plane was moving ..."
24	Weighted factors: "... it took me several rounds to discover the importance of the turbulence rating. Before I discovered this, I paid more attention to fuel and size."
30	Constructed features: "The planes that had all the lowest descriptions together or the highest descriptions all together were accepted."
39	Semantic interpretation: "High turbulence meant to me that smaller aircraft could not change altitude."
41	Constructed features: "I rejected all double positives and double negatives i accepted the ones only with a negative and a positive."
46	Semantic interpretation: "It would make sense that a small plane with low fuel with high turbulence would want to change altitude, and be granted that right in succession."
51	Other features: "... partially by locale."
58	Semantic interpretation: "It was hard not to think logically about whether or not the planes should be allowed to increase their altitude. Smaller planes with less fuel and a high turbulence, to me shouldn't be allowed an increase on their altitude."
60	Other features: "... how close they were to the intersection with other planes ..."
64	Semantic interpretation: "I felt my strategy was more of common sense too; a small plane experiencing heavy turbulence and light on fuel would definitely need make some adjustments."
77	Other features: "... I used percent of the fuel and direction of the airplane as cues ..."
83	Other features: "... First i thought you had to change the altitudes when two planes were about to crash. Then I thought it dealt with the N/S and E/W directions ..."
86	Constructed features: "After the first couple of trials, I noticed a pattern. For example, I knew that if it was 20 S 3 it had to be true and if it was 40 S 3 it had to be false. I just assumed the opposite: If 20 S 3 was true, then 40 S 3 had to be false and so on."
87	Other features: "... At first my strategy was more complicated than necessary. I looked at the direction of the plane, and chose reject for each, until I discovered which was correct in each direction ..."

20 gallons of fuel, rather than 20% of its fuel remaining. Many reported being influenced by the meaning of the features in the context of the task, such as Subject 58, who thought that small planes in high turbulence should be allowed to change their altitude based on a semantic interpretation of the features. Close to 20% of the subjects in the study reported being influenced by one or more of these additional factors.

Further, the features could also be considered as more complex than a simple attribute. Unlike the orthogonal stimuli used by Nosofsky et al. (1994), all of the feature values are alphanumeric, suggesting more fine-grained discrimination between features could be necessary. Some co-occurring feature values have similar shapes (e.g., "S 3" and "L 1"), and the fuel value is represented by two digits (20 or 40). Thus, it is plausible that more than just a single feature could be associated or constructed from an individual input value.

These examples illustrate that information excluded or not considered in the instructions can (and did) influence human subjects. However, the individual data subjective reports are anecdotal and insufficient for determining how to enumerate and codify these effects. To resolve this lack of specificity, we chose to simulate these effects with a number of additional, random values. These values are thus normative rather than descriptive, but are meant to capture the effect of attending to nonrelevant features, considering the meaning, type, and interrelationships among relevant features, constructing new features from combinations of relevant features, and the possibility of perceptual discrimination issues among the alphanumeric feature values.

A better, more detailed model would explain how and why subjects create, consider, and attend to additional features. However, a lack of precision at this level of specification is a limitation of all models of category learning, not only SCA. By adopting this approach, we simply introduce the number of features as a model parameter. However, one of the positive consequences of the constraint of the architecture and model is that they led us to consider these issues. Because the architecture lacks other parameters that might mask these effects, SCA predicted that additional features would play a role in human learning.

Abstraction Strategies

Looking at the individual data also led us to consider a number of potential abstraction orderings, rather than the single method used initially. We observed that for Types 3 and 6, some human subjects exhibited steady progress to zero error, some subjects made little improvements after repeated trials, and some regressed, exhibiting decreasing error for a number of blocks and then suddenly increasing. These patterns corresponded qualitatively to the three possible options for abstraction order outlined previously. A model with a fixed or systematic abstraction order will converge relatively quickly to zero error, even when critical features are abstracted early in the abstraction process, because less of the total feature space needs to be examined. A random abstraction order results in relatively slow progress because a much greater portion of the feature space is examined. This unsystematic strategy leads to slow progress when the number of features (and thus the feature space) is larger. Finally, for Types 3 and 6, relevant feature detection can lead to increases in the error. Even when the relevant feature is incorrect, it will stabilize abstraction order for a time and a consistent portion of the feature space will be examined, leading to a decrease in the error. However, when the model recognizes another relevant feature candidate, it changes the abstraction order and moves to a different part of the feature space. This move can increase the error because the model may have learned few prediction rules in the new area of the feature space.

Populations of Models

Given the possibilities outlined previously, we now had 12 options for instantiating an SCA model (i.e., 0 to 3 extra features and 1 of 3 different strategies). These options spanned the variation in human learning and qualitatively matched specific learning trajectories. The result is a population of models for the category learning task. Because, as described earlier, the human data were insufficient to provide specific guidance for choosing distributions of features and strategies, model instances were instantiated randomly from a uniform distribution of the population of models. As before, the model was run 30 times for each problem type using the uniform distribution for each category.

Model Results

The model was fit only to the learning rate by problem type data (i.e., the human data in Fig. 7.14 and the subject workload data described later). All other matches to the human data are realized without any parameter fitting for the additional phenomena; they arise completely from the fit obtained against the basic human data and the model.

Figure 7.16 illustrates the extended SCA model results for Types 1, 3, and 6. These results provide excellent fits for Types 1 and 3 and a reasonable fit for Type 6. The G^2 statistic for the aggregate fit is 9.96. Qualitative fits improve as well. Although nonuniformly distributed parameter values can improve the fit further, the uniform distributions of model types and feature vectors provided a good fit to the data with minimal additional assumptions. Plots of individual model data, shown in Fig. 7.17, reveal a similar distribution to the individual human.

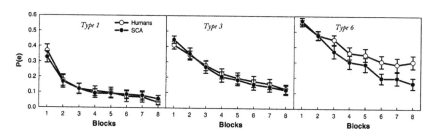

FIG. 7.16.   Extended SCA learning results ($G^2 = 9.96$).

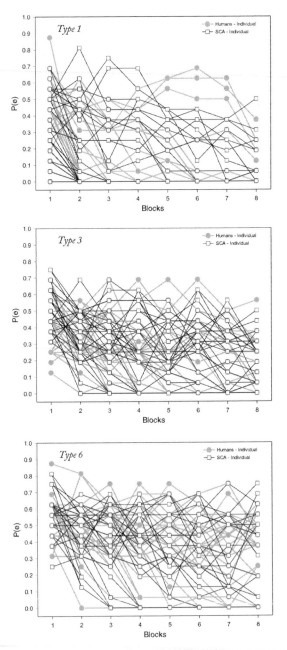

FIG. 7.17.   Comparison of human and model individual learning data.

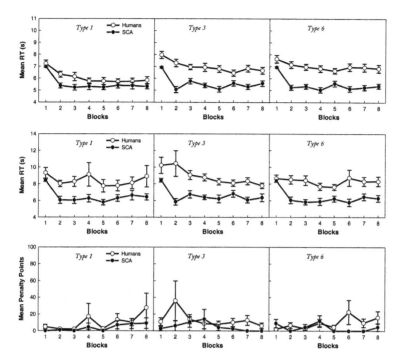

FIG. 7.18. Some predictions of the extended SCA model: primary task mean RT (SSE = 39.33); secondary task mean RT (SSE = 114.73); secondary task penalty points (SSE = 2720.29).

Figure 7.18 shows other performance predictions of the model. The top plot graphs the mean reaction time to respond to a category learning trial.[9] As would be expected, after a few blocks, in the aggregate humans respond faster to Type 1 instances than Type 3 and Type 6. However, SCA fails to capture this effect, responding in roughly the same amount of time for each type of instance. This omission occurs because the abstraction process (the loop in Fig. 7.11) is insensitive to problem type, and thus the time to respond, within SCA, will always be comparable. A model that more deliberately considered strategies and options when switching to the classification task might naturally account for differences in reaction times between Type 1 and Types 3 and 6 because Type 1 tasks, for most subjects, will quickly be perceived to be easier and thus require less strategic deliberation.

---

[9]This time is measured from the moment a blip turns MAGENTA until the subject/model clicks the SEND button to complete the message. Thus, these mean RTs include the perceptual-motor time of composing the message. The time to determine a prediction alone was not recorded.

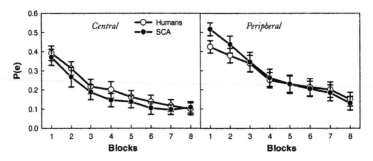

FIG. 7.19. Prediction of "central" and "peripheral" Type 3 stimuli ($G^2 =$ 3.46).

The middle plot in the figure is the mean reaction time measured from when a blip changes color and when the SEND button is pressed for the ATC task. The bottom plot shows the mean penalty points accrued for the ATC task.

Nosofsky et al. (1994) showed that human subjects learn to classify Type 3 peripheral stimuli more slowly than central ones. SCA was previously shown to replicate this effect qualitatively (Miller, 1993). Figure 7.19 shows quantitative predictions for the AMBR learning task.

Number of Perfect Learners

Analysts at BBN introduced the notion of a *perfect learner*—a subject whose Block 8 error was zero. Table 7.6 shows the number of human perfect learners and SCA perfect learners. Prior to its extension, all SCA model runs reached zero error by the eighth block. The number of SCA perfect learners in the extended model was nearly exact for Types 1 and 3, but off by a factor of 2 for Type 6. Comparing the number of perfect learners is important as a simple measure of the variability captured by the model. For example, models tuned very closely to the aggregate learning data might show many fewer perfect learners because the error in the last training block for all three problem types is greater than zero.

TABLE 7.6
Number of Perfect Human and Model Learners by Problem Type

Problem Type	Humans	SCA, Original	SCA, Extended
1	24	30	23
3	15	30	15
6	6	30	12

EXPERIMENT 2: RULEX-EM

Many of the existing category learning models commit to learning as the acquisition of rules (hypotheses) or exemplars exclusively. As is the case with many dichotomies, progress often occurs with a theory that can best reconcile alternative perspectives. Empirical work by Minda and Smith (2001) showed that both representations are used in learning and identifies characteristics of the category that can cause one representation to be more prominent than another. Erickson and Kruschke (1998) and Anderson and Betz (2002) are examples of work to reconcile both representations into a coherent model. Similarly, we developed a model that employed both representations.

The hypothesis-testing process model, RULEX, was selected as a starting point because it is a process model that demonstrated good fits to rule-based classification learning (Nosofsky et al., 1994). The end product is a distinct process model that incorporates both rules and exemplars, includes memory effects such as forgetting, and relies on a smaller, more principled set of parameters. The model we developed is called RULEX-EM, reflecting the addition of **E**xemplars and **M**emory constraints (Chong & Wray, 2003).

Model Description

Like RULEX, the model uses a homogeneous representation for both exemplars and rules. Both are four-tuples consisting of the three instance features (FUEL, SIZE, TURB) and an associated category (ALLOW or DENY). Both declarative representations are subject to forgetting through the base-level learning mechanism.

Exemplars are defined as fully specified four-tuples: Values of all three instance features and the category (determined after receiving feedback) are specified. For example:

EXEMPLAR: [FUEL = 20; SIZE = S; TURB = 3; CATEGORY = ALLOW]

The system contains two kinds of rules. A single-feature rule is one where the value of only one of the three instance features is specified and the remaining features are unspecified (shown next as a *). The following single-feature rule applies to all instances where TURB is 3:

SINGLE-FEATURE RULE: [FUEL = *; SIZE = *; TURB = 3; CATEGORY = ALLOW]

The second kind of rule, an exception rule, is a two-feature rule. Following RULEX, an exception rule is a specialization of a single-feature rule; it tests a feature in addition to the one tested by a failed single-feature rule. The following exception rule could be derived from the prior single-feature rule:

EXCEPTION RULE: [FUEL = *; SIZE = L; TURB = 3; CATEGORY = DENY]

A block diagram of the model is shown in Fig. 7.20. Like RULEX, the model has two distinct phases—prediction followed by learning. Beginning after an instance appears and is perceived, the prediction phase tries prediction strategies—from specific to general—to determine the category of the instance. This approach, inherited from RULEX, is similar to SCA's specific-to-general search for prediction rules. Unlike RULEX, the first step is to try to recall an exemplar for the given instance. If successful, the category specified in the CATEGORY slot of the recalled exemplar is produced. Because exemplars are subject to forgetting, this recall strategy can fail.

If so, the model tries to recall an exception rule. If several exception rules can be recalled, the model tries the most highly activated rule. In general, this is the rule most frequently and/or recently used. If the recalled rule can be applied, a category prediction will be output.

If the exception recall strategy fails (either because no exception rules could be recalled or because none could be applied), the model then tries to recall a single-feature rule. If no single-feature rules can be recalled, the model will guess the instance's category. If a rule can be recalled and applied, the category prediction is output.

If a single-feature rule is recalled but cannot be applied, the model will produce the opposite category as specified in the rule. We surmised that subjects, realizing that the feature values and categories in this task are binary, might choose a category response that is the complement of the one specified in the recalled rule. Subject 86 in Table 7.5 reports performing such an inversion. To illustrate, suppose the instance is [20 S 1] and the model only has the single-feature rule shown before. The rule does not match because the TURB values are complements. A reasonable response might then be to produce the complementary category (i.e., DENY).

After a prediction has been made and feedback provided by the environment, the model enters the learning phase. The learning behavior used depends on the feedback and the strategy used to make the prediction.

If an incorrect prediction were made, the model will always create an exemplar, as defined earlier. (Creating a duplicate of an existing exemplar or rule results in an increase of the activation of the existing exemplar or rule.) Next, the model rehearses the exemplar. Rehearsals boost activation to increase the likelihood a memory element will not be forgotten.

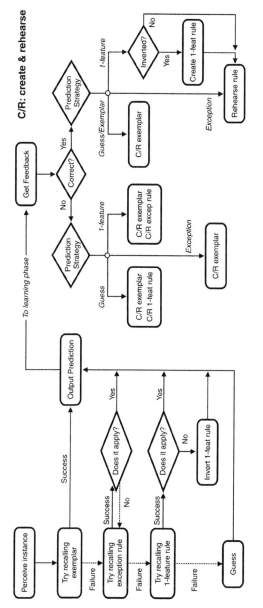

FIG. 7.20. Block diagram of the RULEX-EM model.

281

If the incorrect prediction was due to:

- a *guess*, the model will create and rehearse a single-feature rule by randomly selecting one of the features of the instance and associating it with the current category.
- a *single-feature rule*, the model will create an exception rule. An exception rule is derived from the failed single-feature rule by using the specified feature value in the rule and one other randomly selected feature value from the instance. The exception rule shown earlier could have resulted from the presentation of [20 L 3] and the recall of a previously learned but incorrect single-feature rule such as [*, L, *, ACCEPT] or [*, *, 3, ACCEPT].

If a correct prediction was produced, the learning behavior is dependent on the prediction strategy as follows:

- a *guess* or *exemplar recall*: The model creates and rehearses the exemplar.
- an *exception* rule: The model rehearses the exception rule.
- a *single-feature* rule: If a single-feature rule was directly applied, the rule is rehearsed. If the model uses the complement of a single-feature rule, the model creates and rehearses a single-feature rule representing the inverted rule.

Due to the architectural base-level learning memory mechanism, exemplars and rules can be forgotten unless they are used or rehearsed. Rules that are predictive will be chosen and used more often, further increasing the chance of being used and not forgotten. Rules that are less predictive will experience less use and will eventually be forgotten. In contrast to rules, successful exemplar recall will always produce a correct prediction. Therefore, their activation will increase largely as a function of the number of exposures.

Model Results

Figure 7.21 shows the fit of the model to the learning data as a function of problem type. Aside from the four parameters of the base-level learning mechanism (which were never manipulated), these fits are accomplished using only two free parameters: the rehearsals used to reinforce exemplar and rule memories. The best fits were achieved with rehearsals of four and seven, respectively. A goodness-of-fit analysis produced a G^2 of 5.64. The human data and model show significant effects of problem type and blocks. Figure 7.22 presents a series of model predictions. For the primary task reaction time (the time from when a blip turns magenta until when the "send" button is clicked), the human data showed significant effect of blocks; subjects' per-

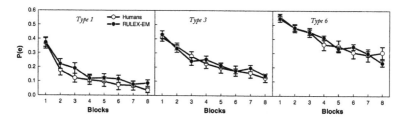

FIG. 7.21. The fit of the RULEX-EM model to the human learning rate data. Error bars designate 95% confidence intervals ($G^2 = 5.64$).

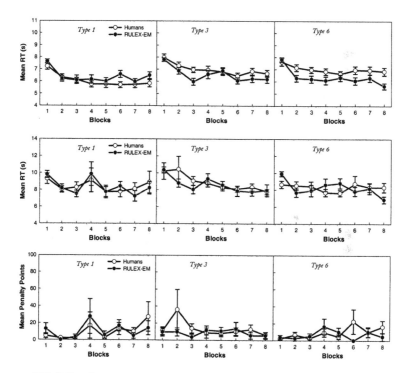

FIG. 7.22. Some predictions of RULEX-EM: primary task RT (SSE = 8.40); secondary task RT (SSE = 15.24); secondary task penalty points (SSE = 2043.46).

formance is improving with practice. However, there was a weak effect by type; Type 1 is different from Types 3 and 6, whereas Types 3 and 6 are not different from each other. For this measure, the model was only able to reproduce the effect by blocks. There was a significant effect by block for secondary task reaction time for both humans and the model. Finally, no effect by problem type or block was found for the mean penalty points in humans. There was a similar absence of effect for the model data.

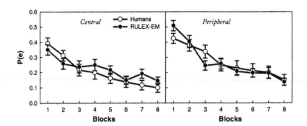

FIG. 7.23.   RULEX-EM prediction of Type 3 learning rates for "central" and "peripheral" stimuli ($G^2 = 5.89$).

Figure 7.23 presents the model's central versus peripheral prediction. There were significant effects of stimulus type and blocks for both the human and model data. Figure 7.24 compares individual human and model data. The model's variability in performance decreases as problem difficulty increases, unlike the human data or the SCA model (Fig. 7.17).

Insights Provided by the Model

To further evaluate the model and gain a deeper insight into its behavior, we instrumented the model to collect data on prediction strategy utilization as a function of experience and problem type. Figure 7.25 shows the collected data as a distribution of strategy use in the model for the three types of problems. Initially, guesses are frequent, but quickly taper off as learning progresses; guesses are more frequent for the difficult Type 6 problems. Single-feature rules are learned quickly and persist in the Type 1 condition as expected. However, for Type 6, single-feature rules are tried, demonstrate little utility, then yield to exception rules. (Recall that exception rules are created when single-feature rules fail.) Exception rules grow to dominate by the end of learning in Types 3 and 6 as would be expected. Exemplar recall is used more in Type 6 problems than Type 1 because the difficulty of Type 6 causes more incorrect predictions, which leads to increased opportunities to memorize and rehearse exemplars. The steady increase in exemplar recall mimics implicit learning or priming effects that can occur merely from repeated exposure to stimuli.

SUBJECTIVE WORKLOAD

Figures 7.26 and 7.27 present the fits for the extended SCA and RULEX-EM models, respectively. Because both models share the same workload implementation and achieve relatively good fits to the learning prediction data, they also share good fits to the human workload data.

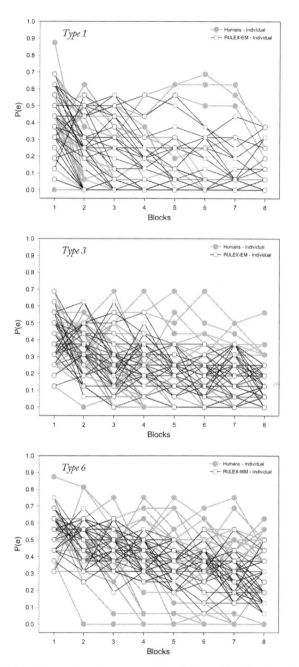

FIG. 7.24. Comparison of human and model individual learning data.

285

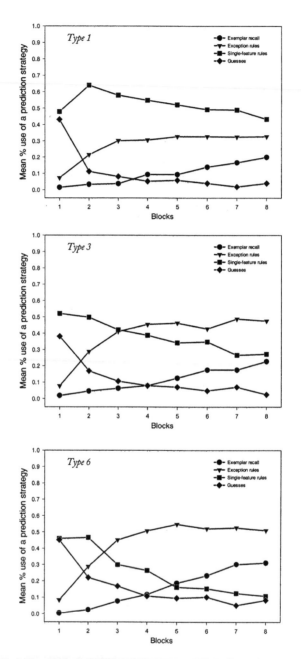

FIG. 7.25. Evolution of strategy use across blocks by problem type.

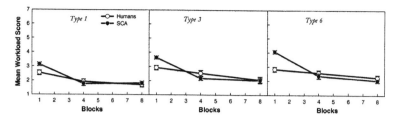

FIG. 7.26. Workload (SSE = 2.66) for the extended SCA model.

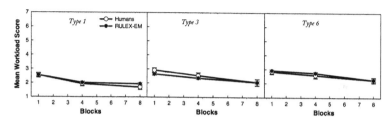

FIG. 7.27. Workload (SSE = 0.21) for the RULEX-EM model.

To achieve these good subjective workload fits, the subjective workload formulation used in Experiment 1 and described earlier was elaborated in two ways. First, the workload value for magenta blips was increased from 2 to 10 to reflect the new primary-task status of responding to altitude change requests. Second, we added a new realization: An incorrect prediction (i.e., when receiving negative feedback) triggers a realization that there is more learning to do. This realization was given a workload value of 15.

We also made two minor changes to the workload equation. To increase the stability of the workload predictions between runs, the t parameter was made a constant, now representing the duration of the scenario in seconds (600). Previously, t represented the cognitive cycle count at the end of training, which varied from 9,000 to 18,000 cycles (depending on the duration of the cognitive cycle), giving an average of 13,500 cycles. The new t value is roughly 1/20th of 13,500, therefore the old α value (100) was scaled accordingly to give a new value of 5. This relationship between the old and new values of t and α suggests that: (a) the new values would have produced the same fits for Experiment 1, and (b) the good fit of workload in Experiment 2 is a validation of our general formulation of workload (Eq. 1).

TRANSFER TASK

We have examined some predictions of SCA and RULEX-EM in the context of the eight learning blocks. This section reports on the model predictions for the transfer task described in chapter 2.

SCA Transfer Task Results

Figure 7.28 shows the initial transfer task results for the SCA model. For this model, knowledge was added to map unknown feature values to the values specified in the task instructions. This knowledge reflects commonsense knowledge about the values of scalars and sizes. For instance, the value 10 is closer to 20 than 40; therefore, 10 will be mapped to 20. It seemed plausible that subjects would use this kind of knowledge to map an extrapolated value to a known value for a prediction. Thus, FUEL = 20, SIZE = XS, TURBU-LENCE = 3 would be mapped to FUEL = 20, SIZE = S, TURBULENCE = 3, a trained instance, and the subject would respond with the prediction learned for this instance.

There were two unresolved issues. First, mapping intermediate values (e.g., 30) included three obvious possibilities: (a) map to the lower value, (b) map to the higher value, and (c) do not change the value. Thus, an instance with a fuel value of 30 could get mapped to the known values of 20 or 40 or not changed at all. For the transfer task, we designed the model to make a random choice among the three options, each option having equal probability.

Second, we considered capacity limitations on the mappings. For example, an instance of 10, 4, XL requires three mappings (to 20, 3, L) and then the retrieval of the prediction rule for this trained instance. There is no ambiguity in this mapping, but rather a question if subjects could readily perform all three mappings and then retrieve a prediction for the instance. This last issue is important because perceptual cues might be included in prediction rules (if so subjects might respond differently to trained instances presented verbally, for example). Because it was the simplest approach (requiring no additional assumptions about capacity limitations or perceptual issues), the initial transfer task model completes all mappings and then makes a prediction.

Superficially, the SCA transfer task results appeared quite discouraging. However, the overall results are skewed by the learning rate in the original

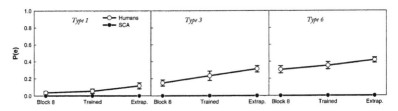

FIG. 7.28. Initial SCA transfer task results in comparison to human results (G^2 = 420.09). Probability of error is plotted for the last training block ("Block 8"), the trained instances during the transfer task ("Trained"), and for those instances that could be unambiguously mapped to trained instances ("Extrap").

SCA model with respect to the basic learning task. Because SCA learns all categories by the eighth training block, its probability of error for the learned instances will be zero and all its transfer task predictions will be based on completely learned categorizations. A comparison of human perfect learners to the SCA transfer task results was much more encouraging. As shown in Fig. 7.30, perfect learners produce an average probability of error close to zero for the trained instances, particularly for Types 1 and 3.

The real failure in the transfer task results is the predictions SCA made with respect to the extrapolated stimuli. SCA shows no change in probability of error for the extrapolated instances versus the trained instances. These results are attributable to the complete mapping we chose. With the complete mapping, all extrapolated instances are mapped to the corresponding trained instances, and thus result in the same probability of error and consistency as the trained cases. Therefore, for the revised model, we sought a simple approach that reduced the number of mappings.

In the original model, the mapping occurred before any prediction. That is, when the model was presented an instance such as (10, L, 4), it would complete the mappings to the trained instance (20, L, 3) before attempting to make a prediction. The only change in the revised model was to allow prediction and mapping to compete. Figure 7.29 illustrates the process. If the model abstracted the size feature in this example (L), it then would consider abstracting either of the remaining values or mapping them to training values. Prediction is accomplished through the deliberate choice to ignore (abstract) a feature, which then allows the model to retrieve any prediction rules matching the partial instance. We changed the mapping knowledge so that the model could, with any decision, choose to map features or abstract them. Abstraction operators are proposed at the beginning of the prediction process as well as any mapping operators (as before, equidistant values lead to the proposal of three mapping operators: map lower, map higher, do not map). The result is that sometimes a particular feature is mapped and sometimes it is ignored.

Figure 7.30 displays the final SCA probability of error results for the transfer task. The result is a much better match to the extrapolated stimuli than was observed in the first round. However, the model fails to predict the increase in error in the trained stimuli when presented during the

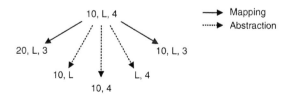

FIG. 7.29.   Example of the competition between abstraction and mapping.

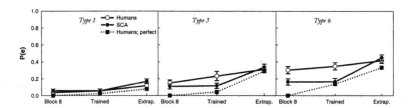

FIG. 7.30.   Final SCA transfer task probability of error results in comparison to human results ($G^2 = 14.37$).

transfer task. SCA provides no inherent explanation of this effect. SCA predicts that the error rates should be the same across Block 8 and trained stimuli in the transfer task. There are a number of potential explanations for the increase in error. The methodology in the transfer tasks is slightly different, and some subjects took a break before completing the transfer task, which would have led to increased delays for these presentations. An intriguing possibility is that subjects are learning something during the transfer task that interferes or inhibits their ability to retrieve their correct predictions. If this hypothesis were true, performance should degrade over the course of the transfer task. Yet another possibility is that some subjects guessed wildly during the transfer task and skewed the results of those subjects who took this task more seriously. Answering these questions might provide some guidance toward extending the model to account for this result. However, SCA alone would not account for these differences, and its failure to account for this trend in the data represents incompleteness in its account of category learning.

RULEX-EM Transfer Task Results

We used the same transfer task implementation as used in the extended SCA model illustrated in Fig. 7.29. Figure 7.31 presents the results. First, the predictions for extrapolated stimuli ("Extrap") are puzzling because RULEX-EM used the same mapping and abstraction process as for the extended SCA model. We presently have no explanation for its nearly uniform prediction across problem types. There might be an unanticipated interaction in the mapping/abstraction procedure and the memory effects present in the RULEX-EM model and not present in the SCA models. This warrants further investigation. The remainder of this section focuses on the prediction of "Trained" instances during the transfer task.

   For Type 6, the model correlates well to the human data. However, in Types 1 and 3, the model predicts small improvements in performance (reduction in P(e)) for Block 8 and Trained, whereas the data reveal a decrement in performance (increase in P(e)).

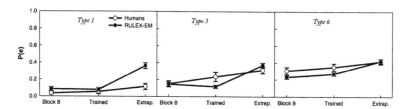

FIG. 7.31.   RULEX-EM transfer task results in comparison to human results
($G^2 = 16.23$).

Although the Types 1 and 3 model trends contradict the data, there are
good reasons to believe the model:

- During the training phase, it is possible to learn a reliable rule or successfully memorize more/all exemplars in the waning moments of Block 8.
The consequence is that performance for Trained stimuli is improved relative to performance in Block 8.
- Types 1 and 3 (as illustrated in Fig. 7.25) rely heavily on single-feature
and exceptions rules. This combination provides a low degree of specificity.[10] Rules, by definition, apply to multiple instances (e.g., a single-feature
rule covers four instances). During the transfer task, the use of a rule increases the rule's activation, making it more likely to be available for the
other transfer task instances covered by the rule. In essence, the model continues to learn (in the absence of feedback), resulting in improved category
prediction performance for the Trained instances. In contrast, Type 6 relies heavily on exceptions and exemplars. The high combined degree of
specificity of exemplars and exceptions—five: three for exemplars plus two
for exceptions—allows less reuse and therefore a lower likelihood of improved performance.

To gain more insight into performance on the Trained stimuli, we
turned to the individual human data. Figure 7.32 shows the individual and
aggregate human data. Similar to the learning data (Fig. 7.15), there was
much more variability than expected. Closer examination of the data revealed other unexpected findings. For example, the Type 1 subject with the
worst Trained performance (0.625) had previously demonstrated perfect
performance—$P(e) = 0.0$—from Block 2 through Block 8. Also six Type 1
subjects showed a decrease in performance on Trained stimuli relative to
Block 8, although they attained perfect performance no later than Block 5.

---

[10]A single-feature rule specifies only one feature, whereas an exception rule specifies two
features, yielding a combined degree of specificity of three.

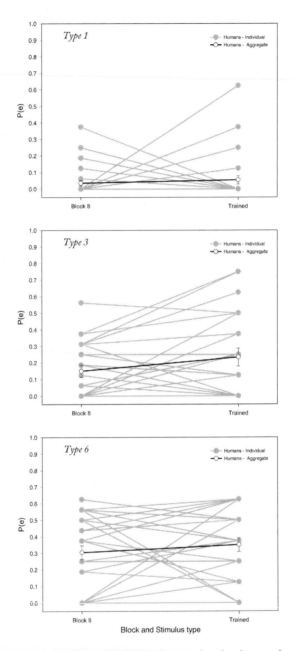

FIG. 7.32.   Individual and aggregate human data for the transfer task.

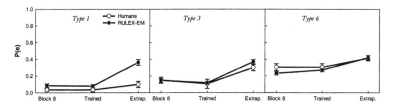

FIG. 7.33. Revised fit after removal of outlier subject data ($G^2 = 14.94$).

This unexpected behavior suggests that some subjects may have been confused about what to do during the transfer task. Recall that subjects were given no practice transfer trials, nor were they told ahead of time that a transfer task would be performed. This confusion may have been compounded by interference between trained and extrapolated stimuli.

When the transfer task data for these outlier subjects are removed,[11] the performance decrement observed in Fig. 7.31 was reduced (Type 1) or reversed (Type 3) to an increase in performance (see Fig. 7.33). Type 6 was unaffected largely because of its reliance on exceptions and memorized exemplars as discussed before. The result of pruning outlier subjects was that the model's predictions of Trained performance are a better match to the human data.

DISCUSSION

"Every model is wrong, but some models are useful" is an epigram attributed to George E. P. Box. Having presented the models and some initial discussion of their fits to human data, this section examines the limitations of the models more critically. It also attempts to show that, although the models had limitations, they provided insights into human performance that made them quite useful.

Critical Analysis of SCA

The original SCA model, representing a single strategy and subject, provided learning within the brackets of the fastest and slowest human learners and matched the learning of some individual subjects qualitatively and quantitatively. The SCA Soar model provided these fits a priori. We achieved these results by reusing an extant model, following constraints im-

---

[11]For this analysis, we remove subjects whose performance in Block 8 was better than chance—$P(e) < 0.5$—but whose performance on Trained stimuli was equal to or worse than chance—$P(e) \geq 0.5$. One subject was removed for Type 1; five subjects were removed for both Types 3 and 6.

posed by theory, and without introducing additional knowledge or parameters. This methodology provides for the cumulation of results necessary for a comprehensive architectural theory (Newell, 1990).

We achieved improved aggregate fits by developing a population of models with different strategies (reflected in the different methods for determining abstraction order) and different feature vectors. These choices were motivated from a more fine-grained analysis of the individual data. This approach begins to approximate the demand for more sophisticated models of human learning that match not only the aggregate data, but also the learning trajectories of individual subjects and successfully predict performance on transfer stimuli (Estes, 2002). The number of direct correspondences between human individuals and individual model runs does improve over the original SCA model.

One positive consequence of taking seriously the constraints of theory, architecture, and a previously existing model is that this constraint led us to consider different strategies and alternate feature encodings. Although we would much prefer to be able to make a priori predictions of the features based on the representation, post hoc estimation of the feature space is consistent with the decisions of other modelers. For example, in an icon search task model, Fleetwood and Byrne (2002) indicated that the features for their task, which include simple shapes as well as more complex icons, were estimated from human data. Currently, models of perception such as EPIC and ACT-R/PM do not inform or constrain the number of features needed for any particular percept (in part because such results are not available in the human factors or cognitive science literature). Thus, although our approach did require post hoc analysis to match the data, it also led us to ask other questions that modelers using other architectures were not led to ask. In general, this is one of the advantages of alternate theories and computational architectures: Different theories and architectures lead to different ways of interpreting and analyzing a data set, thus offering, in sum, a greater perspective on the human phenomena than any individual perspective.

Although the aggregate and individual model fits were good, issues and questions related to the plausibility and completeness of SCA as a descriptive model of category learning were not resolved. If the debrief results can be assumed to be reasonable indicators of a person's self-awareness of cognition, it appears that human subjects learned using both exemplar-like techniques (Subject 2: "I started to notice a pattern") and hypothesis testing techniques that led to rules (Subject 18: "Accept if the plane's fuel was at 20, reject at 40"). SCA models only the former. A potential line of future research would be to combine the hypothesis-testing component of the RULEX-EM model with SCA and compare the results to other hybrid models.

SCA's abstraction process is deliberate, which makes the use of additional, irrelevant features more problematic for a descriptive model. Even if irrelevant features were perceived, SCA, as currently conceived, would ignore them due to their irrelevance (as defined by the task instructions). Although the immediate goal was to model this task within the existing model of SCA, we have begun to investigate an alternative formulation of SCA that will use episodic indexing (Altmann & John, 1999). In this model, feature abstraction occurs as a consequence of attention and recall, rather than via a deliberate abstraction process. Preliminary results suggest this model will provide similar learning results, but avoid the use of a deliberate abstraction procedure, a psychologically unrealistic component of SCA.

The current model also ignores that any extra features considered in early blocks would be decreasingly likely to play a factor in later blocks. Although human subjects did report being influenced by external factors, most acknowledged or implied that they abandoned or excluded these factors as experience with the task deepened. In the attention-based SCA model, an obvious way to model the decreasing influence of extra features would be to learn to attend only to the features that led to positive feedback. Initially, this learning would introduce new features into consideration (because, by random chance, some of them would be useful for a few trials), but over time would allow the model to converge on just those features that are needed for categorization. Such a model will be a step toward a descriptive model that accounts for the consideration of extra features in human learning. However, such a model still would not address other factors like feature value discrimination and semantic interpretation of the features and values.

Hypotheses other than extra features are also useful for developing deep explanations of human learning in this task. For example, in Round 1, we evaluated how learning slowed in SCA if the model did not learn on every trial (SCA learns a new prediction rule with every learning trial). Introducing a probability of learning parameter did allow SCA to better match the aggregate learning curves. The primary reservation with this approach is that we did not find any direct evidence in the data that would explain why the model should not learn on every trial. Subjects did report that they grew bored during the experiment and for a period responded randomly or with the same response. These responses provide a clue as to how to slow learning, but again the challenge is to capture and encode the conditions under which such factors should be considered, requiring models of motivation and interest.

Critical Analysis of RULEX-EM

The development of RULEX-EM relied on synthesis and integration on several dimensions. First, the model is constructed within the constraints of an integrated cognitive architecture. Second, the model contains both exemplar and rule representations. Third, the learning model is integrated with a preexisting model of a dynamic perceptual-motor performance task.

RULEX-EM, evaluated in the context of the AMBR learning and performance task, produced good fits and many predictions confirmed by human data. We attribute the model's success, in part, to (a) the architectural integration of elements of ACT-R, Soar, and EPIC; (b) inheriting the validation of these systems; and (c) accepting the modeling constraints of these mechanisms. Notwithstanding these positive results, there remain many unresolved limitations and methodological issues.

One such issue concerns the uniform representation of rules and exemplars as declarative four-tuples. This representation was similar to that used by Nosofsky, Palmeri, and McKinley (1994) and was sufficient for modeling the AMBR learning task. However, we are not asserting that this representation is used by humans. A comprehensive review of the empirical literature will help inform the proper representations for rules and exemplars as the model evolves.

Another issue concerns the strict specific-to-general approach to category prediction. It is unlikely that humans use such a strict process to determine an instance's category. A consequence of the model always considering exception rules before single-feature rules is seen in Fig. 7.25 by the high use (30%) of exception rules in Type 1 problems, where one might expect near exclusive use of single-feature rules. We are considering an alternative prediction process—one that is based on competition between prediction strategies (exemplar recall, exception rules, single-feature rules). A competitive prediction approach—selecting a prediction strategy based on their utility (activation) and tending to favor new rules or rules successfully used in the previous trial—may produce a more believable strategy distribution. Such an approach would require a control scheme that deliberately chose not to use a recalled rule that had just failed. This would allow the model to better explore the space of hypotheses while not preventing the reuse of previously failed rules.

A weakness of the model is that the episodic recall strategy, if it succeeds, will always return the correct category. This occurs, in part, because exemplar memories are a four-tuple, tightly coupling the instance features with the category. A more ecologically correct representation should perhaps group instance features in a three-tuple, create a distinct memory structure for the category (because the feedback is temporally displaced from the onset of the instance features), and then use an associating memory structure to bind the instance to the category. This dissociation of stimuli feature and category allows the model to recall or recognize a stimulus while not ensuring the availability of the category because the associating memory structure may become unavailable due to inadequate use. Although this solution provides a more distributed representation, it only addresses failure to recall a category. Another issue entirely ignored by the present architecture and model is successful, but confused recall or recognition due to the interference between similar stimuli and category classes. This is an important avenue for future architectural explorations.

The individual model data (Fig. 7.24) are almost uniformly distributed around the mean model data. This occurs because the model's primary source of variability is noise. This reliance on noise is responsible for the unexpected reduction in variability as problem difficulty increased. Wray and Laird (2003) cautioned against attempts to represent the range of human behavior by noise alone. Rather there must also be representations of the variety of strategies humans perform. RULEX-EM only implements a normative strategy; it does not include specific prediction or learning strategies, such as used by a subject who may (a) choose to give the same prediction until they have observed a pattern, or (b) make an a priori decision to memorize the exemplars (e.g., one subject reported an a priori decision to memorize instances). It also does not include the behavior of subjects who did not conform to task instructions and considered nonrelevant task features when formulating their categories (as exemplified in Table 7.5) or who perhaps did not understand the goal of the task (e.g., as discussed earlier).

RULEX-EM is principally a learn-on-failure model. Only exemplar learning and reinforcement, through the creation and rehearsal of exemplars, will occur until a prediction (using the "guess" prediction strategy) fails. This learning approach has implications for modeling human data, most notably for Type 1 problems. The individual human data graphs in Fig. 7.24 show that at least one human subject produced perfect prediction ($P(e) = 0$) in Block 1. In fact this subject made only one error (in Block 8) for the entire training. RULEX-EM cannot reproduce this behavior and offers the implausible explanation that this subject guessed correctly over seven blocks. In contrast, SCA, which learns on every instance presentation, is able to produce perfect prediction in Block 1 for Type 1 as illustrated in Fig. 7.17. It may be possible for RULEX-EM to also produce this behavior with the addition of explicit cognitive strategies such as those mentioned previously for increasing the variability of the model.

RULEX-EM required tuning of only two free parameters: the number of rehearsals for rules and exemplars. These two stand in contrast to the 10 free parameters available in RULEX. However, before this reduction can be considered an achievement, RULEX-EM must demonstrate coverage of the breadth of data previously fit by RULEX. Additionally, the explicit rehearsals controlled by those two free parameters are an example of the placeholder nature of free parameters. We do not believe that subjects are deliberately and consistently rehearsing rules seven times and exemplars four times. Instead it is more likely that subjects are performing productive processing of rules and exemplars that has an effect approximated by explicit rehearsals. As we refine the model, we hope to identify parameter-free processes that eliminate the need for explicit rehearsals.

CONCLUSIONS

Modeling, in all its forms, is a technique by which we operationalize, test, and expand our understanding of phenomena or behavior. Model development has a large number of degrees of freedom. Constraints on the process reduce the space of model development options, resulting in more principled models. One of the themes of this chapter has been the essential role that constraints played in the development of our models.

The methodology and principles that Newell (1990) outlined for unified theories of cognition strongly constrained our modeling decision. The EASE architecture, developed in the course of the AMBR project, came about as a result of "listening to the architecture" and identifying areas where the set of mechanisms of the original architecture (Soar) needed to be amended. Also we have reused the SCA model developed in previous work on category learning. Although the initial fit of the SCA model to the mean human data was poor, the constraint of "listening to the architecture" and seeking solutions within it led to further, deeper analysis of the human data. By minimizing changes to both the architecture and model, we developed the hypothesis that other factors were playing a role in the task (such as additional features and semantic interpretation of the features). This hypothesis was confirmed in the more fine-grained data analysis. The normative effects of these features were then incorporated into the existing model with little change to the model. By following the task and methodological constraints, we preserved the previous validation of SCA and gained a deeper understanding of influences on learning for the AMBR task.

The mechanisms of an architecture also provide strong constraints on the formulation of the model. For example, the visual perception system of EASE (inherited from EPIC) represents retinal zones and the varying availability of perceptual features and objects depending on which zone the object is located. This constraint required that the model include a saccade generation component. EASE also includes the base-level learning memory mechanism from ACT-R. When this mechanism was first added to the model, it immediately required the addition of knowledge for coping with forgotten items. Both of these mechanisms required a more detailed representation of the task. However, the consequence is a deeper understanding of the behavior and the emergence of unanticipated effects (e.g., performance errors).

Another source of constraint present in this work is the adoption of pre-existing mechanisms that have been validated in other architectures and models. EASE contains the sensory, perceptual, and motor mechanisms of EPIC and the ACT-R base-level learning memory mechanism. In both cases, the established free parameters values were also adopted and not tuned to fit human data. By adopting mechanisms from other architectures, EASE inherits the validation of these mechanisms. Additionally, the history of findings that validate those mechanisms, and particularly the established free parameter setting, acts as a strong constraint against tuning the parameters to provide better fits.

Thus far we have only addressed the architectural constraints. However, the architecture only captures the invariant aspects of the human organism—the mechanisms, structures, and processes that are brought to bear in facilitating all behaviors. The architecture does not produce behavior. Rather, it is knowledge that determines what and how behaviors are generated (Newell, 1990). Differences in knowledge and how that knowledge is applied produces a wide range of learning and performance in human behavior.

For many tasks, the greatest constraint arises from the explicit and implicit knowledge available in the task environment and task instructions. Encoding instructions and dependencies identified from a functional analysis can define much of the process necessary to perform the task. This is often true of interactive tasks or subtasks that have a minimal cognitive component, such as the immediate behavior tasks commonly used in psychological experiments. The model of the ATC task (Experiment 1) is an example of such a task. The explicit knowledge was encoded to produce the interactive behavior and implicit knowledge in the penalty scores informed how the model would resolve multitask demands.

However, even in Experiment 1, covert cognitive behavior appeared to be critical to performance (e.g., the choice of a blip on which to fixate). Covert cognitive processes are also central to the learning task of Experiment 2. Tasks or subtasks with such significant cognitive components can seldom benefit from constraints as strong as those available for interactive tasks or subtasks. Although a model can derive weak constraints from task analyses or related research, it is the combination of these weak constraints with those provided by the architecture that can result in more principled models. As architecture-based theories evolve, they will impose increasingly stronger constraints on models of cognitive behavior.

Although we were subject to many sources of constraint on the model-building process, many degrees of freedom remain. This is evident by the two different models of category learning that comparably fit and predict the data. The differences represent alternate learning strategies—strategies that humans may also use. These strategies emerged from our investigation of contrasting hypotheses of the factors that influence category learning. The SCA model investigated the effect of considering extraneous information during learning, whereas RULEX-EM investigated the interaction of memory effects and prediction strategy on learning. In the final analysis, both models have contributions to make to one another, with the end result being a fuller understanding of category learning.

SUMMARY QUESTIONS AND ANSWERS

1. How Is Cognition Represented in Your System?

The cognitive primitives of EASE, derived from Soar, are production rules and declarative structures. Cognition is represented by the operation of the match-fire cycle of the production system. The average duration of cognitive steps in EASE is 50 milliseconds. Learning occurs via two distinct mechanisms. First, chunking is a caching mechanism that encapsulates the results of reasoning. Inductive learning, such as the category learning of the SCA model, results from caching inductive reasoning. A second type of learning, incorporated from ACT-R, modulates the availability of elements in declarative knowledge as a function of the recency and frequency of their use. In other words, the availability of knowledge is a function of its usefulness in generating behavior. Perception and action are implemented using EPIC's sensory, perceptual, and motor processors. These processors impose physiologically and psychologically inspired constraints on the model. The eye has a limited field of view requiring the model to move the eye to points of interest to fully comprehend the task environment. The motor processors provide constraints on the sequencing and coordination of action and produce correct execution times.

2. What Is Your Modeling Methodology?

Our primary modeling philosophy can be summarized by Newell's imperative to "listen to the architecture." In the SCA model, we used only the mechanisms available in Soar and reused the existing model of this phenomenon for the new task, severely constraining the choices we could make as modelers. The constraints led to novel views of the human data and a deeper understanding of the approaches humans take in the task. When an architecture cannot accommodate certain behaviors, it (and the theory it implements) must be carefully elaborated. Both the ATC task model and RULEX-EM models demonstrate how an ACT-R memory mechanism can be leveraged to produce a number of effects and behaviors not easily attainable from the native architecture: forgetting, saccade generation, processing during fixations, error generation, and others. As another example of taking theories seriously, we adopted the empirically determined parameter settings of the ACT-R mechanism into the models, thus inheriting the validation those values represent.

3. What Role Does Parameter Tuning Play?

Our goal is to understand the human phenomena in question, not to fit a function to the resulting data. Listening to the architecture constrains the parameter fitting process. The primary parameter in the EASE models is knowledge, in that redesigning and reformulating knowledge can often lead to great differences in performance measures. For both the ATC and the category learning task, our approach was to develop straightforward models, based on task analysis and architectural constraint, and to then fix the knowledge for the models. Parameters in the base-level learning mechanism of EASE used ACT-R's default or recommended settings and were not tuned to fit the data. Additional free parameters were introduced in the specific learning models—namely, additional features in the SCA model and the number of rehearsals in RULEX-EM. These parameters were fit to the probability of error learning curves. Workload measures were also empirically derived. No other performance and learning data were fit and can be interpreted as predictions of the models, although not all were supported by the human data.

4. What Is Your Account of Individual Differences?

The SCA model accounts for individual differences via different strategies in the SCA feature selection process and normative extra features in the instance description. The extra features represent the additional information on the display (and other possible learning distractors). We adopted a normative approach because the original SCA results (taking into account only the features subjects were instructed to attend to) led us to close examination of the human data, where it became evident that human subjects were attempting to use many different techniques (examining additional features, constructing new features, using world knowledge to construct stories, etc.). RULEX-EM does not account for individual differences. The model is normative in that it uses one general strategy for category learning. There is a stochastic component (transient noise) that produces variability, but this alone is insufficient to capture the broad range of behavior present in the data.

5. What Is Your Account of Cognitive Workload?

Subjective workload is based on the realization that there is work to be done. A realization occurs when a task event or condition occurs that indicates there is or will be work to be done. When blips change from WHITE to some other color, expectations and anticipations are created, and feedback indicates an incorrect prediction was generated. Each kind of work is assigned a workload value representing its relative importance or urgency. These are deduced from the task instruction and the penalty point schedule. When the model realizes there is work to be done, it records the workload value associated with the work to be done. At the end of a model run, the total workload is divided by the scenario duration and scaled by α, a tuning parameter. This formulation captures two intuitive characteristics of workload: Workload is a function of both the amount of work to be done per unit time and the difficulty or urgency of the work to be done per unit time. Workload is presently computed at the end of a trial, so it does not influence strategy selection during task performance. However, our equation casts workload as a function of time and is easily amenable for use as a measure of instantaneous workload, which could then be used to influence task performance.

6. What Is Your Account of Multitasking?

Multitasking is implemented by task switching. The task instructions and priorities, explicit and implied, are encoded as a set of production rules— in the spirit of an executive process—that implements a simple task scheduler. These rules ensure that tasks are executed, preempted, or shed in accordance with the task instructions. The executive process is represented in productions and is executed in the same manner as, and concurrently with, the task models. Therefore, multitasking in EASE does not require a special architectural mechanism. Limits to multitasking arise primarily from the limitations of the perceptual and motor components of the architecture and from the task instructions.

7. What Is Your Account of Categorization?

SCA is an exemplar category learning model, meaning that it does not learn an explicit category representation, but rather learns to associate an instance representation with a particular classification. SCA learns via production composition, but the rules it learns encode semantic knowledge (the category description). Explicit knowledge plays two roles in SCA—it defines the basic prediction and learning procedures, and it specifies a learning strategy. RULEX-EM learns both rules and exemplars. Both are represented as declarative memory structures. Exemplar learning occurs through a process somewhat analogous to priming; retention occurs as a consequence of many exposures to the exemplars. RULEX-EM is primarily a learn-on-failure algorithm. When incorrect predictions are produced, the model learns a new rule. Both rules and exemplars are subject to the architecture's base-level learning mechanism. For learned items to be retained, they must be used frequently (they must have high predictive utility).

ACKNOWLEDGMENTS

This work was supported by the U.S. Air Force Research Lab, contracts F33615-99-C-6005 and F33615-01-C-6077. We thank the program sponsors, other members of the AMBR program, and David E. Kieras, Randolph Jones, Anthony Hornof, Christian Lebiere, and Michael Schoelles for assistance, feedback, and suggestions. Portions of this work were previously presented at the 2000 Human Factors and Ergonomics Conference, the 2001 Conference on Computer Generated Forces and Behavioral Representation, the 2002 Cognitive Science Conference, the 2003 International Conference on Cognitive Modeling, and the 2003 conference of the European Cognitive Science Society.

REFERENCES

Altmann, E. M., & John, B. E. (1999). Episodic indexing: A model of memory for attention events. *Cognitive Science, 23*(2), 117–156.

Anderson, J. R., & Betz, J. (2002). A hybrid model of categorization. *Psychonomic Bulletin and Review, 8*, 629–647.

Anderson, J. R., & Lebiere, C. (1998). *Atomic components of thought.* Mahwah, NJ: Lawrence Erlbaum Associates.

Card, S. K., Moran, T. P., & Newell, A. (1983). *The psychology of human–computer interaction.* Hillsdale, NJ: Lawrence Erlbaum Associates.

Chong, R. S. (2003). The addition of an activation and decay mechanism to the Soar architecture. In the *Proceedings of the Fifth International Conference on Cognitive Modeling,* Bamberg, Germany.

Chong, R. S., & Laird, J. E. (1997). *Identifying dual-task executive process knowledge using EPIC-Soar.* Proceedings of the 19th Annual Conference of the Cognitive Science Society, Palo Alto, CA.

Chong, R. S., & Wray, R. E. (2003). RULEX-EM: Incorporating exemplars and memory effects in a hypothesis-testing model of category learning. In the *Proceedings of the First European Cognitive Science Conference,* Osnabrueck, Germany.

Erickson, M. A., & Kruschke, J. K. (1998). Rules and exemplars in category learning. *Journal of Experimental Psychology: General, 127,* 107–140.

Estes, W. K. (2002). Traps in the route to models of memory and decision. *Psychonomic Bulletin and Review, 9*(1), 3–25.

Fleetwood, M. D., & Byrne, M. D. (2002). Modeling icon search in ACT-R. *Cognitive Systems Research, 3,* 25–33.

Kieras, D. E., & Meyer, D. E. (1997). An overview of the EPIC architecture for cognition and performance with application to human–computer interaction. *Human–Computer Interaction, 12,* 391–438.

Lewis, R. L., Huffman, S. B., John, B. E., Laird, J. E., Lehman, J. F., Newell, A., Rosenbloom, P. S., Simon, T., & Tessler, S. G. (1990). *Soar as a unified theory of cognition: Spring 1990.* Proceedings of the 12th Annual Conference of the Cognitive Science Society, Cambridge, MA.

Love, B. C., & Medin, D. L. (1998). *SUSTAIN: A model of human category learning.* Proceedings of the 15th National Conference on Artificial Intelligence (AAAI-98), Madison, WI.

Meyer, D. E., & Kieras, D. E. (1997a). A computational theory of executive cognitive processes and multiple-task performance: Part 1. Basic mechanisms. *Psychology Review, 104*(1), 3–65.

Meyer, D. E., & Kieras, D. E. (1997b). A computational theory of executive cognitive processes and multiple-task performance: Part 2. Accounts of psychological refractory-period phenomena. *Psychology Review, 104*(4), 749–791.

Miller, C. S., & Laird, J. E. (1996). Accounting for graded performance within a discrete search framework. *Cognitive Science, 20*(4), 499–537.

Minda, J. P., & Smith, J. D. (2001). Prototypes in category learning: The effects of category size, category structure, and stimulus complexity. *Journal of Experimental Psychology: Learning, Memory, and Cognition, 27,* 775–799.

Newell, A. (1990). *Unified theories of cognition.* Cambridge, MA: Harvard University Press.

Nosofsky, R. M., Gluck, M. A., Palmeri, T. J., McKinley, S. C., & Glauthier, P. T. (1994). Comparing models of rule-based classification learning: A replication and extension of Shepard, Hovland, and Jenkins (1961). *Memory & Cognition, 22,* 352–369.

Nosofsky, R. M., Palmeri, T. J., & McKinley, S. C. (1994). Rules-plus-exception model of classification learning. *Psychological Review, 101,* 53–79.

Rosenbloom, P. S., Laird, J. E., & Newell, A. (1993). *The Soar papers.* Cambridge, MA: The MIT Press.

Shepard, R. N., Hovland, C. I., & Jenkins, H. M. (1961). Learning and memorization of classifications. *Psychological Monographs, 75*(13, Whole No. 517).

Wray, R. E., & Chong, R. S. (2003). *Quantitative explorations of category learning with symbolic concept acquisition.* Proceedings of the Fifth International Conference on Cognitive Modeling, Bamberg, Germany.

Wray, R. E., & Laird, J. E. (2003). *Variability in human behavior modeling for military simulations.* Proceedings of the 2003 Conference on Behavioral Representation in Modeling and Simulation (BRIMS), Phoenix, AZ.

Young, R. M., & Lewis, R. L. (1999). The Soar cognitive architecture and human working memory. In A. Miyake & P. Shah (Eds.), *Models of working memory: Mechanisms of active maintenance and executive control* (pp. 224–256). Cambridge, England: Cambridge University Press.

Part III

CONCLUSIONS, LESSONS LEARNED, AND IMPLICATIONS

Comparison, Convergence, and Divergence in Models of Multitasking and Category Learning, and in the Architectures Used to Create Them

David E. Diller
BBN Technologies

Kevin A. Gluck
Air Force Research Laboratory

Yvette J. Tenney
Katherine Godfrey
BBN Technologies

This chapter marks the beginning of the final section of the book, in which we develop our conclusions, describe our lessons learned, and define some of the implications for research. This particular chapter assumes some familiarity with the material that has preceded it, and we recommend the reader refer back to those earlier chapters as necessary. Chapter 2, for instance, describes the air traffic control (ATC) task, the experiment designs, and the human data in detail, and we do not repeat those details here. Similarly, the preceding four chapters (chaps. 4–7) provided detailed descriptions of the multitasking and category learning models developed by each of the modeling teams. The model description chapters were long and thorough by design to allow the modelers the opportunity to provide a complete account, in unusual depth, of their architectures and their modeling approach and implementation. This chapter is designed to provide a side-by-side comparative view of the models across a number of different dimensions.

We start with the models' ability to fit the observed human data—providing a comparative quantitative evaluation of model performance. We illustrate places where the models produce results similar to one another, as well as where they make their own unique predictions. It is these similarities and differences that help us better understand the processes by which we as humans operate effectively in complex tasks and also contributes to our under-standing of the kinds of representations and processes that make such behav-iors possible in computational models. We follow the comparison of model fits to human data with a discussion of other dimensions along which one might compare computational process models and some of the challenges associated with comparing along those dimensions. These dimensions in-clude the degrees of freedom available in the architectures and in specific model implementations, model reuse, interpretability, and generalizability.

From a focus on model comparison, we turn to a discussion of the simi-larities and differences among the modeling architectures. The authors of the model description chapters each addressed a set of common questions that were considered to be of broad theoretical and practical significance for those interested in the science of human representation. We draw from our experience with the models and the answers to the common questions to present a summary in both narrative and table formats.

We conclude the chapter with a discussion of points of convergence and divergence in the models of multitasking and category learning developed for the AMBR comparison and in the architectures used to create them.

QUANTITATIVE FITS TO THE EXPERIMENTAL RESULTS

Experiment 1: Air Traffic Control Procedure

COGNET/iGEN, DCOG, and EASE provided model runs that produced data equivalent to that of four participants. ACT-R provided runs equiva-lent to 16 participants to match the number of human participants in the study. The number of runs was determined by time considerations and modelers' preferences.

Model predictions are compared against the observed human data using either a sum of the squared error (SSE) or a G^2 measure. SSE was used for continuous variables such as reaction time, whereas G^2, sometimes known as *deviance*, was used for categorical or counted data such as accuracy re-sults. G^2 is a log-likelihood ratio statistic designed to measure the goodness of fit between predicted and observed data and, like χ^2, is calculated for contingency tables. See Agresti (2002) for additional details on categorical data analysis.

Accuracy as a Function of Display and Workload.   Figure 8.1 illustrates both human data and each model's predictions of mean accumulated pen-alty points by condition. Error bars represent dual-sided 95% standard er-ror of the mean confidence intervals.

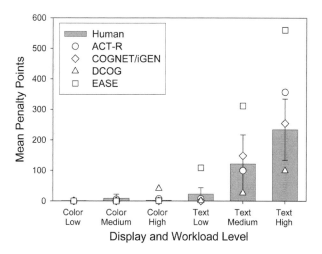

FIG. 8.1. Human and model penalty scores as a function of display and workload.

All four models correctly produced higher penalty points in the text display than in the color display, especially at higher workloads. Color display conditions produced few penalty points in both the observed and predicted data. With the exception of DCOG, models tended to overpredict the number of penalty points in the text display condition. DCOG underpredicted the number of penalty points in the text display condition. COGNET/iGEN came closest to the human norms with an SSE of 1,745 followed by ACT-R with 15,752, DCOG with 29,151, and 150,034 for EASE.

Penalty scores were explored in greater detail in the most demanding condition: text display with high workload. The upper panel in Fig. 8.2 shows the penalty points earned by humans and models in each of the penalty subcategories for the text-high workload condition. It is clear from the graph that the overriding source of points for humans was Hold penalties (at 50 points each). All the models showed this same pattern, although no model fell within the human confidence intervals for each penalty type. Again deviations from the observed data tended to be in the direction of too many penalties. DCOG came closest to the human norms with an SSE score of 35,193, followed by 60,545 for COGNET/iGEN, 94,927 for ACT-R, and 234,665 for EASE.

The lower panel in Fig. 8.2 shows the actual number of occurrences of each type of error. The results suggest that participants prioritized their actions so as to minimize overall penalties. Thus, Welcome Delay, which carries the lowest penalty (1 point per minute), was the most frequent penalty obtained by humans. The next largest category of observed errors was Speed Delay (2 points per unit of time). The "load shedding" strategy of

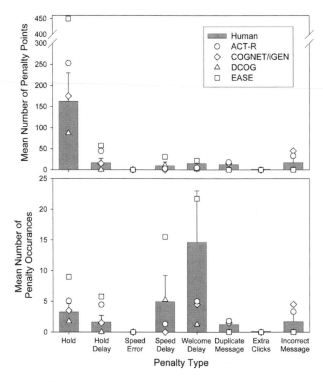

FIG. 8.2.   Human and model performance by penalty category for text-high workload condition.

postponing actions carrying low penalties to focus on preventing aircraft from turning red, which carries a higher penalty (50 points), is a reasonable strategy for coping with high workloads. None of the models managed to consistently fall within the confidence limits of the observed data. However, EASE did show evidence of load shedding. EASE was the only model to have more occurrences of Welcome Delays and Speed Delays than of Holds, resembling the observed data. SSE scores were 288 for DCOG, 313 for COGNET/iGEN, 342 for ACT-R, and 1,083 for EASE. Interestingly, despite being the only model to show load shedding behavior, EASE has the worst SSE value. Clearly the type of measures, such as relative trend or quantitative measures, used to evaluate a model can greatly impact conclusions about the quality of the model. Schunn and Wallach (2001) made the point that it is possible to have an inverse relationship between qualitative trends and absolute fit measures and like EASE fit the trend, but provide a poor fit to the absolute data, or in contrast provide a reasonable fit to the absolute data, but miss the trend, illustrating the need to evaluate both relative trend and absolute deviation from the data.

Response Time as a Function of Display and Workload. Figure 8.3 illustrates the human and model response times for each condition. As can be seen in the graph, participants responded to the events more quickly with the color display than with the text display, and workload effects were more pronounced in the text than in the color condition. These results show a similar pattern to the results seen in accuracy measures, suggesting there was no speed/accuracy trade-off occurring for the conditions. The models all showed similar trends. No model fell within the confidence intervals for all conditions, but again COGNET/iGEN came extremely close. SSE scores were 6 for COGNET/iGEN, 80 for ACT-R, 276 for DCOG, and 285 for EASE. Overall, the models tended to respond too slowly relative to the observed human data.

Subjective Workload Measures. Human subjects provided separate data for each of the six individual workload scales (mental demand, physical demand, temporal demand, performance, effort, frustration) that are part of the Task Loading Index (TLX) workload rating sheet (Hart & Staveland, 1988; Vidulich & Tsang, 1986). Each individual scale rated workload from 0 to 10 representing low to high workload, respectively. COGNET/iGEN produced a workload score for each of the six TLX scales. ACT-R and EASE each produced a single overall workload score. DCOG did not calculate workloads. To allow comparison of the ACT-R, EASE, and COGNET/iGEN workload ratings, an overall subjective workload rating was obtained for each human subject by averaging the six scores on the individual TLX scales. The COGNET/iGEN model values were similarly averaged across the six scales.

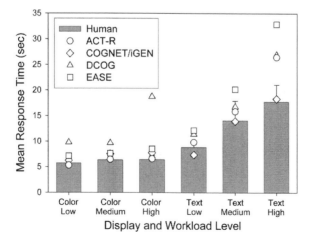

FIG. 8.3.   Human and model mean response times as a function of display and workload.

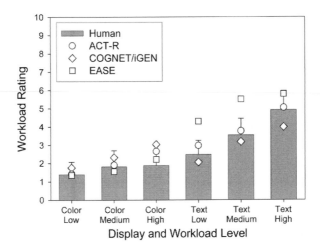

FIG. 8.4. Human and model subjective workload as a function of display and workload condition.

The aggregate human results, shown in Fig. 8.4, demonstrate that participants rated their workload as higher for the text than for the color display. There was also an increase in subjective workload as actual workload increased, especially for the text display. The three models showed the same pattern of results and provided a good qualitative fit to the data. ACT-R provided the best fit with an SSE of 0.92 and falling within the observed confidence intervals for all conditions. COGNET/iGEN and EASE produced SSEs of 2.91 and 8.06, respectively.

Discussion. The assortment of quantitative data reviewed earlier provided a significant set of challenges to the models. All the models were successful in producing the qualitative effects of display type and workload on penalty scores. With respect to reaction time measures, all models showed the general trend of reaction times increasing with workload level. In addition, all models except DCOG produced average response times in the color display conditions that were faster than the easiest text display condition. DCOG failed to produce this result because its model's performance was affected by workload level in the color-high condition. Although a main focus of this experiment was on multiple task management, only one of the models, EASE, showed evidence of load shedding, with more occurrences of Welcome Delays and Speed Delays than of Holds, resembling the observed data. Ironically, despite being the only model to get this particular qualitative result correct, EASE had the worst quantitative fit to the data on penalty points and penalty occurrences. All the models produced the qualitative relationship between subjective workload rating and workload level except DCOG, which produced no workload ratings. In general, although most qualitative trends were produced, close quantitative fits were achieved only infrequently.

Experiment 2: Category Learning

The category learning experiment, which involved a modification to the air traffic control (ATC) task used for Experiment 1, is described in detail in chapter 2. We do not repeat those details here. Data were collected from 90 participants in that study, and each modeling team completed enough runs to simulate the 90 participants. Three of the models produced subject variation through stochastic variation of parameters on each run (COGNET/iGEN, ACT-R, EASE). One developed templates of a smaller number of subjects, defined by parameter values or strategy choice, and then replicated them to produce the requisite number of subjects (DCOG). All the models completed the main task, workload ratings, and transfer test (but not the training blocks, quiz, or debrief). One model, COGNET/iGEN, produced ratings for the six NASA TLX workload scales used by the human subjects, rather than a single composite workload score.

All human results, with the exception of the transfer task, were shared with the modeling teams early in the model development cycle to facilitate their modeling efforts. The results of the transfer task were not revealed to the modeling teams until after the modeling teams produced the initial round of model predictions. This manipulation was meant as a test of the model's ability to predict, not simply replicate, human behavior. The results from this initial round of model prediction were compared to human performance. Modeling teams were then provided with the results of the transfer task and allowed to revise their models in light of these results. During this round of model revisions, the EASE modeling team introduced a second variant of the EASE model. This new variant, called RULEX-EM, was derived from the Rule-Plus-Exception (RULEX) model developed by Nosofsky et al. (1994a). In addition, the EASE team revised their original model based on the Symbolic Concept Acquisition (SCA) model (Miller & Laird, 1996). All of the models were evaluated against the observed data a second time to determine whether they had been successful in creating a better explanation of human performance on the transfer task.

Because the models were tasked to generate 90 simulated participants, we decided to analyze and compare the models against the pattern of main effects and interactions seen in the analysis of variance (ANOVA) on the human data. Each of the 90 model runs was treated as an independent participant, and ANOVAs were generated in the same manner as for the human participants. Results of these ANOVAs for both human and models are presented in table format for each dependent variable evaluated.

Category Learning Task (Primary Task)

Accuracy Measures. The observed category learning data and the data from each of the models are shown in Fig. 8.5. We plot the mean probability of error for each block of 16 categorization judgments for both human and models in each of the Type I, III, and VI problems. Each model's initial and revised predictions and the observed human data are organized into a row of three graph panels, one panel for each problem type.

G^2 analysis of the initial model fits to the Type I, III, and VI data were 15.95 for DCOG, 21.36 for COGNET/iGEN, 49.69 for ACT-R, and 673.62 for the EASE SCA model. Additionally, the models were evaluated using the same ANOVA measures used to evaluate the human data to evaluate how well the models captured the observed pattern of results. These results are

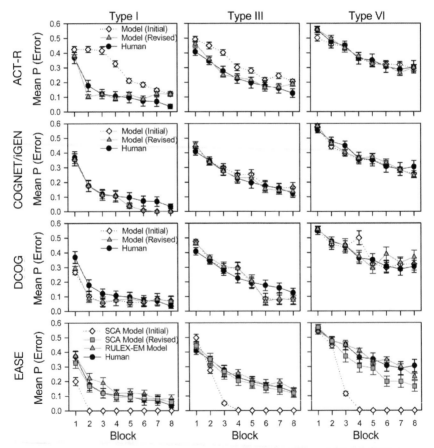

FIG. 8.5.   Human category learning data for Type I, III, and VI problems and initial and revised model data.

TABLE 8.1
A Comparison of Human and Model Data
for Primary Task Accuracy Measures

	ANOVA Main Effects and Interactions		
	Problem Type	*Block*	*Problem Type by Block*
Human	Significant*	Significant*	Not Significant†
Original Model Predictions			
ACT-R	✓	✓	
COGNET/iGEN	✓	✓	✓
DCOG	✓	✓	
EASE SCA	✓	✓	
Revised Model Predictions			
ACT-R	✓	✓	
COGNET/iGEN	✓	✓	✓
DCOG	✓	✓	
EASE SCA	✓	✓	
EASE RULEX-EM	✓	✓	

*$p < .0001$. †$p > 0.05$.

shown in Table 8.1. The first row describes the significant (or nonsignificant, as the case may be) main effects and interactions in the human data. Check marks indicate those instances where the model replicated the observed human results. A significance level criterion of .05 was used for rejecting the null hypothesis. The initial ACT-R model showed the desired main effect of problem type and main effect of block, but also showed an interaction of Problem Type × Block that was not observed in the human data. In particular, the shape of the learning curve, especially for Problem Type I, tended to drop too slowly during the initial blocks, in contrast to the rapid learning seen in the observed data. The initial COGNET/iGEN model showed significant effects of problem type and block, with no interaction of Problem Type × Block. As can be seen in Fig. 8.5, the COGNET/iGEN model matched the observed data well, falling within or close to the observed Standard Error of the Mean (SEM) in all cases except the later blocks for Problem Type I. The initial DCOG model showed the desired effects of problem type and of block, but showed a Problem Type × Block interaction not present in the human data. The initial version of EASE, the SCA model, showed a significant problem type and block effect. However, the SCA model differed significantly from the observed human data in several respects. EASE exhibited an inappropriate interaction of Problem Type × Block. As can be seen, there was a precipitous drop in errors to zero, especially in Problem Type III and VI, as compared with the more gradual learning curve in the observed data.

After a round of model revisions, all of the models showed improvement in their quantitative fit to the human data, some of them dramatic improvements. The ACT-R model showed a marked improvement, lowering its G^2 value from 49.69 to 7.23. The revised ACT-R model again showed significant effects of problem type and block, but still had an inappropriate interaction of Problem Type × Block. The final COGNET/iGEN model showed an improved fit to the observed data, with a G^2 of 20.92, the appropriate main effects, and no interaction. The fit of the DCOG model showed a slightly improved G^2 value of 15.53. There was still an inappropriate significant interaction of Problem Type × Block. As can be observed in the DCOG Problem Type III and VI plots in Fig. 8.5, the learning curves were more irregularly shaped than the observed data. The EASE SCA model showed a dramatically improved fit, lowering its G^2 value to 9.96. However, the EASE SCA model still showed the interaction of Problem Type × Block. The EASE RULEX-EM model showed a G^2 fit of 5.64, with main effects of problem type and block, but also the unobserved interaction of Problem Type × Block.

A more fine-grained analysis of Problem Type III is shown in Fig. 8.6. In Problem Type III, half the stimuli are members of the central set and half are members of the peripheral set.[1] The results show that humans learned central stimuli more quickly than peripheral stimuli. The predictions of the revised models for central and peripheral item types are shown in Fig. 8.6. It is clear from the graph and the item effect from Table 8.2 that all models except EASE RULEX-EM made fewer errors in learning the central than the peripheral items. G^2 results for the revised models were 3.46 for EASE SCA, 4.40 for COGNET/iGEN, 5.89 for EASE RULEX-EM, 9.24 for ACT-R, and 74.49 for DCOG. A separate ANOVA was conducted for each model alone to determine whether the model replicated the human results of significant effects of item (peripheral or central) and block, with no interactions between the two variables. However, none of the models matched the observed data perfectly except for EASE SCA, which showed significant item and block effects and no significant interaction between the two variables. The ACT-R, COGNET/iGEN, and DCOG models all showed significant effects of item and block, but also inappropriate interactions of Item × Block. EASE RULEX-EM, while showing an appropriate effect of block, failed to show a significant difference in learning rates for central and peripheral items and showed an inappropriate interaction of Item × Block.

Response Time Measures. Figure 8.7 shows the mean response times to the primary category learning task for both observed data and each model's

---

[1]The central/peripheral distinction is explained in chapter 2.

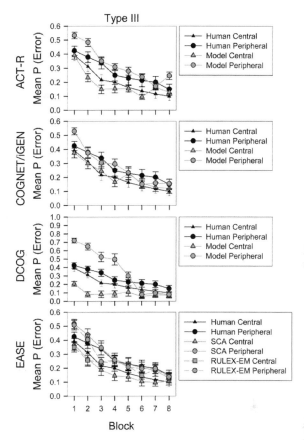

FIG. 8.6.   Human and revised model data for the Type III problem learning data.

TABLE 8.2
Revised Model Results for Central/Peripheral Item Differences

	ANOVA Main Effects and Interactions		
	Item	Block	Item by Block
Human	Significant*	Significant**	Not Significant†
Revised Model Predictions			
ACT-R	✓	✓	
COGNET/iGEN	✓	✓	
DCOG	✓	✓	
EASE SCA	✓	✓	✓
EASE RULEX-EM		✓	

*p < .05. **p < .0001. † p > .05.

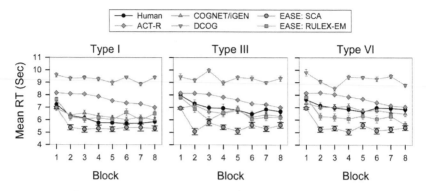

FIG. 8.7.   Human and revised model response times on the category learning task as a function of category learning problem type.

revised fit. Response times to the category learning task were faster for
Problem Type I than Problem Type III or VI, which did not differ from one
another. Models showed a large variation in quality of fit. ACT-R response
times were too slow, producing an SSE score of 30.72. ACT-R showed the
desired effect of block, but not problem type. COGNET/iGEN had the
closest fit with an SSE of 3.21 and showed the desired block effect. However, they failed to show a problem type effect and had an inappropriate interaction of Problem Type × Block. The DCOG model had an SSE of
170.02, reflecting that the response times were too slow. DCOG failed to
achieve faster responses for Problem Type I than for Problem Type III or
VI. EASE SCA had an SSE of 39.33, reflecting that the response times were
too fast for Problem Types III and VI. EASE RULEX-EM had an SSE of 8.40,
reflecting a better fit to response times for Problem Types III and VI. EASE
RULEX-EM and EASE SCA both showed the desired block effect, but failed
to achieve the problem type effect.

Handoff Task (Secondary Task)

Penalty Score Measures.   Figure 8.8 shows the mean penalty score on the
secondary task for Problem Type I, III, and VI for the observed data and revised model predictions. As described in chapter 2, there were no effects of
blocks or problem type. As illustrated by the error bars in the figure, the human data are quite variable. Revised quantitative model fits to the penalty
score data are as follows (in SSEs): 1726.86 for COGNET/iGEN, 1924.06
for ACT-R, 2043.46 for EASE RULEX-EM, 2720.29 for EASE SCA, and
5098.42 for DCOG. In general, the models fit the qualitative data reasonably well. The DCOG model showed a number of blocks with too many penalty points, reflected in an undesirable significant main effect of block,
$F(7, 399) = 2.32$, $p = .0248$, and an inappropriate interaction of Block ×
Problem Type, $F = 4.52$, $p < .0001$. All other models accurately predicted no

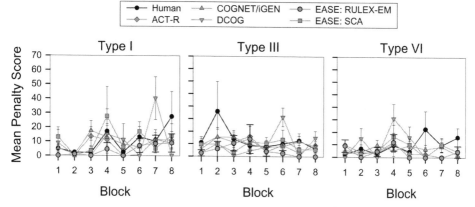

FIG. 8.8.   Human and revised model penalty scores on the handoff task as a function of category learning problem type.

significant main effects or interactions. ACT-R, COGNET/iGEN, and EASE SCA models showed scores that were close to the observed data, whereas EASE RULEX-EM showed too few penalty points.

Response Time Measures.   Human and revised model response times for the secondary task are shown in Fig. 8.9. Human response times were quite variable, illustrated by the large error bars in the graph. Although no main effects of workload level or problem type were found, there was a main effect of blocks, with participants responding more quickly on later blocks. However, this appears to be primarily driven by the results observed in Problem Type III. There was no interaction of Problem Type × Blocks in the human data.

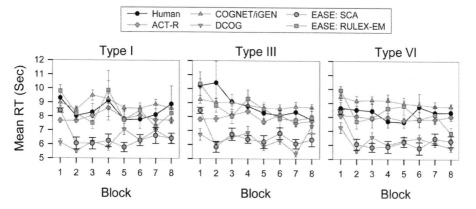

FIG. 8.9.   Human and revised model response times to the handoff task as a function of category learning problem type.

Congruent with the human results, the revised versions of the models all showed a significant blocks effect. Unlike the human results, DCOG also exhibited an interaction between problem type and blocks. G^2 values were 14.20 (COGNET/iGEN), 15.24 (EASE RULEX-EM), 21.25 (ACT-R), 114.73 (EASE SCA), and 135.83 (DCOG). Response times by the DCOG and EASE SCA models were too fast, contributing to their high SSE value. The other models showed reasonably good fits to the observed data.

Transfer Task

We begin our analysis of the transfer data by first comparing performance on the "Trained" transfer items previously encountered, with performance on those same items from the last block of training. We contrast this with performance on "Extrapolated" transfer items more extreme than the Trained items. Extrapolated stimuli were scored in the same manner as the nearest previously Trained item. The Trained versus Extrapolated comparison was designed to assess how well strategies generalized from one type of item to another. The "Last Block" versus Trained comparison allowed for an evaluation of how well performance transferred from the learning portion of the experiment to the transfer condition. Results from the observed data, initial model predictions (made prior to having the observed human results), and revised model data are shown in Fig. 8.10 for each problem type.

An ANOVA on the human data showed there were significant main effects of problem type and items, where the three possible levels of items are Training Block 8, Transfer Trained, and Transfer Extrapolated (see Table 8.3). The pattern of results shows there was a significantly greater number of errors on the Trained items on the transfer test than on the identical items in Training Block 8. Less surprising was the finding that Extrapolated items were missed more frequently than previously trained items on the transfer test. A Tukey analysis showed that all three types of items differed significantly from each other ($p < .05$).

We calculated a G^2 value to determine how well each model predicted these data, without prior knowledge of the observed results: 11.01 for ACT-R, 16.77 for DCOG, 48.96 for COGNET/iGEN, and 420.09 for EASE SCA. The results of ANOVAs performed on the initial model results to look for significant effects of items and problem type are described in Table 8.3. All models showed the desired problem type effect. However, all the models initially failed to produce the observed items effect. COGNET/iGEN produced a significant items effect that was reversed, with the highest probability of error for the Training Block 8 items instead of the Extrapolated items for Problem Types III and VI. COGNET/iGEN also showed an undesirable, significant interaction of Problem Type × Items, reflecting the floor effect seen in Problem Type I. As shown in Fig. 8.10, DCOG's curves appear flat

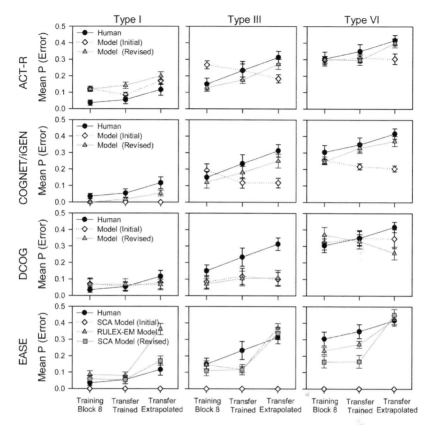

FIG. 8.10.   Human data, initial model predictions, and revised model data
for Block 8 learning data, Trained, and Extrapolated transfer test stimuli.

across item types. Unlike the observed data, EASE SCA showed perfect performance on all three types of items for all problem types. F statistics could not be computed for the EASE SCA results due to this lack of variability.

After making their predictions, the modelers were given the observed data from the transfer task and allowed to revise their models. Most of the model fits improved, some considerably, after model revisions as illustrated by the following G^2 values: 7.99 for ACT-R, 8.53 for COGNET/iGEN, 14.37 for EASE SCA, 16.23 for EASE RULEX-EM, and 21.28 for DCOG.

DCOG's fit was slightly worse than their initial prediction, showing the desired problem type effect, but still not producing the items effect. This time there was an undesirable interaction of Problem Type × Items. As shown in the graphs, there was no items effect for Problem Types I and III and a reversed items effect for Problem Type VI (see Fig. 8.10). COGNET/iGEN improved its fit, showing the observed items and problem type effects with no interactions. ACT-R improved its fit, this time showing significant

TABLE 8.3
A Comparison of Human Data, Original Model Predictions,
and Revised Model Data for Transfer Task Analysis
of Trained and Extrapolated Items

	ANOVA Main Effects and Interactions		
	Problem Type	*Items*	*Problem Type by Items*
Human	*Significant**	*Significant**	*Not Significant[†]*
	Original Model Predictions		
ACT-R	✓		✓
COGNET/IGEN	✓	X[a]	
DCOG	✓		✓
EASE SCA	Not Computable[b]	Not Computable[b]	Not Computable[b]
	Revised Model Predictions		
ACT-R	✓	✓	✓
COGNET/IGEN	✓	✓	✓
DCOG	✓		
EASE SCA	✓	✓	
EASE RULEX-EM	✓	✓	

*$p < .0001$. [†]$p > .05$.
[a]Incorrect direction of effect. [b]Due to a lack of variance (no simulated subjects made any errors, so the variance was 0), F values could not be computed.

effects of items and problem type. However, as is clear from the graph, ACT-R underperformed in Problem Type I. EASE SCA made a huge improvement in their fit to the human data. EASE SCA exhibited a significant effect of problem type, but showed a significant interaction of Problem Type × Items. While showing a significant effect of items, EASE SCA did not show the observed decrease in performance in the transfer condition on previously Trained items relative to performance on Block 8. EASE RULEX-EM also showed a similar pattern of results, with the desired effect of problem type and items, but an undesired interaction of Problem Type × Items. As seen in the graphs, EASE RULEX-EM showed the desired performance decrement on old items in the transfer condition in Problem Type VI condition, but not in the easier conditions, and it showed poor performance on Problem Type I Extrapolated items.

Subjective Workload Ratings

Figure 8.11 illustrates subjective workload ratings taken after Blocks 1, 4, and 8 for both the initial and revised model predictions as compared with the human data. Table 8.4 shows that initial predictions by all models

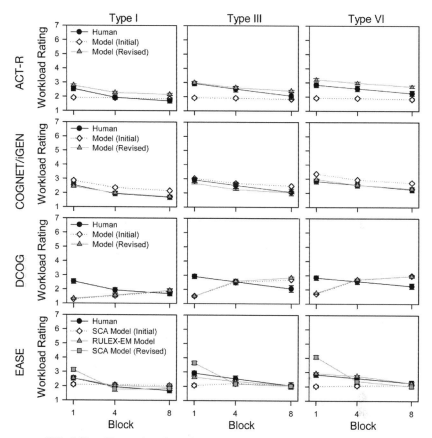

FIG. 8.11. Observed and predicted subjective workload ratings administered after Blocks 1, 4, and 8.

showed significant effects of secondary task workload contrary to the observed data. Also unlike the human results, initial predictions by ACT-R and EASE SCA showed no effect of problem type. In addition, EASE SCA failed to predict the block effect. Although ACT-R showed a main effect of block, this was an artifact of producing extremely low between-subjects variability, producing a large F value even though visual examination of Fig. 8.11 shows virtually no effect of block. The initial predictions of COGNET/ iGEN showed both the problem type and block effects. DCOG showed the desired problem type effect, but had a reverse block effect, predicting a workload rating increasing over blocks unlike the observed results. Additionally, DCOG was the only model to predict an interaction of Problem Type × Block—an interaction not seen in the human results. SSE values for the initial model predictions are as follows: 1.34 for COGNET/iGEN, 2.13 for EASE SCA, 3.37 for ACT-R, and 5.89 for DCOG.

TABLE 8.4
A Comparison of Human Data Results and Model
Predictions for Workload Ratings

	Problem Type	Block	Secondary Workload	Problem Type by Block	Workload by Block
		ANOVA Main Effects and Interactions			
Human	Significant*	Significant**	Not Significant[†]	Not Significant[†]	Significant**
		Original Model Predictions			
ACT-R		✓		✓	
COGNET/iGEN	✓	✓		✓	
DCOG	✓	X[a]			✓
EASE SCA				✓	
		Revised Model Predictions			
ACT-R	✓	✓			
COGNET/iGEN	✓	✓	✓	✓	
DCOG	✓	X[a]			✓
EASE SCA	✓	✓			
EASE RULEX-EM	✓	✓			

*$p < .05$. **$p < .0001$. [†]$p > .05$.
[a]Incorrect direction of effect.

The model revisions achieved closer fits in all cases. The final SSE values were: 0.21 for EASE RULEX-EM, 0.33 for COGNET/iGEN, 1.05 for ACT-R, 2.66 for EASE SCA, and 5.83 for DCOG. All models, with the exception of DCOG, showed a block effect in the correct direction. DCOG still predicted an increasing workload difficulty rating. Additionally, all models showed the effect of problem type, with Problem Type I having a lower workload than Problem Type III or VI. All models, except COGNET/iGEN, continued to show an unhuman-like effect of secondary task workload. Additionally, only DCOG showed a secondary task workload by block interaction. However, this was offset by DCOG's incorrect prediction of an interaction between problem type and blocks. In fact model revisions resulted in ACT-R, EASE SCA, and EASE RULEX-EM showing unhuman-like Problem Type × Block interactions, something not seen in their initial models.

SUMMARY OF MODEL FITS

These models' ability to postdict and predict (in the case of the transfer task predictions) the primary human results is summarized in Table 8.5. The table shows each model's best shot at replicating the results, after the

TABLE 8.5
Summary of Model Comparison Results

Desired Result Type	Predicted Result				
	ACT-R	COGNET/ iGEN	DCOG	EASE SCA	EASE RULEX-EM
Primary Task Learning Results					
Problem Type Effect	✓	✓	✓	✓	✓
Block Effect	✓	✓	✓	✓	✓
No Type by Block Int.		✓			
Problem Type III Central Versus Peripheral Item Results					
Item Effect	✓	✓	✓	✓	
Block Effect	✓	✓	✓	✓	✓
No Item by Block Int.				✓	
Primary Task Response Time Results					
Problem Type Effect					
Block Effect	✓	✓	✓	✓	✓
No Type by Block Int.	✓			✓	✓
Secondary Task Penalty Point Results					
No Prob. Type Effect	✓	✓	✓	✓	✓
No Prob. Type Effect	✓	✓		✓	✓
Other					Too few points
Secondary Task Response Time Results					
No Prob. Type Effect	✓	✓	✓	✓	✓
Block Effect	✓	✓	✓	✓	✓
No Type by Block Int.	✓	✓		✓	✓
Other			Too slow	Too slow	
Transfer Task Prediction					
Problem Type Effect	✓	✓	✓	X[b]	—[c]
Items Effect		X[a]		X[b]	—[c]
No Type by Items Int.	✓		✓	X[b]	—[c]
Transfer Task Postdiction					
Problem Type Effect	✓	✓	✓	✓	✓
Items Effect	✓	✓		✓	✓
No Type by Items Int.	✓	✓			
Workload Rating					
Problem Type Effect	✓	✓	✓	✓	✓
Block Effect	✓	✓	X[a]	✓	✓
No Secondary Workload Effect		✓			
No Type by Block Int.		✓			
Workload by Block Int.			✓		
Percent Match	74.1%	77.8%	51.9%	63.0%	62.5%

[a]Incorrect direction of effect. [b]Due to a lack of variance (no simulated subjects made any errors, so the variance was 0), *F* values could not be computed. [c]EASE RULEX-EM did not exist in the set of initial model predictions.

opportunity for revisions, except in the case of the transfer task predictions, which include both initial and revised model predictions.

As can be seen in the table, ACT-R matched 74.1% of the main results. In the primary task, ACT-R showed an interaction of Problem Type × Block unlike the human results. Also it did not show an effect of problem type in response times in the primary task (i.e., it did not show an increase in reaction times with increased problem type complexity, as seen in the observed data). Like most other models, ACT-R showed a number of problems with predicting workload rating results: predicting a secondary workload effect and interaction of Problem Type × Block, but no interaction of Secondary Task Workload × Block.

Overall, COGNET/iGEN showed the best fit to the data, matching 77.8% of the primary results and having the best G^2 or SSE on four of eight performance measures. Like ACT-R, COGNET/iGEN did not show an effect of problem type in primary task response time results. Additionally, it predicted an unobserved interaction of Problem Type × Block for the primary task response time measure and also incorrectly predicted an unobserved interaction of Item × Block as part of the detailed analysis of Problem Type III.

DCOG matched 51.9% of the main findings, with most of its incorrect predictions due to predicting unobserved interactions between effects, including (a) Problem Type × Block in primary task accuracy, (b) Problem Type × Block in primary task reaction time, (c) Problem Type × Items in the transfer task, (d) Problem Type × Item in the detailed analysis of Problem Type III, (e) Problem Type × Block in secondary task response time, and (f) Problem Type × Block in subjective workload ratings. Finally, DCOG predicted an unobserved secondary workload effect on subjective workload ratings and did not predict an effect of problem type on primary task response time results.

EASE SCA matched the observed data on 63.0% of the primary indicators, producing a reasonable qualitative fit to much of the data. Like the three other models, EASE SCA predicted an unobserved interaction of Problem Type × Block on the category learning accuracy measure. Unlike any other model, EASE SCA correctly replicated all three findings in the detailed analysis of Problem Type III. EASE SCA did not predict the effect of problem type on the primary task reaction time measure seen in the observed data. EASE SCA consistently underpredicted secondary task reaction times and predicted an interaction of Problem Type × Items in the transfer task, unseen in the human data. EASE SCA also mismatched the workload ratings findings in a manner consistent with ACT-R and EASE RULEX-EM: incorrectly predicting a secondary task workload effect and an interaction of Problem Type × Block, but not predicting a secondary task workload interaction with blocks.

EASE RULEX-EM matched 62.5% of the principal results.[2] EASE RULEX-EM's pattern of results was typical in many respects. It showed the same pattern of workload rating results as ACT-R and EASE-SCA. Like ACT-R, DCOG, and EASE-SCA, it predicted an unobserved interaction of Problem Type × Block for the primary task accuracy measure and did not predict an observed problem type effect in primary task reaction times. EASE RULEX-EM was the only model not to predict a significant difference between central and peripheral items in Problem Type III. Like DCOG and EASE SCA, it predicted an unobserved interaction of Problem Type × Items in the transfer task.

There were a number of surprising findings in the modeling predictions. First, no models predicted differences in primary task response times across problem types, unlike humans, who produced longer response times for the harder problem types (III & VI) than for the easiest problem type (I). Second, no model initially predicted the decrease in performance accuracy on trained items when presented in the transfer condition, and the COGNET/iGEN model actually predicted the opposite of the observed effect (predicted performance improvement, when in fact humans showed a performance decrement in the transfer condition). However, model revisions for ACT-R and COGNET/iGEN models were able to reproduce the general pattern of results. Third, no model initially predicted worse performance on the new Extrapolated items relative to previously observed items. Last, we were surprised at the initial deviations from the category learning curves by many of the models. ACT-R initially learned too slowly in Problem Type I, whereas EASE SCA learned much too quickly in all problem types. Additionally, DCOG produced a non-monotonic learning curve in Problem Type VI.

OTHER FACTORS IN MODEL COMPARISON

The AMBR models showed varying qualitative and quantitative fits to an assortment of data subsets (see Table 8.5 and the goodness-of-fit measures earlier in this chapter), with the revised COGNET/iGEN model postdicting the highest overall percentage of the qualitative effects and the DCOG model postdicting the lowest overall percentage. This begs the question, "Is the COGNET/iGEN model a better model than the DCOG model?" Or the EASE models? Or the ACT-R model? As we discuss in this section, the quality of a model is in the eye of the beholder. The quality/acceptability/appropriateness of a model, and any effort to rank order it relative to other

---

[2]Transfer task prediction results were not included in the evaluation of RULEX-EM because the model was developed after the release of the transfer data to the modelers.

models developed with other architectures, depends on what one values in a model and an architecture. There are several other factors to consider in evaluating and comparing models, beyond goodness of fit.

Thus far, the comparison of the AMBR models has focused entirely on the quality of their fits to the experimental data. It would be easy for the reader to get the mistaken impression that it is our position that a comparison of these models should be based entirely on goodness of fit, and that goodness of fit to empirical data is the most important dimension on which to compare models. That is not the case. In a recent series of articles, Roberts and Pashler (2000, 2002) and Rodgers and Rowe (2002a, 2002b) debated the role of goodness of fit in theory testing. Roberts and Pashler (2000) started the discussion with an attack on goodness of fit as the metric for assessing the quality of psychological theories. Rodgers and Rowe came to the defense of goodness of fit, and by the end of the interaction all parties seem to have agreed that goodness-of-fit measures serve as a good starting point (but not ending point) in the evaluation process. We strongly agree that quantitative and qualitative measures of goodness of fit are good starting points in evaluating models. We are also quick to point out that there are several other important factors one might consider when comparing models of human behavior. These include the degrees of freedom available in implementing the model, how much of the model was reused from previously implemented models, the interpretability of the model's behavior during run time, and the generalizability of the model. Next we discuss why each of these is a dimension of interest and how the AMBR models compare on each of them.

Degrees of Freedom

The degrees of freedom available during model implementation are important to consider because they provide a context in which to interpret the impressiveness of a particular fit. There is a positive correlation between degrees of freedom and expectations for fit statistics. As the degrees of freedom increase, so should goodness of fit because the modeler has a great deal more flexibility in the implementation of the model.

Researchers involved in mathematical modeling of psychological phenomena often emphasize the importance of considering degrees of freedom during model evaluation (e.g., Myung, 2000; Pitt, Myung, & Zhang, 2002). They generally refer to this issue as one of complexity, and numerous approaches are available for quantifying the complexity or degrees of freedom available in a closed-form mathematical model (e.g., Bozdogan, 2000; Busemeyer & Wang, 2000; Grünwald, 2000; Wasserman, 2000).

The AMBR models are not closed-form mathematical models, but this does not mean that complexity is not an issue. It just means we need to consider alternative approaches to identifying and quantifying degrees of freedom. In the behavior representation and cognitive modeling communities, a distinction is often made between the architecture (relatively fixed structure) used to develop models and the knowledge that we represent with those architectures to model behavior in a specific context or domain. This creates a useful classification scheme for degrees of freedom in computational process models like those developed for AMBR: architecture degrees of freedom and knowledge degrees of freedom.

Architecture. Creating entirely new architectural capabilities, like spreading activation where none existed before or an instance-based learning mechanism where none existed before, is a powerful way to achieve additional degrees of freedom in the implementation of a model. There are so many decisions made in the implementation details of new architectural capabilities that it might be fair to consider it to be the case that they involve multiple additional degrees of freedom. Among the AMBR models, the ACT-R architecture added no new capabilities (all necessary modeling capabilities were already in place), COGNET/iGEN and EASE both added new learning capabilities, and the entire DCOG architecture was under development. Lest the reader get the impression that the previous sentence was a rank ordering of the degrees of freedom associated with the use of each of these architectures, we should note that not all architectural additions are created equal in terms of how much freedom they provide the modeler. Things like strict adherence to specific theoretical constraints and/or code reuse from other models can have a significant impact on the degrees of freedom associated with the implementation of any particular architectural feature. An example of this is that the EASE SCA model borrowed an existing learning mechanism from SCA-Soar, thereby tightly constraining the addition of their new architectural learning capability. By contrast, the COGNET/iGEN learning mechanism was constructed from scratch and was not strictly constrained by specific theoretical commitments, which provides quite a lot of freedom in its implementation.

An alternative to creating architectural features is removing them, which serves as a second type of architectural degree of freedom. For example, Soar's powerful learning mechanism (called *chunking*) was deactivated in the TacAir-Soar model (Jones et al., 1999) because that was considered to be a model of expert performance and was to be used in situations where new learning was considered unimportant and perhaps even undesirable. In ACT-R modeling, it is customary to deactivate components of the architecture that are not central to the psychological focus of a particular model. Irrespective of the architecture, anytime the modeler is making a choice about activating or deactivating an architectural component, it is a degree of freedom in the model's implementation. A caveat is when it is conclusively demonstrated that the performance of the model is entirely insensitive to the presence of a particular architectural component, in which case that component arguably is not a degree of freedom.

Numerical parameters are a third type of architectural degree of freedom. These are things like retrieval threshold (ACT-R and EASE) and patience (DCOG). Interestingly, the COGNET/iGEN team reports that COGNET has no numerical parameters in its baseline architecture (chap. 6, this volume). It is important to point out, however, that they make up for this through the use of micromodels that are tailored to the demands of each specific modeling context in which COGNET/iGEN is used. Additionally, COGNET/iGEN did add three numerical parameters in their implementation of a learning capability. If these parameters are used in future COGNET/iGEN models, perhaps they will come to be seen as architectural parameters.

Among the three teams who do report having architectural parameters available to them in the AMBR models, ACT-R used all default values for the multitasking model in Experiment 1, but changed three architectural parameters (retrieval threshold, value of the goal, and goal activation) for the category learning model in Experiment 2. DCOG used one free parameter (time-factor) for the multitasking model in Experiment 1 and seven additional free parameters for the category learning model—to create individual differences among operator representations. EASE used all default architectural parameters for the multitasking model in Experiment 1, but EASE-SCA and EASE-RULEX-EM each were allowed one free parameter for the category learning model in Experiment 2.

Knowledge. Architecture-based computational process modeling involves adding knowledge to the architecture to get behavior in specific contexts. The architecture is supposed to constrain the allowable structures in the knowledge (e.g., production rules, chunks, operators, frames), but does not necessarily constrain the content of those structures. It is in the knowledge where task strategies, domain expertise, and general knowledge are implemented. There are (potentially) both symbolic and numeric degrees of freedom in knowledge representation, such as activation values for declarative chunks or utilities for production rules, to draw on a couple of examples from ACT-R. Baker, Corbett, and Koedinger (2003) proposed some guidelines for quantifying knowledge degrees of freedom (i.e., parameters) for comparing different models developed in ACT-R. The basic approach is that they count every production rule and chunk that influences the behavior of the model, and they also count every numerical parameter that is not fixed to some default or other a priori value. As one would expect, this results in large numbers of parameters even for relatively simple domains. No doubt any similar exercise undertaken with COGNET/ iGEN, DCOG, or EASE would also result in large numbers of parameters for models developed with those architectures. This might be a fun exercise, but comparing the results across the AMBR models would be misguided. Baker et al. noted that differences in representational granularity make it inappropriate to compare models written in ACT-R 4.0 to those written in ACT-R 5.0. In other words, because ACT-R 4.0 represents cognition at a coarser granularity, whereas ACT-R 5.0 represents cognition at a more atomic level of representation, counting free parameters in the manner suggested by Baker et al. necessarily results in a higher number of free parameters in ACT-R 5.0 models than ACT-R 4.0 models. We have the same problem in comparing across the AMBR architectures. The different architectures modeled performance and learning at different granularities, and so a quantitative comparison of knowledge degrees of freedom would be inappropriate and misleading.

Model Reuse

Code reuse is highly desirable in software engineering because it increases cost effectiveness and standardization. Model reuse is highly desirable in human behavior representation for the same reasons, and also because it can teach us something about the generalizability of the representations used in other models (more on generalizability in a moment). However, model reuse is difficult to accomplish and is almost never done in any large-scale way. This is because human performance and learning occur at the intersection of knowledge and environment, and as the context and task domains vary from one model to the next, the knowledge in the model must also vary. The knowledge required for Task B must be almost identical to the knowledge required for Task A to have any chance of successfully porting the model for Task A over to Task B. The pattern of model reuse (or lack thereof) was fairly predictable in the AMBR model comparison with a couple exceptions. None of the models reused existing code for the multitasking model in Experiment 1. All of the models reused their code from the Color/Aided condition in Experiment 1 when implementing their category learning models for Experiment 2, except for the DCOG team, which reimplemented its entire architecture in Java (from Lisp) during the transition from Experiment 1 to 2. The EASE SCA model also reused the SCA model (i.e., the production code) developed by Miller and Laird (1996). The developers made only the minimum number of changes required to the model for the current version of EASE (SCA was originally developed in a much earlier version of Soar), and they confirmed that the learning results generated by the new model were exactly the same as those produced by Miller and Laird (1996).

Interpretability

Model interpretability is a significant issue for human behavior representation models, in the sense that it typically is difficult to know why the model is doing what it is doing and sometimes is even difficult to know what it is doing at a particular time. This is an issue of run-time interpretability, and it plagues all human behavior representation architectures. Only the EASE team took steps to address this issue during the AMBR model comparison. They did so by adding a color-coded legend to the task display that marked which of several possible cognitive activities was taking place at any moment in time. It served not only as a helpful debugging tool for the model developers, but also as a helpful learning tool for those trying to become familiar with the model's implementation.

Generalizability

This final factor to consider in comparing computational models is really quite simple. We would like for it to be the case that a model that is developed for or fit to one set of data will generalize to another set of data. We would like for it to be the case that model predictions (or postdictions) extrapolate with some predictive accuracy to contexts/situations/stimuli beyond those for which the model was specifically developed. Our modest attempt at pushing the models in this direction during Experiment 2 revealed that the field has quite a lot of room for improvement in this area. None of the models accurately predicted even the direction of the results in the transfer condition.

MODEL ARCHITECTURAL COMPARISONS: THE SEVEN COMMON QUESTIONS

This section examines the similarities and differences found across the four model architectures employed in the AMBR project; the goal is to illustrate the architectural implications for modeling multitasking and category learning phenomena. We base this discussion around a set of seven questions given to each modeling team, the answers to which are presented at the end of each of the modeling chapters (chaps. 4–7). Before comparing responses to each of the seven questions, it is useful to examine the historical origins and theoretical assumptions of these model architectures because it provides insight into their fundamental capabilities and their architectural strengths and weaknesses.

EASE is the latest in a line of hybrid models, with its roots in the Soar architecture (Newell, 1990), but also borrowing and integrating elements from EPIC (Kieras & Meyer, 1997, 2000) and ACT-R (Anderson & Lebiere, 1998) to augment less well-developed portions of the Soar architecture.[3] Work on the Soar architecture has historically focused on developing intelligently behaving systems, with less emphasis on modeling detailed psychological phenomena. That is not to say, however, that Soar and Soar hybrids such as EASE have not been used to model detailed psychological results— they have—only that this is more the exception than the rule in the Soar community, and the historical bias has been on general intelligence, rather than specifically human intelligence, with an emphasis on demonstrating mechanisms and functions sufficient for general intelligence.

ACT-R, in contrast, has its roots in psychological theories of memory, learning, and problem solving (Anderson, 1983, 1990, 1993). ACT-R places an emphasis on modeling task accuracy and reaction time, incorporating both symbolic and subsymbolic mechanisms. Like Soar, ACT-R has a long research tradition and has been used to explain a range of cognitive phenomena.[4]

Unlike EASE or ACT-R, COGNET/iGEN has not grown out of any desire to develop a general approach to psychological theory or cognition, but was developed as a framework for the development of human behavior representations in practical, real-world applications such as intelligent interfaces as well as training and decision-support systems. COGNET/iGEN was designed to provide a great deal of flexibility with which to create models, and it is intentionally theory-neutral with respect to many of the underlying processes.

DCOG does not have an extensive history. It was actually under development during the AMBR comparison. Unlike the other three architectures, DCOG does not advocate an information-processing viewpoint, but describes itself as a distributed, state-change system where "mind states themselves give rise to information, based on energetic stimulation from other local mind regions and the external environment" (chap. 6, this volume). DCOG is also unique in its implementation as a distributed software agent architecture. As a new modeling architecture, DCOG is less comprehensive than the other model architectures, and it has not been evaluated against behavioral or cognitive phenomena outside the AMBR project.

---

[3]EASE extends its predecessor, EPIC-Soar, by adding elements of ACT-R to the EPIC/Soar hybrid model.

[4]See the ACT-R Web site for a fairly comprehensive list of phenomena and task domains (http://act.psy.cmu.edu).

THE SEVEN QUESTIONS

1. How Is Cognition Represented in Your System?

Perception. The EASE model has the most highly developed perceptual system of any model in the AMBR project. Based on the EPIC model, EASE's visual processing system represents retinal processing limitations as well as eye-scan patterns, which are based on both top–down and bottom–up processing. Limitations on featural perception are modeled through the use of retinal zones, with certain classes of features such as object direction requiring foveal processing and other events such as stimulus onsets processed in all retinal zones. Additional limits are due to perceptual memory decay mechanisms. Eye-scan patterns are based on priority values associated with perceptual events. Both perceptually and knowledge-based priorities are represented, with precedence given to knowledge-based priorities. Explicit strategies for scanning message history lists were also developed.

The COGNET/iGEN system developed visual scanning mechanisms based on cognitive task analysis (CTA), leading to the development of simple scanning mechanisms, which assumed changes in a display pane can be processed directly and in their entirety. Additionally, CTA suggested no perceptual memory mechanisms were required, and none was implemented. Different scanning strategies were developed for the text and color display conditions. The color display scanning strategy contained only a single goal of detecting color changes in the radar display. The text display condition incorporated a more complex strategy involving scanning the radar display for red stimuli, followed by checking the text panes in a fixed sequence for information different from that found in memory.

Perceptual processing in ACT-R was implemented as a set of production rules and subgoals that systematically scanned the display panes and added display information to memory. For the model to respond to event onsets, a new visual onset detection mechanism was implemented with a number of processing limitations. First, onsets can only be detected during a limited time window; if the system is busy during that time, the onset will not be detected. Second, only a single-onset event is detected during a production cycle—subsequent onsets are ignored.

In the DCOG model, an agent is assigned the task of monitoring and processing the display and making perceptual information available to other agents in the system. The radar agent stores perceptual features, such as color and aircraft name, into an iconic memory. Additionally, higher knowledge-level, task-relevant events such as the aircraft is entering or leaving the airspace are encoded and stored in a global memory. A visual scanning strategy was implemented that scans the four boundary regions in the radar display followed by the text message history panels. Scanning sequences repeat every 5 seconds. A scanning sequence can be interrupted and attention paid to a specific display region when the number of aircraft soon to require attention exceeds the worry factor strategy variable.

Knowledge Representation and Cognitive Processing. COGNET/iGEN distinguishes among and represents five different types of knowledge or expertise: declarative, procedural, action, perceptual, and metacognitive. Declarative and metacognitive memory elements are represented in separate blackboard systems. Procedural, action, and perceptual expertise are represented using GOMS-like goal hierarchies and a specialized task description language. The cognitive processor executes a single cognitive task at a time, but there can be multiple active tasks in various states of completion. Tasks are activated when its conditions are met by elements in memory, and task completions are a means to accomplish a goal. Fast-task switching simulates multitasking capabilities.

In ACT-R, declarative knowledge is represented as structured memory elements or chunks, whereas procedural knowledge is represented as production rules. Cognitive processing is a function of activity at both the symbolic and subsymbolic levels. At the symbolic level, ACT-R is a serial-firing production rule system where all productions whose conditions match elements in memory are instantiated, but only a single production is selected using ACT-R's conflict resolution mechanisms and fired. Subsymbolic mechanisms determine the speed and success of memory access and also participate in conflict resolution mechanisms. Cognition is goal driven, and a goal stack is used to track goals in the AMBR models, which were implemented in ACT-R 4.0. More recent releases of ACT-R do not include a goal stack. The goal stack was used in the AMBR models for historical reasons and really played a minor role. In particular, the goal stack was not used to remember where to restart processing after handling an interruption.

Like ACT-R, EASE represents declarative knowledge as structured memory elements and procedural knowledge in production rules. Although EASE's cognitive processing system is also a production rule system, in contrast to ACT-R, it is a parallel firing production system where every rule that matches is fired. Rules are used to propose or register preferences for operators—of which only a single operator is selected using conflict resolution mechanisms and fired. EASE integrates ACT-R's subsymbolic memory mechanisms for improved modeling of memory effects. Like ACT-R, control is organized around a goal hierarchy. Unlike ACT-R, where goals arise from productions, in EASE goals or subgoals are created when an operator cannot be selected, resulting in an impasse.

DCOG was designed as a framework for developing software agents to model human performance. The framework is based on four principles: (a) distributed knowledge and control, (b) emergent forms of knowledge,

(c) communication through broadcast signaling, and (d) cognitive strategies form the basis for complex behaviors. DCOG views cognitive processing as a state-change system, with software agents executing parallel computational threads of activity. Knowledge emerges as a pattern of activations over distributed regions.

Memory. Memory in the DCOG-2 model is based on an associated memory system where feature- and symbol-based knowledge, such as stimulus exemplars and hypotheses, are represented as nodes in the system. The co-activation of nodes forms and strengthens associative links among the nodes, providing pathways for spreading activation across nodes. Procedural or functional knowledge is stored as procedures executed by a software agent.

In COGNET/iGEN, memory elements are represented within a blackboard, with a number of separable and distinct areas for different classes of information (e.g., perceptual, domain knowledge). COGNET/iGEN also postulates a metacognitive memory representing the state of the cognitive, perceptual, and motor systems. A number of extensions were developed to the COGNET/iGEN memory systems for the AMBR comparison—specifically to support the learning mechanism—and were only used within the learning mechanism. In those extensions, separate memory systems were developed for short- and long-term memory, and memory constraints were implemented based on the principles of decay, rehearsal, and proactive interference. Memory elements are maintained in short-term memory through rehearsal, and each rehearsal provides an opportunity to transfer the element to long-term memory, which does not decay. Retrieval from short-term memory is based on the complexity of the memory element and the amount of rehearsal afforded it.

ACT-R contains three separate memory structures. Declarative memory consists of chunks or memory elements, with activation levels and weighted associations to other chunks. Procedural memory is made up of production rules. Together these make up long-term memory. Finally, a last-in-first-out goal stack is used to track goals and guide behavior.[5] The goal stack and the most active declarative memory elements make up working memory. Memory limitations are based on sophisticated subsymbolic quantities, which represent chunk activation and production utilities.

EASE's memory mechanisms are similar to those found in ACT-R. Like ACT-R, procedural memory consists of rules or operators representing task

---

[5]The goal stack is no longer an architectural feature in ACT-R 5.0, but that version was not available when the AMBR model comparison started, and Lebiere chose to stick with 4.0 throughout the project. Lebiere reports that the goal stack was not used as a significant memory structure in the AMBR models (personal communication, July 27, 2004).

behaviors. Declarative or working memory contains memory elements obtained directly from sensory subsystems or through the firing of production rules. ACT-R's subsymbolic chunk activation components are incorporated to provide limits to working memory. A goal stack is also used to track goals and focus problem solving.

Learning. The AMBR project required the addition of a learning mechanism to COGNET/iGEN. Although specific to the category learning paradigm, its mechanisms for learning the goals and actions to be undertaken were designed to be general and extensible to other forms of learning. A separate category-learning module was developed, with access to short- and long-term memory structures, which learned category representations using a rule-based hypothesis testing approach. The COGNET/iGEN team added a decay mechanism as a memory moderator.

Learning in DCOG is based on building activations and associations among nodes in its associative memory. DCOG employed four distinct category learning strategies, emphasizing different learning styles observed in individuals. In every learning style, associations are built up between units representing response categories and other knowledge structures such as primitive features, exemplars, or category hypotheses.

Learning in ACT-R is a fundamental process, with most components of the model able to be learned, including rules, memory elements, and subsymbolic values. Learning in the AMBR model is based on the learned utility of production rules as well as the activation and associative strengths of declarative memory instances based on their usage history. Limits to learning capabilities are based on subsymbolic memory decay and utility computation mechanisms, as well as limits on the creation of new memory structures as a function of processing.

EASE incorporates ACT-R's declarative memory learning mechanisms, modulating the availability of declarative memory elements based on the recency and frequency of use. In addition, EASE inherited Soar's learning mechanism, in which the results of a subgoal search can be cached as part of a production rule, eliminating the need to generate a subgoal when a similar situation is encountered.

Action. In ACT-R, motor actions are presented by production rules whose latencies are based on the time required to select and apply the production. The application or execution of a production generally has a default latency of 50 msec. However, certain classes of productions related to motor actions, perceptual encodings, and feedback productions were assigned longer latencies. Latency times were not fixed, but instead were drawn from a uniform distribution with a range of +/- 25% around the mean.

In COGNET/iGEN, action procedure latencies are estimated through the use of micromodels, the results of which are used to delay the processing thread and the associated amount of time. Different latencies were assigned to different types of actions, with latencies a function of the task load levels and display complexities. Errors were introduced into motor response mechanisms with the possibility of pressing the wrong button.

Actions in EASE were represented by task operators, which made use of motor processing mechanisms incorporated from EPIC. Constraints are placed on these operators, such as requiring the hand and eyes to work together to achieve a behavior. Response latencies are a function of stochastically varied motor response parameters as well as the duration of each production cycle, which varied uniformly. The DCOG model does not yet have a principled method for including latency measures and did not predict response time measures for either Experiment 1 or 2.

2. What Is Your Modeling Methodology?

A fundamental principle for the ACT-R and EASE modeling teams was the importance of working with their respective cognitive architectures to develop the most natural and effective model of the task. Lebiere (chap. 4) states their modeling methodology is "based on emphasizing the power and constraints of the ACT-R architecture," while Chong and Wray (chap. 7) quote Newell and his imperative to "listen to the architecture." In fact Lebiere goes on to say that they did not analyze the empirical data and protocols to ascertain the strategies used by human participants, but instead "asked ourselves which ACT-R model would best solve the task given the architectural constraints." This is in contrast to the approach taken by COGNET/iGEN and DCOG, both of which emphasized the important role that detailed analysis of human data played in guiding the implementation of their models.

Although the ACT-R and EASE modeling teams emphasize the importance of architectural constraints, the COGNET/iGEN team emphasizes the flexibility of the COGNET/iGEN system, enabling them to develop models at the level of granularity best suited for the task. A guiding assumption was to develop models at the most coarse level of granularity required to achieve the modeling goals. The COGNET model was developed from the top down using the iGEN graphical development environment.

The EASE modeling team emphasizes the careful elaboration of the existing architecture only when it is unable to account for behavioral phenomena. As suggested by the name (Elements of ACT-R, Soar, and EPIC), architectural extension is often performed by integrating elements of other previously validated architectures, inheriting their power and constraints as well as their validity.

3. What Role Does Parameter Tuning Play?

The role of parameter tuning by each of the modeling teams follows rather consistently from their individual modeling methodologies. Both the ACT-R and the EASE modeling teams tried to work within the constraints imposed by their respective architectures, including the reuse of architectural components and default parameter values. In contrast, the COGNET/iGEN modeling architecture and tool suite is explicitly designed to be unconstrained with respect to model development—the modeler is welcome to implement whatever is necessary to fit the data at whatever level of granularity seems appropriate. With DCOG's emphasis on individual differences, parameterization was largely used as a mechanism for developing different model instances representing different populations of individuals.

The presence of preexisting architectural components and their associated parameters enabled both ACT-R and EASE to reuse parameter values. ACT-R used default parameter values in all cases where default values existed, and it coarsely set other parameters such as the memory retrieval threshold, perceptual and motor action times, stimulus similarity values, and workload scalers.

EASE reused ACT-R's memory activation and decay mechanisms and carried over the default parameter values. Additional parameters such as aircraft color priorities were coarsely estimated, while others such as the number of rehearsals in RULEX-EM, number of extra features in SCA, and workload scaling factors were fit to the empirical data. COGNET/iGEN also adapted other architectural components—reusing the HOS memory moderation model—and carried over two of the four parameter values from prior HOS models.

COGNET/iGEN made more extensive use of parameters as part of micromodels within the architecture. These micromodels contained parameters that reflected perceptual, cognitive, and motor action times, practice effects, confusion factors for degrading transfer task performance, and workload scaling factors.

As the only model not based on a preexisting architecture, the DCOG modelers did not draw on any prior modeling components or their parameters in the development of DCOG. As noted earlier, DCOG did use free parameters to represent individual differences.

Both Lebiere (chap. 4) and Chong and Wray (chap. 7) acknowledge that the knowledge structures constructed as part of the model can add additional degrees of freedom to the model. Chong and Wray (chap. 7) state this most strongly, saying, "The primary 'parameter' in the EASE models is knowledge, in that redesigning and reformulating knowledge can often lead to the greatest differences in performance measures." This is evident by the fact that a number of model revisions in Experiment 2 involved changes to knowledge structures and processes. For example, a rule learning mechanism was added to the ACT-R model to account for fast learning in the Problem Type I condition. This point is also illustrated by the construction of two EASE models—EASE SCA and EASE RULEX-EM—as part of the model revision process. Both models were developed within the constraints of the EASE architecture. Although each model used different knowledge structures, both ultimately produced similar overall fits to the data.

Lebiere (chap. 4) is unique in providing a detailed analysis of the influence of the three parameters involved in memory retrieval processes on category learning accuracy in category Problem Type I. Lebiere systematically evaluates a range of parameter values, revealing the range of data that can and cannot be accounted for by the model.[6]

The lack of quantitative parameter optimizing among these AMBR models is unusual for the development of models of multitasking and category learning. The majority of category learning models found in the literature are highly tuned to the data. Models of category learning such as RULEX (Nosofsky, Palmeri, & McKinley, 1994b), ALCOVE (Kruschke, 1992), and SUSTAIN (Gureckis & Love, 2003; Love & Medin, 1998) all used parameter estimation techniques to precisely determine the best fitting parameter values. The AMBR modelers, for the most part, did not highly tune their parameter values, emphasizing a desire to develop a mechanistic understanding of the phenomena, rather than simply fitting a model to the data. The exception to this is the COGNET/iGEN approach that eschews architectural constraints in favor of implementation flexibility through the use of micro-models.

4. What Is Your Account of Individual Differences?

It is generally agreed in the cognitive modeling and behavior representation communities that there are two ways to represent individual differences: as knowledge differences and as architectural differences. To represent knowledge differences observed in the human data, several of the modeling teams developed a variety of different strategies, with individual models representing distinct populations of individuals. DCOG made extensive use of strategy differences, employing four distinct learning strategies and mechanisms for shifting between them. EASE SCA developed three different strategy variations for learning which stimulus features to ig-

---

[6]These parameter analyses were performed on the original model prior to adding production rules for single-dimension rules. It is interesting to note that no parameter values shown were capable of producing the fast learning shown for human participants in the Type I problem. However, the addition of the single-dimension production rules (a knowledge-level change) produced good fits using default architectural parameter values.

nore during the category learning experiment. In contrast, EASE RULEX-EM was designed as a normative model and did not attempt to account for individual differences. ACT-R and COGNET/iGEN developed models employing a single strategy.

The second source of individual differences variation employed by a number of the AMBR modelers was the explicit manipulation of architectural parameter values. EASE SCA altered the number of features attended by an individual from zero to three, which when combined with the three strategy variations resulted in 12 different individual models. DCOG developed two strategy-mediating variables (worry factor and process two) for DCOG-1 and three personality variables (preference, patience, and tolerance) for DCOG-2. They used the three personality variables, which mediated category learning strategy shifts, to produce 12 different category learning profile strategies.

A final source of variability employed in all the models was stochastic noise built into various architectural components. This is a form of the architectural parameter approach to modeling individual differences. ACT-R has global noise parameters that influence chunk activations and production rule utilities at model run time. Despite only using a single knowledge-level strategy, the ACT-R modeling team took the view that each run of the model was equivalent to a separate human participant run. EASE employs stochastic elements in both perceptual and motor elements, as well as noise in memory activation levels—a property inherited from ACT-R. Both EASE SCA and EASE RULEX-EM employ stochastic mechanisms for feature selection in category learning. COGNET/iGEN also had stochasticity built into its feature selection mechanisms. Additionally, COGNET/iGEN made use of randomness as part of micromodels, including generating motor response errors and incorporating confusions in transfer task judgments. There are no architectural noise parameters in DCOG.

5. What Is Your Account of Cognitive Workload?

All of the architectures in the AMBR model comparison had to design new workload prediction mechanisms to account for the subjective workload ratings in Experiments 1 and 2. None of the architectures had been used to account for workload ratings prior to this, although COGNET/iGEN previously developed a representation of metacognition. The definitions and implementations of subjective workload are surprisingly different across the three models.[7]

The ACT-R model initially represented workload as a scaled ratio of the time spent on critical tasks (process and scan-text goals) to the total time on

---

[7]EASE SCA and EASE RULEX-EM used the same workload mechanisms.

task. Although this representation was sufficient for Experiment 1, it performed poorly in Experiment 2, leading to the addition of a success-based measure of effort in which the number of errors were weighted and added to the critical time on task.

EASE defined *workload* as the realization that an activity or event occurred, which indicates some work needs to be performed. Workload is not the amount of time or effort spent performing critical tasks, but rather the perception that there is work to be done. Different kinds of work were assigned load values representing its relative importance or urgency. Workload was then implemented as the scaled sum of the total realized load divided by the scenario duration.

DCOG used yet another representation for workload. Their approach was to identify 11 factors that appeared relevant to workload estimation, which when present added weighted contributions to the associated NASA TLX scale. These factors included actions such as altitude requests processed, perceived task complexity such as the average number of aircraft on the screen, and performance measures including the number of altitude request errors. The DCOG model did not produce workload ratings for Experiment 1. Although workload estimates were generated for Experiment 2, the modelers suggest that the current DCOG architecture does not yet provide satisfactory representations of metacognitive state.

In contrast to the others, the COGNET/iGEN model previously developed metacognitive capabilities representing underlying state information through a metacognitive memory system—making it unique among the AMBR models. Also, unlike any other model, COGNET/iGEN produced workload assessments across all six workload dimensions as defined by the TLX workload scales. In COGNET/iGEN, prediction of subjective workload is a complex computation, taking into account factors such as the weighted time spent performing actions, the number of goals and methods performed during the task, the amount of time without an active task, the number of perceived errors, and the number of task interruptions, all calibrated to the reporting scale through calibration parameters.

6. What Is Your Account of Multitasking?

ACT-R, EASE, and COGNET/iGEN all have similar accounts of multitasking based on the serial nature of some portion of their central cognitive processing mechanisms. Each architecture's cognitive multitasking mechanisms are based around goal or task switching. In ACT-R, cognitive behavior is goal oriented, with the current goal playing a key role in the selection of production rules from one cognitive cycle to the next. Only a single production rule can fire on any given cycle. Concurrent tasking can be accomplished by combining multiple goals into a single goal through extensive training. However, the architecture places limitations on both goal switching and goal combination capabilities. The incorporation of an explicit representation of sensitivity to visual onsets (see the earlier section on perception) in ACT-R allowed for the possibility of task interruptions, and therefore increased reactivity in the model. This is an important milestone for the ACT-R group because much of the cognitive modeling community assumed that ACT-R's goal-focused orientation precluded the possibility of task interruptions, thereby limiting the utility of ACT-R as an architecture for modeling multitasking. That the addition of sensitivity to visual onsets made this possible serves as additional evidence for the modeling benefits to be gained by using an embodied cognitive architecture.

Unlike ACT-R, EASE is a parallel firing production rule system where each rule that matches fires on every production cycle. In EASE, rules register preferences for operators. It is these operators, representing tasks, that operate in serial and manipulate or transform goal states. By encoding arbitration and priority guidelines for operator selection into production rules, the system is able to represent cognitive task switching. Critical to the success of multitasking in EASE was the addition of a capability for task interruption driven by perceptual input. Constraints on multitasking come largely from task instructions and strategies encoded in production rules or limitations in the perceptual or motor components of the architecture.

COGNET/iGEN was designed with multitasking as a primary component of the system. In COGNET, the cognitive, motor, and perceptual subsystems operate in parallel. Within the cognitive system, only a single procedural knowledge unit or task can be executed at one time. However, multiple tasks can simultaneously be active with differing states of completion. Changes to memory knowledge structures can facilitate the interruption, suspension, or execution of tasks. Multitasking is facilitated through parallel task activation and rapid task switching and execution. The COGNET/iGEN team added a separate knowledge type (metacognitive knowledge), which in conjunction with declarative and procedural knowledge facilitates the ability of the model to multitask on a strategy-driven basis. Alternative metacognitive strategies for multitasking are built into individual models by the developers via changes to the metacognitive knowledge. However, even without an explicit multitasking strategy, a model can still multitask using iGEN's built-in metacognitive strategies. A metacognition module makes for an effective means to manage activity during multitasking, and it is unquestionably a useful architectural component. One might question the theoretical parsimony of a separate metacognitive knowledge mechanism. However, it is important to keep in mind that the COGNET mission is not one of theoretical improvement, but rather to create a behavior representation system with practical applicability in a variety of modeling contexts.

With its primary emphasis on cognition as a distributed state-change system, DCOG has inherent mechanisms facilitating multitask performance.

In DCOG, tasks consist of activities performed by software agents operating in parallel and independent from one another. Behavior is coordinated and constraints imposed, either through task sequencing occurring within an individual software agent or through signals broadcast between agents. Without these constraints, tasks executed by different agents are all processed in parallel.

7. What Is Your Account of Categorization?

Although there have been instance- or exemplar-based accounts of category learning in the literature (e.g., Kruschke, 1992; Love & Medin, 1998), all the AMBR models were either rule-based or hybrid, combining both rule- and instance-based learning.

Originally developed using an instance-based approach, the initial ACT-R model could not replicate the steep learning curve found in the Problem Type I data. The revised ACT-R model included the addition of six single-dimension production rules whose subsymbolic production utility values compete with each other and with the instance-based learning mechanism to succeed at the categorization task. In the Type I condition, one of these single-dimension categorization rules will always be successful, and its utility value therefore dominates the others very quickly, leading to rapid improvements in categorization performance. Limits to instance-based category learning capabilities are based on memory decay and retrieval (e.g., partial matching) mechanisms.

The EASE SCA approach to categorization is a specific-to-general search for a production rule matching the instance. It first looks for a rule matching all features. If unsuccessful, it ignores a feature and again attempts to find a match. This is performed until either a match is found or all features have been eliminated, resulting in a guess being generated. Learning occurs by constructing a new specialized production based on the production used to generate the response. The last feature unspecified by the old production is set to the value specified in the stimulus. In this manner, the system will eventually saturate, learning fully specified rules for each stimulus. This approach was learned too quickly, relative to the human data, so the modeling team hypothesized participants were attending to additional features irrelevant to the task. These noise features reduced performance to levels matching the human data.

The RULEX-EM model learns both instances and rules, both of which are represented as declarative memory structures. Like EASE SCA, RULEX-EM performs a specific-to-general search strategy, first attempting to recall instances, then two-feature rules, followed by single-feature rules. In the event a complementary single-feature rule is found (i.e., the single-feature value is the opposite of that found in the stimulus), the model responds with the complementary category. If no applicable rule is found, the model makes a guess. RULEX-EM is a learn-on-failure algorithm, with new instances or rules learned in response to failures. Existing rules and instances are rehearsed when successfully applied. Based on the memory mechanisms of ACT-R, items used frequently are more likely to be retrieved from memory, whereas unused items decay and are forgotten.

The COGNET/iGEN model also takes a rule-based approach to category learning. However, unlike EASE SCA or EASE RULEX-EM, COGNET/iGEN performs a general-to-specific search strategy—first attempting single-feature rules, followed by two-feature rules, and last three-feature rules or unique instances. Rules in COGNET/iGEN are specified only for a single-category response—acceptance. If no applicable rules are found, the stimulus is categorized into the rejection category. Rule learning occurs using a general-to-specific strategy. New single-feature rules are hypothesized if no existing rules match the stimulus. Incorrect rules are further specialized based on negative feedback or removed if already fully specialized. Limits on the speed and power of learning are due to constraints placed on memory mechanisms. Only a limited number of rules are retained in short-term memory, with the likelihood of recalling a rule from short-term memory the product of rule complexity and the amount of rehearsal afforded the rule. Rules are maintained in short-term memory through rehearsal and transferred to long-term memory based on memory load and rule complexity. Rules in long-term memory are always available to the categorization process and are not subject to decay, but can be deleted deliberately.

The DCOG model employs four different learning strategies (rote, emergent, deductive, and abductive). DCOG claims that humans learn by using strategies, and subjects may shift learning strategies as they interact with their environment. They also claim that people have individual differences in their preferred learning strategy, in their patience with the learning process, and in their tolerance of exceptions. DCOG characterizes these individual differences with the parameters for mode, patience, and tolerance, which are called *personality* variables.

SUMMARY

Table 8.6 summarizes the features found in the architectures and models involved in the AMBR project.

Even with their diverse origins and varied length of existence, there are a number of commonalities and points of convergence among the models. As aspiring unifying and integrative cognitive architectures, ACT-R and EASE share the greatest amount of architectural commonality. Both are built on production systems with similar cognitive representations, with EASE even utilizing some of ACT-R's memory mechanism. Both EASE and

TABLE 8.6
Architecture Summary Table

	ACT-R	COGNET/iGEN	D-COG	EASE
Representation of Cognition	Modular architecture interacting through a central production system. Declarative memory is represented as structured chunks, whereas procedural knowledge is represented in production rules.	Flexible architecture with multiple representations for knowledge. Cognitive processing is serial with rapid attention switching based on changes in memory components.	Software agent architecture with agents executing parallel computational threads. Emphasis on strategies, which are a foundation for behaviors.	Match and fire production system with rules and declarative memory structures.
Modeling Method	Model construction emphasizing the power and constraints of the architecture.	Use cognitive task analysis to capture strategies from human experts. Development driven by task demands and constructed at appropriate level of granularity.	Perform task analysis to develop models specialized for work/task.	Emphasis on listening to the architecture and building models within the constraints imposed by the architecture. Some use of cognitive task analysis.
Parameters	Work within the constraints of the architecture. Use default parameter values where available. Knowledge structures the greatest source of degrees of freedom for the model.	Core architecture has no parameters. Makes extensive use of parameterized micromodels to fit empirical data.	Parameters reflect different learning strategies and personality factors. Strategies and parameter values selected based on empirical data and task analysis.	Knowledge structures considered the primary "parameter." Reformulation of knowledge has large impact on performance. Default ACT-R parameter values used for memory mechanisms.

Individual Differences	Differences due to variations in knowledge structures, architectural parameters, and stochasticity built into system components.	Stochasticity built into micromodel components and feature selection mechanisms. Dominant differences based on knowledge and task strategy differences, although only one strategy was implemented in AMBR.	Large emphasis on multiple learning strategies. Twelve individual models were developed, each reflecting different learning strategies and personality factors.	The SCA model developed 12 different model instances with different learning strategies and parameter values. RULEX-EM was a normative model and did not account for individual differences.
Workload	Scaled ratio of time spent on critical task goals to total time on task, combined with a weighted measure of errors made.	Detailed workload assessment across all six workload dimensions using a complex set of factors.	The presence of up to 11 factors were weighted and combined into a single measure of workload.	Scaled sum of the perceived amount of work required. Different types of work were differentially weighted.
Multitasking	Cognitively controlled goal switching. Concurrent tasking is possible by combining goal representations.	Parallel processing across motor, perceptual, and cognitive components. Within the cognitive system, multiple tasks can be active, but only one is executing at one time.	Inherently multitasking architecture. Tasks are activities performed by software agents operating in parallel. Constraints occur via task sequencing within an agent or by waiting on event signals.	Multitasking is implemented as task switching between task operators. Operator/task preferences encoded in production rules.
Categorization	Hybrid approach combining instance-based memory retrieval with rule-based productions for single-feature rules. Performance limitations based on memory decay and retrieval mechanisms, as well as production utility learning mechanism.	General-to-specific rule-based hypothesis testing. Constraints based on short-term memory limitations and knowledge transfer to long-term memory.	Four strategies for learning and mechanisms for switching between them, including feature and exemplar learning and hypothesis testing. Categorization implemented as a spreading activation model.	SCA is a specific-to-general search for production rules matching the instance. Learning occurs by production specialization. RULEX-EM is a hybrid model using both exemplars and rules.

ACT-R primarily use task or goal switching to model multitasking performance. Conversely, DCOG and COGNET/iGEN were designed from the onset for parallel processing with inherent multitasking capabilities. ACT-R and EASE are also similar in that both architectures emphasize the importance of working within architectural constraints while building models and taking an architecturally centered approach to model development. Even with these constraints, both architectures provide a significant degree of freedom to develop knowledge representations across diverse modeling tasks. Conversely, DCOG and COGNET/iGEN emphasize a more task-oriented approach to model development. For these architectures, task analysis is used to provide the foundation on which to develop models specialized for a particular task.

Although the pair-wise points of divergence between the architectures and the models developed with them are numerous, there are a few points of divergence that are particularly noteworthy. First, each model's implementation of workload varied considerably, with each model using a variety of factors and processes for calculating workload. Second, DCOG's architectural framework as a set of parallel, interacting software agents is unique among the architectures. Last, COGNET/iGEN's lack of core architectural parameters and consequent use of parameterized micromodels to fit empirical results was also unique among the architectures.

REFERENCES

Agresti, A. (2002). *Categorical data analysis* (2nd ed.). New York: Wiley.

Anderson, J. R. (1983). *The architecture of cognition.* Cambridge, MA: Harvard University Press.

Anderson, J. R. (1990). *The adaptive character of thought.* Hillsdale, NJ: Lawrence Erlbaum Associates.

Anderson, J. R. (1993). *The rules of the mind.* Hillsdale, NJ: Lawrence Erlbaum Associates.

Anderson, J. R., & Lebiere, C. (1998). *The atomic components of thought.* Mahwah, NJ: Lawrence Erlbaum Associates.

Baker, R. S., Corbett, A. T., & Koedinger, K. R. (2003, July 25–27). Statistical techniques for comparing ACT-R models of cognitive performance. In *Proceedings of the 10th Annual ACT-R Workshop* (pp. 129–134). (Retrieved January 30, 2004, from http://act-r.psy.cmu.edu/workshops/workshop-2003/proceedings/39.pdf.)

Bozdogan, H. (2000). Akaike's information criterion and recent developments in information complexity. *Journal of Mathematical Psychology, 44,* 69–91.

Busemeyer, J. R., & Wang, Y.-M. (2000). Model comparisons and model selections based on generalization criterion methodology. *Journal of Mathematical Psychology, 44,* 171–189.

Grünwald, P. D. (2000). Model selection based on minimum description length. *Journal of Mathematical Psychology, 44,* 133–152.

Gureckis, T. M., & Love, B. C. (2003). Towards a unified account of supervised and unsupervised learning. *Journal of Experimental and Theoretical Artificial Intelligence, 15,* 1–24.

Hart, S., & Staveland, L. (1988). Development of the NASA-TLX: Results of empirical and theoretical research. In P. Hancock & N. Meshkati (Eds.), *Human mental workload* (pp. 139–184). Amsterdam: North-Holland.

Jones, R. M., Laird, J. E., Nielsen, P. E., Coulter, K. J., Kenny, P., & Koss, F. V. (1999). Automated intelligent pilots for combat flight simulation. *AI Magazine, 20*, 27–41.

Kieras, D. E., & Meyer, D. E. (1997). An overview of the EPIC architecture for cognition and performance with application to human–computer interaction. *Human–Computer Interaction, 12*, 391–438.

Kieras, D. E., & Meyer, D. E. (2000). The role of cognitive task analysis in the application of predictive models of human performance. In J. M. C. Schraagen, S. E. Chipman, & V. L. Shalin (Eds.), *Cognitive task analysis* (pp. 237–260). Mahwah, NJ: Lawrence Erlbaum Associates.

Kruschke, J. K. (1992). ALCOVE: An exemplar-based connectionist model of category learning. *Psychological Review, 99*, 22–44.

Love, B. C., & Medin, D. L. (1998). SUSTAIN: A model of human category learning. In *Proceedings of the 15th National Conference on Artificial Intelligence (AAAI-98*; pp. 671–676). Madison, WI: American Association for Artificial Intelligence.

Miller, C. S., & Laird, J. E. (1996). Accounting for graded performance within a discrete search framework. *Cognitive Science, 20*(4), 499–537.

Myung, I. J. (2000). The importance of complexity in model selection. *Journal of Mathematical Psychology, 44*, 190–204.

Nosofsky, R. M., Gluck, M., Palmeri, T. J., McKinley, S. C., & Glauthier, P. (1994a). Comparing models of rule-based classification learning: A replication and extension of Shepard, Hovland, and Jenkins (1961). *Memory & Cognition, 22*, 352–369.

Nosofsky, R. M., Palmeri, T. J., & McKinley, S. C. (1994b). Rule-plus-exception model of classification learning. *Psychological Review, 101*, 53–79.

Newell, A. (1990). *Unified theories of cognition.* Cambridge, MA: Cambridge University Press.

Pitt, M. A., Myung, I. J., & Zhang, S. (2002). Toward a method of selecting among computational models of cognition. *Psychological Review, 109*, 472–491.

Roberts, S., & Pashler, H. (2000). How persuasive is a good fit? A comment on theory testing. *Psychological Review, 107*, 358–367.

Roberts, S., & Pashler, H. (2002). Reply to Rodgers and Rowe (2002). *Psychological Review, 109*, 605–607.

Rodgers, J. L., & Rowe, D. C. (2002a). Theory development should begin (but not end) with good empirical fits: A comment on Roberts and Pashler (2000). *Psychological Review, 109*, 599–603.

Rodgers, J. L., & Rowe, D. C. (2002b). Postscript: Theory development should not end (but always begins) with good empirical fits: Response to Roberts and Pashler's (2002) reply. *Psychological Review, 109*, 603–604.

Schunn, C. D., & Wallach, D. (2001). *Evaluating goodness-of-fit in comparisons of models to data.* Online manuscript. http://www.lrdc.pitt.edu/schunn/gof/index.html.

Vidulich, M. A., & Tsang, P. S. (1986). *Collecting NASA workload ratings: A paper-and-pencil package* (Version 2.1). Working Paper. Moffett Field, CA: NASA Ames Research Center.

Wasserman, L. (2000). Bayesian model selection and model averaging. *Journal of Mathematical Psychology, 44*, 92–107.

Chapter 9

In Vivo or In Vitro: Cognitive Architectures and Task-Specific Models

Bradley C. Love
The University of Texas at Austin

The AMBR project has a worthy and lofty goal—to create systems that can successfully simulate human behavior. In service of this goal, AMBR teams created category learning systems that were embedded within a cognitive architecture. To test and more fully develop these architectural proposals, human performance data were collected in a behavioral study that paired structures utilized in Shepard, Hovland, and Jenkins's (1961) classic category learning studies with secondary tasks that evoked air traffic control (ATC) scenarios.

More narrowly defined models developed in the category learning literature have successfully accounted for human performance on Shepard, Hovland, and Jenkins's (1961) six problem types (e.g., Kruschke, 1992; Love & Medin, 1998; Nosofsky, Palmeri, & McKinley, 1994). One interesting question is how these task-specific models compare to the architectural solutions proposed by the AMBR teams. After a brief discussion of the surface commonalities and differences between task-specific and architectural approaches, this chapter considers how models from each approach are developed, utilized, and evaluated. The manner in which models from each class integrate diverse behavioral findings is also discussed. Finally, I suggest when one approach is preferable to the other and argue that task-specific and architectural models are destined to converge.

COMMONALITIES AND DIFFERENCES

Salient commonalities and differences exist between these two classes of models. On the convergence front, many of the AMBR models successfully borrow from the category learning literature. For example, the ACT-R team posits an exemplar-based representation of category information, which is the most popular modeling framework in the category learning literature (e.g., Kruschke, 1992; Medin & Schaffer, 1978; Nosofsky, 1986). The ACT-R model also adopts an exponentially shaped function for relating psychological distance to perceived similarity. This choice, motivated by the work of Roger Shepard (Shepard, 1964, 1987), is often employed in category learning models (e.g., Kruschke, 1992; Love & Medin, 1998; Nosofsky, 1986).

Convergence is not limited to the ACT-R proposal. DCOG, like some current models in the category learning literature (e.g., Ashby, Alfonso-Reese, Turken, & Waldron, 1998; Erickson & Kruschke, 1998), holds that multiple memory and learning systems underlie category learning performance. Perhaps the best example of transfer from psychological models to AMBR is the EASE team's choice of the RULEX model (Nosofsky et al., 1994) as one of its category learning modules.

The category learning experiment directed by BBN is a force for convergence and divergence. In terms of convergence, BBN's results for the difficulty ordering of the Shepard et al. (1961) Problems I, III, and VI replicated findings used to develop category learning models. This is a testament to the robustness of the original findings given the differences in the BBN experiment (e.g., stimuli, secondary tasks, etc.). Unfortunately, time and resource constraints prevented BBN from including all six problem types from the original Shepard et al. study. This is somewhat problematic because the Type II problem, a highly nonlinear category structure (i.e., XOR with an irrelevant stimulus dimension), is easily learned by humans (more easily than the Type III problem), yet many models predict that Type II should be more difficult than Type III. Type II is unusual because its relative difficulty ordering is not predicted by similarity-based generalization models that do not include rule or attentionally driven components. Corroborating this conclusion, Rhesus monkeys who cannot entertain verbal rules have more difficulty learning Type II than all other problems except Type VI (Smith, Minda, & Washburn, 2004). The omission of Type II denied the AMBR teams the opportunity to directly confront one of the most challenging data points from the original Shepard et al. study.

Of course the AMBR models faced other significant challenges because the BBN data involved tasks other than category learning. Although the psychology literature in general has considered dual-task manipulations that create working memory loads (see Pashler, 1994, for a review), the category learning literature has not exploited such methods (though see Love & Markman, 2003, for an exception). Furthermore, current category learning models do not have a component that directly corresponds to working memory capacity. Perhaps consideration of dual-task data would create an additional point of convergence. For instance, the COGNET team chose to augment their system with a working memory component in light of the dual-task manipulation. Although the BBN data offer a well-thought-out method for incorporating secondary tasks with category learning tasks, unfortunately the secondary task loads were not sufficient to disrupt learning performance, and thus the actual data do not provide strong constraints for extending existing category learning models.

The differences discussed earlier between category learning and AMBR models are symptomatic of a basic difference in approach. The AMBR models propose a complete cognitive architecture. These models are intended to be applicable to all relevant aspects of performance from perception to action. Category learning is simply one application for these architectures. In contrast, category learning models are task-specific and focus on explaining human category learning performance. This chapter brings the relationship between these two approaches into focus.

MODEL OBJECTIVES, DEVELOPMENT, AND EVALUATION

In this section, we consider the function of models in the category learning literature and the AMBR program. Model evaluation is also discussed. A later section considers how category learning and AMBR models differ in architectural commitments and in the sense in which they are integrative.

What Are Models For?

Psychologists, including modelers, strive to develop theories that will lead to a mechanistic understanding of cognition. Category learning models can serve multiple functions on the path to this ultimate goal. One function is to offer an instantiation of abstract theories to enable rigorous evaluation. Often the full import of a theory is not understood until it is actualized as a model. For example, until the context model (Medin & Schaffer, 1978), psychologists did not appreciate that an exemplar-based model could account for abstraction results (e.g., Posner & Keele, 1968) that on the surface appear to uniquely support a prototype account of category representation. Once implemented, it became clear that activating numerous studied exemplars stored in memory could lead to strong endorsement of a category prototype (the central tendency of the studied exemplars) even in the absence of studying the prototypical stimulus.

Beyond prediction, category learning models serve as conceptual tools that help researchers understand the determinants of behavior. As such models that are easily understood often prove the most useful. Transpicuous models assist in conducting thought experiments that can yield ideas for actual experiments. The Shepard et al. original studies were partially motivated by similarity-based generalization models. When the Shepard et al. results proved inconsistent with these models, a renewed cycle of model construction and testing began. As can be seen by this example, models in psychology play a critical role in theory development and revision.

In contrast, the goal of AMBR is to develop software systems that can successfully simulate human behavior. Some AMBR teams do not view their systems as psychological theories. For example, the COGNET teams state that their model is an engineering tool for creating practical applications rather than a platform for generating and testing psychological theories. Despite these striking surface differences in the goals of category learning models and the AMBR program, both communities are destined to converge if they remain true to their goals. As the psychological theories underlying category learning models are extended and refined, they will improve in their ability to predict behavior, and related models will provide more complete and accurate simulations of human behavior. Conversely, as simulation test beds become more accurate in making a priori behavioral predictions, they will likely converge to the mechanisms underlying human behavior. In this sense, the two communities are taking two paths to the same destination.

The different paths these two communities have chosen are reflected in how they evaluate models. Because category learning researchers are primarily concerned with theory development, there is a greater focus on which aspects of the model drive overall model behavior. Although this attribution process has the desirable outcome of building a firm foundation for future progress, it can have the negative consequence of stifling bold proposals and leading to theoretical quagmires. As models converge, a greater number of experiments become necessary to tease apart the alternatives, and the return of investment in terms of predicting behavior diminish rapidly. For example, the ongoing debate between exemplar and prototype theorists focuses on a deep, but narrow, set of findings (from the viewpoint of those outside the field). The debate is difficult to resolve through human experimentation and model simulation because of the subtleness of the predictions the models make (e.g., Nosofsky & Zaki, 2002; Smith, 2002). Although such debates make us keenly aware of the assumptions and capabilities of different formalisms, they are not associated with rapid advances in our ability to simulate human behavior under general conditions.

Of course the downside of the approach adopted by the AMBR participants is that it is impossible to know with certainty which aspects of the model are driving performance and if all assumptions are warranted. The data simply underconstrain the models. Aspects and specific predictions (which can be ascribed to certain mechanisms in the models) are not adequately tested through controlled and systematic human experimentation. In this sense, the AMBR models exist as indivisible units, which can make it difficult to know with confidence what specific lessons are to be gleamed from a simulation.

One proposed solution to this problem is to evaluate cognitive architectures across a wide range of tasks and criteria (Newell, 1980, 1990). By addressing multiple criteria simultaneously, as opposed to specializing in one task, architectural proposals can be viewed as the "decathletes" of cognitive modeling (Vere, 1992). Unfortunately, the criteria proposed for evaluating architectures (e.g., Anderson & Lebiere, 2003; Newell, 1980, 1990) are vague and their application subjective. For example, Anderson and Lebiere (2003), revisiting Newell's earlier work, listed "Integrate diverse knowledge" and "Be realizable within the brain" as 2 of 12 criteria for evaluating architectures. Evaluating such criteria is far from trivial. Furthermore, when the primary research goal is to understand human category learning in particular, knowing that an architecture addresses a number of other tasks in general is only satisfying to the extent that these other successes make one confident that the architecture's account of category learning is sound. Unfortunately, such confluence is likely unwarranted given that numerous solutions to a particular task (such as category learning) can be built within a single architecture. An example of this scenario is discussed later in this chapter.

Model Development and Revision

The differences in approach between task-specific and AMBR models can also be seen in how models are developed. Category learning models tend to undergo a competitive and incremental evolution, whereas AMBR models tend to take bold steps and reuse significant components from existing models. For example, DCOG represents a radically new proposal that has many novel components that are not fully evaluated. Other models, like those from the EASE group, recycle large components from previous efforts or incorporate existing models as submodules. Both of these developmental paths are consistent with the idea that systems in the AMBR community are evaluated at a coarse level (i.e., the architecture or its modules are the unit of evaluation) in comparison with category learning models.

This is not to say that lessons learned over time are not incorporated into an architecture. Architectures undergo evolution and borrow elements from one another (see Anderson & Lebiere, 2003, for a brief history of ACT-R's development). However, simulations of a particular task (such as category learning) do not follow this pattern of development, perhaps reflecting that proponents of cognitive architectures are more concerned with addressing a wide array of tasks than focusing on a particular task.

In contrast, category learning models tend to develop in a more evolutionary manner. For example, the context model is an early example of an exemplar model (Medin & Schaffer, 1978). Nosofsky developed the generalized context model (GCM) by combining the context model with Roger Shepard's work on stimulus generalization (Nosofsky, 1986; Shepard, 1964, 1987). Subsequently, Kruschke combined connectionist learning rules (Rumelhart, Hinton, & Williams, 1986) with the work of Nosofsky to create ALCOVE (Kruschke, 1992). None of these steps in the evolution of the exemplar model involved combining or recycling modules. Each step represented a new model that integrated successful principles from existing models into a coherent whole.

Like evolution, modeling proposals often branch in divergent directions. For example, the exemplar-based random walk (EBRW) model combines GCM with instance-based models of automaticity (Logan, 1988) and work in diffusion decision models (Ratcliff, 1978) to create a new exemplar-based model that can account for reaction time distributions. Branches in category learning research can also crisscross. For example, the SUSTAIN (a clustering model) model's development was influenced by work in exemplar, prototype, clustering, and rule-based approaches (Love & Medin, 1998; Love, Medin, & Gureckis, 2004). The trajectory of model development reflects the theoretically driven nature of work in psychology. Just as there is usually an element of truth in yesterday's dominant theory, there is also some truth in past leading models that is reflected in successive generations of models.

Evaluating Models Through Group and Individual Data

The AMBR project's goal of a priori parameter-free prediction is also embodied to a certain extent in category learning modeling. In many ways, it is as important to know what a model does not predict as it is to know what it does predict. A model that can predict every possible pattern of results through different settings of its parameters is not explanatory. Although psychologists have often erred in the direction of favoring more complex and flexible models, there is a growing awareness of the importance of a priori prediction and considering model complexity. One approach has been to reuse parameters across a number of different simulations (e.g., Love et al., 2004). Another approach has been to consider whether a model can predict a pattern of results not observed (e.g., Love et al., 2004; Markman & Maddox, 2003). A computationally intensive approach is to integrate over the entire parameter space to determine the qualitative predictions of a model (e.g., Johansen & Palmeri, 2002). Psychologists have also developed and applied sophisticated model selection statistics that take into account both the fit and functional complexity of a model (e.g., Pitt, Myung, & Zhang, 2002). Of course the process of deriving predictions from a model and then testing them through experimentation is an exercise in a priori prediction.

As the AMBR project unfolded, AMBR teams became aware of the prevalence and importance of individual differences. Comprehensive simulations of human behavior require accounting for individual differences. Likewise comprehensive theories of categorization must address individual differences. Although the majority of psychological research has relied on group averages, there is a growing appreciation of the importance of characterizing individual differences. Exploring individual differences offers another avenue for discriminating between theories. For example, a theory that holds that people stochastically discover rules and one that holds that people incrementally strengthen connections both predict smooth learning curves for the averaged data, but make different predictions at the level of individual subjects (cf. Estes, 2002).

In the AMBR project, as is often the case in category learning research, individual differences were explored only after their magnitude became apparent. Ideally, the goal of understanding individual differences would be reflected in the basic experimental design. One excellent example of this methodology is the work of Johansen and Palmeri (2002). Johansen and Palmeri trained subjects on a category structure that could be learned by applying an imperfect rule or generalizing across exemplars. They predicted that people's behavior would be rule governed early in learning and exemplar driven late in learning. To evaluate this possibility, they introduced transfer trials without feedback after every few blocks of training. These transfer trials required subjects to apply their category knowledge to new examples. The patterns of transfer performance could easily be characterized as rule- or exemplar-based or following several other patterns. Subjects were binned by strategy; as predicted, the distribution of transfer pattern shifted toward the exemplar-based pattern from rule-based patterns over the course of training. Rather than relying on average performance, Johansen and Palmeri presented their data as a distribution of outcomes over subjects. Models that account for the average data may not account for the distribution of individual subject performance. For example, a model which predicts that subjects are using a blend of rules and exemplars will not account for a transfer distribution that indicates that subjects are basing their responses on either rules or exemplars.

Another approach to individual differences in the category learning literature has been to study a small number of subjects over many (i.e., hundreds of) trials. This tradition traces its roots back to work in psychophysics, where individual subject analysis (over many trials) is stressed. With so much data per subject, parameters can be fit to individual subjects.

Those using this methodology often employ models in a descriptive manner. For example, General Recognition Theory (GRT), which is a generalization of signal detection theory, can be used to estimate parameters for single subjects (Ashby & Townsend, 1986). These parameters become the data representation for the subject. In other words, it is not the model's job to simulate or fit human data. Rather the model's job is to redescribe data in a more understandable form so that the theoretical significance of the results can be appreciated. In such analyses, different patterns of parameter values are expected for subjects in different learning conditions.

ARCHITECTURE AND INTEGRATION

In this section, we consider architectural differences between category learning and AMBR models, as well as different senses in which models from these two communities are integrative. Many of the differences are reflected in the disparate functions models serve in these two communities (as discussed in the previous section).

Different Senses of Integration

Category learning models trace their roots back to work in mathematical psychology and animal learning (e.g., Spence, 1936). Animal learning studies tend to be fairly simple. After all there are only so many paradigms an animal can be trained in. For example, animals cannot be trained in a simulated ATC task as the BBN subjects were. A lot of early (and recent) work in human category learning, including the Shepard et al. studies, have been influenced by previous work in animal learning. The combined influence of mathematical psychology, with its emphasis on rigor, elegance, and transparency, along with experiments that provide limited ways for subjects to interact with the stimuli, have driven the field toward simple models suited to addressing a narrow range of tasks. The scientific motivations for pursuing such a path are discussed in the previous section.

The end result is models that are simple and built exclusively for category learning (as defined by laboratory paradigms). Category learning models are not architectural proposals like AMBR models are. They tend to test a core set of ideas. For instance, many category learning models are test beds for determining the nature of our category representations. Models have been useful in determining whether categories are represented by exemplars, clusters, prototypes, rules, or combinations thereof. The models tend not to integrate many other mental functions except for those directly relevant to category learning, such as attentional mechanisms. Perception and action are usually removed from the mix by modeling tasks in which these processes are not pivotal in determining category learning performance. By simplifying the data and models, core issues in category learning and representation can be brought into focus.

AMBR models and other proposals for the cognitive architecture have grander ambitions. These models attempt to provide a complete account of cognition. For example, the EASE team's model performs eye movements across the ATC display to actively gather information. These models also have a notion of goal and a control structure to determine what to do next. The DCOG model goes as far as to suggest how personality factors govern strategy shifts. In these ways, AMBR models are much more general and integrative than category learning models.

Still there is more than one way to be integrative. Category learning models tend to be fairly integrative in terms of relating findings from different studies to one another. Shepard et al. is just one study amid hundreds. Category learning models serve to integrate findings into common theoretical frameworks. One way to view the difference in focus between AMBR and category learning models is a choice between depth and breadth.

Integration also occurs at the level of relating different induction tasks to one another. There are more ways to learn about categories than the supervised classification learning procedure used in Shepard et al. and the BBN experiment. For example, people often learn through inference-based learning. In inference learning, the category membership of a stimulus is known, but the value of an unknown stimulus dimension must be predicted (Yamauchi, Love, & Markman, 2002; Yamauchi & Markman, 1998). An example inference trial is, "This is a bird. Is it warm-blooded? Does it eat worms?" Other category learning studies have explored how people learn categories in the absence of supervision and how such unsupervised learning compares with supervised learning (Love, 2002). The results from these studies are not reviewed here, but one important thread that runs through all the results is that human performance is determined by the interaction of induction task (e.g., inference or classification) and learning problem (e.g., Type II or VI) so that studying a single induction task (e.g., classification learning) leads to an incomplete account of human category learning. Category learning models have successfully accounted for these interactions (Love, Markman, & Yamauchi, 2000; Love et al., 2004).

In addition to addressing a wider range of real-world learning situations, these alternative learning tasks have also been useful in model selection. For instance, a number of category learning models with different theoretical commitments can successfully account for human performance on Shepard, Hovland, and Jenkins's (1961) six problem types (e.g., Kruschke, 1992; Love & Medin, 1998; Nosofsky et al., 1994). Consideration of other learning tasks and other measures, such as item recognition following category learning, has proved useful in selecting candidate models (Love et al., 2004; Sakamoto & Love, in press). One would be mistaken to think that the simulation of one data set verifies a model's account of category learning given the varied and challenging nature of the data.

Other modeling efforts have explored integrating learning from examples with prior knowledge (Heit, 2001). Understanding the influence of prior knowledge on learning is critical because prior knowledge can reverse the difficulty ordering of acquiring different category structures (Pazzani, 1991; Wattenmaker, Dewey, Murphy, & Medin, 1986) and can even alter the representations of stimulus items (Wisniewski & Medin, 1994).

Another area of integration for psychological models has been the juncture of brain and behavior. In recent years, there has been a flourish of activity directed at understanding which neural circuits support category learning. Some researchers have proposed models that are closely tied to learning systems in the brain (Ashby et al., 1998). Architectural proposals have also begun to consider cognitive neuroscience data (Anderson et al., 2003).

In summary, integration is occurring in both cognitive architecture models and psychological models of category learning. The different senses of integration often reflect the different goals of these two communities. The fact that category learning researchers, like those working within a cognitive architecture, prize integration might reflect that category learning is a fairly encompassing task with many manifestations.

Who Needs a Cognitive Architecture?

Clearly, an integrative cognitive architecture is required for applications that aim to simulate human behavior from perception to action. Developing cognitive architecture models is a necessity for the AMBR teams. A more interesting question is what the category learning community potentially loses from not working within an architecture. For instance, is working within a cognitive architecture necessary for developing a complete model of category learning? Does working within a cognitive architecture provide useful theoretical constraints on developing a model of category learning?

At this point, the answer to both questions appears to be no. The AMBR teams' results suggest that cognitive architecture plays little role in specifying models of category learning. For instance, the EASE team has constructed two different learning models within their system. It is likely that other category learning models could also be implemented within their system with equivalent results. Similarly, the ACT-R team proposes an exemplar-based category learning system within ACT-R. Also working within the ACT-R architecture, Anderson and Betz (2001) forward a different exemplar-based category learning system, a rule-based category learning system, and a hybrid system. Anderson and Betz's rule-based category learning system is identical to the rule-based category learning system constructed within EASE. In summary, multiple and different category learning systems are proposed within a single architecture, and identical learning systems are proposed in different architectures. At this stage, architecture provides little constraint on the development of category learning models.

Although architecture per se does not constrain the development of category learning models at this juncture, future category learning research may benefit from work in cognitive architecture. Architectures, like ACT-R and EASE, specify how much time cognitive, perceptual, and motor operations require. These parameter values can be used within category learning models to make response time predictions. Also future experimental results may increase the importance of cognitive architecture in developing models of category learning. For instance, dual-task learning data demonstrating interactions between category structure (e.g., Types I, III, VI) and secondary task load may be most readily addressed by working within an existing architecture. As data of this type become available, work in category learning and cognitive architecture will likely merge.

Until such interactions emerge, the best strategy for architecture proponents is to implement existing category learning models within a chosen architecture. In the future, as data become available demonstrating shared resources between category learning systems and other cognitive systems, architectural approaches will serve as more than programming languages with timing constraints. In light of such findings, the divide and conquer approach to understanding category learning and other aspects of cognition and perception might not be as appealing. Those working outside an architecture would need to address concerns that the category learning systems they construct will be inoperable with other cognitive systems. Even at this future juncture, one potentially fruitful approach could be to "grow" existing category learning models to encompass other facilities and cognitive bottlenecks such as a working memory. These facilities could be adjusted to reflect the impact of concurrent tasks on category learning performance. As these interactions with other systems sharing resources become more pervasive, the best approach will likely be to build category learning models within an existing architecture.

CONCLUSIONS

Architectural models of cognition that seek to successfully simulate human behavior and task-specific models that are tools for developing theories of cognition adopt two different paths that will both hopefully lead to successful a priori predictions about human behavior under a variety of conditions. The sense in which these two classes of models are integrative differs greatly. Architectural proposals are integrative by definition. They must simulate behavior from perception to action. Task-specific models, such as models of category learning, are integrative by virtue of placing disparate findings from numerous experiments into a common theoretical framework, considering multiple induction tasks, subsequent item recognition, the effects of prior knowledge on learning, and the relationship between brain and behavior.

Despite adopting different paths, work in one community is relevant to the other. As can be seen in the AMBR proposals, formalisms from the category learning literature are utilized in AMBR models. Similarly, the challenges faced by AMBR models highlight future challenges for category learning modelers. Although cognitive architecture does not strongly constrain theories of category learning at this juncture, it is likely to in the near future. As appropriate dual-task data become available, psychological models of category learning are likely to merge with cognitive architecture proposals.

Finally, applications of cognitive architecture models to realistic behavioral simulations provide valuable information to all of psychology. Theories and experiments created in the laboratory can fail to address variables that contribute to significant variance in real-world settings. To the extent that architectural proposals borrow from theories developed in the laboratory, theorists working in the laboratory gain a valuable check on their efforts. Without such checks, models developed in the laboratory face the danger of not generalizing. Clearly, progress in one community benefits the other.

REFERENCES

Anderson, J. R., & Betz, J. (2001). A hybrid model of categorization. *Psychonomic Bulletin & Review, 8,* 629–647.

Anderson, J. R., & Lebiere, C. (2003). The Newell Test for a theory of cognition. *Behavioral and Brain Sciences, 26,* 587–640.

Anderson, J. R., Qin, Y., Sohn, M.-H., Stenger, V. A., & Carter, C. S. (2003). An information-processing model of the BOLD response in symbol manipulation tasks. *Psychonomic Bulletin and Review, 10,* 241–261.

Ashby, F., Alfonso-Reese, L., Turken, A., & Waldron, E. (1998). A neuropsychological theory of multiple-systems in category learning. *Psychological Review, 105,* 442–481.

Ashby, F. G., & Townsend, J. T. (1986). Varieties of perceptual independence. *Psychological Review, 93,* 154–179.

Erickson, M. A., & Kruschke, J. K. (1998). Rules and exemplars in category learning. *Journal of Experimental Psychology: General, 127,* 107–140.

Estes, W. (2002). Traps in the route to models of memory and decision. *Psychonomic Bulletin & Review, 9,* 3–25.

Heit, E. (2001). Background knowledge and models of categorization. In U. Hahn & M. Ramscar (Eds.), *Similarity and categorization* (pp. 155–178). New York: Oxford University Press.

Johansen, M. K., & Palmeri, T. J. (2002). Are there representational shifts during category learning? *Cognitive Psychology, 45*, 482–553.

Kruschke, J. K. (1992). ALCOVE: An exemplar-based connectionist model of category learning. *Psychological Review, 99*, 22–44.

Logan, G. D. (1988). Towards an instance theory of automatization. *Psychological Review, 95*, 492–527.

Love, B. C. (2002). Comparing supervised and unsupervised category learning. *Psychonomic Bulletin & Review, 9*, 829–835.

Love, B. C., & Markman, A. B. (2003). The non-independence of stimulus properties in human category learning. *Memory & Cognition, 31*, 790–799.

Love, B. C., Markman, A. B., & Yamauchi, T. (2000). Modeling classification and inference learning. *Proceedings of the Fifteenth National Conference on Artificial Intelligence*, 136–141.

Love, B. C., & Medin, D. L. (1998). SUSTAIN: A model of human category learning. In *Proceedings of the Fifteenth National Conference on Artificial Intelligence* (pp. 671–676). Cambridge, MA: MIT Press.

Love, B. C., Medin, D. L., & Gureckis, T. (2004). SUSTAIN: A network model of human category learning. *Psychological Review, 111*, 309–332.

Markman, A. B., & Maddox, W. T. (2003). Classification of exemplars with single and multiple feature manifestations: The effects of relevant dimension variation and category structure. *Journal of Experimental Psychology: Learning, Memory, & Cognition, 29*, 107–117.

Medin, D. L., & Schaffer, M. M. (1978). Context theory of classification learning. *Psychological Review, 85*, 207–238.

Newell, A. (1980). Physical symbol systems. *Cognitive Science, 4*, 135–183.

Newell, A. (1990). *Unified theories of cognition.* Cambridge, MA: Harvard University Press.

Nosofsky, R. M. (1986). Attention, similarity, and the identification-categorization relationship. *Journal of Experimental Psychology: General, 115*, 39–57.

Nosofsky, R. M., Palmeri, T. J., & McKinley, S. C. (1994). Rule-plus-exception model of classification learning. *Psychological Review, 101*(1), 53–79.

Nosofsky, R. M., & Zaki, S. F. (2002). Exemplar and prototype models revisited: Response strategies, selective attention, and stimulus generalization. *Journal of Experimental Psychology: Learning, Memory, & Cognition, 28*, 924–940.

Pashler, H. (1994). Dual-task interference in simple tasks: Data and theory. *Psychological Bulletin, 116*, 220–244.

Pazzani, M. J. (1991). Influence of prior knowledge on concept acquisition: Experimental and computational results. *Journal of Experimental Psychology: Learning, Memory, & Cognition, 17*, 416–432.

Pitt, M., Myung, I., & Zhang, S. (2002). Toward a method of selecting among computational models of cognition. *Psychological Review, 109*, 472–491.

Posner, M. I., & Keele, S. W. (1968). On the genesis of abstract ideas. *Journal of Experimental Psychology, 77*, 241–248.

Ratcliff, R. (1978). A theory of memory retrieval. *Psychological Review, 85*, 59–108.

Rumelhart, D. E., Hinton, G. E., & Williams, R. J. (1986). Learning representations by backpropagating errors. *Nature, 323*, 533–536.

Sakamoto, Y., & Love, B. C. (2004). Schematic influences on category learning and recognition memory. *Journal of Experimental Psychology: General, 133*(4), 534–553.

Shepard, R. N. (1964). Attention and the metric structure of the stimulus space. *Journal of Mathematical Psychology, 1*, 54–87.

Shepard, R. N. (1987). Toward a universal law of generalization for psychological science. *Science, 237*, 1317–1323.

Shepard, R. N., Hovland, C. L., & Jenkins, H. M. (1961). Learning and memorization of classifications. *Psychological Monographs, 75*(13, Whole No. 517).

Smith, J. (2002). Exemplar theory's predicted typicality gradient can be tested and disconfirmed. *Psychological Science, 13*, 437–442.

Smith, J. D., Minda, J. P., & Washburn, D. A. (2004). Category learning in rhesus monkeys: A study of the Shepard, Hovland, and Jenkins tasks. *Journal of Experimental Psychology: General, 133*, 398–414.

Spence, K. W. (1936). the nature of discrimination learning in animals. *Psychological Review, 43*, 427–449.

Vere, S. A. (1992). A cognitive process shell. *Behavioral and Brain Sciences, 15*, 460–461.

Wattenmaker, W. D., Dewey, G. I., Murphy, T. D., & Medin, D. L. (1986). Linear separability and concept learning: Context, relational properties, and concept naturalness. *Cognitive Psychology, 18*, 158–194.

Wisniewski, E. J., & Medin, D. L. (1994). On the interaction of theory and data in concept learning. *Cognitive Science, 18*, 221–281.

Yamauchi, T., Love, B. C., & Markman, A. B. (2002). Learning nonlinearly separable categories by inference and classification. *Journal of Experimental Psychology: Learning, Memory, & Cognition, 28*, 585–593.

Yamauchi, T., & Markman, A. B. (1998). Category learning by inference and classification. *Journal of Memory and Language, 39*, 124–149.

Chapter 10

HBR Validation: Integrating Lessons Learned From Multiple Academic Disciplines, Applied Communities, and the AMBR Project

Gwendolyn E. Campbell
Amy E. Bolton
NAVAIR Orlando

It would be difficult to find a topic associated with human behavior representations (HBRs) that brings forth more spirited and lively discussion than the topic of validation. Many assertions on this topic elicit almost violent agreement. For example, it is generally agreed that validation is tremendously important, and the risk of drawing erroneous conclusions from unvalidated models is unacceptable (e.g., U.S. Department of Defense, 2001a). Authors of one recent report (Committee on Technology for Future Naval Forces, National Research Counsel [NRC], 2003) stated that the need to ensure valid model content is so critical it is worth an investment of $20 to $30 million per year. In addition, there is general agreement that HBR validation is a difficult and costly process (e.g., Ritter & Larkin, 1994; U.S. Department of Defense, 2001b). Finally, most in the community would probably agree that HBR validation is rarely, if ever, done (e.g., Harmon, Hoffman, Gonzalez, Knauf, & Barr, 1999). The issue that elicits disagreement, on the other hand, is exactly what activities and results constitute a demonstration of satisfactory HBR validation. The goal of this chapter is to focus on this issue and attempt to incorporate insights from several disciplines, including software engineering, mathematics, statistics, and psychology, bringing in examples from the AMBR project whenever appropriate.

This chapter is divided into six major sections. In this introductory section, we lay the foundation for a discussion of cognitive model validation by reminding readers of the distinction between a model and an architecture, present the Defense Modeling and Simulation Office (DMSO) definitions of *verification* and *validation,* and elaborate on perspectives on validation that can be found in the psychological literature. In the next two sections, we discuss a wide variety of techniques for collecting qualitative and quantitative evidence associated with assessing the validity of an HBR, inspired by the psychological notion of *construct validity.* The fourth section acknowledges that, although there is much that the military community can gain from the psychological community's definition of construct validity, there are also limitations of this notion when applied to HBRs. The fifth section returns to the DMSO definition of validity, illustrating how this definition provides guidance for additional HBR assessment measures and processes that are highly appropriate for the military user community. Finally, the last section discusses HBR validation in the context of the AMBR program and provides a brief summary of the chapter.

LAYING A FOUNDATION

Architectures Versus Models

The distinction between a cognitive architecture and a model has been made before (Gluck, Pew, & Young, chap. 1, this volume), but needs to be reiterated here because *validation* means different things in these two contexts. Possibly the easiest way to describe this distinction is by making an analogy to standard office software. Consider Microsoft® Excel. It is a software tool that allows individual users to build specific spreadsheets. Excel is analogous to a cognitive modeling architecture like ACT-R or Soar, and any particular spreadsheet that a user builds is analogous to a specific model that someone builds in one of those architectures.[1] Obviously, it is necessary to demonstrate that, if a person enters a mathematical formula into a cell in Excel, the program will correctly calculate the answer. However, it is impossible to guarantee that every spreadsheet built in Excel will be a good one. (A spreadsheet may be flawed for many reasons, including users who simply do not know the correct mathematical relationships that need to be established, the inclusion of typographical mistakes that create calculable yet inappropriate formulas, and the more subtle and vexing situation that arises when working in a domain such as accounting, which includes principles that are open to interpretation.) Similarly, it is impor-

---

[1]This analogy also helps illustrate the oversimplification inherent in any discussion that treats the model/architecture distinction as a straightforward dichotomy. Not surprisingly, it is more of a continuum, and a software program for personal financial management like Quicken®, which falls somewhere in between the Excel software tool and a specific spreadsheet in terms of both the guidance and the flexibility it provides to a user, represents the nature of a potential midpoint along this continuum.

tant to demonstrate that a cognitive architecture will implement processes predictably and reliably across all models developed within that architecture. However, it is simply not possible to guarantee that every model built in an architecture will be an accurate representation of its referent in the real world.

Like all analogies, this one is not perfect. Some modeling architectures impose constraints that prevent the development of models with particular unrealistic outcomes. For example, psychological research suggests that human memory for the most recent items in a serial list is a function of the ratio of two intervals: the interval between the presentations of items in the list and the interval between the last presentation of the list and the memory test. This function has been incorporated into the ACT-R cognitive architecture, and it would be difficult, if not impossible, to develop a model in the current ACT-R architecture that does not produce behavior consistent with this function (Anderson, personal communication, July 31, 2003). However, the bottom line is that different architectures impose different levels of constraints, and there is no architecture that perfectly constrains all model development to only valid models.

In this chapter, we address the validation of models, rather than the architectures in which these models are created. The topic of cognitive architecture validation is well beyond the scope of any single chapter because this level of validation would be equivalent to proving a complete, integrated theory of all aspects of human functioning that the architecture is intended to cover (e.g., cognition, emotion, personality).[2] More specifically, we focus on the validation of one particular class of models, HBRs, with *HBR*s defined as software simulations of human performance that can be integrated into existing simulated environments and run in real time.

Verification Versus Validation

The second distinction that needs to be made is between the concepts of *verification* and *validation*. Returning to our Excel example, consider a spreadsheet that has been programmed with a particular depreciation schedule. It is possible to demonstrate that all of the formulas entered into this spreadsheet are being calculated correctly, and this is similar to the process known in the modeling and simulation community as *verification*. DMSO defines *verification* as "the process of determining that a model implementation and its associated data accurately represent the developer's

---

[2]Of course there is actually an intimate relationship between validating a model and validating a cognitive architecture. Attempts to validate a model sometimes led to suggestions for architectural changes. Conversely, a powerful process for validating an architecture is to develop and evaluate models within that architecture.

conceptual description and specifications" (U.S. Department of Defense, 2001c, p. 36). However, there are different depreciation schedules for different types of assets, and showing that this particular spreadsheet for calculating depreciation is appropriate for the specific asset being depreciated roughly corresponds to demonstrating the validity of that spreadsheet. *Validation* is formally defined as "the process of determining the degree to which a model or simulation is a faithful representation of the real world from the perspective of the intended uses of that model or simulation" (U.S. Department of Defense, 2001c, p. 35). Another way to describe the relationship between verification and validation is that the former demonstrates internal consistency, whereas the latter demonstrates correspondence with the way the world, including its human participants, really works. This characterization is useful in that it provides some insight as to which disciplines may be able to provide guidance for these two efforts.

First, consider verification. Software verification is a problem that software engineers have been struggling with for a long time. Although no one would claim that it is an easy process, they have developed some tools that appear to have applicability to the M&S community (MacKenzie, Schulmeyer, & Yilmaz, 2002). In addition, there are also a number of tools and techniques that have been developed to support the verification of a particular class of software systems—knowledge-based systems (KBS). These include tools to assess the content of a KBS along the dimensions of completeness, consistency or coherence, and redundancy (Harmon, Hoffman, Gonzalez, Knauf, & Barr, 1999). These verification tools may be relevant for HBRs because many HBRs have knowledge bases.

Next, consider validation. Again the software engineering community has methods and tools for validating software and, in particular, simulations (e.g., Rakitin, 2001; Software Engineering Standards Committee of the IEEE Computer Society, 1994, 1998; Wallace, Ippolito, & Cuthill, 1996). However, many sources suggest that HBR validation is more complex than validating simulations of the physical world, and approaches typically used for validating physical simulations fall short of the requirements for validating HBRs (e.g., Harmon, Hoffman, Gonzalez, Knauf, & Barr, 1999; U.S. Department of Defense, 2001b). Part of the challenge in validating HBRs comes from features that they share with other complex physical systems such as weather systems—high inherent complexity, nonlinear relationships among variables, and the chaotic principle that small changes to inputs may produce wildly discrepant outputs. Beyond that, Harmon and his colleagues (1999) argued that the real distinction between HBRs and other physical system simulations—the distinction that makes HBR validation the most challenging—is that HBRs are actually made up of two sets of computer programs: a behavior engine and a knowledge base. According to Harmon et al. (1999), it is the combination of the inherent complexity of HBRs with the requirement to address those two separate and complete software components of an HBR that ". . . easily makes them the most complex components of a simulation system, even when compared to simulated environments" (p. 3). Thus, we need to look beyond the tools and techniques available within the software engineering community to validate HBRs.

Validation in the Psychological Community

If an HBR is thought of as an executable theory of human behavior, then the correspondence between assessing an HBR's validity and testing a hypothesis about human behavior is striking. This suggests that we can turn to psychology for additional tools and methodologies to support HBR validation efforts. Psychologists have actually been testing theories and hypotheses about human behavior for even longer than software engineers have been trying to verify and validate software! In fact the psychological literature is teeming with discussions of validity—particularly how to define and assess it.

One classic reference (Cronbach & Meehl, 1955) focuses on the validation of psychological tests. These authors were interested in the question of how we can know that a person's score on a test has any meaning. Within this context, they present a taxonomy of types of validity. The *criterion validity* of a test is the extent to which a person's score on that test predicts that person's performance or score on some other (single) independent measure of interest. For example, demonstrating that a person's score on an entrance exam accurately predicts their level of performance in a private school is equivalent to demonstrating criterion validity for the entrance exam. The *content validity* of a test is the extent to which the test items form a representative sampling of the potential universe of all relevant content. The *construct validity* of a test is a measure of the extent to which a test score is an accurate reflection of some underlying psychological trait or characteristic of the test taker. Typically, evidence in support of the construct validity of a test can only be slowly accumulated by producing a variety of demonstrations that the relationships between the test score and many other test scores and behaviors under a diverse set of conditions appear to be appropriate. Researchers are required to demonstrate that the test score is both (a) consistent with behaviors it should be associated with, and (b) unrelated to behaviors that it should not be associated with (Campbell & Fiske, 1959).

Another classic reference (Cook & Campbell, 1979) discusses the validation of an experiment or experimental design. Rather than focusing on the meaning behind a person's test score, they were interested in how we can know that an experimental result has any meaning. More specifically, these authors were interested in the question of whether we can have confidence in the accuracy of the inferences about causal relationships between variables that are based on the results of an experiment. Their taxonomy, although similar in some ways to Cronbach and Meehl's (1955) taxonomy, is not identical. The types of validity that they cover include: *statistical conclusion validity*, the extent to which statistical requirements (such as a sufficiently large sample size) are met in the experimental design; *internal validity*, the extent to which causal relationships have been accurately identified among the manipulated variables; *construct validity*, the extent to which those same causal relationships generalize to the underlying psychological traits of interest; and *external validity*, the extent to which the identified causal relationships generalize across populations and environmental conditions.

Although the two perspectives on validity are not equivalent, they are similar in some important ways. The most obvious similarity is that both taxonomies include a form of validity called *construct validity*. More important than the similarity in terminology, both definitions of construct validity are based on the premise that humans have psychological traits that cannot be measured or studied directly, but can only come to be understood through inferences based on imperfect indicators. The extension of the concept of construct validity to an HBR is obvious: A construct valid HBR would be one in which the knowledge base and behavior engine implemented in the model correspond to the knowledge structures and cognitive and psychomotor processes of the person or people being modeled.

A second important similarity is that both taxonomies treat construct validity as a continuum rather than an all-or-nothing judgment. This means several things. Evidence is accumulated gradually over time. It is rare to find a test, experimental design, or model with absolutely no validity at all. There is no way to prove that something is valid. Instead the relevant community must establish a threshold of acceptability or sufficiency that individual efforts can be compared against.

Finally, both perspectives suggest a variety of types of evidence that could be collected to assess construct validity. Over the next two sections, inspired by psychologists' approaches for assessing construct validity, we discuss many different types of evidence that could be collected to evaluate an HBR.[3] The first section focuses on qualitative or subjective evidence, and the second section discusses quantitative or objective evidence. The discussion includes a consideration of each type of evidence along two dimensions: first, the extent to which that type of evidence is considered to provide "strong" support for a claim of validity; and second, the extent to which

---

[3]Recall that after these two sections we bring up some limitations of the notion of construct validity as applied to HBRs, and provide guidance as to additional sources of evidence that should be collected when assessing an HBR.

that type of evidence serves the pragmatic purpose of providing insight into ways in which a particular model might be improved. This second dimension is included because evidence suggesting that a model lacks validity, without providing any indication as to how that model might be improved, is not particularly useful (Grant, 1962; Ritter, 2004).

QUALITATIVE EVIDENCE FOR MODEL VALIDITY

One of the most commonly used approaches to collect validation evidence for an HBR in the modeling and simulation community is to ask subject matter experts (SMEs) to make judgments about the content and/or behavior of the HBR (U.S. Department of Defense, 2001b, 2001d; Young, 2003). The extent to which a thing under consideration (measure, model, etc.) agrees with someone's common experience and intuition about how it should look and/or work is often referred to as *face validity*. When SME judgments are being collected to assess the validity of a model, every attempt must be made to follow a process that is standardized, objective, systematic, repeatable, and independent. By standardized, objective, systematic, and repeatable we mean that the analysts should develop a formal procedure involving questionnaires, checklists, or structured interviews in advance. Then this procedure would be applied identically to each of several SMEs who are selected for their specific knowledge of the subject matter, and only after they have been introduced to the modeling application in as much depth and completeness as possible.

There are two requirements for achieving a desirable level of independence. First, the SMEs who were used to help develop the model should not be the only SMEs involved in the evaluation of the model because they have a vested interest in the outcome of the validation process. Second, several SMEs should make their judgments independently of each other before the results are compared and combined. Qualitative evidence for validity can be attributed to those aspects of the model that elicit positive feedback independently from all the SMEs, but not to model components that elicit disagreement or consistent concern. Above all else, the key is to avoid the BOGSAT (bunch of guys sitting around a table) process (Committee on Technology for Future Naval Forces, NRC, 2003).

Unfortunately, regardless of how carefully one collects these types of data, it is a well-documented fact that human judgments are prone to a number of limitations that make these data suspect (Tversky & Kahneman, 1974). There are a number of ways in which people, even SMEs, come to form erroneous judgments (Gilovich, 1993). For instance, we are cognitively predisposed to perceive order and patterns in life even when confronted with random sequences of unrelated events. In addition, we typically only notice events and miss "nonevents," making our informal data collection processes biased. Unfortunately, once an opinion has been formed, we tend to only look for evidence that confirms that opinion, and we find ways to discredit any conflicting evidence that arises, thus strengthening our conviction in the original opinion.

Gilovich (1993) documented a number of examples that span a diverse assortment of topics, including sports, medicine, and interpersonal relationships. For example, many people, including obstetricians, believe that adopting a child increases the odds that a couple with a history of fertility problems will subsequently become pregnant. In fact this is not true, but it is easy to see how such a belief could arise. A couple becoming pregnant is an event that occurs at a specific time. More than that, if the couple has had fertility problems in the past, it is an event worthy of notice and celebration. Thus, each occurrence of pregnancy that follows a time of infertility and adoption is likely to be brought to people's attention, be emotionally charged, and highly memorable. In contrast, not becoming pregnant is a nonevent that is not officially established to have happened at a particular time and is rarely brought to our attention. Thus, our internal scorecard racks up another point each time we hear of a couple who becomes pregnant after adopting, but rarely counts couples who do not, and we are left with a biased opinion about the actual probabilities.

Thus, in the academic community, human judgments are not believed to provide strong evidence for the construct validity of a theory of human behavior. However, there are still several good reasons to collect these data in an applied military M&S environment. One is that it encourages buy-in from the user community. More important, this type of analysis provides a wealth of data indicating how an HBR could be improved. Beyond identifying specific ways in which the model does not behave as expected, the act of participating in the evaluation process may inspire the SMEs to identify new testing conditions, additional input variables and constraints, and so on.

In theory, a similar type of qualitative evidence could be collected from a different group of SMEs—psychologists could be called on to judge the correspondence between an HBR and psychological theories of human behavior and cognition. For example, a model that can only maintain a limited amount of information in an active memory store and experiences decay of those items over time would be more consistent with current cognitive theory than one with an infinite memory store.

Unfortunately, things are not usually this simple as was borne out by our experiences in the AMBR project. "Consistent with theory" was in the eye of the beholder; even given an established theory of memory, there were multiple ways to instantiate decay (for example) and no clear way to judge one technique better than another. Finally, even if one component of an HBR, such as its memory module, could be validated this way, HBRs are sufficiently complex that it would be impossible to evaluate all of the separate components and all of the interactions between all of the components in this way. In fact Nunnally (1978) went so far as to categorically deny that validation can ever be accomplished logically: "There is no way to prove the validity of an instrument purely by appeal to authority, deduction from a psychological theory, or any type of mathematical proof" (p. 87). Thus, as with domain SMEs, qualitative evidence in the form of judgments about the apparent reasonableness of a model's content, processes, and/or behavior are limited in their ability to provide strong evidence for a model's validation, but may provide insight into ways in which a model could be improved.

QUANTITATIVE EVIDENCE FOR MODEL VALIDITY

An obvious alternative to collecting qualitative evidence in the form of human judgments of the apparent reasonableness of an HBR's behavior is to collect quantitative evidence in the form of a statistical assessment of the similarity between an HBR's behavior and a human's behavior. In fact there is a long-standing tradition of comparing model predictions to empirical data. Roberts and Pashler (2000) cited examples from the psychological literature going back over 60 years. Interestingly, although the general notion of comparing predictions with data has been around for many years, the community has not settled on a standardized, quantitatively rigorous procedure for conducting these comparisons (Schunn & Wallach, 2001).

Traditional Statistical Approach: Hypothesis Testing

One position that is generally accepted is that traditional hypothesis testing techniques cannot be used to assess the ability of a model to fit empirical data. Grant (1962) reminded readers of the logic underlying hypothesis testing and explained why it is not appropriate for evaluating models. First, consider hypothesis testing as it is applied to a traditional experiment. Imagine a simple experimental procedure in which a number of participants are randomly drawn from some larger pool of candidates and half are randomly subjected to a treatment of some sort. If, the treatment has no impact on these participants, their data should appear quite similar to the data collected from the untreated participants. This state of affairs is captured in the null hypothesis, which states that the two sets of data were drawn from the same underlying population. If in contrast, the treatment has an impact, then the two sets of data should appear different. This outcome is represented by the alternative hypothesis, which states that the two sets of data came from different underlying populations.

The difficulty arises from the fact that each person behaves a bit differently from every other person even when everyone is treated similarly. Thus, regardless of whether the treatment had an effect, the two data sets are likely to look at least a little different from one another. A statistical test is used to determine whether the observed difference between the two data sets is large enough to conclude that the treatment actually had an impact. More specifically, the statistical test determines the probability that two samples could have been randomly drawn from a single underlying population and still appear as different from each other as the two samples under investigation. This probability is compared against an agreed-on standard. If there is less than a 5% chance that the two samples could have been drawn from the same population, the researcher may conclude that the treatment made a difference.

In traditional experimental psychology, of course, we expect to show that our treatment had an effect by demonstrating that it would be highly unlikely that our two data sets would look so different if they came from the same population. Thus, we want to reject the null hypothesis. When evaluating a model, however, we are in the opposite situation and anticipate that the model's predictions will be indistinguishable from empirically collected data. This is equivalent to wanting to prove that the null hypothesis is true. Unfortunately, it is not possible to prove that the null hypothesis is true (Fisher, 1942). The statistical test only provides an estimate of the probability that a single population could have produced two samples that appear as different from one another as your experimental sample and control sample are from each other. It does not provide an estimate of the likelihood that the two samples actually came from the same population. In fact there is no way to calculate such an estimate because in theory there could be an infinite number of different underlying populations that are similar enough to one another that they could produce highly similar samples. In practice there is no way to know that all of the other possible populations have been ruled out.

A (highly simplified) concrete example may help illustrate the distinction. Imagine that two new lawyers are applying for a job. Both claim to have graduated from Harvard Law School. One scored 97% on the bar exam and the other scored 21%. You happen to know that Harvard Law School graduates score, on average, 95% on the bar exam with a standard deviation of 5 percentage points. The null hypothesis for each applicant would state that he did come from the population of Harvard Law School graduates. The alternative hypothesis would state that he came from a different population (or different school). Consider the applicant with the 21% score. This number is so different from the typical Harvard graduate performance that you would probably be willing to challenge his claim to have gone to Harvard. Granted, there is a small chance that he actually did go to Harvard. (Maybe there is a building on campus named after his grandfather.) Yet, with that low score, it is so unlikely that you would probably be willing to assume the low risk of being wrong, reject the null hypothesis, and conclude that he did not go to Harvard.

Now consider the applicant with the 97% score on the bar. That score is indeed similar to scores produced by Harvard graduates. Does that mean you can confidently conclude that this applicant did actually graduate from Harvard? In other words, can you accept the null hypothesis? Unfortunately, the answer is no. There are many other ways in which the applicant could have earned such a high score. The applicant could have graduated from law school at Stanford or Yale. Students from those universities also score, on average, quite well on the bar. The applicant could have attended a local public university due to circumstances beyond his control (financial, family obligations, etc.), but still be quite brilliant in the law.

When there is no statistical significance, the researcher is left unable to conclude anything about which underlying population the applicant was drawn from. In other words, the lack of statistical significant difference between a model's predictions and a set of empirical data does not constitute evidence for the validity of the model. Thus, the use of traditional hypothesis testing procedures to compare model predictions to empirical data is, quite simply, inappropriate.

Grant (1962) also pointed out that attempting to apply these statistics to evaluate a model would result in the situation in which small studies with insensitive measures and insufficient power would be most likely to produce statistical support for a model, whereas studies with sensitive measures and sufficient power would be likely to reject models. Obviously, this is not the way in which a discipline advances.

Alternative Statistical Approach: Goodness-of-Fit Measures

Fortunately, there are a wide variety of alternative statistical approaches to traditional hypothesis testing for the evaluation of HBRs. Specifically, there are many different ways in which the similarity between two sets of data can be quantified, and these are referred to as *goodness-of-fit* measures. Recently, Schunn and Wallach (2001) proposed that the goodness-of-fit between a model's predictions and empirical data should be assessed along two dimensions: trend consistency and exact match. They discussed the strengths and weaknesses of a number of statistical options for assessing these aspects and ultimately recommended, when possible, calculating r^2 to assess trend consistency and the Root Mean Squared Scaled Deviation (RMSSD) to assess the exact match. In the AMBR program, we assessed both aspects of goodness-of-fit, although we used somewhat different statistics from the ones recommended by Schunn and Wallach. Specifically, we assessed the exact match of each model's predictions to empirical data with the G^2 statistic (deviance) for categorical dependent variables and with the Sum of the Squared Error (SSE) for continuous dependent variables (Diller & Gluck, chap. 8, this volume). (It is important to note that we did not use the G^2 statistic to draw conclusions about accepting or rejecting a model. Instead, as can be seen in Diller and Gluck [chap. 8, this volume], values of G^2 were compared between models to assess relative fit and across modifications of the same model to assess changes in fit.) In addition, we assessed trend consistency by applying separate analyses of variance (ANOVAs) to the human data and the model data, and noting whether the same pattern of significant results was found in each data set.

Of course using the correct statistic will only produce meaningful results if you are comparing your model's predictions to the right data. Traditional experimental psychologists use aggregated data (i.e., group means) almost reflexively. Conventional wisdom has it that the process of averaging data cancels out the randomly distributed error and magnifies the common, systematic variance. However, as previously discussed in this book (e.g., see Love, chap. 9, this volume; Zachary et al., chap. 6, this volume), as well as in other sources (e.g., Estes, 2002; Ritter & Larkin, 1994; Siegler, 1987), aggregated data may not be the most appropriate for assessing the validity of an HBR. An intuitively obvious case in which aggregating data would not be appropriate is the situation in which different participants are applying different cognitive processes to produce their data. In this case, the data sets do not share common, systematic variance, and thus aggregating the data cannot magnify or elucidate anything.

A more subtle case sometimes arises in which data from individuals may have been generated by highly similar underlying processes, but averaging these data obscures or distorts this process. Estes (2002) described a concrete example of this phenomenon taken from learning research. According to Estes, a number of studies using artificially generated data sets demonstrated that ". . . there is a pervasive tendency for averaged data to be fit better by power functions, even when performance of the individuals is known to conform to exponential functions" (p. 6). In other words, the model with the best fit to aggregated data was not construct valid.

In the case of the development of HBRs for the military community, the desire to model individuals rather than aggregated data may reflect more practical goals. For example, if an HBR is being used to support simulation-based design, the output of interest may be performance at the extreme ends of the continuum, such as slowest reaction times expected, to support decisions based on safety considerations and worst-case scenario planning. Similarly, if an HBR is being used to simulate adversaries in a training system, models that faithfully represent aggregate performance quickly become predictable and easy for trainees to outmaneuver, minimizing their training effectiveness. Whatever the reason, if there is interest in modeling individual differences, rather than just aggregate performance, then additional data collection and analysis techniques (e.g., Gluck, Staszewski, Richman, Simon, & Delahanty, 2001; Newell & Simon, 1972; Siegler, 1987) are required to establish an appropriate set of empirical data.

A Mathematical Issue: Overfitting

Unfortunately, and perhaps surprisingly, even after the most appropriate set of data has been selected, a demonstration that your model achieves a high goodness-of-fit score, compared with those data, does not automatically constitute strong evidence for the validity of that model. Confidence in that evidence depends in part on how the model was developed relative to those data. The weakest case arises when that model, and only that model, is compared to a limited[4] set of data after the model developer has used that same set of data to help build and refine the model. In this situation, interpreting the resultant goodness-of-fit value is problematic. Although a larger value always corresponds to a better fit to a particular set of data, this does not always translate to a model with a higher degree of validity. To understand why this is so, we need to turn to measurement theory and mathematics.

Measurement theory specifies that empirical data always contain an element of error, and we know from mathematics that it is possible for a model to be so powerful that it fits both the systematic variance (which we are interested in) and the error variance within a given data set. The problem with this situation, known as *overfitting*, is that this same model is now not likely to generalize to a new data set, in which the error variance (often a depressingly large amount of variance in data collected from human participants) is unrelated to the error variance from the first set. The goal is a model that captures the regularities in the systematic variance, but not in the error variance associated with a particular data set. This would achieve the level of generalizability that would be associated with capturing the underlying processes associated with creating the data (i.e., with validity).

There are techniques that are routinely used in the mathematical modeling community to assess the extent to which a model is overfitting a data set. A common technique—cross-validation—is to divide the empirical data set into two subsets and use one subset to build (or train) the model and the other subset to evaluate (or test) the model. The best indicator of a model that has only captured the systematic variance in empirical data is a model

---

[4]*Limited* could mean several things here, including: (a) only one type of data, (b) only data collected under one set of very narrow circumstances, and/or (c) very few data points.

that demonstrates similar goodness-of-fit values on the two subsets of data. A model that fits the training data well, but does not demonstrate good fit to the testing data, has probably been overfit and is unlikely to be valid.

This basic cross-validation technique can be extended quite nicely by repeating the whole process many times. If the fit of the model to the testing subset of the data is treated as a single data point and the cross-validation process is repeated many times (each time using a random process to split the entire data set into subsets), then a set of these fit statistics produces an estimate of a sampling distribution. The mean of this distribution is a more reliable indicator of the extent to which a modeling technique is overfitting the training data. A nice illustration of this process, called *bootstrapping*, can be found in Dorsey and Coovert (2003).

Another Mathematical Issue: Model Complexity

There are additional lessons that the HBR community can learn from the mathematical modeling community about using fit to data as an indicator of validity. Mathematicians have long known that there are two potential explanations for the ability of a model to demonstrate a close fit to a set of empirical data. It may be that the model is an accurate representation of the underlying processes that produced the empirical data (i.e., that the model is construct valid). Yet it may also be that the model is sufficiently powerful that it could fit any set of data—even data that could not conceivably have been produced by a group of human participants. Obviously, that type of model would not be a valid representation of underlying human processes. The components of a model that contribute to its level of power include the number of free parameters in the model and its functional form. Taken together, these are often referred to as a model's level of complexity. This suggests that a model's goodness-of-fit to data should be interpreted in light of the model's level of complexity, and more credit should be given to a less complex model that is able to fit empirical data.

Pitt, Myung, and Zhang (2002) evaluated a number of different quantitative techniques for adjusting goodness-of-fit measures to take model complexity into account, including the Akaike information criterion (AIC), the information-theoretic measure of complexity (ICOMP), cross-validation (CV), and the minimum description length (MDL). Their approach, replicated across three domains, was to select two competing mathematical models of a cognitive phenomenon—one being more computationally powerful or complex than the other—and use each model to generate a data set (with random error injected afterward). Then they tried to fit each of the two data sets with each of the two models, yielding four comparisons to be evaluated by multiple measures of goodness-of-fit. Their premise was that the more complex model would demonstrate the best pure goodness-of-fit to both data sets, and thus would appear to be the winner when a goodness-of-fit measure that did not adequately control for model complexity was used. However, a goodness-of-fit measure that controlled for model complexity should correctly recognize which model generated which data set. As they hypothesized, MDL was the only goodness-of-fit measure that correctly identified the true underlying model for each data set. The other measures were sometimes fooled into giving a higher score to the more complex mathematical model even when it was not the model that had been used to generate the data. Thus, MDL proved to be the best technique for adjusting goodness-of-fit to take model complexity into account.

This work may appear to be only tangentially related to HBRs, as Pitt and his colleagues focused on mathematical models, and many HBRs (including the ones used in the AMBR program) are embodied in complex software programs that cannot easily be translated into closed mathematical forms. In fact Pitt and his colleagues called out the need for extensions of this work to address other types of models; indeed there is already some progress being made in this direction. Recently, for example, Baker, Corbett, and Koedinger (2003) described an attempt to extend complexity assessments to ACT-R models without first reformulating those models into their closed mathematical forms.

Summary: Weaknesses of Simple Goodness-of-Fit Approach

Although the assessment of HBR complexity is a relatively new area of investigation and there is still much work that needs to be done, the immediate lesson for HBR developers is that achieving a large goodness-of-fit value when comparing an HBR's performance to human data could indicate one of several different things. Although we would like to believe that it provides evidence of the model's validity, it may reflect overfitting, especially if those same data were used to build or refine the HBR, or the sheer computational power of the modeling approach. Thus, the psychological community does not generally consider the ability of a model to demonstrate good fit to a single set of data to provide compelling evidence for the validity of that model.

Roberts and Pashler (2002), for example, argued that, "Consistency of theory and data is meaningful only if inconsistency was plausible" (p. 605). In other words, before they would be impressed that the model "passed the test," they require independent confirmation that the test was actually difficult. Roberts and Pashler went on to describe several situations that could result in an "easy test," by reducing the plausibility of inconsistency between a model and data. One, the data itself might be too variable. Fitting data is like trying to hit a target, with data variability corresponding to target size. The larger the target, the less likely it is that a shot will miss. Similarly, the more variability in the empirical data, the less plausible it would be for the model's predictions to fall outside of the boundaries of those data.

Another situation, already discussed in some detail, occurs when a model is so powerful that it is capable of fitting any data set. Again inconsistency between that model and data is implausible. A model that can fit any set of data can never be disproved or, in the term used by philosophers of science, is not falsifiable. Estes (2002) provided an example of just this situation that has arisen in the domain of memory research. Specifically, Estes described the history of research on recognition memory and contended that the result of approximately 50 years of investigation is ". . . a number of models that have been shown to predict most of the well-established facts of recognition memory." Estes continued, "Satisfaction with this embarrassment of riches is tempered, however, by there being apparently no prospect of constructing decisive experimental tests for relative evaluation of the models" (p. 14). He pointed the finger of blame at the models, which he said are simply not falsifiable.

Roberts and Pashler (2002) were not the only ones concerned about the practice of relying solely on goodness-of-fit measures to assess model validity. Pitt and his colleagues (2002) also emphasized that other factors, such as "plausibility, explanatory adequacy and falsifiability," must be taken into account when assessing a model (p. 486). Similarly, Schunn and Wallach (2001) called out generalizability, relative complexity, and falsifiability as key factors in model assessment. In other words, the ability to fit data, especially a single stream of data, is not sufficient to validate a model.

We would also like to point out that a single statistical score representing the fit of a model's outcomes to empirical data does not provide much information about the ways in which the model could be improved. Grant (1962) proposed some solutions to this problem, such as plotting confidence intervals around the empirical means and focusing attention on those points (or intervals) for which the model's predictions fall outside of the confidence intervals. A careful analysis of this information may provide insight into specific weaknesses of the model. (An additional advantage of this technique is that it provides some insight into the variability of the data, which speaks to the plausibility of inconsistency.) In other words, the bottom line is that a single goodness-of-fit score does not provide strong evidence for the validity of a model, nor does it provide a rich source of information about potential ways to improve the model.

Moving Beyond Simple Goodness-of-Fit Measures

Luckily, there are at least three ways to strengthen the validity evidence that can be accumulated by assessing the fit between model output and empirical data. Each of these techniques may also increase the amount of information regarding potential model improvements that is gained. One is to extend the investigation by comparing the fits of several different models. Another is to increase the scope of the investigation by assessing the fit of the model to multiple streams of empirical data. Before mentioning the third way, we would like to remind the reader that in all of the techniques and efforts discussed so far, the modeler has access to a representative subset of the data that must be fit and is able to make adjustments to the model before its goodness-of-fit is statistically assessed. The third way to strengthen the credibility of goodness-of-fit evidence is to assess the fit of model predictions that were generated before the modeler has access to those data. We applied all three of these techniques in the AMBR project, and we briefly address each one in the remainder of this section on quantitative evidence.

Model Comparisons. Consider the process of comparing the fit of several different models. The goal of the effort helps determine which models should be included in this comparison process. When the primary issue of interest is (or is related to) model complexity, the goodness-of-fit of the primary model should be compared to the goodness-of-fit values achieved by variations of that model with modified functional forms and/or different numbers of free parameters. For example, Sohn, Douglass, Chen, and Anderson (2004) had empirical learning data for a complex task from a group of participants. They were interested in evaluating a learning model that hypothesizes that a single learning rate will fit learning data at different levels of task decomposition. They decomposed the complex task into four unit tasks and assessed the statistical fit of four models to these data. Their primary model used a single exponent (representing the learning rate) for performance on all four unit tasks, but allowed the other two model parameters (a scale factor and an asymptote) to vary by task. The main competitor model allowed all of the parameters, including the exponent, to vary by task. This represented the more complex hypothesis that everything about a person's learning curve may be completely different from one subtask to the next. Two additional models filled in the gaps by holding one of the other two parameters (the scale factor or the asymptote) constant across tasks and allowing the remaining two parameters (one of which was always the exponent) to vary by task. None of the other models achieved a statistically higher goodness-of-fit value to the empirical data than their primary model, and one of the other models was significantly worse. This is a nice illustration of an effort that compared the goodness-of-fits achieved by variations of a primary model to accumulate evidence for the validity of that model.

Of course when the issue under investigation is not that of model complexity, comparisons are often made among substantively different models. For example, theoreticians often compare the most current competitive theories of the behavior of interest (e.g., Love, chap. 9, this volume). Users from applied communities, in contrast, are most likely to be interested in comparisons among the most readily available alternatives. For this group, issues like cost, commercial availability, and ease of use often determine the set of models included in a comparison. Within the AMBR project, a number of considerations were brought to bear when selecting models to participate in the comparison. One of our goals, for example, was to select models that differed from each other in interesting and significant ways. (It should also be pointed out that we were only able to choose from the set of proposals that were submitted in response to the request/call for proposals.)

Pattern Matching. A second way to strengthen a validity argument based on fit to empirical data is described by the pattern-matching perspective (e.g., Trochim, 1985, 1989). According to this perspective, the more complex the pattern of data fit by one model, the more confidence you can have that your model is construct valid. A nice example of this type of approach can be found in Gluck, Ball, Krusmark, Rodgers, and Purtee (2003). These authors built a model of expert-level basic aircraft maneuvering in ACT-R and compared the model's behavior to human performance data in a number of different ways. They started by assessing the extent to which the model's performance fit human performance when aggregated across all flight maneuvers. Next they analyzed the data on a maneuver-by-maneuver basis. Acknowledging that it was hard to know how to interpret their fit statistics without a benchmark, they used individual participants to derive one. Specifically, they calculated the extent to which data from each human participant fit the aggregated human data, and they asked how those numbers compared to the fit of their model's data to the aggregated human data. The result was that the model was almost as good a fit to the human sample as most of the individual humans were, and the model was a better fit than one of the humans, making the model's performance essentially indistinguishable from expert pilot performance.

They also investigated the variability in the model's performance relative to the variability in human performance, at both an aggregate and a maneuver-by-maneuver level. Finally, they applied within-subjects ANOVA tests to the human data and the model's data and noted that both sets of data showed the same pattern of significant results (performance as a function of maneuver difficulty). In a subsequent article, Purtee, Krusmark, Gluck, Kotte, and Lefebvre (2003) used concurrent and retrospective verbal protocols from the same sample of expert pilots as a means to assess whether the process used by the model to fly the aircraft maneuvers was similar to the aircraft maneuvering process used by expert pilots. In total, this set of process and outcome measures provides substantial converging evidence that their cognitive model of aircraft maneuvering is construct valid.

Of course the AMBR program illustrates an even more ambitious attempt to take a multivariate pattern-matching approach when assessing an HBR's consistency with human behavior. As described by Diller and Gluck (chap. 8, this volume), models were assessed on their ability to fit and/or predict: (a) a diverse set of performance measures, including reaction time and performance accuracy on primary and secondary tasks and self-reported workload, (b) performance data at multiple levels of aggregation, and (c) performance under a wide variety of conditions, including manipulations of the system interface, task load, and cognitive complexity of category learning task.

Although this approach is capable of providing substantial evidence regarding the validity of a model, it is not a panacea. One unresolved issue is that we do not have a way to reliably and objectively quantify the level of statistical confidence that should be associated with the ability of a model to fit any particular set of multivariate data. More important, as was amply demonstrated in the AMBR program, even with a large, multivariate set of data for assessment purposes, it still may be the case that different models can fit the data equally well or each model fits some subset of the data better than the other models, leaving you unable to draw definitive conclusions about the relative validities of the models.

A Priori Predictions. Finally, one of the most powerful types of quantitative evidence for the validity of a model is the capability of the model to go beyond fitting empirical data post hoc and actually predict data a priori. This should not be confused with statistical techniques for cross-validation. In those techniques, a single set of data (typically collected from multiple participants under the same conditions) is split into subsets. One subset is used to build the model, and the other subset is used to test the model. The key here is that the modeler has access to a (presumably) representative subset of the data that will have to be predicted. A much more difficult and impressive test of a model's validity occurs when the model is asked to make predictions of human behavior under novel conditions before the modeler has access to any empirical data collected under those conditions.

In the AMBR project, we collected this type of evidence when we asked our modelers to predict the performance of human participants in the category learning task under the transfer conditions. In the transfer task, participants were asked to categorize stimuli with values they had never seen before. AMBR modelers were able to use empirical data collected during the category learning phase of the experiment to develop their models. However, they were asked to predict the participants' responses to these novel stimuli without being provided with any representative performance data from this phase of the experiment. The difficulty of this challenge can be seen by comparing the ability of the models to fit the learning data to their ability to predict the transfer data (Diller & Gluck, chap. 8, this volume).

Other modelers use evidence that their models successfully predict counterintuitive findings to support their claims of model validity. For example, Gigerenzer and Goldstein (1996) described how one of their "fast and frugal" models of human reasoning, the recognition heuristic, predicts the rather surprising "less is more" effect that has been found in the experimental literature. Specifically, under certain circumstances, human decision-making performance has been shown to deteriorate as the amount of information known about each option increases. The recognition heuristic was developed to explain human reasoning in situations in which the only information available to make a decision is whether either of the options is recognized, and the prediction of the "less is more" effect was a serendipitous byproduct of the model. The accuracy of this prediction, therefore, increases researchers' confidence in the model.

It is interesting to note that the AMBR transfer data included an unexpected finding. This finding was that categorization performance on previously seen (and well-known) items dropped in the early trials of the transfer task. (Unfortunately, none of the AMBR models predicted this outcome [Diller & Gluck, chap. 8, this volume].) Although the ability to make accurate prediction of data (especially unexpected data) a priori is a strong indicator of the validity of a model, exclusively pursuing this type of assessment, like the pattern-matching approach, it is not a perfect solution to the problem of establishing that a model is valid. The main problem is that a conclusive demonstration of construct validity would require showing that a model can predict everything. Obviously, this is an impossible task.

In summary, statistically assessing the similarity between the output of an HBR and human behavior is an obvious alternative to using SME judgments as evidence of a model's validity. This type of evidence tends to be more objective and reliable than human judgments, although it is still susceptible to a number of potential flaws, such as the misapplication of statistical tests and data overfitting. There are techniques that both strengthen the quality of the evidence and increase the amount of information on potential model improvements that may be generated, including comparing the fits of multiple models, assessing fit across multiple streams of data, and requiring that the models truly predict at least some data a priori. Although this type of evidence is usually valuable and powerful for HBR users in the applied military community, many in academia do not believe that raw measures of fit to data by themselves will ever be sufficient to truly establish the construct validity of a theory of human behavior (e.g., Estes, 2002; Grant, 1962; Ritter, 2004; Ritter & Larkin, 1994; Roberts & Pashler, 2002).

CONSTRUCT VALIDITY AND COGNITIVE MODELS

In the previous two sections, we described many different types of evidence (including both qualitative and quantitative information) that could be collected to assess a model's validity and/or identify ways in which a model could be improved. Hopefully the breadth of available techniques, combined with the discussion of the weaknesses of each approach, has underscored the claim made earlier in the chapter—that validation is never definitively proven. Rather evidence is accumulated incrementally until it reaches a point that is considered satisfactory by some community.

Recall that much of the previous discussion was based on work conducted in the psychological community, with the goal of establishing that a particular theory is construct valid. In this context, *construct validity* means that the theory embodies an accurate description of the actual underlying processes that explain human behavior, and that alternative theories can be disregarded.[5] Although the task of collecting sufficient evidence to support a conclusion of construct validity is certainly daunting enough to discourage those in the modeling community from pursuing this goal, in fact the goal is not even appropriate for this community.

As Anderson (1993) explained, the process of developing a computational model that represents a particular theory requires the modeler to make a large number of implementation decisions that are irrelevant from the perspective of the theory. Not only are these details theoretically irrelevant, there are many different implementations capable of producing the same model output or behavior. For example, given a set of production rules, it has been shown that the decision to match them in parallel or in series does not lead to different predictions of behavioral measures including processing time, and thus there is no behavior-based way to determine which implementation is "correct" (Anderson, 1993, p. 12). In other words, although the state of the art can be advanced through the process of comparing different models (as was demonstrated in the AMBR program), the goal of finding the single correct computational model is misguided.

So we have argued that the types of evidence described in this chapter are valuable for assessing an HBR, but that the goal of demonstrating that an HBR is the one and only valid model is inappropriate. This leaves us with a question: What is an appropriate goal for the developers and users of HBRs in applied, military settings? What does it mean to say that our models must be validated? In the next section, we begin by reminding the

---

[5]Of course science philosophers and historians have shown that these convergences on accepted theories within a scientific community are temporary states of affairs, and reigning theories are eventually unseated, often through dramatic paradigm shifts (Kuhn, 1962).

reader of the DMSO definition of validity, and we go on to explain how unpacking this definition provides insight into the measures and processes for assessing HBRs that are most appropriate for this community.

APPLICATION VALIDITY: ASSESSING A MODEL
FOR ITS INTENDED USE

DMSO defines *validation* as ". . . the degree to which a model or simulation is a faithful representation of the real world from the perspective of the intended uses of that model or simulation" (U.S. Department of Defense, 2001c). It is easy to focus on the first part of the definition, "faithful representation of the real world," which sounds quite a bit like the traditional notion of construct validity. In fact the second part of the definition, "from the perspective of the intended uses," is a critical qualifier with the potential to significantly impact the processes, metrics, and requirements associated with assessing the validity of an HBR.

Unlike the psychological community, whose goal is to advance theory and thereby elucidate the determinants of human behavior, the military community has a somewhat more pragmatic goal, which is to improve military capability by, among other things, improving human performance. Different subcommunities will use HBRs in different ways to serve this goal. One way in which the military training community uses HBRs is as synthetic adversaries in training simulators to increase the effectiveness of the training activities, and thus improve trainees' performance. The military acquisition community, on the other hand, uses HBRs to evaluate candidate system designs and identify those designs that are likely to lead to the best human–system integration, and thus improve human performance. The military operational community uses HBRs as core components of decision-support systems (DSS), which are intended to provide explicit support to improve human decision making in the field and thus performance. The point is that each community has an intended use, and an HBR can be assessed directly as to its ability to support that intended use.

Interestingly, there is at least some evidence that improving human performance does not necessarily require a construct valid model. For example, a training study conducted by Campbell, Buff, and Bolton (in press) found that each of several qualitatively different models derived from the same expert performance data led to the generation of training feedback that improved performance (compared with two different control conditions). More specifically, all of the models investigated in this study were able to fit a set of expert data reasonably well. However, the models represented qualitatively different reasoning strategies, and so it is not possible that they were all accurate representations of the actual reasoning process used by this expert (i.e., construct valid). Despite this fact, they all produced task strategy instruction that resulted in improved trainee performance. In other words, even the models that were not construct valid were capable of meeting the goals of this particular application. This suggests that a model's capability to serve an applied goal (DMSO's definition of validity) is not necessarily equivalent to its construct validity. To distinguish these two types of validity, we use the term *application validity* to capture DMSO's meaning.

It is our contention that the requirements for demonstrating application validity for a model typically prove more tractable than the requirements associated with establishing a significant level of construct validity for a theory. Clearly, no HBR assessment is ever a trivial undertaking. However, taking an "intended use" perspective serves two purposes: (a) it bounds the scope of the validation problem, and (b) it provides insight into the activities, metrics, and measurement paradigm that could be used to demonstrate application validity. In the following paragraphs, we elaborate on how understanding an HBR's intended use can produce a bounded requirement on HBR validity.

Application: Training

Consider the use of HBRs within a military training community. This is probably the application that provides the most support for HBR validation efforts. Although not all training systems meet these criteria, when designed correctly, training systems will have mechanisms in place for the assessment of their effectiveness.[6] In addition, the ultimate goal of these training systems—to improve human performance—will already have been cast in terms of a number of well-defined learning objectives, learning activities will have been planned, the conditions under which performance will be assessed will have been established, performance measurement techniques will be in place, and criteria will have been set.

Demonstrating application validity of an HBR within a training community would require demonstrating that the incorporation of an HBR into a training system leads to some benefit, with improved human performance being the most obvious.[7] There are many possible ways to measure this. Some common approaches include: (a) the average performance of a group of students increases, (b) the number of students who fail to meet

---

[6]These measures are typically treated as measures of the trainees' learning and/or performance, rather than assessments of the system, but that is just a question of interpretation.

[7]There are other potential benefits, such as reducing the personnel costs associated with conducting a training exercise. However, other benefits are only meaningful if the training effectiveness of the system does not suffer. As we have stated previously, demonstrating that there is "no difference" in the training effectiveness of two systems is statistically problematic. For extensive guidance on evaluating a new training system, see Boldovici, Bessemer, and Bolton (2002).

some minimum criterion decreases, and (c) the amount of time it takes the average student to reach a criterion decreases. In some cases the original training system (sans HBR) can serve as the control condition and baseline data may even exist, reducing the burden associated with demonstrating an HBR's application validity even further.

Application: System Design and Acquisition

Next, consider the use of HBRs within a military acquisition community. An obvious use for HBRs in this community is to support the simulation-based acquisition process. Simulations of warfighters must be able to be integrated into simulations of hardware and software systems to predict the overall system performance (or mission outcomes) associated with candidate system designs. Here the application goal is to support the acquisition team (design engineers, lead system engineer, program manager, etc.) as they develop, evaluate, modify, and finalize the design of a new military system. The most direct test of the capability of an HBR to support simulation-based acquisition would be to assess whether systems designed with an HBR were better than systems designed without an HBR. Unfortunately, it is unlikely that this question could really be addressed. The difficulty is based primarily on the fact that the acquisition process is quite lengthy, with a relatively low base rate (e.g., compared with the base rate of scenarios run in a training simulator). Thus, from a practical perspective, it is not feasible to show statistically that the output of the entire process conducted with an HBR is of higher quality than the output of the process conducted without an HBR.

A partial solution to this problem is to divide the acquisition process into phases and determine whether the use of an HBR supports the team's goals in each stage. For example, the use of an HBR should be able to complement the more traditional practice of building a prototype and conducting human-in-the-loop studies to assess a candidate design. Thus, one requirement for the application validity of an HBR in this context is that the results of a simulation with an HBR must be comparable (to some degree of precision) to the results that would have been obtained by building a prototype and conducting human-in-the-loop studies. (It should be noted that, in some cases, an accurate rank ordering of candidate designs based on mission outcomes will suffice.)

The previous example may suggest that assessing application validity in this context is equivalent to the quantitative validation processes already discussed. However, providing support to the acquisition team is actually a complex endeavor with multiple requirements. For example, an additional requirement is that the use of an HBR (in conjunction with simulations of the other system components) provides the team members with the capability to quickly and easily explore a much larger region of the space of all possible candidate designs than could be covered with prototype testing. Positive evidence on this point would increase our confidence in the quality of the final design. Another important but easy to overlook requirement is that the HBR must be able to help identify those aspects of a candidate design that could be improved. Evidence that an HBR could meet these requirements would weigh heavily in favor of its application validity.

Ultimately, assessing the application validity of an HBR for this community is not as straightforward as it is in the training community. However, a careful consideration of the application does suggest additional types of evidence that will be useful in this process. In addition, a specific acquisition program may help constrain the boundaries of the model validation effort that would be required in certain ways. For example, the set of design reference scenarios provided for the assessment of candidate system designs establishes boundaries on the conditions under which the model's behavior must be consistent with empirical data.

Application: Decision Support System

Finally, consider the use of HBRs within a military operational community. One potential operational application of an HBR is to serve as the reasoning engine within a decision support system (DSS). In addition to quantitative analyses assessing the reliability of the output of the HBR-driven decision support tool, a study assessing the application validity for this effort would appear similar to the validation effort for the training system described earlier. That is, everyday performance on the current operational system could serve as the baseline condition, which would be compared to the performance of operators using the decision support tool. More specifically, a simulation of the operational environment could be run in a laboratory setting while the DSS is feeding decision information to the operators. To demonstrate the application validity of the HBR, we would hope to observe a decrease in the number of incorrect decisions, an increase in the timeliness of decisions and action responses, and a resulting increase in overall mission performance with the use of the DSS.

Summary

Although the exact nature of the assessment activities will vary from situation to situation, the point is that the intended use of an HBR can provide insight into the types of evidence and assessment processes that should be used to validate that HBR. This intended use perspective speaks directly to validity as DMSO defines it for our community. There is one cautionary note to be presented; unfortunately, assessment techniques that focus on the impact of the use of a model on human performance may not provide much explicit information on ways to improve the model. This suggests that an assessment of application validity should be conducted in combination with the collection of other types of evidence, such as the ones described earlier in the chapter.

THE AMBR PROJECT, VALIDATION, AND CHAPTER SUMMARY

The AMBR project was a research effort that was not tied to a particular application such as training or system design, and thus did not include an assessment of application validity. However, AMBR provided a powerful demonstration of many of the other validation processes recommended in this chapter, as well as providing support for some of the other, more general assertions we have made.

Considering first validation processes, a number of best practices were implemented in AMBR. First, the AMBR project team included a panel of subject matter experts who provided qualitative assessments of the models and identified ways in which the models could be improved. More important, however, we did not rely solely on this qualitative evidence, but applied many of the recommended quantitative approaches to assessing the AMBR models. For example, we assessed both the exact match and trend consistency of model predictions to empirical data. Also, although the nature of (and variability among) the cognitive architectures included in the project did not allow for a rigorous assessment, we made an effort to at least qualitatively acknowledge the relative complexity of the models by noting the number of free parameters used in fitting data. In addition, we did not limit ourselves to considering a single stream of empirical data. Instead we took a pattern-matching perspective and assessed the models' abilities to fit performance data, timing data, learning data, and workload data under several different environmental conditions. Moreover, we did not restrict ourselves to assessing model fit to aggregate data. Models were also expected to match the variability found in human data.

Finally, perhaps one of the strongest aspects of the AMBR project is that we "pushed" the models to make predictions of performance under novel conditions prior to presenting the actual data to the modelers (Diller & Gluck, chap. 8, this volume). This goes well beyond the more typical requirement that models are able to predict data from additional participants under the same conditions and represents a significant challenge for any HBR, as can be seen in our results.

The AMBR project also provides strong support for several of the more general assertions about cognitive modeling made in this chapter. For example, the AMBR project contains several nice examples of how the process of building, evaluating, and comparing different models can play an important role in improving architectures and advancing the state of the art in cognitive modeling. The requirement to build the ATC model (combined with a particular philosophical outlook) led to modifications to the EPIC-Soar memory mechanisms, enabling the resultant EASE architecture to implement activation and decay processes similar to those in the ACT-R architecture (Chong & Wray, chap. 7, this volume). Similarly, the requirement to develop a model for the category learning task led to the addition of a general learning mechanism in the COGNET/iGEN architecture (Zachary et al., chap. 6, this volume).

The single assertion that was perhaps most vividly illustrated within the AMBR project is that there are many different ways to implement a model that can produce highly similar behavioral outcomes. This, of course, supports the contention that the goal of selecting the single correct or best HBR is inappropriate and misguided. The requirement that AMBR models represent performance variability as well as aggregate performance provides a nice example of this assertion. Each of the AMBR modeling teams found qualitatively different ways to introduce performance variability into their model of the category learning task. The DCOG architecture, for example, generated performance variability through a combination of personality variables and the simulation of different learning strategies (Eggleston, McCreight, & Young, chap. 5, this volume), whereas the SCA model built in the EASE architecture simulated different feature abstraction strategies (Chong & Wray, chap. 7, this volume). The COGNET/iGEN model relied on micromodels to induce performance variability during the model runs (Zachary et al., chap. 6, this volume), and variability in the ACT-R model performance was a result of the stochasticity inherent in the subsymbolic mechanisms of the architecture (Lebiere, chap. 4, this volume).

Chapter Summary

The main goal of this chapter was to address an issue associated with the validation of HBRs that generates controversy and concern in the community—the nature of the activities and evidence required to validate a model. Specifically, we explored definitions of validity and assessment techniques from several disciplines, with an emphasis on the perspective from psychology. Although there are limitations to the applicability of the psychological notion of theoretical construct validity to specific, individual HBRs, we argued that the types of evidence associated with establishing construct validity are potentially quite relevant and useful to the applied military M&S community.

The first general class of validation techniques we described included qualitative methods for assessing a model's validity. This type of effort relies on domain SMEs (and sometimes psychological SMEs) to provide a subjective assessment of the accuracy and completeness of an HBR's content and behavior. Although qualitative analyses are generally discounted by the psychological community as providing limited (or no) evidence for the construct validity of a theory, the modeling community can use this approach to collect a great deal of information regarding ways to improve a model. In addition, the more systematically, rigorously, and objectively it is done, the better the evidence for model validity.

Next, we provided a detailed discussion of quantitative approaches to assessing model validity. In particular, we began with a discussion of statistical considerations associated with assessing the fit between a single model's predictions and a single stream of empirical data. We then went on to describe ways in which this type of process could be strengthened, such as comparing the relative fits of various plausible models, assessing the fit to a complex pattern of outcomes across many different variables, and requiring the model to predict (a priori) empirical results collected under novel circumstances. In general, these changes are likely to not only increase the strength of the validity evidence collected, but also to improve the quality of the information gained about specific ways in which a model could be improved.

Finally, we argued that in the applied military community, focusing on the desired application could both identify additional types of validation activities and bound the requirements associated with collecting evidence for a model's validity. For example, if an HBR is intended to serve as a simulated adversary in a training system, investigations that ask whether the HBR's behavior seems reasonable or is consistent with the performance of a human instructor/role player only provide indirect evidence on the question of whether the HBR will support the application. A more direct approach is to assess the impact of incorporating the HBR into the training system on student learning and performance. This approach has the additional advantage of being able to leverage existing metrics of student performance. We introduced the term *application validity* to refer to an assessment of the capability of the model to support the goals of an application.

This type of approach, in fact, speaks directly to DMSO's definition of *validity*, and it may become a requirement as the military moves closer to its goal of accrediting all models and simulations prior to use. DMSO defines *accreditation* as "the official certification that a model, simulation, or federation of models and simulations and its associated data are acceptable for use for a specific purpose" (U.S. Department of Defense, 2001c, p. 1). Although accreditation of models and simulations is currently only a requirement for major military applications (U.S. Department of Defense, 2003), it may eventually become a requirement for all military HBRs. Establishing criteria for accreditation requires determining acceptable types of evidence and setting sufficiency thresholds for each type and, we believe, should be an interdisciplinary effort that involves not only the military community, but also cognitive scientists, modelers, and software engineers.

In closing, despite the difficulty and expense associated with validating an HBR (U.S. Department of Defense, 2001b), the risk of drawing erroneous conclusions from unvalidated models is simply unacceptable (U.S. Department of Defense, 2001a). In this chapter, we tried to provide examples of many different types of evidence that could be collected to assess HBRs, as well as information about the capabilities of each to achieve two goals: that of providing supporting evidence for a claim of validity, and that of providing insight into ways in which a model could be improved. Although the collection of both qualitative and quantitative evidence should play an important role in any validation effort, we argued that the military community, in accordance with DMSO's guidance, must also consider the specific goals for the use of the model(s) and allow the application to help shape the validation plan.

ACKNOWLEDGMENTS

We gratefully acknowledge the sponsorship of Dr. Harold Hawkins at the Office of Naval Research (Contract #N0001403WX20275), which allowed us to participate in the AMBR program. We would also like to extend particular thanks to Dr. Kevin Gluck and Dr. Richard Pew, whose insightful feedback on an earlier draft of this chapter went beyond the contribution expected of editors and significantly improved this work.

REFERENCES

Anderson, J. (1993). *Rules of the mind.* Hillsdale, NJ: Lawrence Erlbaum Associates.

Baker, R. S., Corbett, A. T., & Koedinger, K. R. (2003). Statistical techniques for comparing ACT-R models of cognitive performance. In *Proceedings of the 10th Annual ACT-R Workshop,* 129–134. (Retrieved April 1, 2004, from http://www-2.cs.cmu.edu/~rsbaker/BCKACTR 2003v24.pdf.)

Boldovici, J. A., Bessemer, D. W., & Bolton, A. E. (2002). *The elements of training evaluation* (DTIC Publication No. ADA402961). Alexandria, VA: U.S. Army Research Institute for the Behavioral and Social Sciences. Available online at <http://www-ari.army.mil/pdf/ bk2002-01.pdf>

Campbell, D. T., & Fiske, D. (1959). Convergent and discriminant validation by the multitrait-multimethod matrix. *Psychological Bulletin, 56,* 81–105.

Campbell, G. E., Buff, W. L., & Bolton, A. E. (in press). Viewing training through a fuzzy lens. To appear in A. Kirlik (Ed.), *Adaptation in human-technology interaction: Methods, models and measures.* Oxford, England: Oxford University Press.

Committee on Technology for Future Naval Forces, National Research Counsel (NRC). (2003). *Technology for the United States Navy and Marine Corps, 2000–2035 becoming a 21st-century force: Volume 9: Modeling and simulation.* National Academics Press. (Retrieved April 1, 2004, from http://books.nap.edu/catalog/5869.html.)

Cook, T. D., & Campbell, D. T. (1979). *Quasi-experimentation: Design and analysis issues for field settings.* Boston: Houghton Mifflin.

Cronbach, L. J., & Meehl, P. E. (1955). Construct validity in psychological tests. *Psychological Bulletin, 52,* 281–302.

Dorsey, D. W., & Coovert, M. D. (2003). Mathematical modeling of decision making: A soft and fuzzy approach to capturing hard decisions [Special issue]. *Human Factors, 45*(1), 117–135.

Estes, W. K. (2002). Traps in the route to models of memory and decision. *Psychonomic Bulletin & Review, 9*(1), 3–25.

Fisher, R. A. (1942). *The design of experiments.* London: Oliver & Boyd.

Gigerenzer, G., & Goldstein, D. G. (1996). Reasoning the fast and frugal way: Models of bounded rationality. *Psychological Review, 103*(4), 650–669.

Gilovich, T. (1993). *How we know what isn't so: The fallibility of human reason in every day life.* New York: The Free Press.

Gluck, K., Ball, J., Krusmark, M., Rodgers, S., & Purtee, M. (2003). A computational process model of basic aircraft maneuvering. *Proceedings of the 5th International Conference on Cognitive Modeling* (pp. 117–122). Bamberg, Germany: Universitats-Verlag Bamberg.

Gluck, K. A., Staszewski, J. J., Richman, H., Simon, H. A., & Delahanty, P. (2001). The right tool for the job: Information-processing analysis in categorization. *Proceedings of the 23rd Annual Meeting of the Cognitive Science Society* (pp. 330–335). London: Lawrence Erlbaum Associates.

Grant, D. A. (1962). Testing the null hypothesis and the strategy and tactics of investigating theoretical models. *Psychological Review, 69,* 54–61.

Harmon, S. Y., Hoffman, C. W. D., Gonzalez, A. J., Knauf, R., & Barr, V. B. (1999). *Validation of human behavior representations.* (Retrieved April 1, 2004, from https://www.dmso.mil/public/library/projects/vva/found_02/sess_papers/b3_harmon.pdf.)

Kuhn, T. S. (1962). *The structure of scientific revolutions.* Chicago: University of Chicago Press.

MacKenzie, G. R., Schulmeyer, G. G., & Yilmaz, L. (2002, October 22–24). Verification technology potential with different modeling and simulation development and implementation paradigms. Paper presented at the *Foundations for V&V in the 21st Century Workshop,* Johns Hopkins University Applied Physics Laboratory, Laurel, MD.

Newell, A., & Simon, H. A. (1972). *Human problem solving.* Englewood Cliffs, NJ: Prentice-Hall.

Nunnally, J. C. (1978). *Psychometric theory* (2nd ed.). New York: McGraw-Hill.

Pitt, M. A., Myung, I. J., & Zhang, S. (2002). Toward a method of selecting among computational models of cognition. *Psychological Review, 109*(3), 472–491.

Purtee, M. D., Krusmark, M. A., Gluck, K. A., Kotte, S. A., & Lefebvre, A. T. (2003). Verbal protocol analysis for validation of UAV operator model. *Proceedings of the 25th Interservice/Industry Training, Simulation, and Education Conference,* 1741–1750. Orlando, FL: National Defense Industrial Association.

Rakitin, S. R. (2001). *Software verification and validation for practitioners and managers (2nd ed.).* Boston: Artech House.

Ritter, F. E. (2004). Choosing and getting started with a cognitive architecture to test and use human–machine interfaces. *MMI-Interaktiv-Journal's special issue on Modeling and Simulation in HMS, 7,* 17–37. [in English, abstract in German] useworld.net/mmiij/musimms

Ritter, F. E., & Larkin, J. H. (1994). Using process models to summarize sequences of human actions. *Human-Computer Interaction, 9*(3), 345–383.

Roberts, S., & Pashler, H. (2000). How persuasive is a good fit? A comment on theory testing. *Psychological Review, 107*(2), 358–367.

Roberts, S., & Pashler, H. (2002). Reply to Rodgers & Rowe (2002). *Psychological Review, 109*(3), 605–607.

Schunn, C. D., & Wallach, D. (2001). *Evaluating goodness-of-fit in comparison of models to data*. On-line manuscript. (Retrieved April 1, 2004, from http://www.lrdc.pitt.edu/schunn/gof/GOF.doc.)

Siegler, R. S. (1987). The perils of averaging data over strategies: An example from children's addition. *Journal of Experimental Psychology: General, 116*(3), 250–264.

Software Engineering Standards Committee of the IEEE Computer Society. (1994). *Guide to software verification and validation plans*. IEEE STD 1059–1993.

Software Engineering Standards Committee of the IEEE Computer Society. (1998). *IIE standard for software verification and validation*. IEEE STD 1012–1998.

Sohn, M.-H., Douglass, S. A., Chen, M.-C., & Anderson, J. R. (2004). *Characteristics of fluent skills in a complex, dynamic problem-solving task*. Manuscript submitted for publication.

Trochim, W. (1985). Pattern matching, validity, and conceptualization in program evaluation. *Evaluation Review, 9*(5), 575–604.

Trochim, W. (1989). Outcome pattern matching and program theory. *Evaluation and Program Planning, 12*, 355–366.

Tversky, A., & Kahneman, D. (1974). Judgment under uncertainty: Heuristics and biases. *Science, 185*, 1124–1131.

U.S. Department of Defense. (2001a). *A practitioner's perspective on simulation validation: RPG reference document*. Washington, DC: Defense Modeling and Simulation Office. (Retrieved April 1, 2004, from http://vva.dmso.mil/Ref_Docs/Val_Lawref/Val-LawRef-pr.pdf.)

U.S. Department of Defense. (2001b). *Validation of human behavior representations: RPG special topic*. Washington, DC: Defense Modeling and Simulation Office. (Retrieved April 1, 200,4 from http://vva.dmso.mil/Special_Topics/HBR-Validation/nbr-validation-pr.pdf.)

U.S. Department of Defense. (2001c). *VV&A recommended practices guide glossary*. Washington, DC: Defense Modeling and Simulation Office. (Retrieved April 1, 2004, from http://vva.dmso.mil/Glossary/Glossary-pr.pdf.)

U.S. Department of Defense. (2001d). *V&V techniques: RPG reference document*. Washington, DC: Defense Modeling and Simulation Office. (Retrieved April 1, 2004, from http://vva.dmso.mil/Ref_Docs/VVTechniques/VVTechniques-pr.pdf.)

U.S. Department of Defense. (2003, May 13). *DoD modeling and simulation (M&S) verification, validation and accreditation (VV&A)*. DoDI 5000.61. Washington, DC: Department of Defense. (Retrieved April, 1, 2004 from https://www.dmso.mil/public/library/policy/policy/i500061p.pdf.)

Wallace, D. R., Ippolito, L. M., & Cuthil, B. (1996, April). *Reference information for the software verification and validation process*. NIST Special Publication 500–234, National Institute of Standards and Technology. (Retrieved April 1, 2004, from http://hissa.ncsl.nist.gov/HHRFdata/Artifacts/ITLdoc/234/val-proc.html.)

Young, M. (2003). Human performance model validation: One size does not fit all. Presented at the *Summer Computer Simulation Conference* (SCSC2003), Montreal, Canada.

Chapter 11

Accomplishments, Challenges, and Future Directions for Human Behavior Representation

Richard W. Pew
BBN Technologies

Kevin A. Gluck
Air Force Research Laboratory

Stephen Deutsch
BBN Technologies

In chapter 1 (this volume), Gluck Pew, and Young describe three goals for the AMBR model comparison: (a) to advance the state of the science in human behavior representation (HBR), (b) to develop HBR models that are relevant to the Department of Defense (DoD) mission, and (c) to make all of the research tasks, human behavior models, and human process and outcome data available to the public. As evidence of progress on the first two goals, in this book we have presented an exemplary set of models and the modeling architectures in which they were built. In Experiment 1, the models pushed the frontiers in the representation of multitasking in HBR architectures. In Experiment 2, we stimulated the incorporation of category learning into architectures that previously did not have this capability. These accomplishments are certainly a contribution both to the state of the science and the development of more capable models to meet DoD HBR needs.

This book and the accompanying CD represent the accomplishment of Goal 3. Early in the project, we opened a Web site and BBN made available runnable copies of the software supporting the project. On the CD, in addition to the runnable simulation software, we have included data files and material from each model developer documenting their model implementations.

Beyond progress toward the primary goals, the project has also confirmed that it is feasible to conduct comparisons among models at this level of complexity on a common problem, and that doing so is a useful way to assess current capabilities and stimulate further advancements and cross-fertilization among proponents of the various architectures and modeling approaches. The comparison paradigm is an effective way to advance the field. In the course of conducting the comparisons, we learned a lot and also identified a number of issues that need to be addressed to enhance the contribution that such comparisons can make. These are addressed in subsequent sections.

CHALLENGES TO THE CONDUCT
OF MODEL COMPARISONS

We have been advocates of the comparison approach to pushing the frontiers of models for some time. When it came to actually accomplishing it, we had to address a number of issues.

Choice of Domain and Task

At the outset, we had the challenge of selecting the human performance tasks to be modeled. Even when we had agreed on the thrust of the comparisons (multitasking and category learning), there were difficult trade-offs to be considered in choosing a task context. We could select a task that was of practical interest, realistic complexity, and required highly trained operators to be our participants, such as a high-fidelity simulation. Or we could select a task that was highly abstracted, like a traditional laboratory task from experimental psychology that anyone could be expected to learn in a short time and that would isolate the cognitive phenomena of interest.

Clearly the first alternative has greater practical significance and is more challenging from a modeling perspective. However, it would have required extensive knowledge acquisition on the part of each development team—an investment that would detract from the time and effort that could be put into the actual coding of models. The BBN moderator team could have supplied that knowledge, but we were concerned that knowledge supplied by a third party might not be sufficient. An overlay on this debate was whether we should require the developers to model experienced or novice operators. There were strong arguments against modeling novices doing highly complex, real-world tasks because the likely variability they would produce in the data would mask the behaviors we were trying to measure.

Using a high-fidelity task also would have had implications for the moderator team. We had limited resources for collecting data. Either we would have had to identify and recruit experienced (and expensive) operators from the domain under study to employ as participants, or we would have to invest in an extensive period of training (which also is expensive).

As a compromise between a high-fidelity simulation and an abstract laboratory task, we opted to use an abstracted version of an air traffic control (ATC) task. The task is probably not as representative of multiple-task management or category learning requirements as we could have achieved with a more realistic task, but we obtained stable data from novice human participants in 4-hour sessions, and the modelers were able to develop the requisite knowledge based on their own experience or that of a small set of previously untrained subjects.

What Human Data to Collect

A major goal of our approach was to collect data from humans and the models to (a) make model–human and model–model comparisons, and (b) give the modelers human data to allow them to tune their models to the details of the task requirements. As has been amply demonstrated in chapter 8, this is not as straightforward as it might seem. There is a need to satisfy multiple criteria for choosing the data as well as for comparing results. First we wanted to collect data sets that all the model developers would find useful for tuning their models. Because each model began from different theoretical bases and software infrastructures, the data potentially useful for one model may not be useful for any other. For example, two of the models would have found eye movement records of the human subjects useful data. However, at least one of the models did not make any assumptions about the details of eye movements at all.

Second, we took as a requirement that we be able to obtain the same data from both the human subjects and the models. This is more constraining on the humans than on the models. One could imagine a range of data that can be collected from the models that would not be available from humans, such as the average number of tasks queued waiting for execution. This led us to focus on the more or less standard measures—aggregate measures of observable outcome performance, such as task completion time and number of errors. We collected data on response times for the most elemental task decomposition elements for which we could reliably identify both a stimulus event and a response event. We also required the model developers to provide an estimate of workload level derived from their theory and their models' performance, and we compared that with human participant subjective workload data as measured by the NASA TLX instrument (Hart & Staveland, 1988; Vidulich & Tsang, 1986). We found this a useful addition to the direct performance measures, and it challenged the developers to think about how they would represent workload. In addition, we provided a trace of the time history of every action of each scenario for each subject in case the model developers wished to analyze it to obtain some other parameter or index. These traces also made it possible for the developers to rerun a trial as performed by a participant and watch the resultant activity on the ATC-like displays.

Third, we wanted the data to be useful for discriminating among the features of various models. For the same reasons—namely, a lack of commonality in the decomposition of either human performance or the tasks to be performed—we did not figure out how to specify measurements at the level of model features that would be universally comparable even if we dropped the constraint that the same data had to be collected from humans. Instead we settled for asking each of the model developers to answer a common set of questions, the results of which are reported at the end of each of the model chapters (chaps. 4–7) and summarized in chapter 8.

Finally, we wanted to collect data that would challenge the predictive capabilities of the models. To do so required that some of the data from human subjects be given to the developers to support tuning their models, but that a condition be added to the experiment that was not announced to the developers until after the models were declared complete. There was a real challenge to devising this additional condition. It could not be so different as to create a new task for which the developers had not prepared their model, but it could not be so similar that it did not represent a stretch for the models. In Experiment 1, we created a second set of scenarios that were substantially similar to the original ones except that the arrival times and locations of the incoming planes requiring control were changed. This proved to be so similar to the model development scenarios that it did not represent a challenge at all. In Experiment 2, we created a categorization transfer condition wherein the subjects were to respond to new specific stimuli that were either interpolated among or extrapolated from the original ones. For these stimuli, neither the human subjects nor the models had previous exposure. These conditions proved to be so difficult that none of the models was able to predict the behavior of the human subjects successfully. Nevertheless this proved to be a useful condition to introduce because, when given an opportunity to revise their models to do better on this transfer condition, a great deal was learned through an understanding of the specific nature of the changes that were required to make the models perform better.

Whether to Compare or Compete the Models

The large number of human behavior representation architectures available for use today (see chap. 1, Table 1.1) understandably leads to the common speculation that certain of these architectures are better than others, or at the very least certain of them should be better at representing particular human abilities or behaviors. Such speculation results in the desire for competitions to help decide which is the best architecture to use. It was exactly this sort of interest that motivated an orientation toward competition early in the AMBR model comparison. However, as the project began to take shape, it became clear that selecting the HBR system that is objectively the best for representing human behavior is not an achievable objective.

There are three reasons for this. The most obvious is that we did not have the resources to have every available HBR architecture participate. At best we could only hope to provide a rank ordering among those architectures participating in the project. A second reason is that all current HBR architectures are moving targets. They are constantly under development and subject to modification to expand their range of application and/or level of psychological validity. Therefore, any conclusion regarding the rank ordering of the architectures would be a fleeting conclusion—true only until the developers of the various systems had improved on any deficiencies revealed in the course of the project. The third reason is that each alternative is likely to have its own strengths and weaknesses. Choosing among those strengths and weaknesses adds a layer of subjective valuation that marginalizes any claims regarding which of the architectures is "the best." For these reasons, a rank ordering of architectures did not seem to be the appropriate goal.

Some consideration was then given to the possibility of using the project as an opportunity to compare the characteristics and capabilities of different HBR architectures that make it possible (or impossible) for them to represent the human capabilities of interest in the project. The proliferation of human representation systems in the modeling and simulation community has prompted others to adopt this goal before (Anderson & Lebiere, 1998, 2003; Johnson, 1997; Jones, 1996; Morrison, 2003; Pew & Mavor, 1998; Ritter et al., 2003), and it certainly is reasonable to think that we could follow suit. One positive aspect of this approach is that it shifts the emphasis somewhat from the brand names to the (more important) underlying architectural characteristics.

Architectural characteristics and capabilities are not the full story, however. Recently the point has been made that modeling style or idiom is at least as important to the success of a model as are the underlying architectural characteristics (Kieras & Meyer, 2000; Lallement & John, 1998). This means that any particular model's ability to simulate human behavior is a function not only of what the architecture allows the modeler to do, but also of how the modeler uses the architecture. Modeling style effectively becomes a confound in any effort to compete across architectures.

An additional consideration is that the best way to objectively demonstrate the relative utility of HBR architectures is to use them to build models. These architectures make predictions about human performance only through the models that are developed with them, which means that any competition really would be among models, not architectures. This suggests a focus on the models that are developed rather than the characteristics of the architectures that support their development, and a consequence is the requirement to develop human behavior process models as part of the project.

Once it was clear that the process models were to be the focus of the project, there still was the issue of deciding whether the project was to be a model competition or a model comparison. This is a distinction with implications we did not fully appreciate early on. The two terms were used interchangeably, which created some confusion regarding the goal of the project. A competition implies the goal is to identify a winner. However, several concerns led us to the conclusion that a model competition was not what we wanted. First, an infinite number of models can be developed to describe or predict human behavior, some or all of which might do an equally good job of accounting for that behavior. Anderson (1993) referred to this as the *uniqueness* problem. To complicate matters further, there is no guarantee that the models created for such a competition are necessarily the best possible models that could have been created with those architectures. Therefore, any rank ordering that is based on modeling results must be considered tentative and arguably could be considered misleading. Third, winning depends on one or more evaluation criteria, which raises the issue of what criteria to use. Candidate criteria might include empirical model fits to data, the parsimony with which the model represents the behavior, amount of reuse of knowledge, design principles or parameters from previous models, usability, interpretability, robustness, or development cost. Once the criteria are chosen, of course, decisions must be made regarding relative weighting. Models are developed for different purposes, with architectures created from various underlying motivations. These different architectural motivations and model purposes make it difficult to get people to agree on what is important in HBR models, which further makes it hard to reach consensus on the weighting of evaluation criteria. Finally, there was the pragmatic issue: There was nothing to win—no follow-on contract or cash prize. Thus, although identifying a winning model is an attractive idea on the surface, the uniqueness problem and debates regarding model assessment methodology and what should be valued in HBR models make it a problematic and potentially empty objective.

In the end, the decision was made to organize the project as a model comparison. Just as in the case of architectural comparisons, one benefit of this approach is that it emphasizes mechanism as opposed to name branding. It is more important to gain insight into the representational assumptions and processing mechanisms that enable the representation of human behavior than it is to establish that a particular brand-name architecture has a better fit to a sample of data than does another architecture. This does not mean goodness of fit is irrelevant in a model comparison because a model's ability to predict or explain some aspects of human behavior is critical in the development of HBR models, and a useful means to assess this is through a measure of fit. Nevertheless, the ultimate goal is to shift the emphasis away from the name brand and toward the underlying assumptions and mechanisms that produce certain predictions. Another advantage of the comparison approach is that it promotes communication among modelers using different architectures, which in turn encourages architectural improvements. This is good for the modeling and simulation community because it results in improved HBR capabilities.

Some might still argue (and they have in both public and private conversations with the authors) that the AMBR project should have pursued some form of head-to-head competition among the models to determine which is the "most correct." However, Estes (2002) pointed out that, although this argument seems sensible on the surface, it becomes problematic on closer inspection. One problem is that models created by different people using different modeling architectures differ in numerous ways and make it extremely difficult, if not impossible, to determine which are the necessary assumptions that allow for successful prediction of the data. Another problem is that, as model complexity increases, it becomes more likely that the one that "wins" will simply be the model that is favored by the sampling error in those data. This tells us less about the necessary human behavior representation requirements for predicting specific behavioral phenomena than it does about which of the models happened to win the statistical lottery.

Summary

These challenges and others will be faced by anyone attempting future large-scale model comparisons, and many of them are also faced daily by people involved in the cognitive modeling and human behavior representation communities. We use the remainder of this chapter to offer two forms of guidance for further advancement in HBR modeling: (a) programmatic guidance for development of future model comparisons, and (b) science and technology guidance regarding specific directions for improvement in the theory and practice of modeling.

GUIDANCE FOR FUTURE MODEL COMPARISONS

As described in chapter 1, the model comparison process employed in this project began with selecting the driving goals for improved models, identifying a suitable task domain, and creating a simulation of it that could be operated either by a human in the loop or a model. Then a workshop was held to exchange ideas, interfacing requirements and constraints among the moderator and developer team members so that everyone was on the same page. Following this step, the moderator team collected and disseminated human performance data for the task, and the modeling teams generated models that sought to replicate the data. Finally, an expert panel was convened with the entire team to review the data and compare and contrast the models; the results were shared with the scientific community. On the basis of comments made after the completion of Experiment 1, it was recognized that the simulation could have been more complete before the workshop and the expert panel should have been involved earlier. For Experiment 2, some progress was made in accomplishing both of these goals, but it was concluded that still more needed to be done to get the developers and expert panel on board.

More Modeler Input

Although for Experiment 2 the simulation was more complete before the workshop, we believe that much more collaborative effort should be invested among the model developers and moderator team, particularly after the task is selected and the task simulation has been created and signed off. At this point, the developers are the only ones who know their models well enough to suggest the level at which to define measures that might discriminate among the model features and yet be applicable across models. Initially the Developers Workshop was held at a time when the task was not signed off, and it focused mostly on what parameters had to be exchanged with the simulation for the model and simulation to execute together. The moderator team dictated what data the modelers were to provide, rather than engaging in an exchange that might have led to a more creative definition of performance measures.

Get Objective Expert Guidance

We also believe that the use of an expert panel was an extremely beneficial feature of the comparison process. They brought a high level of knowledge and experience to the project. Even after they were brought in earlier in Experiment 2, they had great difficulty understanding the models in sufficient depth to consider comparative strengths and weaknesses realistically. In future such comparisons, it is critical that the panel be identified at the beginning of the project and brought into the process early, certainly by the time of the Developers Workshop.

Focus on Prediction

The use of a predictive phase in the model development and revision cycle, in which the modelers were required to predict the results of the transfer task, provided another mechanism by which to compare the models. It also provided a significant challenge to the modelers, illustrating the fragility that most models exhibit at the boundaries of their intended performance envelopes. We suggest that this strategy of evaluating the predictive capabilities of a model can be quite valuable and should be considered as part of the evaluation of any model or modeling architecture.

Just Do It

In our opinion, the importance of undertaking such comparisons out-weighs the challenges that we have encountered in accomplishing this one. It is a productive way to push the frontiers in terms of model architecture development as well as our understanding of stable, productive methodologies for moving from architecture to detailed, robust human performance models.

NEEDED IMPROVEMENTS IN THE THEORY AND PRACTICE OF MODELING

Significant scientific and technological progress is needed on a variety of fronts. First, we need to continue to improve our theory and practice for building robust models. Second, we need to strengthen the research base concerning human integrative behavior on which robustness can be built. Third, we need to continue to improve the validation process, including the metrics against which we evaluate. Fourth, an important contribution to validation would be to reduce the opacity of models through improved inspectability and interpretability. Finally, as we improve the theory and practice, we need to develop and assess better methods for improving cost-effectiveness with respect to the ways in which the models are created and used. In subsequent paragraphs, we address each of these requirements.

Improving Robustness

The quote, "Robustness is the ability of a system to maintain function even with changes in internal structure or external environment,"[1] provides a good working definition of *robustness*, where the systems are our human

---

[1]http://discuss.santafe.edu/robustness/; Definition 2 (SFI RS-2001-009 Posted 10-22-01).

performance models. Making models more robust in this sense is a high-priority goal for future development that should be funded both at the application and basic research levels. Researchers are at work on several paths by which to improve model robustness. The challenge will certainly stimulate ideas for new initiatives. For the present, we provide an outline of one strategy composed of elements at three levels of complexity, each with the potential to contribute to model robustness. The focus of this strategy is greater tactical variability.

The methodological norm for all architecture-based model development today is that developers, using their preferred cognitive architecture, start from a task definition and environment description, elaborate the contingent elements of the task, the decision points, and attempt to anticipate different potential outcomes. They then program the models to meet their challenges conditional on the series of real-time cues that define the context in which they operate. We refer to these sequential task executions as *threads* because they may span multiple levels in the task hierarchy and may involve execution of multiple productions or procedures. What developers don't do often enough is think tactically about the multiple ways the same threads under the same constraints could be performed or how slight variants in the constraints or cues might lead to different behaviors and outcomes. Developers tend not to represent a large number of tactical variants because of the added complexity and associated costs in coding time. The small number of variants represented is a significant concern because the availability of an assortment of tactics for accomplishing any given task has significant advantages over the limited repertoire more typical of most models developed today. These kinds of variations contribute in several ways. They are required to represent inter- and intraindividual tactical variation from execution to execution. In training simulations, such variability makes it more difficult for trainees to "game" the system by easily anticipating synthetic force actions. Additionally, interindividual variation is needed to represent cultural and personality differences. All of these kinds of variations contribute to robustness in a general sense, but do not address the ultimate problem of dealing with unanticipated events.

There are three different levels of sophistication in the methods by which tactical variation can be introduced and monitored. At the simplest level, at significant decision nodes, the developer should anticipate the reasonable alternate ways that a modeled human could accomplish the given task. There may be alternate means to achieve the same outcome or an appropriate alternate outcome that might be pursued. The decision on the outcome to be achieved and the means to achieve it can be based on contextual cues or even simple stochastic selection. This kind of variation can be accomplished in just about any architecture, but it takes significant time and effort.

At a more challenging level of sophistication, we can add an adaptive selection mechanism so the model learns from the choices it makes at the decision points where it chooses among alternate outcomes and the means to achieve those outcomes. The advantage here is that once the tactical variants are coded in, the model can learn to select among them to improve probability of success. Three elements are necessary to support the learned selection:

1. A rich array of executable behaviors, not all of which lead to the same result, but that better represent the range of actions a human might take.
2. A real-time selection mechanism that chooses among possible behaviors appropriate in the present situation to achieve the goals of the particular thread.
3. A real-time learning mechanism supported by performance indexes that measure success or failure and credit the appropriate thread decision relative to the situation in which it was made.

Ideally, the selection and learning would take place internal to the cognitive mechanisms that make up the model. That is, they might involve task activities such as planning or workload estimation, which will change the course of action well before the final procedure or production is executed to produce the behavior. This places demands on the performance indexes to represent success at appropriate intermediate as well as final levels in the completion of the threads. The challenging scientific issue is how to handle the credit and blame assignment—selecting the threads that can benefit from this treatment, identifying the appropriate decision nodes, and creating and scoring the effectiveness measures that are appropriate to each thread or context.

The most difficult challenge lies in adapting existing behaviors or creating new behaviors to address unanticipated situations. If we wish to genuinely improve model robustness—that is, the ability of the models to continue to execute reasonable behaviors in contexts not anticipated by the developers—the models will need to do what people routinely do every day: combine elements of old threads in new ways and create new threads to meet the situations at hand. This is the most significant scientific challenge facing the human behavior representation community and one that is seldom acknowledged. It is a capability largely untouched by today's architectures. Some believe that it can be achieved within one or more of the existing architectures, whereas others believe an entirely different and as yet undeveloped architecture will be necessary. It is a topic worthy of significant research investment.

Improving Our Understanding of Integrative Behavior

By integrative behavior we mean the aspects of skills that transcend perception, cognition, and motor performance. In the last several years, as cognitive psychologists have moved away from the componential view of information processing and toward more integrative views based in neuroscience, there has been growing interest in understanding the coordinative and integrative functions that bring together the wide range of basic human abilities. Theories of workload and multitasking fall into this category. People monitor their own ongoing performance. People dynamically prioritize, schedule, and replan. Somehow they know when they are running out of time or falling short of succeeding and they have the means to try something different. How are these objectives accomplished? People's cognitive skills, as well as their motor skills, improve with practice. Novices are different from experts. All of these characteristics of real human performance reflect something more than basic perceptual-motor skills. Advancing this understanding and manifesting it in models represents a second requirement for more robust models. Eva Hudlicka's (2002) work on modeling emotion represents a start toward identifying and representing the impact of emotion at the level of cognitive mechanisms, and we see the integration of emotion into HBR architectures as an important step.

Improving Validation

At this point, we should pause and take stock of exactly what we should be expecting of our models. It is often argued that the *sine qua non* of human behavior representation is for the models to behave exactly as humans do. The authors' experience suggests otherwise. We believe the criteria for success of models should be usefulness, not veridical representation of humans. We must remember that models are only approximations. Is it not true that one of the reasons that we believe models are useful is because they are simpler to build and, once built, to run than actually to collect the corresponding data on humans?

What makes a model useful? First and foremost, it should serve the purpose for which it was designed. In other places, these purposes have been defined to include training, evaluation at the level of conceptual design, supporting system acquisition decisions, and in test and evaluation. Campbell and Bolton (chap. 10, this volume) refer to this characteristic of models as *application validity*. In chapter 10, we read about the limitations in the capabilities for validating models of the complexity and comprehensiveness of HBR models. It is worrisome that current DoD HBRs rarely receive anything more than cursory face validation, if that. Models whose results are to be relied on for training or system effectiveness assessment really need to be accredited for the purposes to which they will be applied, but quantitative accreditation guidelines do not currently exist. Much further creative work must be accomplished, and we need to work toward a consensus for what classes or perhaps what aspects of models we expect to be able to validate quantitatively through goodness of fit to data or careful systematic qualitative analysis to ensure they are reflecting what people really do and what classes can only be validated through a usefulness demonstration. Usefulness is a fine criterion, and it is influenced by the quality of our HBRs, but it also depends on many other aspects of a simulation.[2] When it fails, it is difficult to pinpoint the source of the failure. Even if it can be attributed to the HBR, without more detailed validation data, it is difficult to identify what it was about the HBR that needs improvement.

As we move toward ever more complex models and toward models that learn and adapt over time, validation can only be said to be meaningful at the level of representing the behavior of individuals, not aggregates of non-homogeneous individual performances (Gobet & Ritter, 2000). In the AMBR category learning experiments, we found it helpful to classify subsets of participants in terms of their strategies (i.e., those that cited using rules and those that did not) and evaluate the models' success at mimicking the corresponding strategies. The DCOG model explored the possibility of parameterizing personality differences that might lead to different behavior or even different strategies (see Eggleston, McCreight, & Young, chap. 6, this volume). Yet no other models that we are aware of have attempted to characterize different strategies and branch on the basis of some individual difference characteristic to follow different strategies in accomplishing a task. We need to generalize and formalize the procedures for evaluating models of this type.

Establishing the Necessity of Architectural and Model Characteristics

We already mentioned several times the importance of emphasizing the identification of computational mechanisms capable of reproducing desired human behaviors. If we wish to be diagnostic about where or why an HBR failed or succeeded, we need to further mature our methods for validating the characteristics of models that claim to represent the unobservable properties of cognitive mechanisms. In AMBR, the emphasis has been on encouraging development of models that are sufficient for postdicting and predicting human performance data. Establishing the necessity of ar-

---

[2]If it is a training simulation, the usefulness is captured in measures of training effectiveness. If it is an evaluation associated with system acquisition, usefulness rests in the ability to discriminate real differences between alternative designs.

chitectural and model characteristics has not been a goal. Estes (2002) made clear the distinction between necessity and sufficiency in model testing, and he described this distinction in the context of the search for a correct (i.e., appropriate) model to account for experimental data. *Appropriate* is defined as a model that "... is necessary and sufficient for prediction of the data" (p. 5). If a model's predictions are correct, one can conclude that the model is sufficient for predicting the data. One cannot conclude, however, that the assumptions of the model are necessary. Necessity can only be demonstrated by modifying the model's assumptions and showing that the modified version no longer predicts the data. If this can be shown, the assumptions and processes built into the model are, in fact, necessary and sufficient for predicting the data, and therefore they comprise an appropriate model. Estes wrote:

> ... an improved strategy is, at each step, to compare a reference model with an alternative version of the same model that differs from it with respect only to inclusion or exclusion of a single parameter or process. One gains information, not only about the sufficiency of the reference model for predicting the test data, but also about the contribution of the component whose exclusion leads to (relative) disconfirmation of the model. (p. 8)

This form of comparative testing of models is to be done within an architecture, varying only one free parameter at a time. Due to budget and time constraints, we have not adopted this approach in AMBR. However, we agree with Estes that this is a productive approach for testing the necessity of the components of computational process models, and perhaps it is possible to follow this recommendation in future research that builds on the existing AMBR models.

Improving Inspectability and Interpretability

Opaqueness was an issue with the models in AMBR, as with all complex computational process models. Diller, Gluck, Tenney, and Godfrey (chap. 8, this volume) refer to this as *model interpretability*, and Love (chap. 9, this volume) refers to this as *transpicuity*. When it came time to compare the models, the developers were given 2 to 4 hours to present their models before a panel of experts who were generally familiar with HBR. The panel's conclusion was that they did not learn enough in 4 hours to really evaluate the models. We need to develop means to make the internal performance of HBR models more transparent. This capability is useful for developers to support model debugging, it is needed to support validation, and it helps users understand what a model is doing. One should never make use of software without understanding how it works. This point is often cited with respect to statistical programs, but is equally applicable to decision support and to models. The EASE model described by Chong and Wray (chap. 7, this volume) includes a run-time interface that provides a visualization of where the model's eyes are looking, what buttons are being pushed, and what perceptual/cognitive process is operating at each point in time. In an earlier model development effort, Nichael Cramer and Stephen Deutsch introduced a run-time interface with "Kate," a simple stick figure seated at a workplace whose eyes and hands moved tracing the model's execution of the task (Deutsch, Cramer, & Feehrer, 1994). These features were helpful in gaining confidence in how the model worked. Much more can be done to make a model's functionality transparent.

Improving Cost-Effectiveness

As cited earlier, to be cost-effective, a model should accomplish the intended purpose well enough and with less effort than one or more candidate alternative methods for accomplishing the same purpose. In the context of DoD applications, cost-effectiveness of HBR models is established when the total life cycle cost of a system with the HBR model can be shown to be less than the total life cycle cost of a system without the HBR model.

What we mean by accomplishing the task well enough is a challenge. Just as in engineering design, there are literally hundreds of decisions and choices that are made in assembling a human-like model. Only a subset of them really make a difference in the behavior that is relevant to the context and task of interest. The challenge, maybe an insurmountable one, is to determine those decisions that really matter and put the development effort into accomplishing them well. One useful direction for further work might be to draw on the experience of successful models and model developers to catalogue those features of working models that have turned out to be the most critical for achieving useful models. Because each modeling approach involves different decompositions of the requirements, there may be limited cross-fertilization possible, but the AMBR program has provided several examples where features have migrated from one model architecture to another (see chap. 8).

One way to promote cost-effectiveness is to invest in one model that can serve multiple purposes. One can create a model infrastructure and modular components that can be assembled as needed. This approach was adopted by Robert Wherry and his colleagues in the original conception of the human operator simulator (HOS; Lane, Strieb, Glenn, & Wherry, 1981). It is similar to the approach used by those who create HBR architectures. Architectures exist along continua of completeness, scope, and generality. At one extreme, illustrated by MicroSaint (Micro Analysis and Design, 2004), they are a programming infrastructure in which to create models. At the other extreme, illustrated by ACT-R, they embody relatively complete theories of human performance and, in principle, require only adding the domain knowledge and constraints associated with the specific task context.

As presented in chapter 1, there are already more than two dozen alternative architectures advertised in various stages of completeness. Some have suggested that this is a bad thing and, rather than continue to invest in such a broad range of architectures, the United States should concentrate its resources on just a few. In our view, it is premature to settle on a small set of modeling approaches. The range of needs is broad. Different modeling architectures and approaches are needed because this is not a domain where one size fits all. There will be opportunities for cross-fertilization from one approach to another and even the potential for aggregation across architectures, such as the integration of concepts from EPIC into ACT-R to produce ACT-R/PM (Byrne & Anderson, 1998) or the work of Chong to integrate EPIC with Soar to study learning of simple perceptual motor actions (Chong & Laird, 1997).

We found the development paradigm we evolved in the AMBR program to be one way to promote cost-effectiveness, especially because human performance data were available for the same tasks. Given an architecture, the method began with an understanding of the task requirements. Next, the context-dependent features were added to the model. Then the model was run as a predictor of the human data before revising or tuning it to the specifics of the data. That way one promotes an understanding of the capacities and limitations of the basic model and can more intelligently determine what is needed to improve it. In the process, one gains an understanding of how robust it is in those cases for which data exist, and this provides a forecast of how robust it is likely to be in situations for which data are not available. In AMBR, we were only able to accomplish this with the transfer condition of the category learning task (see chap. 8). However, the inadequacies of the models before they were revised was striking and revealing.

CONCLUDING THOUGHTS

The message in this discussion for those funding and performing R&D on HBRs is that, at the current state of development, resources need to be allocated not just to building the models, but also to (a) collecting the knowledge and human performance data needed to make them function realistically; (b) iteratively conducting formative and summative evaluations to ensure robustness, usefulness, and validity; and (c) continuing to support new science leading to breakthroughs in concepts for improved architectures and more robust models. If the military services intend to continue to increase their reliance on human behavior representation to improve the cost-effectiveness of training, system acquisition, and decision-support, and there is every indication that they do, it is short-sighted to support only the specific development of the models to the exclusion of supporting the research, quantitative validation studies, and infrastructure needed to improve the sophistication and scope of behaviors that can be represented in high-quality models. As evidenced in this book and in the broader scientific community, considerable progress has been made in the development of integrated cognitive architectures. As also evidenced in this book and in the broader scientific community, considerable additional research is needed to achieve the desired levels of robustness, integrative fidelity, validity, parsimony, inspectability, interpretability, and cost-effectiveness. These research directions are more than worthwhile. They are imperative.

REFERENCES

Anderson, J. R. (1993). *Rules of the mind.* Hillsdale, NJ: Lawrence Erlbaum Associates.

Anderson, J. R., & Lebiere, C. (1998). *The atomic components of thought.* Mahwah, NJ: Lawrence Erlbaum Associates.

Anderson, J. R., & Lebiere, C. L. (2003). The Newell test for a theory of mind. *Behavioral & Brain Science, 26,* 587–637.

Byrne, M. D., & Anderson, J. R. (1998). Perception and action. In J. R. Anderson & C. Lebiere (Eds.), *Atomic components of thought* (pp. 167–200). Mahwah, NJ: Lawrence Erlbaum Associates.

Chong, R. S., & Laird, J. E. (1997). Identifying dual task executive process knowledge using EPIC-Soar. In M. G. Shafto & P. Langley (Eds.), *Proceedings of the 19th Annual Conference of the Cognitive Science Society* (pp. 107–112). Mahwah, NJ: Lawrence Erlbaum Associates.

Deutsch, S. E., Cramer, N. L., & Feehrer, C. E. (1994). *Research, development, training, and evaluation support. Operator model architecture (OMAR).* BBN Report 8019. Cambridge, MA: BBN Technologies.

Estes, W. K. (2002). Traps in the route to models of memory and decision. *Psychonomic Bulletin & Review, 9*(1), 3–25.

Gobet, F., & Ritter, F. E. (2000). Individual data analysis and unified theories of cognition: A methodological proposal. In N. Taatgen & Aasman (Eds.), *Proceedings of the 3rd International Conference on Cognitive Modelling* (pp. 150–157). Veenendaal (NL): Universal Press.

Hart, S., & Staveland, L. (1988). Development of the NASA-TLX: Results of empirical and theoretical research. In P. Hancock & N. Meshkati (Eds.), *Human mental workload* (pp. 139–184). Amsterdam: North-Holland.

Hudlicka, E. (2002). This time with feeling: Integrated model of trait and state effects on cognition and behavior. *Applied Artificial Intelligence, 16*(7–8), 1–31.

Johnson, T. R. (1997). Control in ACT-R and Soar. In *Proceedings of the 19th Annual Meeting of the Cognitive Science Society* (pp. 343–348). Mahwah, NJ: Lawrence Erlbaum Associates.

Jones G. (1996). The architectures of Soar and ACT-R, and how they model human behaviour. *Artificial Intelligence and Simulation of Behaviour Quarterly, 96,* 41–44.

Kieras, D. E., & Meyer, D. E. (2000). The role of cognitive task analysis in the application of predictive models of human performance. In J. M. C. Schraagen, S. E. Chipman, & V. L.

Shalin (Eds.), *Cognitive task analysis* (pp. 237–260). Mahwah, NJ: Lawrence Erlbaum Associates.

Lallement, Y., & John, B. E. (1998). Co+gnitive architecture and modeling idiom: An examination of three models of the Wicken's task. In *Proceedings of the 20th Annual Conference of the Cognitive Science Society*. Mahwah, NJ: Lawrence Erlbaum Associates.

Lane, N., Strieb, M., Glenn, F., & Wherry, R. (1981). The human operator simulator: An overview. In J. Moraal & K.-F. Kraiss (Eds.), *Manned systems design: Methods, equipment, and applications* (pp. 121–152). New York: Plenum.

Micro Analysis and Design. (2004). http://www.maad.com/index.pl/products.

Morrison, J. E. (2003). *A review of computer-based human behavior representations and their relation to military simulations* (IDA Paper P-3845). Alexandria, VA: Institute for Defense Analyses.

Pew, R. W., & Mavor, A. S. (Eds.). (1998). *Modeling human and organizational behavior: Applications to military simulations*. Washington, DC: National Academy Press.

Ritter, F. E., Shadbolt, N. R., Elliman, D., Young, R. M., Gobet, F., & Baxter, G. D. (2003). *Techniques for modeling human performance in synthetic environments: A supplementary review* (HSIAC-SOAR–2003-01). Wright-Patterson Air Force Base, OH: Human Systems Information Analysis Center.

Vidulich, M. A., & Tsang, P. S. (1986). *Collecting NASA workload ratings: A paper-and-pencil package* (Version 2.1, Working Paper). Moffett Field, CA: NASA Ames Research Center.

Author Index

Subject Index

A

A priori predictions, *see* Predictions, a priori

Abductive mode, 202, 203, 205, 220

Abstract symbols, 205

Abstracting, 266, 267, *see also* Symbolic concept acquisition

Abstraction operators, 289

Abstraction order, 268

Abstraction strategies, 274–275, 294

Abstraction transfer task, 290

Accreditation, 392, 409

Accuracy measures
  AMBR, 21–22, 34–35
  COGNET/iGEN and multitasking, 142
  human versus model comparison
    category learning primary task, 314–317
    quantitative fits to experimental results, 308–310

Acquisition, simulation-based, 388

Action
  ACT-R cognitive architecture, 64, 65, 66, 69
  COGNET/iGEN model, 119
  DCOG-1 framework, 185, 187, 189

EASE model, 300
  model comparisons, 337–338

Action-condition learning, 148–149

Action times, 80, 138–139

Actionable/nonactionable conditions, 192

Activation
  ACT-R cognitive architecture, 242, 243–244
  DCOG architecture, 230, 337
    DCOG-2 learning, 206, 208, 215
  RULEX-EM model, 280, 291

Activation equation, 65

Activation noise, 101, 103

Activation processes, 66

Activation strength, 230

Active memory store, 372

Activity threads, 122

ACT-R cognitive architecture
  AMBR
    comparison and degrees of freedom, 329, 330
    D-OMAR native-mode distributed simulation, 53
    HLA impact on model performance, 57, 58
    initial model, 85–91
    model, 71–81

421

Q, R